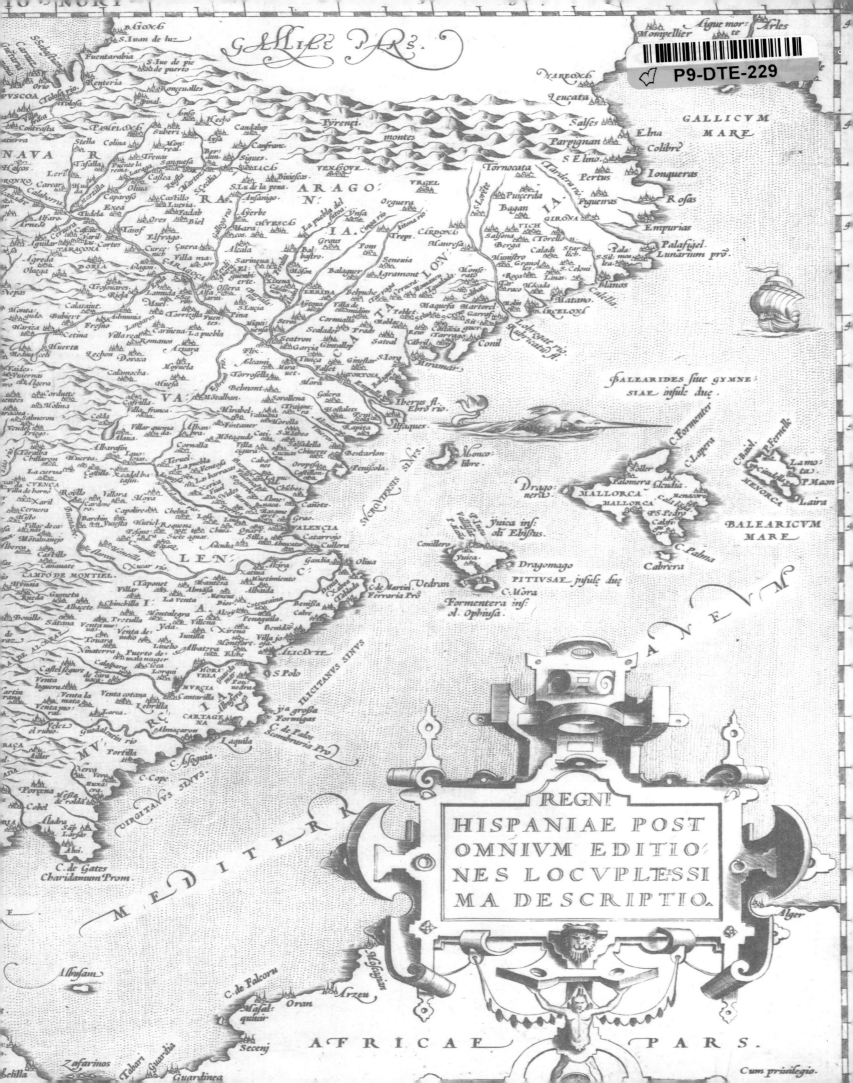

GALLIÆ PARS.

GALLICVM MARE

NAVARRA

ARAGON.

CATALONIA

VALENCIA

MVRCIA

MEDITERRANEVM

BALEARIDES siue GYMNESIAE insulæ duæ.

MALLORCA

MENORCA

BALEARICVM MARE

PITIVSAE insulæ duæ

Formentera ins: ol. Ophiusa.

Yuica ins: ol. Ebissus.

REGNI HISPANIAE POST OMNIVM EDITIONES LOCVPLESSIMA DESCRIPTIO.

AFRICAE PARS.

Cum priuilegio.

Cultural Atlas of
SPAIN
and
PORTUGAL

Senior editor and project director
Susan Kennedy
Editor Hilary McGlynn
Art editor Chris Munday
Design Adrian Hodgkins
Picture editor Linda Proud
Picture manager Jo Rapley
Cartographic manager Richard Watts
Senior cartographic editor Sarah Phibbs
Cartographic editors Pauline Morrow,
Tim Williams
Editorial assistant Marian Dreier
Index Ann Barrett
Production Clive Sparling
Typesetting Brian Blackmore

AN ANDROMEDA BOOK

Planned and produced by
Andromeda Oxford Limited
9–15 The Vineyard, Abingdon
Oxfordshire, England OX14 3PX

Facts On File, Inc:
460 Park Avenue South
New York NY 10016
USA

Vincent Mary.
        Cultural atlas of Spain and
    Portugal / Mary Vincent.
        p.   cm.
    Includes bibliographical references
    (p.   ) and index.
    ISBN (invalid) 0-8160-3014-6
    (alk. paper)
        1. Spain.   2. Portugal.   I. Title.
DP17.V56   1995
946--dc20   94-31211

Facts On File books are available at
special discounts when purchased in
bulk quantities for businesses,
associations, institutions or sales
promotions. Please call our special
Sales Department in New York at
212/683-2244 or 800/322-8755.

Origination by Eray Scan, Singapore

Printed in Spain by Fournier Artes
Gráficas, S.A., Vitoria

10 9 8 7 6 5 4 3 2 1

Frontispiece Street-sellers of Madrid,
from a 19th-century children's
alphabet primer, Municipal
Museum, Madrid.

Cultural Atlas of
SPAIN
and
PORTUGAL

Mary Vincent and R. A. Stradling

Facts On File®

AN INFOBASE HOLDINGS COMPANY

CONTENTS

Special Features

List of Maps

Regional Maps

CHRONOLOGICAL TABLE

	500 BC	1 AD	500 AD	700	900	1100

Part of bronze bridle, Iberian period

Emperor Marcus Aurelius, from Roman Tarragona

Christian knight, 10th century

Iberia and the Outside World

237 Hamilcar Barca brings Carthaginian rule to Cádiz
218–201 2nd Punic War between Carthage and Rome leads to peninsula becoming part of Roman world (Hispania)
50–45 Roman civil wars. Fighting between Pompey and Caesar's armies in the peninsula
29–19 Emperor Augustus completes conquest of peninsula

170 First African invasions of peninsula
258 Franks invade peninsula
409 onward Invasions of Vandals, Suevi and Alans. Rome invites Visigoths into the peninsula as allies
476 Fall of Roman Empire in west

507 Visigothic kingdom in Gaul conquered by Franks; Spain becomes center of Visigothic power
552–624 Byzantine stronghold in south of peninsula

711 Muslim invasion of peninsula
716–732 Muslims carry invasion into France until halted by Charles Martel at the battle of Poitiers
778 Battle of Roncesvalles (western Pyrenees). Charlemagne establishes Frankish March in northeastern peninsula
844–866 Series of Viking raids successfully resisted by Muslims

1208 Albigensian Crusade in southern France leads to waning of Aragonese influence there
1257 Alfonso X of Castile elected Holy Roman Emperor, but hostility of papacy forces him to renounce title
1282 Conquest of Sicily by Pedro III of Aragon

Politics and Constitution

227 Foundation of Carthago Nova by Carthaginians
206 Fall of Cádiz to Romans: expulsion of Carthaginians and foundation of Italica, first Roman settlement in peninsula
197 Peninsula divided into 2 provinces: Hispania Citerior and Hispania Ulterior
c.155–133 Lusitanian revolt against Roman rule
81–72 Sertorius sets up independent state in Spain
c.24 Spain reorganized into 3 provinces: *Baetica*, *Lusitania* and *Tarraconensis*

75 Granting of *ius Latii* by Vespasian gives entire peninsula partial rights of Roman citizenship
298 Spain reorganized into 5 provinces: *Gallaecia* and *Carthaginensis* added
456 Visigoths defeat Suevi, who withdraw to Gallaecia
476–484 Visigoths under Euric finally extinguish Roman rule in peninsula

569–586 Leovigild conquers Suevic kingdom of Gallaecia and establishes united Visigothic state with its capital at Toledo
654 *Liber Iudiciorum* brings a unified legal system to the peninsula

712–718 Muslim armies gain virtual control of entire peninsula
718/722 Battle of Covadonga establishes the kingdom of Asturia
739 Reconquest of Galicia
756 Foundation of emirate of Córdoba
801 Frankish armies capture Barcelona
Mid 9th century The Christians move out of Asturias into León

914? Ordoño II establishes the kingdom of León
929 Establishment of Umayyad caliphate of Córdoba
Mid 10th century Reconquest reaches the River Douro
1031 Fall of the caliphate
Mid 11th century Emergence of Christian kingdoms of León, Castile, Aragon and Navarre, and the County of Barcelona
1064 Capture of Barbastro marks new stage in Reconquest
1085 Capture of Toledo from Muslims
1086 Almoravids take control of Muslim Spain and halt Christian advance

1137 Union of Aragon and Catalonia
1139 Portugal declared an independent kingdom
1146–72 The Almohads replace the Almoravids as dominant power in Muslim Spain
1212 Defeat of Muslim army at Navas de Tolosa
1230 Definitive union of León and Castile
1236–48 Capture of Andalusia by Fernando III of Castile
1238 Muslim kingdom of Granada founded

Religion and Culture

5th to 3rd centuries Flowering of Iberian civilization. Phoenician and hellenistic influences present in art
2nd century onward Progressive Romanization of peninsula

1st century Spain produces Latin writers: Seneca, Lucan, Martial
3rd century onward Gradual spread of Christianity
400 1st Council of Toledo
456 onward The Visigoths bring Arian Christianity to peninsula

569–680 Settled period of Visigothic civilization, with widespread building of churches and monasteries
589 King Reccared converts to Catholic Christianity at the 3rd Council of Toledo
600–636 St Isidore bishop of Seville
633 4th Council of Toledo

785 Construction of the Great Mosque of Córdoba
9th century onward Spread of Mozarabic art and architecture in Christian kingdoms
899 Consecration of the cathedral of Santiago de Compostela

10th to 11th centuries Flowering of Islamic culture in the peninsula, with its center in Umayyad capital of Córdoba
11th century Beginnings of Romanesque architecture in the north

12th century Toledo center of Christian, Muslim and Jewish learning
13th century Appearance of Gothic architecture; Mudéjar style in the south
1212 Foundation of Spain's first university, at Palencia
1219 Establishment of Dominican Order
1252–84 Arts and sciences encouraged under Alfonso X
1290 University of Lisbon founded (later moved to Coimbra)

Society and Economy

5th century onward Period of Iberian city-building with some form of feudal organization. Phoenician and Greek trading colonies established in south and east of peninsula
1st century *Coloniae* founded as settlements for Roman ex-legionaries

1st to 3rd centuries Establishment of Hispano-Roman civilization; construction of major architectural monuments
4th century Decline of civic building
5th century Collapse of Late Roman society

680–710 Collapse of Visigothic society into internecine strife

Mid 8th to 11th centuries Period of *convivencia* – generally peaceful coexistence of Islam, Judaism and Christianity in Muslim al-Andalus

10th to 11th centuries Growth of an urban middle class in the reconquered towns leads to granting of municipal *fueros*
Mid 11th century Disintegration of caliphate into *taifas* (petty kingdoms)

12th to 13th centuries Feudalism established in Christian kingdoms, with serfdom on landed estates. The existence of more settled societies encourages population growth
13th to 15th centuries Flourishing commerce between Catalan regions and the Mediterranean through the port of Barcelona

Portuguese ship, c. 1500

Portrait of Miguel de Cervantes in 1600

Catalan tile, 18th century

Church of the Sagrada Familia, Barcelona

1323–24 Aragonese conquest of Sardinia
1341 Portuguese expedition to the Canary Islands
1419–27 Portuguese colonization of Madeira and the Azores
1442–43 Aragonese acquire Naples
1487–88 Portuguese sail round the Cape of Good Hope
1492 Columbus' 1st voyage to America
1494 Treaty of Tordesillas
1497–99 Vasco da Gama reaches India

1500 Alvares Cabral reaches Brazil
1519–21 Magellan's ships circumnavigate the globe; Cortés conquers Mexico
1531–55 Wars of religion in Germany
1532–34 Pizarro conquers Peru
1543 Portuguese navigators reach Japan
1568 The Netherlands revolt against Spanish rule
1571 Battle of Lepanto
1588 Defeat of the Armada

1618–48 Thirty Years War
1635–59 Franco-Spanish War
1648–61 United Provinces win independence from Spain
1667–97 Further wars with France

1702–13 War of the Spanish Succession involves Austria, France and Britain. Spain loses Gibraltar to Britain and the remaining Spanish Netherlands to Austria
1776–86 Administrative reform of Spanish colonies in America
1789–94 French Revolution
1793–94 War against French revolutionary government
1796 Re-establishment of Franco-Spanish alliance

1804–15 Napoleonic Empire in France
1807 Portuguese royal family flee to Brazil
1810–24 Independence gained by most of Spanish empire in America
1822 João, crown prince of Portugal, declares Brazil's independence with himself as emperor
1882–91 Portugal consolidates African colonies
1898 Spanish-American War leads to loss of Cuba, Puerto Rico and the Philippines

1914–18 Spain neutral in World War I; Portugal on Allied side
1936–39 Intervention of Germany, Italy and USSR in Spanish Civil War
1939–45 Spain and Portugal both neutral in World War II
1974–75 Portuguese colonies granted independence
1986 Spain and Portugal join EC
1992 Olympic Games held in Barcelona

1350–1474 Dynastic and civil strife in Castile
1385 Battle of Aljubarrota consolidates Portuguese independence
1464 Marriage of Isabella of Castile with Ferdinand of Aragon
1474 Isabella I becomes queen of Castile
1479 Ferdinand II becomes king of Aragon
1492 Capture of kingdom of Granada

1517 Charles I assumes crowns of Aragon and Castile, uniting Spain
1519 Charles elected Holy Roman Emperor (Charles V)
1519–21 Revolt of the *comuneros* in Castile
1556 Charles abdicates: Philip II becomes king of Spain
1580 Extinction of Portuguese ruling house of Aviz: Philip II assumes Portuguese crown

1621–43 Count-Duke of Olivares controls Spanish policy
1640 Revolts in Catalonia and Portugal. João IV re-establishes Portuguese independence
1659 Peace of the Pyrenees ends Catalan revolt: Roussillon and Cerdagne ceded by Spain to France
1660 Accession of Carlos II (last Spanish Habsburg)
1669 Spain recognizes Portuguese independence

1700 Death of Carlos II. Philip of Bourbon crowned Philip V of Spain – contested by Charles of Austria, with support of Catalonia and Aragon
1716 Abolition of the *fueros* of Aragon, Valencia and Majorca
1746–88 Political and administrative reforms in Spain
1750–77 Reforms of Pombal in Portugal

1807 Napoleonic invasion of peninsula
1808–14 Spanish War of Independence
1812 Constitution of Cádiz
1814 Restoration of Bourbon monarchy
1828–34 Miguelist civil war in Portugal
1833–40 Carlist civil war in Spain
1868 Abdication of Isabel II of Spain
1873–74 1st Spanish Republic
1874 Restoration of monarchy

1908 Assassination of King Carlos I of Portugal
1910 Proclamation of Portuguese Republic
1923–30 Dictatorship of Primo de Rivera in Spain
1931–39 2nd Spanish Republic
1933–74 New State in Portugal
1936–39 Civil war in Spain
1939–75 Francisco Franco Spanish head of state
1974 Revolution in Portugal
1975 Death of Franco. Spanish monarchy restored
1976 New constitution in Portugal (modified in 1982)
1978 New Spanish constitution
1980–83 17 autonomous regions created in Spain

1390s Pogroms against Jews in Castile and Aragon
1416 Prince Henry of Portugal founds first school of navigation
1474 First printing press established in Valencia
1477–90 Introduction of Spanish Inquisition
1492 Jews expelled from Spain
1497 Jews expelled from Portugal

Manueline architectural style in Portugal; plateresque in Spain. "Golden Age" of Spanish literature
1536 Inquisition introduced into Portugal
1540 Jesuit Order founded
1563 Council of Trent launches Counter-Reformation in Spain
1572 Camões publishes *Os Lusíados*
1580–1535 Lope de Vega writes some 1800 plays

"Golden Age" continues
1605–15 Cervantes publishes *Don Quixote* in 2 parts
1609 Expulsion of the *Moriscos*
1623–60 Velázquez court painter to Philip IV of Spain
1629–81 Pedro Calderón de la Barca produces more than 100 *comedias* and a further 76 religious dramas

1720 Portuguese Academy of History founded
1735 Spanish Academy of History founded
1759 Jesuits expelled from Portugal
1767 Jesuits expelled from Spain
1786–1824 Goya court painter to 4 successive kings of Spain

1814–32 Emigration of many Spanish and Portuguese liberal intellectuals
1840–70 Revival of Catalan language and literature
1860s onward Replanning of Madrid and Barcelona. Emergence of Barcelona as cosmopolitan cultural center
1898 "Generation of 1898" writers in Spanish include Unamuno, Ortega and Antonio Machado

1900 Pablo Picasso moves to Paris to join other Spanish emigré artists
1927 "Generation of 1927" in Spain includes Lorca, Albertí and Aleixandre
1933–75 Repressive regimes in Portugal and Spain force many artists into exile
1975 onward Revival of regional culture in Spain; lifting of political and moral censorship

---

c.1350 Black Death appears in peninsula, followed by a worsening in social and economic conditions and a major decline in population
Late 15th century Some improvement in rural conditions following reforms of Catholic Monarchs
1499 *Moriscos* revolt in Andalusia

Spanish and Portuguese economy revitalized by American trade. Beginnings of the price revolution
1550 onward Flow of bullion fails to pay for Spain's aggressive foreign policy. Economic strains lead to periodic royal bankruptcies
1568–70 2nd *Morisco* revolt

Spanish economic decline continues, with periodic bankruptcies declared, leading to administrative and economic collapse in Castile by the end of the century
1632–40 Failure of Olivares' attempts at economic reform

1700–1755 Brazilian trade brings period of prosperity to Portugal. Beginnings of Spanish economic revival
1703 Methuen Treaties lay basis for Anglo-Portuguese trade
1749–88 Economic reforms in Spain
1755 Earthquake devastates Lisbon

Later 19th century Rural economic stagnation in Spain and Portugal. Growing politicization of working class and rise of anarchism as vehicle of social protest
Growth of regionalism in Spain

1945–70 Gradual state-directed economic revival in Spain
1950 onward Reemergence of nationalist movements: ETA launches terrorist campaign
1974 onward Return of democracy opens up society to liberalizing movements

9

PREFACE

"Spain is different." This tourist slogan of the 1960s drew on foreign perceptions of a sun-soaked land where life continued as it had for centuries. Pictures of village life and Arab architecture became the staple fare of holiday brochures. The Iberian peninsula was marketed as a forgotten region, as befitted one of the least known and least understood areas of Europe. Yet, behind the popular images lies an immense cultural diversity. Both Portugal and Spain created great empires, and the links forged during their periods of expansion have left a rich cultural legacy, as have the earlier settlements of the peninsula by Phoenicians, Celts, Greeks, Romans, Visigoths and Arabs. The *Cultural Atlas of Spain and Portugal* explores this remarkable inheritance.

Part One of the *Atlas* sets out the physical features of the peninsula, stressing its size, its mountainous character and the hostility of much of the terrain. This dramatic geography has shaped the historical development of both Spain and Portugal. Within the peninsula, the contrast between the arid south and temperate north provides a key to the profound regional diversity that is a recurring theme in the history of the Iberian lands. The mountain barrier of the Pyrenees, separating the peninsula from France, and its long coastline, have played a major part in forming its contacts with the outside world, which for long periods of its history have lain by sea with the Mediterranean countries to the east, Africa to the south, and west into the Atlantic and beyond, rather than with western Europe.

Part Two traces the political and cultural development of Spain and Portugal from prehistoric times to the present day. It shows how the succession of early colonizers from the Phoenicians to the Visigoths interrelated with the populations already living there, and how the Arab invasion of 711 divided the peninsula between the Christian north and Islamic south. The co-existence of Muslims, Jews and Christians led to a flourishing of learning and culture unique in the Europe of that period, but as the Christian monarchies strengthened, so territorial gains were made at the expense of the Arabs: Granada, the last Muslim kingdom on the peninsula, fell to Ferdinand and Isabella in 1492, the year that Columbus made his first voyage to the New World.

Both Portugal and Spain were at the forefront of the European age of discovery, establishing empires in Asia and America. The wealth that flowed into the peninsula led to a remarkable flowering of art and literature. Unified under the Habsburg monarchs, during this "Golden Age" Spain extended her European possessions; for a time Portugal came under its rule before reclaiming its independence in 1640. With the passing of the Spanish throne to the Bourbons in 1700, Spanish court life became increasingly Francophile; the old regime could not resist the forces of the French Revolution and crumbled before Napoleon's invading armies – a period of turmoil and transition chronicled by Goya's dramatic paintings. The 19th century was marked by the loss of the American colonies and by civil wars and military *coup d'etats*, while the rapid industrialization of Catalonia and the Basque Country fueled the growth of regional nationalisms, which found remarkable artistic expression in the rebuilding of Barcelona at the turn of the century.

In Portugal, Manuel II's abdication in 1910 gave rise to a republic; in Spain, Alfonso XIII lost his throne in 1931. The text describes the constitutional crises and – in Spain – civil war that paved the way for the authoritarian dictatorships of Salazar in Portugal and Franco in Spain when stifling insistence on political conformity and conservative morality effectively suffocated artistic and cultural experimentation. The return to democracy in both countries in 1974-5 was accompanied by cultural and social changes that have revolutionized the peninsula. Iberian society is now secularized; women have an increasingly important role to play outside the home, and family life itself has changed considerably.

Part Three looks at the geographic regions of the peninsula. Detailed maps shows the different characters of the regions at a glance, while the text describes their physical background and cultural and historical development, and looks at the continuing strength of local identities on the peninsula.

Maps throughout the *Atlas* provide the physical, economic and political background, while the illustrated special features highlight particular topics within each chapter and bring them into closer focus. Most of the writing has been divided between Mary Vincent, who was responsible for Part One, the last two chapters of Part Two, and Part Three, and Robert Stradling, who covered the history of the peninsula from 1470 to 1812. Dr Andrew Fear wrote the chapter on the early history and Dr John Edwards the medieval period. Dr Roger Collins provided the special features on Visigothic and Asturian Churches, Early Spanish Frescoes, the Great Mosque at Córdoba, Medieval Toledo, and the Alhambra, and gave great help with captioning. Linda Proud contributed the features on the Altarpiece of St Vincent and the Traveler in Spain. Finally, acknowledgement must be made to the editorial support given by Robert McNeil of the Bodleian Library who generously checked dates, drew up the chronology, lists of ruling houses and glossary, and wrote the special features on Batalha, Portuguese Navigators, Pombal and the Rebuilding of Lisbon, Goya, and Portuguese Tiles.

Mary Vincent
Robert Stradling

PART ONE
THE PHYSICAL BACKGROUND

THE LAND AND THE PEOPLE

The peninsula

The position of the Iberian peninsula – which contains the countries of Spain and Portugal – is, in every sense, peripheral. It lies at the southwest corner of Europe, on the very edge of the continent, part of both its western and its southern fringe. Yet, in geopolitical terms, it should be a formidable power. At 504,782 square kilometers, the kingdom of Spain is – excluding Russia – the second largest country in Europe, being only fractionally smaller than France and nearly half as large again as the new Germany. Moreover, with its Atlantic coastline and its unique proximity to the African continent – the Strait of Gibraltar is a mere 13 kilometers across at its narrowest point – the Iberian peninsula might have been expected to act as a bridge between Europe and the Americas and Europe and Africa. Instead, the great bulk of the Iberian peninsula has proved a bulwark, separating west and east, south and north. For much of their history, the nations of the peninsula have occupied a marginal position in European affairs. It has often been said that the Iberian peninsula may be *in* the European continent, but it is not truly *of* it.

Frontiers

Seven-eighths of the peninsula is bounded by sea. Though the ocean waters have proved formidable defenses, they have also contributed to the insularity of Spain and Portugal, particularly as the only land boundary, with France, is formed by the great peaks of the Pyrenees, the broadest and highest mountain range in the peninsula. Dating from the Tertiary and Quaternary periods (65 to 2 million years ago), the Pyrenees rise to 3,404 meters at their highest point (Aneto Peak) and, except at their coastal flanks, are difficult to cross, their complex structure of steeply scarped sierras, or ranges, and deep river valleys making them virtually impenetrable.

The peninsula is divided between the sovereign territories of Spain and Portugal. The only exceptions are the Pyrenean valley that forms the independent fiefdom of Andorra and the 6 square kilometers of rock midway along its southern coast that is Gibraltar – a British possession since 1713. Portugal is by far the smaller nation, occupying around 15 percent of the peninsula. Its boundary with Spain – unchanged since the 13th century – is political in origin but still reflects certain geographical features. For much of its length it runs through the thinly populated borderlands of Extremadura while other stretches are marked by waterways. Though most of these are minor rivers, the great Douro (Duero), which rises in Castile and flows into the sea at Porto, forms the border in Portugal's northeastern corner, while in the far south the Guadiana separates the Portuguese Algarve from Spanish Andalusia before draining into the Gulf of Cádiz. Indeed, 54 percent of Portugal's eastern border runs along steep-sided river canyons; between Paradela and Barca d'Alva, the Douro falls 500 meters through a canyon whose walls are 30 meters high in places. Deep

river gorges, combined with the unpopulated arid terrain that forms much of the borderland, have always ensured that Portugal is the remotest part of a remote region. Divided from the interior by geography, if not by distance, Portugal has always looked to the coast. Its territory includes the volcanic Atlantic islands of Madeira and the Azores, 600 and 1,200 kilometers off the coasts of Morocco and Portugal respectively, legacies of the nation's maritime past.

Mountains

Spain occupies 85 percent of the peninsula as well as the Balearic Islands off the Mediterranean coast – the extension of the peninsula's southern highland ranges, known as the Baetic Mountains – the North African enclaves of Ceuta and Melilla, and the volcanic archipelago of the Canaries, far to the south in the Atlantic. Its development has been profoundly affected by what has been referred to as its "intractable geography". In marked contrast to Portugal, which is predominantly low-lying, Spain is the second highest country in Europe after Switzerland. The peninsula's tallest peak is Mulhacén (3,478 meters) in the Sierra Nevada, part of the Baetic Mountains. Yet, though both the high Pyrenees and the alpine slopes of the Sierra Nevada provide dramatic scenery, Spain's altitude is largely accounted for by the vast tableland, or *meseta*, that

Below The coast around Cartagena in southeastern Spain is littered with abandoned industrial buildings – a legacy of the area's mining heritage. The minerals found here were first exploited by the Phoenicians and Romans (Cartagena means "New Carthage"). The ancient silver mines are long since exhausted, though there are still working mines in the area. Perhaps because of its industrial associations, this stretch was among the last parts of Spain's Mediterranean coastline to be developed for tourism. Now, however, white-fronted hotels and villas are springing up in formerly deserted coves.

Right Huesca, the northernmost province in Aragon, is dominated by the high Pyrenees. National reserves now protect much of the mountain land and its wildlife (including the last small colony of Pyrenean brown bears); they are popular with hikers. Towns nestle in the shadow of the imposing mountains. Communications in the region have improved rapidly in recent years but, previously these communities were very isolated.

Below right This parched Mediterranean *sierra* is characteristic of much of the landscape of southern Spain. Though the mountains of Murcia's Sierra del Molina are quite low, the arid climate ensures that most vegetation is sparse and scrubby. Only the most sure-footed of animals, such as goats, are secure scrambling about on the rocky hillsides, while birds of prey wheel overhead.

44°

Adour

Bay of Biscay

La Coruña

Oviedo

Santander

Bilbao

San Sebastián

Peña Cerredo
2642

Santiago de Compostela

CANTABRIAN MOUNTAINS

Pamplona

Mte

León

Carrion

Pisuerga

Arlanzón

Burgos

Ebro

42°

Miño

Sierra Cabrera

Esla

Sierra de la Demanda

Gállego

Lima

Támega

Valladolid

Douro

IBERIAN MOUNTAINS

Huerva

Zaragoza

Porto

Douro

Embalse de
Almendra

Salamanca

Sierra de Guadarrama

Tagus

ATLANTIC
OCEAN

Mondego

Tormes

Serrania
de Cuenca

Coimbra

Sierra da Estrela

Sierra de la
Peña de Francia

Sierra de
Gata

Sierra de Gredos

Madrid

Embalse de
Buendia

40°

Pico de Almanzor
2592

Alberche

Jarama

PORTUGAL

Tagus

Embalse de
Alcántara

Tagus

SPAIN

Záncara

Valencia

Tagus

Sorraia

Júcar

Lisbon

Badajoz

Guadiana

Setúbal

Evora

Barragem
de Alqueva

Guadalimar

Alicante

Sado

38°

Ardila

Sierra Morena

Segura

Murcia

Córdoba

Sierra
de Segura

Guadalfentin

Cartagena

Guadiana

Guadalquivir

Genil

BAETIC MOUNTAINS

Seville

Faro

Granada

Gulf of
Cádiz

Mulhacén
3482
Sierra Nevada

Almería

Guadalete

Málaga

Cádiz

36°

Costa del Sol

Gibraltar (UK)

Strait of Gibraltar

Ceuta (Sp)

Melilla (Sp)

MOROCCO

8°   6°   4°   2°

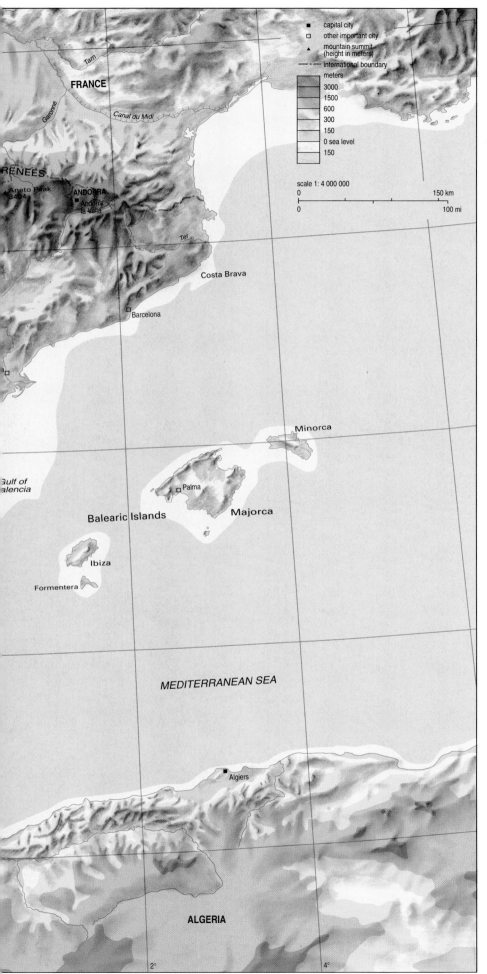

capital city
other important city
mountain summit
(height in meters)
international boundary
meters
3000
1500
600
300
150
0 sea level
150

scale 1: 4 000 000

0   150 km

0   100 mi

FRANCE

Tarn

Garonne

Canal du Midi

PYRENEES

Aneto Peak
3404

ANDORRA

Andorra
la Vella

Ter

Costa Brava

Barcelona

Gulf of
Valencia

Minorca

Palma

Balearic Islands   Majorca

Ibiza

Formentera

MEDITERRANEAN SEA

Algiers

ALGERIA

2°   4°

forms the interior of the peninsula. This great plateau stands at over 600 meters; its high plains and huge skies form one of the peninsula's flattest, most relentless, yet most distinctive landscapes.

Though the tablelands stretch into the Portuguese provinces of Trás-os-Montes, Beira and Alentejo, the *meseta* covers almost the same area as the historic kingdom of Castile, the nucleus of modern Spain. Physically and, from the late Middle Ages, politically dominant, Castile is nevertheless a harsh, sparsely populated land, whose inhabitants are renowned for their stoicism. The soil is dry and thin; in the steppe-lands of La Mancha the underlying rocks break through the topsoil, while other areas of the *meseta* are subject to wind erosion.

Except to the west – where the *meseta* slopes toward the wide coastal plains of Portugal – the central plateau of Castile is bounded by high mountain ranges. To the north, the Mesozoic Cantabrian Mountains, which reach 2,642 meters at Peña Cerredo, isolate the tableland from the Atlantic coast; in the south, the plains end at the Sierra Morena, whose parched, undulating highlands are among the oldest in the peninsula. The eastern edge of the *meseta* is marked by the Iberian Mountains, one arm of which extends into a series of high, dislocated sierras – Guadarrama, Gredos, Gata, Peña de Francia – that bisect the central tablelands and end in Portugal's highest mountain range, the Serra da Estrêla. These "East–West ramparts", in the words of the English writer Laurie Lee, "go ranging across Spain and divide its people into separate races". For many observers, the strength of local loyalties and identities, over and above national ones, has been one of the most distinctive features of modern Spain and Portugal.

Communications
This persistent localism is, in part, a reflection of geography. The Castilian interior is effectively cut off from the traditionally prosperous coastal fringe by numerous mountain ranges, while a lack of navigable waterways has further impeded internal exchange. None of the five major rivers – the Douro, Ebro, Tagus, Guadiana and Guadalquivir – that drain the *meseta* and, with the exception of the Ebro, flow west to the Atlantic, are naturally fully navigable. Iberian rivers have often proved to be boundaries rather than channels of communication; both Portugal and Spain have regions known as Extremadura (Estremadura in Portuguese), meaning "beyond the Douro", while the name given to the Alentejo plains in southern Portugal means "beyond the Tagus" Indeed, the Tagus, running just to the south of the Serra da Estrêla, reinforces the bisection of Portugal.

Spain has 3,144 kilometers of coastline, and Portugal a further 974 kilometers. It is therefore unsurprising that maritime communications have played a vital part in both countries' development. At least until the coming of motor transportation, the quickest, cheapest and most convenient routes were by sea. Yet, even on this lengthy coastline, geography has not been kind. With the exception of Lisbon – which is among the greatest of Europe's historic ports – the natural harbors of the Atlantic coast are isolated from the hinterland. The Galician coastline of Spain, stretching along the Atlantic coast north of Portugal, is deeply indented with drowned estuaries, or *rías*. While these provide superb natural anchorages for the fishing boats that have worked off this dangerous coast for

mean January temperature
°C
12
8
4
0

scale 1 : 10 240 000

mean July temperature
°C
28
24
20
16

scale 1 : 10 240 000

centuries, until the 20th century they were primarily of local benefit. Moreover, the fiord-like landscape hinders internal communications. The region is also isolated from the rest of the mainland by the Cantabrian Mountains, the northern limit of the *meseta*, which are in parts almost inaccessible.

Climate and cultivation

In a land of contrasts, the difference between wet and dry Spain is one of the most acute. The northwest is the peninsula's wettest area. In places the annual rainfall exceeds 1,650 millimeters and, unlike other parts of the peninsula, there is no summer drought. The rugged, rainy terrain lends itself to herding and is the only part of the peninsula that supports dairying. It is wooded with oak, pine and chestnut, and agricultural land can be poor. Despite the beauty and apparent

softness of its lush landscapes, life is often harsh in this part of Spain.

There can be no doubting the harshness of the dry lands to the south. At their most extreme, they become semi-desert, as in parts of the provinces of Almería and Murcia in Spain's southeastern corner – the area known as "mini-Hollywood" proved the ideal setting for the "spaghetti westerns" made in the 1960s and 1970s. Its parched landscape is home to the peninsula's only indigenous palm tree (*Chamaerops humilis*), but naturally supports little other vegetation. Elsewhere in the peninsula, rain falls in winter; there is little or none in summer.

All the dry regions of the peninsula have an abundance of sun, giving brilliant blue skies and a clear, piercingly intense, light. Summers are punishingly hot while, in the interior tablelands of Castile, where the

Climate of the peninsula
The peninsula experiences great variations in temperature (*above left*) and precipitation (*above right*) caused by the influence of the vast continental interior, the surrounding oceans and the mountains. Most rain falls in winter, when westerly winds blowing from the Atlantic bring cool, wet conditions to the Atlantic coasts. Before reaching the interior, they are pushed north and south by a high pressure system that develops over the *meseta*, keeping it drier and very cold: all parts of the peninsula can experience cold conditions when air from the *meseta* pushes down to the coasts. The westerly wind belt moves northward in summer, restricting rainfall to the mountains of the north and northwest. Farther south

Left In Almería, as in other hot, arid parts of the peninsula, market garden crops are extensively cultivated under plastic. Tomatoes, peppers, aubergines and melons are grown year-round to supply a profitable export market.

Below Galicia's Atlantic coast has long been famed for its abundant seafood. Fish-canning and mollusk-farming are important local industries. These mussel rafts are in the Ría de Arosa. Dramatic chases frequently take place at night around them as customs vessels go in pursuit of smugglers' speedboats – often with fatal consequences. Some smugglers bring in contraband tobacco, but most are involved in the drug trade.

Overleaf Vast areas of Spain are given over to the cultivation of vines; in the 1970s, it had more land under the vine than any other country in Europe – though, paradoxically, as wine production has increased, the vineyard acreage has shrunk. Plowing between the rows of vines takes place in March and April when a solitary tractor may cover large expanses of ground.

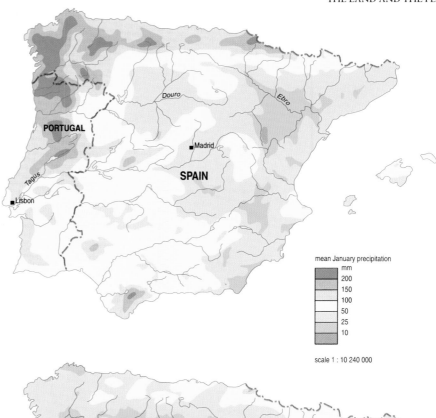

mean January precipitation
mm
200
150
100
50
25
10

scale 1 : 10 240 000

mean July precipitation
mm
150
100
50
25
10

scale 1 : 10 240 000

the Atlantic coast is hot and dry, influenced by the Azores high pressure system over the Atlantic to the west. The interior warms up quickly and remains largely dry: aridity is increased by periodic warm, dry winds from Africa. The northeast Mediterranean coast receives most of its rain in the fall when moisture-carrying winds blow in off the sea. Farther south there is greater local variation: coastal plains and basins in the rainshadow of the mountain ranges are arid, but the mountains themselves are wetter. Snow cover on the Sierra Nevada may last for 7 months or longer. On the high slopes of the Pyrenees snow lies all year.

moderating influence of the sea is not felt, winter is just as hard: the local climate is popularly referred to as "nine months of winter, three months of hell". Even though the coasts have no true winter, Catalonia is racked by the cold north wind known locally as the *tramontana*. Paradoxically, the Atlantic coast of southern Portugal is the only part of the peninsula to enjoy a truly "Mediterranean" climate of hot, dry summers and mild, wet winters.

It is the coastal plains, together with the fertile river valley of the Guadalquivir, that contain the peninsula's richest farmland. Rice, cotton, dates and even bananas, as well as the more familiar citrus fruits, tomatoes and melons, are all grown. Away from these oases, the southern peninsula – especially the uplands of Andalusia – is dominated by the cultivation of olives. With over 190 million olive trees, Spain is the

world's largest olive producer. The tree is native to the region and is particularly suited to a Mediterranean climate; it will tolerate summer drought, but not the frosts of winter.

As the interior of the peninsula suffers from severe winters, it has very different vegetation. Rather than the oaks of the north or the palms of the south and east, the *meseta*'s most typical tree is the ilex or evergreen oak, while cork oaks flourish in the borderlands of the Spanish Extremadura and Portuguese Alentejo. Traditionally, the tablelands of the *meseta* were used for sheep pasturage, but they have proved one of the few areas of western Europe able to support the prairie-style cultivation of wheat, and are now dominated by huge grain-fields. These apparently endless wheatlands enhance the naturally flat landscape of the northern plains, the rippling grain confusing the doves

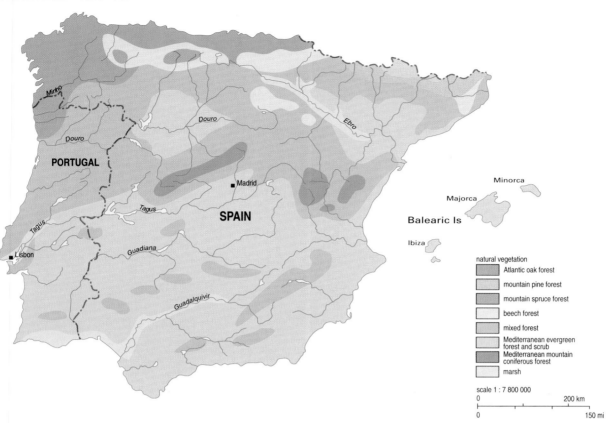

Natural vegetation of the Iberian peninsula
Deciduous woodland, predominantly of oak, is the natural vegetation of the north and northwest, with beech and conifers at higher altitudes: in the Pyrenees pine forests extend up to the treeline. Today this northern area supports forestry and dairying. To the south, little of the natural evergreen oak forests survives. Much of the northern *meseta* is given over to wheat-farming, with sheep pasturage where soils are too poor for cultivation. Olives and vines are widely cultivated in the south. As a result of centuries of human activity, a Mediterranean scrub vegetation consisting of herbs and evergreen shrubs and trees predominates in much of the region. In some arid areas of the southeast a subtropical vegetation more typical of northern Africa is to be found.

natural vegetation

- Atlantic oak forest
- mountain pine forest
- mountain spruce forest
- beech forest
- mixed forest
- Mediterranean evergreen forest and scrub
- Mediterranean mountain coniferous forest
- marsh

scale 1 : 7 800 000

0   200 km

0   150 mi

by resembling the waves of the sea – at least according
to one of the greatest of Spain's 20th-century poets,
Rafael Alberti (b. 1902).

People

In contrast to the peninsula's dramatic variety of landscape and climate, its peoples are ethnically homo-
genous. Latin descent dominates: nearly all the
peninsula's inhabitants have the Mediterranean coloring of olive complexion, dark hair and brown eyes,
though lighter coloring is by no means uncommon,
particularly in the Celtic northwest. Before the coming
of the Romans in the 2nd century BC, much of the
peninsula was inhabited by the Celtiberians, the name
given to the mixture of Celtic peoples – originally from
central Europe, who entered the peninsula through the
Pyrenees in about the 7th and 6th centuries BC – and
the Iberians, already settled there, who are thought to
have originated either in North Africa or in the eastern Mediterranean. Intermarriage with the Roman
settlers provided the common Latin ancestry so apparent among the modern peoples of the peninsula. Only
the Basques, already long established in the western
Pyrenees, escaped these assimilations, preserving their
unique pre-Indo-European culture from both Roman
and the later Visigothic invaders.

The cultural legacy of the Celts is strongest in Galicia. It is often compared to the west of Ireland, not
only because of its rain-sodden scenery, but because
the people listen to bagpipes, tell tales of mermaids
and are generally credited with a romantic, artistic dis-
position. Both Galicia and the west coast of Ireland are
frequently described as "mournful", though Galicians
are not thought to share the Irish fighting temper. All
the Celtic regions of western Europe have, over the
years, proved a fertile source of emigrants, particularly to the new world: in Argentina, all Spaniards are
routinely referred to as *gallegos*.

Unlike the south, the northern peninsula was not
long occupied by the Arabs, or Moors, who invaded
from North Africa in the 8th century AD. Their legacy
may be seen in the darker coloring and Arab features
of many southerners, especially in Andalusia. The very
names of Andalusia and the Algarve are derived from
Arabic words, and the white-walled houses, tiled
courtyards and formal gardens that are a distinguish-
ing feature of the south are also a direct inheritance
from its Islamic past.

Except for Basque – which appears to be unrelated
to any other known language – all the languages spoken on the peninsula are derived from Latin, though
many individual words are borrowed from Arabic.
The dominant languages are the official state languages, Portuguese and Castilian Spanish (*castellano*).
Portuguese is the only language spoken in Portugal,
but though local languages have been discouraged in
the past, and at times actively suppressed, Spain has
several thriving minority tongues. Their survival
reflects the continuing vigor of regional identities
within the modern Spanish state even if, today, all citizens speak *castellano* as well as the local idiom. The
language of Galicia, *galego*, is an old form of Portuguese while the ancient and difficult Basque tongue
– Euskera – survives in the western Pyrenees. Catalan,
a close relative of Provençal, the language of southern
France, is the most widespread of the minority languages, being spoken in Valencia and the Balearic
Islands as well as Catalonia.

Urbanization

Until the beginning of the 20th century, the population of the Iberian peninsula was predominantly a
rural, agricultural one. Historically the location of the
cities – many of them founded by the Romans –
depended upon trade routes and the need for defense.
The importance of interior fortified towns like Elvas
and Ciudad Rodrigo – both of which guarded the
much fought-over frontier lands – declined after the

boundary between Spain and Portugal was settled and the peninsula reconquered from the Arabs.

The rigors of the harsh *meseta* have long pushed the population of the peninsula toward the coasts. Though Philip II chose Madrid in the center of Castile as his political capital in 1560, it did not become Spain's economic capital until this century. As commerce and industry developed, they became concentrated in the hinterlands of the peninsula's coastal cities, particularly Barcelona on the Mediterranean, Bilbao in the north, and – to a lesser extent – Porto and Lisbon in Portugal. In the 19th century, Barcelona was Spain's leading metropolis, when its prosperity was based on trade and textiles. For similar reasons Porto, Portugal's second city, was growing faster than Lisbon but the Portuguese capital soon recovered; unlike Madrid, Lisbon – with its fertile hinterland and natural harbor – is an obvious site for a capital. Not until the expressway and airplane revolutionized communications in the second half of the 20th century did Madrid emerge as Spain's foremost city. In 1950 Madrid was only fractionally larger than Barcelona, but by 1990 it had far outstripped it.

This growth is the result of agricultural decline and rural depopulation, which since the beginning of the century – and even more rapidly since 1950 – have had the effect of increasing urbanization throughout the peninsula. The rise of tourism, has transformed both the look and the prosperity of the eastern and southern coasts. Urban development – characterized by high-rise hotels and time-share apartments – covers the coasts from the Algarve to Catalonia. Old towns like Faro, Málaga, and Alicante have developed sprawling suburbs; former fishing villages like Torremolinos and Benidorm have been transformed into holiday resorts. Ports such as Vigo in Galicia have grown rapidly, particularly when – as in the case of Cartagena in Valencia – they were home to a naval base – or, as in Setúbal, south of Lisbon, to industry.

Away from the coasts, virtually all the provincial capitals have increased their populations since the end of the last century. Though many of them serve predominantly rural areas, the growth of local government, banking and service industries offered new job opportunities as agricultural employment declined. Light industry in cities like Valladolid, capital of Old Castile, or Zaragoza in the Ebro valley also attracted population. Today, Madrid is fast developing Spain's first commuter belt as affluent young families break the habit of generations and move out to live beyond the city limits. Madrid and its hinterland is, however, a rare success story in Castile; modern communications have hastened the drift away from the interior, and the region is increasingly empty of inhabitants.

PART TWO
A HISTORY OF THE PENINSULA

THE PENINSULA TO THE FALL
OF THE VISIGOTHS

Prehistory

Throughout its history, the Iberian peninsula, a large and high diverse geographical land mass, has been settled, not surprisingly, by a wide range of peoples. When studying the early history of the peninsula it is important not to impose an artificial unity on these groups, nor to assume that they followed one another in successive cultural waves. Many of these people lived alongside one another and their cultures interacted and intertwined in many different ways.

What we call prehistory ("before history") is appro-

priately named. It is impossible to recover a narrative of peoples from archaeological traces alone; the best we can do, before the advent of written evidence, is to record the scattered fragments of worlds and peoples that have now vanished. The most spectacular evidence of human occupation in the Palaeolithic period is provided by the cave paintings of bison and other animals at Altamira in the Cantabrian Mountains. These vivid depictions were produced by people of the Magdalenian culture, which dates from c.16,000–10,000 BC, at the end of the last Ice Age. Even older

Right The Els Tudens naveta, or collective tomb, of Minorca is the oldest architectural monument still standing in Spain, dating back to c. 1500–1300 BC. A product of the Bronze Age, its inner chambers were found to hold the remains of over 100 individuals.

Below The cave-paintings at Altamira, executed in full color and showing an understanding of perspective, are among the finest known examples of Palaeolithic art anywhere in the world. Though the motives of their Stone-Age creators will never be securely known, a popular theory is that the paintings were associated with rituals performed to ensure successful hunting.

paintings dating from the Auriginacian period (before 30,000 BC) have been found nearby at Covalanas.

Also impressive are the large stone monuments, particularly chambered tombs, of the megalithic culture that developed among the early farmers of northern and western Europe in the Neolithic period. They were once thought to have derived from cultures in the eastern Mediterranean – the chambered tombs in particular bear a resemblance to the *tholoi* (beehive tombs) of Mycenaean Greece, dating from the Late Bronze Age of the 2nd millennium BC. However radiocarbon dating now places them well before their posited "models". In the Iberian peninsula, megaliths run in a giant horseshoe around the Atlantic and southern coasts, and include large chambered tombs such as those found at Carapito in Portugal, which have been shown to date from the 4th millennium BC, and at Cueva de Romeral near Antequera in southern Spain. The latter tomb possesses a corbelled central chamber rising almost 4 meters in height that is built of drystone walls and covered by an earthen mound, or barrow, 70 meters in diameter. Fortified settlements surrounded by walls with defensive bastions are also to be found. Those at Zambujal and Vila Nova de São Pedro in the Tagus region of Portugal and at Los Millares in Almería, date from the early 3rd millennium BC. It was in this period that copper was first worked in the Iberian peninsula.

The Iberians

The origins of the people known today as the Iberians remains a matter for dispute. They first appeared in the peninsula c. 1600 BC. For many years it was thought that the proto-Iberians were migrants from North Africa, but many scholars now suggest an origin in southern Europe. Iberian settlement is found along the southern coastal strip of Spain, extending into the Guadalquivir valley, and along the Mediterranean coast up to Catalonia and beyond; Iberian settlements, such as that at Enserune, have been found in the south of France.

Like many other Mediterranean peoples, the Iberians seem to have developed a preference for living in urban sites early in their history. This tendency appears to have strengthened as time went on, to give rise to sophisticated fortified and internally planned towns. These were defended with walls built of massive slabs of masonry, often with bastions, such as those at Ullastret (occupied c.500 BC–c.200 BC) in the northeast and at Osuna (occupied in the 1st century BC) in Seville. We know little of the Iberians' political arrangements. They appear to have been a diverse group with no national consciousness. Tribes seem to have been ruled over by kings, and some form of feudal hierarchy may have existed – the name has come down to us of a King Culchus who ruled over twenty towns in Andalusia. The Iberian warrior's obligation of loyalty to the death to his leaders, the *devotio iberica*, which impressed later classical commentators, perhaps suggests such an arrangement.

The Iberians developed a system of writing, later adopting and modifying the Phoenician script to produce a 29-symbol semi-syllabic alphabet. Their writing is known from many inscriptions, but they have yet to be deciphered. However, there appear to have been two distinct versions of the language, one found in Andalusia and the other on the Mediterranean coast. The language does not appear to be Indo-European in origin. At one time, the Basque language was considered an obvious descendant, but it is now agreed that the two are not related, leaving the origins of the latter still unexplained.

The Iberians were not the only inhabitants of the peninsula. In the late 7th and 6th centuries BC large numbers of Celts of the Hallstatt culture of central Europe migrated through the Pyrenees into northern and western Spain, spreading into the central *meseta* to occupy about half of the peninsula's total land mass. They merged quite rapidly with the peoples already there, to produce a distinct Celtiberian culture. This exhibited a much more rural pattern of settlement than that of the Iberians.

The Art of the Iberians

Iberian art is the source of most of our information about life in the peninsula in the 1st millennium BC, providing details about dress, weaponry and so on. With a careful interpretation of the contexts in which the artifacts are found (usually funerary or religious), we can also deduce a good deal about the structure of Iberian society. But more than this, it represents a major artistic achievement in its own right.

Sculpture features prominently in this art. Its most common subject is the human figure, though representations of animals are also frequently found. While large pieces were worked in stone, votive figurines of bronze are also common. In addition, substantial amounts of pottery and jewelry were produced. Iberian art shows both Phoenician and Greek influence, but it has its own distinctive style and is by no means merely imitative. It is difficult to date the material with any precision. The 4th century BC is often regarded as the summit of Iberian creativity; however, high-quality Iberian carving probably dating to the 1st century BC has been found at Osuna, Seville. The arrival of the Romans in the peninsula in the 3rd century BC did not extinguish the indigenous artistic tradition. Iberian painted pottery is found as late as the 1st century AD, and Iberian influence is discernible in much sculpture from the Roman period.

Below Free-standing sculptures of bulls are a common feature of Iberian art. This bull-man from Balazote is much rarer (traces of horns can be seen above the ears). The carving is entirely Iberian in style and its somewhat rude execution suggests that it is an early work. The subject, however, appears to be foreign. Its inspiration could be Phoenician (fantastic semihumans were a common part of oriental religion) or Greek – an archaic Greek figurine of a centaur (man-horse) has been found at Rollos in Spain. The lack of parallels suggests that such pieces did not appeal greatly to Iberian taste.

The so-called Dama de Elche (*above*) and the Dama de Baza (*right*) are funerary statues: the latter is shown in situ in the tomb it was found in in 1971. Cavities at the rear of both statues held a cinerary urn. The statues were originally covered with a fine white plaster and were richly painted. Substantial amounts of this painting still survives in the case of the Dama de Baza. The statues were not portraits of the deceased, as is clear from the presence of a warrior's equipment in the tomb. They may represent an Iberian goddess of the underworld, or perhaps the Phoenician goddess Astarte.

Left This votive bronze warrior is typical of many small Iberian statuettes. His small shield (*caetra*), sword and broad belt may represent the equipment carried by the Iberian warriors of Andalusia. But the piece was found in a religious context, so caution should be taken in using it as evidence for Iberian life.

Below The decoration of Iberian pottery may tell us about life in the peninsula. Here we see a number of warriors. Their use of large shields and javelins is clear, but the interpretation of their differently hatched tunics is more problematic. Do they represent different kinds of clothing, or is body armor being shown?

Below Iberian craftsmen produced gold and silver jewelry of a high quality, borrowing techniques from the orient and Greece to produce work that conformed to their own artistic canons. This horde from Jávea would have been a woman's personal collection of jewelry. The large diadem shows a command of oriental filigree work, the spiral patterns are of Celtic inspiration, but the vegetal motifs, and the jeweler's use of panels to display them, are Iberian in origin.

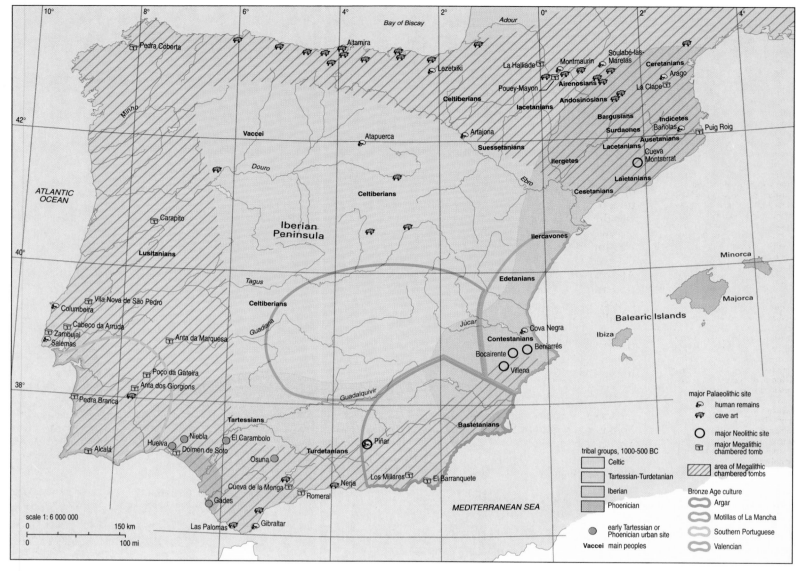

Widening contacts: the Phoenicians

A major development in the cultural life of the peninsula took place in the southwest from c.1300 BC onwards. This was the emergence in the Alentejo region of southern Portugal of a culture that buried its dead in cists marked by stone grave stelae (engraved memorial pillars). These depict in the main warlike objects such as spears, swords, and curious anchor-shaped objects. The stelae gradually spread eastward into Andalusia and Extremadura and further objects came to be depicted on them. These include shields with a curious indentation that seem to mirror those depicted on the Warrior Vase from Mycenae, chariots and – on an example dating to c.800–650 BC found at the northernmost edge of the stelae's zone of distribution – a lyre. That this Bronze Age culture was not isolated from other European societies is clearly shown by the wreck of a ship (dating to c.800 BC) found in the river Odiel at Huelva. The wreck contained more than 400 artifacts, over half of which were weapons. Many of these were swords of the "carp's tongue" variety, which is believed to have originated in the Loire valley of central France.

However, the most important of the peninsula's widening foreign contacts were with the Phoenicians, semitic traders from Tyre in the eastern Mediterranean. Cádiz, whose name derives from the Phoenician word Gaddir meaning "fortified place", was

Left This funerary stele from Solana de Cabanos, dating to 850–750 BC, is one of a series of such monuments providing evidence for the emergence of an aristocratic warrior elite in the southwest of the Iberian peninsula. The deceased is seen surrounded by his weapons, a curious indented shield, and his chariot. Many of these stelae have inscriptions which as yet remain undeciphered.

Right The wealth and metal-working ability of the Iberians is apparent in these gold vessels from a horde found at Villena in the province of Alicante. The complete horde included 66 metal pieces of which all but six were of solid gold. The inclusion of two small pieces of iron among the gold shows the high value placed by the Iberians on this metal. The treasure was buried deliberately around c. 730 BC; it may represent the fortune of a local chieftain or loot acquired in war.

The early settlement of Iberia
The earliest inhabitants of Iberia, not surprisingly, tended to avoid the harsh uplands of the central *meseta* and settled along the more hospitable fringes of the peninsula, as the distribution of megalithic monuments shows. The Iberian Bronze Age produced a mosaic of different cultures. The known areas of the four main ones are illustrated here. These societies were primarily agricultural – irrigation techniques were in use in the Argar cultural area as early as 2200 BC – and showed an ability to establish settlements in harsh terrain; the Motillas culture built stone "castles" on the plains of La Mancha. Here agriculture would have mainly taken the form of stockraising. Copper, lead, and tin were also mined. The Iberians were divided into large numbers of small independent tribal groups. Our information (which is often just their name) about these groups is derived from classical sources and so is most detailed where there was frequent contact with classical civilization – the Mediterranean and south coasts. In fact such tribal divisions would have existed across the entire peninsula. The major disruption to Bronze Age life came with the migration of iron-working Celtic peoples into the north and center of the peninsula and with the arrival of foreign traders, particularly Phoenicians, in the south. Interaction with Phoenician culture was responsible for the emergence of the spectacular native "Tartessian" culture centered in Andalusia.

traditionally founded by Phoenician settlers in 1100 BC. However, the earliest archaeological evidence for Phoenician settlement here dates from the 8th century BC, and it is at this date that other Phoenician settlements appear to have been founded on the southern coast of the peninsula, particularly in the region of Málaga. Cádiz initially seems to have been little more than a trading station, but some of these other sites (for example, Toscanos) appear to have been intended as permanent settlements from the beginning.

The Tartessian culture
The new Phoenician presence provoked major developments in the region's indigenous Bronze Age culture. The end product of this "orientalizing" period was the emergence of the "Tartessian" culture. Tartessus (whose name is known to us from Greek writers) was long thought to be a major city, and some have believed it to have been the genesis of the myth of Atlantis – the fabled city that according to legend sank beneath the sea. However, after many futile attempts to locate Tartessus, most modern scholars now prefer to talk of a "Tartessian culture".

A dynamic combination of Phoenician and native traditions, the Tartessian culture spread over a large area of southern Spain. The central Tartessian area lay in the lower Guadalquivir and Guadiana valleys, but its influence extended farther north. This central region contained major planned and fortified settlements such as those at Niebla, Huelva, and El Carambolo in the region of Seville, the latter being the site of a spectacular hoard of gold jewelry. Tartessian metalworking was of a high quality and shows a thorough understanding of Punic (Phoenician) techniques. A

distinct script was also developed that was unlike either of the other two versions of Iberian already mentioned. Curiously, examples of this script center not on the heartland of the Tartessian culture but in the Algarve in southern Portugal.

The wealth of the region was based on mineral reserves of silver, lead and tin from the Sierra Morena and Rio Tinto areas. Some would hold that Tartessus is the Tarshish of the Old Testament, implying that the area engaged in long-distance trade with the Near East. However this identification is uncertain. The culture seems to have faded away, for reasons that remain unclear, in the 6th century BC.

The Greeks
The mineral riches of Iberia attracted others beside the Phoenicians. The early Greeks certainly knew of the region. The account given in the Odyssey of the entrance to the underworld places it beyond the Pillars of Hercules (the Strait of Gibraltar), seemingly on the Spanish coast. However, its inclusion in the fairyland of the Odyssey shows that at the time the poem was composed (c.750 BC) Spain remained a semi-mythical place for the Greeks. Nevertheless, it is in the *Histories* of Herodotus (c.484–c.420 BC) that we first learn the name of Tartessus: he tells the story of a Greek merchant, Colaeus of Samos, who was blown off course to Spain, where he traded with King Argathonius of Tartessus. Argathonius means the "man of the silver mountain", a name that is suggestive of the mineral wealth of this area. Judging by archaeological remains, which include a battered Corinthian helmet found at Jerez, Greek interest in the peninsula centered around the Huelva region where a large amount of

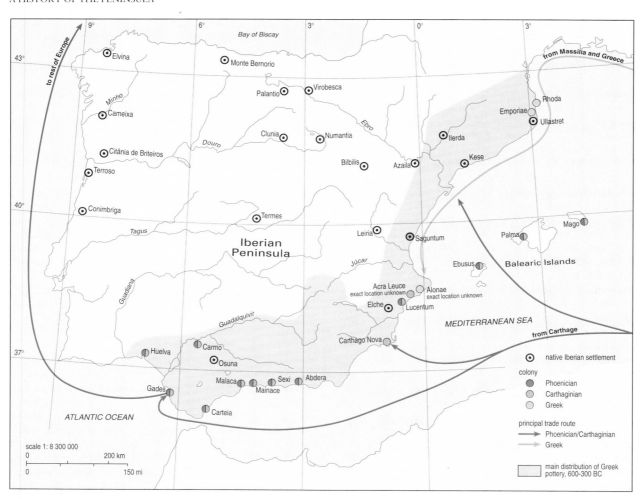

Greek pottery has been found. However, it is impossible to say whether these artifacts were brought there by Greeks or by other traders dealing in Greek goods.

The incidence of Greek pottery in the south disappears after c.550 BC. This must surely be connected to the Carthaginian and Etruscan victory over the Greeks at Alalia off the coast of Corsica – an event that effectively sealed off the western Mediterranean from contact with Greece. Greek influence in the south of Spain never seems to have provoked the cultural efflorescence in the native community as did Phoenician intervention, and after this period it was negligible.

A more important Greek venture was the founding in c.575 BC of settlements on the northeast coast at Emporiae (Ampurias) – the name means market-place – and Rhoda (Rosas) by colonizers from the Greek town of Massilia (Marseille) in southern France. Large amounts of Greek pottery began to spread from these colonies to the rest of the peninsula, but those responsible for its distribution appear to have been Phoenician middlemen rather than Greeks, judging by the Punic graffiti on many of the pots. Particularly large amounts of Greek pottery have been found in the Iberian town of Ullastret, which lies close to Emporiae; indeed it is often asserted that the town's construction owes much to Greek techniques. However, care is needed here, as such influence is often in the eye of the beholder. Similarly, while Greek art has been seen as a major influence on Iberian art, it may be that the Phoenician influence in this area has been underestimated and stands in need of assessment, just as modern opinion judges settlements such as Mainace (Mainake) and Abdera (Adra) – formerly considered Greek – to have been Phoenician in origin.

The wars between Carthage and Rome

The peninsula became a pawn in a much larger power game played out between Carthage, the town in North Africa founded by the Phoenicians that had become the dominant force in the western Mediterranean, and Rome, then beginning to flex its muscles as a rising power. The conflict between them for supremacy is known to historians as the Punic Wars. In the first war (264–241 BC) Carthage lost overseas possessions in Sicily and Sardinia to Rome and decided to rebuild its power by creating a new empire in the Iberian peninsula – given the Phoenician settlements in the south of the peninsula, a natural choice for the Barcid family then ruling in Carthage.

In 237 BC Hamilcar Barca (d.229/8 BC) landed with an army at Cádiz, and the following years saw a steady expansion of Carthaginian rule along the coast and northward into the interior of the peninsula. Some 30,000 Carthaginian settlers, the "Blastophoenicians", arrived in Spain in this period, giving its southern coast a Punic cultural substratum that was still remarked on in the Roman imperial period some 300 years later. Care was taken to fortify key sites in the area. The gate of Seville at Carmona, later rebuilt by both the Romans and the Arabs, dates in its initial form from this period. In 228 BC Carthago Nova ("New Carthage", the modern Cartagena), was founded on the southeast coast as the capital of this new empire, command of which passed in 221 BC to Hannibal (247–183 BC). He pursued a vigorous policy of expansion, extending Carthaginian domains perhaps as far as Salamanca in the west of the peninsula, and married an Iberian wife, Imilce, from Castulo (Cazlona) in the south. Carthaginian rule was

said to be brutal, but since we only learn this from Roman sources, the evidence should be approached with some skepticism.

The rapid extension of Carthaginian power in Spain alarmed Rome, and in 226 BC a treaty was struck between the two powers. This established the river Ebro as a limit for Carthaginian expansion, with an understanding that it was to have a free hand within this area. It was the town of Saguntum (Sagunto) in Spain that provoked the Second Punic War (218–201 BC) and the beginning of continual Roman involvement in the peninsula. Saguntum, a town of the Arsetani tribe of the Iberians some 100 miles south of the Ebro, was determined not to fall under Carthaginian domination and allied itself to Rome. If it is accepted that the Ebro of the treaty between Rome and Carthage was the same as the present river of that name, the town lay well within the zone of interest conceded by Rome to Carthage. Hannibal, intent on ensuring the stability of Punic possessions in Spain, pressed ahead with the capture of the town, despite Roman warnings that Carthage should not interfere with its ally.

In the war that followed Hannibal led an army containing many Iberian troops as well as 37 war-elephants across the Pyrenees and the Alps to Italy, while Rome despatched two legions under Cnaeus Cornelius Scipio to campaign in Spain. Cnaeus, who established his base at Tarraco (Tarragona) in Catalonia, was joined by his brother Publius in 217 BC and for the next five years the "twin thunderbolts", as they became known, waged successful campaigns against the Carthaginian commanders in Spain, penetrating as far south as the Gualdalquivir valley. Crucially for Rome, they prevented reinforcements being sent to Hannibal from Spain. This string of successes came to a halt in 211 BC when Cnaeus was killed near Cartagena after being deserted by the Celtiberian

forces in his army (the natives of the peninsula fought for both sides). A month later Publius also died in an engagement at the head of the Guadalquivir valley. Much later, popular antiquarian sentiment was to assign a tower tomb that lies just to the north of Tarragona as their burial place. Though it is still known as the Tower of the Scipios, this identification is undoubtedly incorrect.

The Roman losses were soon offset by the appointment of Publius' son, also named Publius – and, as the future conqueror of Carthage, later to be better known as Scipio Africanus (236–184/3 BC) – to the Spanish command. He landed on the coast of Catalonia in 210 BC with an army 10,000 strong and, despite his youth and inexperience, soon demonstrated his military ability. In 209 BC he besieged and captured Cartagena. After this the Carthaginian star in Spain waned rapidly. They were pushed ever farther south by a series of military defeats, and after the battle of Ilipa (probably the modern Alcalá del Río in the lower Guadalquivir valley) in 205 BC abandoned the peninsula to Rome.

The Roman settlement of Spain

Scipio settled some of the wounded from the battle of Ilipa in a village to the north of the town of Seville, which he named Italica. This settlement marks the beginning of Rome's permanent interest in the peninsula. The reason that Rome did not abandon Spain, but annexed it to its overseas domains, was economic. From 205–198 BC, some 4,500 pounds of gold and 225,000 of silver reached the Roman treasury from Spain. In 197 BC Rome divided its Iberian possessions into two provinces. The largest of these, known as *Hispania Citerior* ("Nearer Spain"), stretched down the east coast from the Pyrenees to Linares in the south; its administrative capital was the former Carthaginian capital of Cartagena. The second province *Hispania Ulterior* ("Further Spain") comprised most of the eastern half of modern Andalusia and had its capital at the town of Corduba (Córdoba), lying at the head of the navigable portion of the Guadalquivir river.

Over the next 200 years, Roman rule was gradually extended north and west. The reasons for this expansion are controversial. According to some commentators, Rome planned from the outset to bring all the peninsula under its sway; others believe that it was continually drawn into expansion through the need to secure safe boundaries. There is yet another view that holds that expansion, rather than being planned centrally, was the product of individual governors seeking wealth and glory during the course of their one-year span of office in order to further their subsequent political careers at Rome. Whatever the reasons for expansion, the Iberian peninsula proved difficult for Rome to tame. In contrast to the conquest of Britain, which was subdued within 50 years, Rome took almost four times as long to establish control throughout the Iberian peninsula.

The story of the conquest is one of almost unremitting treachery and savagery. Almost as soon as the provinces were established, a widespread revolt began in *Hispania Ulterior*. It soon spread to *Hispania Citerior* as it dawned on the Iberians that they were not about to be freed, but merely subjected to a change of masters. The strength of this rebellion led the Roman consul Cato (234–149 BC) to intervene personally in Spain. Placing himself at the head of an army of

Below As its name (the Greek for "marketplace") suggests, the town of Emporiae was founded by the Greeks of Massilia (Marseille) as a trading post in around 575 BC. The venture was a success and the town rapidly acquired a native Iberian quarter. A Roman town was built adjacent to the original Greek settlement, part of the forum of which is shown here.

70,000 men he crushed the rebellion, reaping a substantial financial reward in the process, as well as a triumphal parade at Rome. However, the revolt and the savagery of its suppression were merely foretastes of the problems that were to dog the Romans in Spain for many years to come.

Celtiberian resistance

The Celtiberian tribes of central Spain continually raided Rome's possessions, making the stabilization of Roman rule almost impossible. While an understanding was reached with the tribes bordering on *Hispania Citerior*, the problem became acute in *Hispania Ulterior*. In the 150s BC the province was subjected to raids by the Lusitani in Extremadura that culminated in 151 BC in the defeat of the province's governor Sulpicius Galba and the loss of 7,000 men. Galba responded by uniting with the governor of *Hispania Citerior* to launch a pincer attack against the Lusitani. The Lusitani soon sued for peace, and Galba thereupon treacherously slaughtered some 9,000 of their number, selling another 20,000 into slavery.

Galba's actions provoked an outcry at Rome. Cato demanded in vain that he be handed over to the Lusitanians. By 141 BC the Lusitanians – rallied by a leader called Viriathus – once again had *Hispania Ulterior* at their mercy. Foolishly, Viriathus was persuaded to strike a treaty with Rome, according to which Rome would respect Lusitanian territory and recognize Viriathus as a "friend of the Roman people". The treaty was broken the next year. Rome resumed the attack on the Lusitanians and Viriathus himself was killed, stabbed through the throat by two confidants bribed by Rome.

On Viriathus' defeat, the focus of opposition to Rome's rule in the peninsula shifted farther north, where various Celtiberian tribes had united to fortify the town of Segeda. A Roman army was despatched to destroy the town and its inhabitants fled to the neighboring town of Numantia, near modern Soria on the river Douro. The subsequent siege of Numantia lasted almost 20 years, before the town finally succumbed to Roman arms in 133 BC. In a pattern all too familiar in Spain, Scipio Aemilianus, the victorious Roman commander, razed the town to the ground and sold the remaining Numantines into slavery. The ramifications of this war were perhaps in the long run greater than either side could have imagined. It was when journeying to take up a command at Numantia that the young Tiberius Gracchus (c.169–133 BC) became distressed at the depopulation of the countryside in northern Italy. This provoked him to launch a series of reforms in Rome that were to shake the Republic to its foundations and eventually lead to its disintegration.

A theater of war

With the fall of Numantia, the backbone of serious resistance to Rome had been broken. However, Spain was now drawn into Rome's internal quarrels. In 83 BC Quintus Sertorius (c.123–72 BC) was appointed governor of *Hispania Citerior*. As a consequence of his faction losing the political power struggle at Rome, he fled his province, but in 81 BC was asked by the Lusitanians to become their leader and returned to the peninsula. Sertorius was an able and charismatic general, and at the head of a mixed force of Celtiberians and refugee Romans he rapidly succeeded in detaching Spain from central Roman power. By 77 BC he was the effective ruler of Spain, establishing a capital

at Huesca in the northeast. He was popular amongst the indigenous population of the peninsula, providing Roman-style education for ambitious local nobles. Nor was Sertorius adverse to using native custom for his own ends – he was accompanied everywhere by a tame stag that was believed by many of his native followers to be a familiar spirit.

Sertorius' military ability allowed him to hold out for 10 years against armies sent against him by the central Roman authorities. His successes included inflicting defeats on the ambitious young Pompey (106–48 BC) who had secured the command against him. However, Sertorius was gradually worn down. After being deserted by many of his native allies, he was murdered by one of his own subordinates, Perpena, who succeeded him but, lacking both the charisma and ability of his former commander, was soon despatched by Pompey.

Brought back into the Roman fold, before long Spain became a theater for the civil wars that were pulling the Republic apart. In 49 BC Julius Caesar (100–44 BC) defeated the forces supporting Pompey at Ilerda (Lérida) in the north of the peninsula; he then swept through the length of Spain setting up officials who could be relied on to support him. However, the governor he appointed in *Hispania Ulterior*, Quintus Longinus Cassius (d. 47 BC), upset the province so much by his insensitive treatment that it reverted to the Pompeian cause. Córdoba was burnt to the ground in the subsequent rebellion and in 45 BC Caesar returned in person to inflict the final blow on Pompey's supporters at Munda, a site somewhere in Andalusia. The struggle was bitter, and Munda thereafter became a by-word for a bloody battle in the Roman world.

The impact of Roman rule under the Republic

By the end of the Republican period (31 BC) Rome had come to rule all but the farthest northwestern regions of the peninsula. The impact of this rule on the native population was varied. Unlike the empires of the 19th century, Rome did not perceive itself as having a civilizing mission, and so the adoption and adaptation of Roman culture was a process that was initiated by the Iberians themselves, rather than being imposed from the top. Roman law was used by Rome in dealing with the peninsula's native inhabitants – for example, in a case at Botorrita in 87 BC. However, this reflected Rome's intransigent approach to its subject peoples, and should not be taken to provide any great evidence that an understanding of Latin and the Roman law was growing amongst the Iberian population at this time.

Iberian culture was not extinguished by the arrival of Rome; indeed, much of the surviving archaeological material concerning the Iberians dates from this "Roman" period. The massively built town wall of Tarragona was long thought to be of pre-Roman date. However, it has now been shown to have been constructed at the beginning of the Roman period and is a good example of how the different cultures mingled together. The wall is built in Iberian fashion of cyclopean stone slabs, but a sculpture of the Roman goddess Minerva was placed over one of the gateways; the positioning of a guardian deity in this way was a common Italian practice. However, on close inspection the aegis or symbol of the Roman goddess has been transformed from the customary gorgon's head to an Iberian wolf. In general, Roman-style buildings dating to

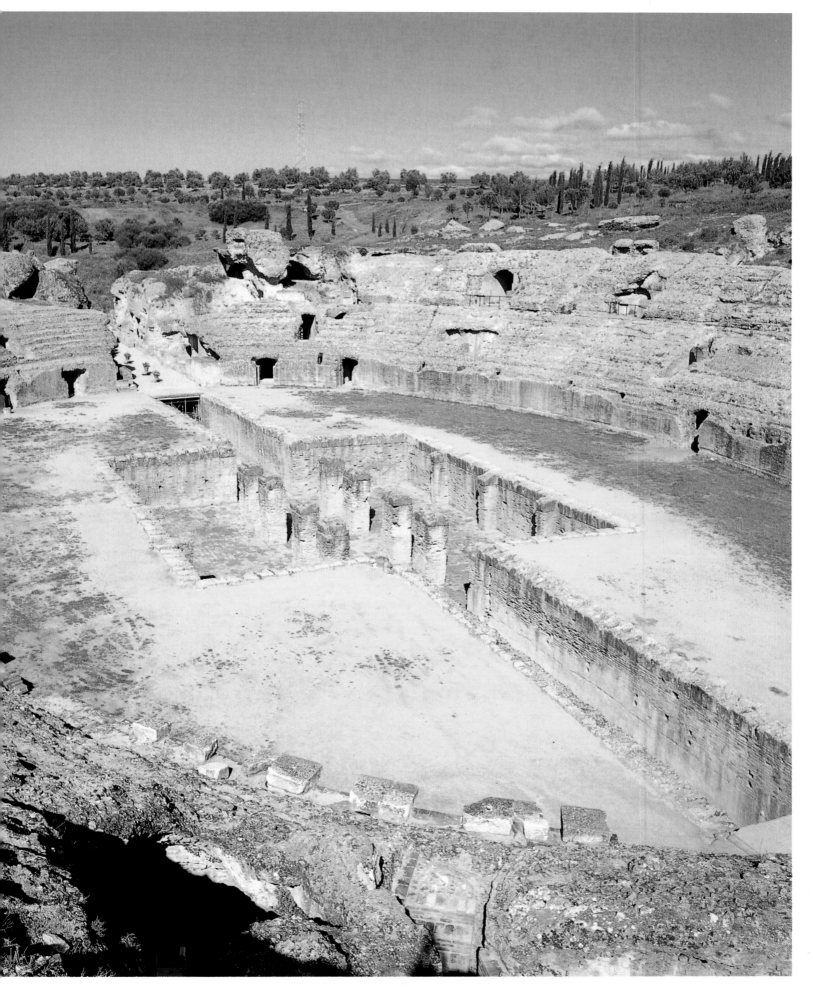

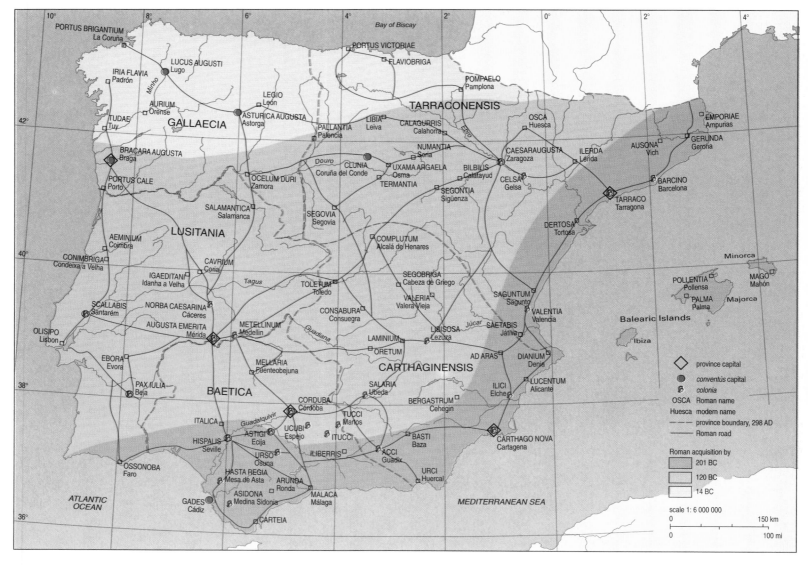

the Republican period are few in number. A colonnaded mud-brick structure at Botorrita may reflect a growing Roman influence, but the building is still only semi-Roman in form.

The period also saw the appearance of Iberian coinage, some struck, like the so-called Iberian *denarii*, to Roman standards. The issuing of this coinage probably began in order to ensure that the native soldiers enlisted in the army were paid in a way that was readily quantifiable by Rome, and again shows a mixture of Iberian and Roman elements. Nor was cultural borrowing a one-way process. In the course of her wars in the peninsula Rome adopted the Iberian sword as the model for the legionaries' *gladius* and their javelin, the *pilum*, which was designed to bend on impact, was based on an Iberian weapon of a similar form, the *soliferrum*.

In 171 BC the inhabitants of the southern town of Carteia (close to the modern Algeciras) successfully petitioned the Roman senate to be awarded partial rights of Roman citizenship. It is, however, the only case of this nature recorded at this early date. In general there was little migration of Romans into Spain, though influential groups of traders (*conventūs*) established themselves in large towns such as Córdoba and Hispalis (Seville). Roman administrative structures were not, on the whole, widely adopted in their entirety. It is true that Gades (Cádiz) by the end of this period was run like a standard Italian municipality,

but this probably reflected the ambitions of the powerful Phoenician Balbi family rather than a strong "Romanizing" tendency among the population at large. The Balbi, who helped to finance Caesar's campaigns, can be contrasted with another of his supporters in Spain, a King Indo, whose name and title are both non-Roman. The two show the wide range of responses to Roman rule in the peninsula in the Republican period. The Balbi were among the few Iberian-born individuals who appear to have integrated into Roman society, though the poet Catullus (c.84–c.54 BC) seems to have been upset in love by a Celtiberian rival, Egnatius – if his use of the epithet "Celtiberian" here is not simply a term of racial abuse aimed at a Roman who had spent some time in Spain.

After campaigning successfully in Spain, Caesar settled large numbers of former soldiers in the peninsula in *coloniae*, towns for Roman citizens that were intended to be microcosms of Rome itself; the close parallel between the two can be seen from the local law code of one such *colonia*, Urso (Osuna), which partially survives engraved on bronze tablets. This policy has been regarded by some as a visionary attempt to unite the Roman world, but is more likely to have been initiated by the need to pay off large numbers of troops and provide them with land. Spain had been in the main hostile to Caesar in his wars with Pompey, and the confiscation and redistribution of land in this way enabled him to reward his troops and

Roman Iberia
Roman possessions in Iberia were originally divided into two provinces, or commands: *Hispania Ulterior* in the south and *Hispania Citerior* in the north. In the reign of Augustus *Ulterior* was subdivided into *Baetica* and *Lusitania*, and *Citerior* renamed *Tarraconensis*. The latter was itself subdivided into three in the late 3rd century AD. Before 298 AD the provinces were entirely separate units. Each had its own governor and was divided into assize districts known as *conventūs*. Local political life centered on the towns, which had their own local councils and jurisdiction over minor cases. The highest status towns were *coloniae*, normally settlements of former Roman legionaries, which enjoyed full Roman citizen status. Though provincial governors frequently also had military functions, the Iberian peninsula contained few troops, the only legion base being at Legio in the north. In the later Roman period, the five provinces – while retaining their own independent administrations – were grouped, along with Mauretania Tingitana in North Africa, into the diocese of the Spains whose overall governor, or *vicarius*, was based at Augusta Emerita. This group formed part of the prefecture of the West, presided over by a praetorian prefect at the emperor's court.

Previous page Italica, just to the north of Seville, was the first Roman *colonia* in Iberia, founded by Scipio Africanus to house the wounded from the battle of Ilipa. Later it was the birthplace of the emperor Hadrian (117–138 AD), who decided to honor his home town by constructing a luxurious new suburb there. This included one of the largest amphitheaters of the Roman world. The arena and the *hypogeum*, or underground area where animals were kept prior to their appearance, can be seen here. The amphitheater was cut into the rock of the hillside and must have suffered problems from flooding as it is built on a natural line of drainage.

Below The Celtic element of the early population of the peninsula is shown by this *castro* site from the northwest of Spain. The circular huts contrast sharply with the rectangular and more ordered Iberian sites found to the south. *Castro* settlements remained in occupation well into the Roman imperial period.

punish those who had fought against him at one and the same time. The policy was continued in the reign of the emperor Augustus (27 BC–14 AD), who also had large numbers of troops to discharge, creating 26 *coloniae* in all in Spain, but stopped abruptly thereafter. Caesar also awarded some native towns full or partial Roman citizen rights. Again the awards appear to have been made for pragmatic not ideological reasons. Many of the towns so favored were not the most "Romanized" settlements in the peninsula, but occupied important strategic positions. In other cases, such as the award of full Roman citizenship to Cádiz, the seat of the Balbi, the personal nature of Caesar's motivation is clear.

Imperial Spain

The rise to power of the emperor Augustus in 31 BC and the establishment by him of the principate, or Roman empire, saw the final conquest of the only part of the peninsula not yet under Roman control, the far northwest. The campaigning in this area was carried out in part by Augustus himself – he fell ill here in 24 BC, coming close to death – and was completed by his general Agrippa (c.63–12 BC). Augustus revised the administrative arrangements of the peninsula, replacing the two Republican provinces with three new ones. *Hispania Ulterior* was divided into two separate parts. The new province of *Baetica*, consisting of most of modern Andalusia and parts of Extremadura, had its

capital at Córdoba, while *Lusitania*, which roughly corresponded to modern Portugal, had as its capital the new *colonia* of Augusta Emerita (Mérida) on the river Guadiana. The remainder of the peninsula, roughly the area covered by *Hispania Citerior*, became the province of *Hispania Tarraconensis* with its capital at Tarragona. *Lusitania* and *Tarraconensis* were governed by *legati*, directly nominated imperial appointees. *Baetica*, on the other hand, was governed by proconsuls appointed by the senate.

Spain now settled down to 200 years of peace. The area provided large numbers of recruits and units for the Roman army. Only one legion (in contrast to the three later found in Britain) was stationed in the entire peninsula, the VII Gemina, based at Legio (León). Though Galba (emperor 69 AD), governor of *Tarraconensis*, launched his successful coup against the emperor Nero (54–69) from the province, Spain did not on this occasion become a theater of battle, escaping the anarchy of the year of the four emperors.

Economic development varied a great deal within the peninsula. The richest area was the province of *Baetica*, its prosperity resting in part on the mineral reserves of the Sierra Morena (the name of which is probably derived from a wealthy Roman owner of mine franchises, Marianus), and the Huelva region. Its principal source of wealth, however, came from the production of olive oil in the Guadalquivir valley. The enormous volume of this trade can be seen from the

Augusta Emerita (Mérida)

Below Despite continuous occupation of its site, considerable evidence of the Roman town survives in present-day Mérida. The most impressive remains are those of the theater, amphitheater and the Los Milagros aqueduct. Other aspects of public life are represented by the Temple of Diana and the "Arch of Trajan" – the entrance to the forum. The sites of numerous wealthy late Roman private houses have also been identified. Visigothic remains can be seen at the church of Santa Eulalia and in the Moorish Alcazaba.

Augusta Emerita was founded in 25 BC, in the reign of the emperor Augustus, by Publius Carisius as a *colonia* for discharged veterans of the V Alaudae and X Gemina legions and to serve as the capital of the newly created Roman province of Lusitania. Built on the site of a small native settlement, Emerita was equipped with all the amenities of a typical Roman town – a town square or forum, temples, aqueducts, a theater, an amphitheater, and a circus for chariot racing. These buildings were constructed primarily for the use and entertainment of the veteran legionaries. However, by their sheer size alone, they would have brought home to the native Lusitani the power of their Roman masters. The town remained a major site throughout the Roman period and beyond – Mérida was briefly the capital of the Suevic kingdom in Spain, and between 549 and 555 AD served as the capital of the Visigothic kingdom of Spain.

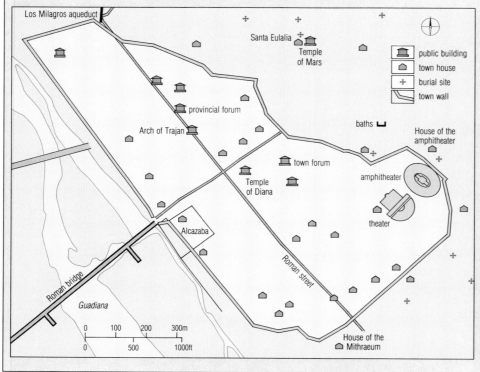

fact that a sizable hill in Rome, the Monte Testaccio, is composed solely of the broken sherds of the distinctive bulbous jars or amphora (known to archaeologists as Dressel 20 amphora) in which the oil was taken to Rome. However, even in *Baetica*, development was not uniform. In the highland areas to the north and south of the Guadalquivir valley settlements remained much less Roman in form and many pre-Roman sites, *recintos*, continued in occupation.

The disparity in degrees of wealth and cultural assimilation was even greater in the other two provinces. Though parts of both were considerably Romanized, other areas showed little sign of adopting Roman ways. In Cantabria the old hill-top *castro* sites

consisting of circular Celtic huts thrived throughout the Roman period, while Punic culture remained very much alive on the southern coast. This was particularly the case at Cádiz where the great temple of the Phoenician god Melqart, which enjoyed considerable fame throughout the empire, retained its oriental usages. Some coastal towns such as Adra were still striking coins with Punic legends in the reign of the emperor Tiberius (14–37). The rock-cut tombs in the cemetery at Carmona, dating from the early imperial period, also show the durability of Punic culture.

In the reign of emperor Vespasian (69–79) the entire peninsula was granted partial Roman citizen rights (the *ius Latii*). By this privilege, the magistrates of

Below The theater at Augusta Emerita was built soon after the foundation of the town with money given by Augustus' leading general Marcus Agrippa. The building seated 5,500 spectators and remained in use, with various modifications, until the second half of the 4th century AD. The restored facade seen here dates from the 2nd century AD. The theater is a good example of the way private individuals in the early Roman period were prepared to use their wealth for the construction of public works. By the late Roman period, however, citizens were more likely to divert their wealth to building luxurious private houses for themselves. These were richly decorated with frescoes and mosaics, such as this one (*left*), depicting a grape harvest, from one of Emerita's many town houses of this period.

Iberian towns, along with various members of their families, would become full Roman citizens on completing their year of office, and their fellow citizens were to be raised to "Latin" citizenship, allowing them a share in a large number of the rights enjoyed by full Roman citizens. The emperor's motives, and even the date of the grant, are unclear. His intention cannot have been to reward progress towards Romanization, since the blanket nature of the grant extended these rights to areas where little or no movement in this direction had taken place. And, given Rome's lack of a civilizing ideology, it also seems unlikely to have been awarded to stimulate Romanization. Most probably, like Caesar's earlier awards, the grant was made for pragmatic reasons. At the beginning of his reign Vespasian may well have felt the need to placate Spain in order to secure his rear while dealing with rebellion in Gaul. It is worth noting that Vespasian was the only one of the four rivals for emperor in 69 who did not have connection with, or had not made concessions to, the peninsula.

Whatever the reason, the Iberian provinces were the only ones in the empire to enjoy this privileged status en masse. The law embodying the grant was only finally put in place by Vespasian's son, the emperor Domitian (81–96). Several substantial fragments of the law, again engraved on tablets of bronze, have survived, all of them from sites in *Baetica*. The law itself is highly technical and is a product of Roman legal thinking. It would be unwise to assume from this, however, that a high standard of Latin literacy and understanding of Roman legal practice existed in the peninsula. We know that the law was produced centrally, and this may simply indicate that in this, as in other things, Rome was unwilling to make any concessions to native practice. A letter at the end of the best preserved example of the law, the *Lex Irnitana*, shows that the important provisions on marriages had been broken soon after the law came into effect.

The early imperial period saw a substantial amount of Roman-style building. Examples include the development of the towns of Belo and Conimbriga (Condeixa a Velha), the spectacular terraced temple at Munigua (Castillo de Mulva), and the aqueduct at Segovia, one of the most impressive anywhere in the Roman world. The funding for the vast majority of this building came not from Rome but from local worthies – many of whom began to adopt Roman names at about this time – who wished to demonstrate their power and wealth to their fellow townsmen. The way towns were administered also took on a firmly Roman form after the granting of the *ius Latii*.

The Spanish provinces contributed to the cultural life of the empire. The literary Seneca family were natives of Córdoba. However, while the philosopher and writer Seneca the Younger (c.4 BC–65 AD) and the poet Lucan (39–65 AD) hardly set foot in the peninsula after their youth, Seneca the Elder (c.55 BC–39 AD) the author of textbooks on the practice of rhetoric, lived in the town. Quintilian (35–c.96), who held the first chair of rhetoric at Rome in the reign of Vespasian, was a native of Calagurris (Calahorra), and the poet Martial (c.38–c.103) hailed from Bibilis (Calatayud), where he chose to spend his retirement. The Spains (*Hispaniae*), as Roman authors knew the provinces, also produced at least two emperors, Trajan (98–117) and Hadrian (117–138) his adopted son, both of them natives of Italica. Hadrian was responsible for substantial redevelopment of his home town,

including the construction of a massive temple to his predecessor and the fourth largest amphitheater in the Roman empire. If a late source is right in tracing the family of Marcus Aurelius (161–180) back to the southern town of Ucubi (Espejo), a third emperor may be attributed to the peninsula.

Growing unrest and reorganization

The peace of the Iberian peninsula came to an abrupt end in the late 2nd and early 3rd centuries. *Baetica* was ravaged by invasions of Moors from North Africa in the 170s and in 210. They established a brief foothold in the peninsula around Málaga before being chased out of the province by the procurator of the North African province of Mauretania. An inscription thanking this official erected at Italica suggests that the incursion had serious effects all along the Guadalquivir valley. Nor was this the only area of the peninsula to suffer at this time. In the northeast, deserters from the Roman army in Gaul crossed into Catalonia, to be driven out by the VII Gemina.

Between 258 and 270 the peninsula was removed from the control of the central Roman authorities to form – along with Britain and the provinces of Gaul – the Gallic empire of Postumus (258–268). Frankish tribesmen poured through Postumus' domain sacking Tarragona and other towns in the peninsula as they made their way to Africa, later returning as pirates to attack the coasts of *Hispania* in 297. The violence of the period caused irreparable damage to the economy of the peninsula. Trade rapidly contracted to within the boundaries of the peninsula itself, and further economic damage was done by a massive debasement of the currency.

In 298 the administration of the peninsula was reorganized in common with reforms that took place in the rest of the Roman world. The province of *Tarraconensis* was divided into three, the north and the west being split off to form the new province of *Gallaecia* with its capital at Bracara (Braga), and *Carthaginensis* being created in the south with its capital at Cartagena. All five Spanish provinces were grouped together with the province of *Mauretania Tingitana* in North Africa to form the diocese of the Spains. This was presided over by a supra-provincial governor, known as the *vicarius*, whose headquarters were situated at Mérida. The reforms gave the central authorities much closer control over the region but at the expense of creating a far larger and more expensive bureaucracy. The burdens of this were borne in the main by wealthy local aristocrats – the very class on whom Rome had previously relied for the good governance of her provinces.

The net result of these upheavals was to change considerably the landscape of the region. Towns became walled, and contracted in size – at Condeixa a Velha, the town wall from this period cuts through early town-houses. Moreover the form of the towns changed significantly. As in other parts of the late Roman empire, the wealthy – instead of spending ostentatiously on increasingly costly public works that brought ever smaller honorific returns – turned instead to build larger and more sumptuous private houses. Public buildings fell into neglect. In c.350 the *basilica* (town hall) of Tarragona burnt down, but no effort was made to replace it or redevelop the site. At the same time the town's theater fell out of use. Some 50 years later the traveller Avienus commented on the ruinous appearance of the once prosperous town of

Cádiz. Wealthy private town houses, such as those at Mérida and Complutum (Alcalá de Henares), were being built throughout this period. Perhaps more importantly, the growth of large landed estates with opulent villas at their center, such as those at Olmeda near Palantia (Palencia) and Foz de Lumbier near Pompaelo (Pamplona), represented the abandonment by the rich of the urban ideal of classical antiquity.

The conversion to Christianity

The last great change of the late Roman period was the conversion to Christianity. The Theodosian family, which supplied the Roman empire with its last ruling dynasty, was of Spanish origin. The best-known member of the clan, Theodosius the Great (379–395), the last emperor to preside over a united empire, was responsible for the outlawing of paganism throughout its domains.

Little is known of the early church in Spain. St Paul wrote of his intention to visit the peninsula, but it is not known if he managed to achieve his wish. Similarly, though the apostle James is said to have visited Spain, there is no evidence that this is more than a legend. Whatever the case, Christianity seems to have taken hold rapidly in Spain. By the mid 3rd century there were substantial Christian communities at Mérida, León and Asturica (Astorga). These had links with fellow-believers in Africa and Rome. In 259 bishop Fructuosus of Tarragona and two of his deacons were burnt to death in the town ampitheater for refusing to recant their faith. Their deaths can be paralleled by those of the potters Justa and Rufina in Seville, and few Spanish towns seem to have lacked martyrs. The strength of the early Spanish church is shown by the fact that a close confidant of the emperor Constantine (312–377) during his path to the purple was bishop Hosius of Córdoba.

The faith grew rapidly after Constantine's edict of toleration throughout the empire was passed at Milan in 313. The most spectacular Christian monument of this period is the mausoleum at Centcelles near Tarragona, possibly the resting place of Constantine's son, the emperor Constans (337–350), the vaulted main chamber of which is decorated with mosaics depicting scenes from the Old Testament. A significant contribution was made by Roman Spain to early Christian literature. The wide-ranging poetry of Prudentius of Calahorra is perhaps the best known example, but he was not alone. His compatriot Iuvencus wrote a paraphrase of the Gospels in Latin verse, and in the 5th century Orosius of Braga, the pupil of St Augustine, composed an influential history of the world written from a Christian viewpoint. Egeria, whose vividly written account of a pilgrimage to the Holy Land and Egypt in 381–384 is one of the earliest contributions to pilgrim literature, was a wealthy noblewoman from *Gallaecia*.

The barbarian invasions

The beginning of the 5th century saw the collapse of this Late Roman society. The empire itself was disintegrating as Germanic tribes, uprooted by the westward migration of mounted nomads such as the Huns and Goths from Central Asia, pushed relentlessly across its frontiers. In 407 AD a British usurper of the imperial throne, Constantine III, sent his son Constans and commander-in-chief (*Magister militum*) Gerontius to seize the peninsula. This was achieved with little difficulty. Constantine then denuded the region of regular troops, leaving the Pyrenean frontier to be

Below Originally a Celtic site, Conimbriga evolved into a Roman town from the age of Augustus onward. A major incentive for building was provided when the town was given partial Roman-citizen status, along with the rest of the towns in the peninsula, by the emperor Vespasian in 71 AD. As well as public buildings, the town contained wealthy private houses. Shown here is one of the mosaic pavements that decorated the central courtyard garden of the House of the Fountains, built in the 2nd or 3rd century AD.

Visigothic Spain

As the Western Roman Empire slowly disintegrated in the 5th century, various barbarian tribes entered the Iberian peninsula. The Suevi originally settled in the northwest, with their capital at Bracara. A brief period of rapid expansion reached its apogee under King Rechila, when almost all the peninsula lay in Suevic hands and a new capital was established at Mérida. After Rechila's death in 448 the Suevi were gradually pushed back into the northwest by the other main barbarian tribe, the Visigoths, though a rump Suevic kingdom continued to exist in *Gallaecia* until 585. The Visigoths never succeeded in securing firm control over the peoples of the Cantabrian Mountains and the Basques. Visigothic Spain was at first merely a part of a much larger Visigothic kingdom centered on Toulouse in southern France. After this fell apart under pressure from the Franks, Spain became a protectorate of the Ostrogothic kingdom of Italy, from which it took the Spanish Visigoths considerable time to reassert their independence. Even after this, Visigothic politics were always turbulent; a permanent capital was only established in 569 at Toledo by King Leovigild. This instability allowed the Byzantine emperor Justinian to re-establish a small province in the southeast of the peninsula as part of his unrealized plan to recover the entire Western Roman Empire. This Byzantine enclave survived for over 70 years and was finally destroyed by the Visigothic king Sisebut in 624. The political instability of the area allowed the church to play a far more important role in society than previously. Much wealth was invested in ecclesiastic buildings, and intellectual life centered around the church. As the Visigoths, unlike their subjects, were Arian rather than orthodox Christians, the peninsula had two rival ecclesiastical establishments. This ended with the conversion of the Visigoths to orthodoxy under King Reccared in 589.

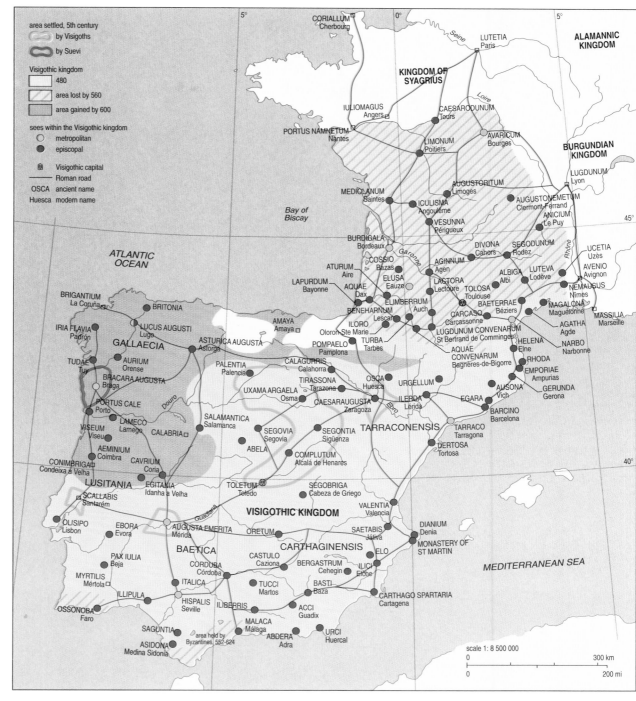

guarded by a garrison of barbarian mercenaries called *honoriaci*. In 409 AD, either through incompetence or collusion, they allowed enormous numbers of Germanic tribesmen to pour into the peninsula.

No action was taken against the invaders for two years while Constantine's campaigns petered out in the south of France. In the meantime, Roman Spain had disappeared. The peninsula now presented a mosaic of barbarian settlements: *Baetica* was occupied by tribes of Vandals; *Gallaecia* was divided between Vandals and Suevi; while *Lusitania* and parts of *Carthaginensis* were occupied by Alans. Some areas along the eastern coast remained under nominal Roman control: in particular, the provinces of *Tarraconensis* and parts of *Carthaginensis*.

This state of affairs was highly volatile and, by playing the barbarian powers off against one another, the Roman authorities managed successfully to remove all but one of them, the Suevi. The latter, under a succes-

sion of leaders, spread out rapidly from their base in *Gallaecia* during this period. Mérida, which was taken in 439, was made the capital of their expanding kingdom. This had grown to take in Seville by 441. A final attempt was made by what was left of the central Roman authorities to recapture the peninsula in 446, but failed.

The power of the Suevi did not last long. The Visigoths, who had sacked Rome in 410 and settled in parts of Gaul, were invited by the Romans to enter the peninsula as a counterweight to the Suevi. In 456 they defeated the Suevi at Astorga and went on to capture Braga and Mérida, thus making themselves masters of the peninsula, apart from a rump Suevic kingdom in *Gallaecia* and an equally diminished Roman province of *Tarraconensis*. In the 470s the Visigothic king Euric (466–484) put an end to the Roman province. The Suevic kingdom, however, was to survive in *Gallaecia* for another 100 years.

Visigothic and Asturian Churches

Below Only the western end of the church of San Miguel de Lillo, Oviedo, survives, the crossing and chancel having collapsed in the later Middle Ages. Argument continues as to whether it was the chapel of the palace complex founded by King Ramiro I (842–850), or was built in the preceding Visigothic period.

Compared with most other parts of western Europe, Spain is particularly well endowed with churches that can be dated largely or in part to the 6th and 7th centuries. Several, such as San Juan de Baños, Palencia, whose foundation in 661 is recorded in an extant inscription, have long been known, but others have only recently been discovered or have been re-dated to this period thanks to archaeological investigation. Such work means that elements of earlier buildings are still being found in churches extensively rebuilt in later centuries. The Visigothic churches vary in plan: all are rectilinear, without apses or domes, but some have unusually prominent and high transepts; the ground plan of one, San Fructuoso de Montelios in Portugal, is based on the equal-armed Greek cross. Decoration also varies: San Pedro de la Nave, Zamora, is notable for the biblical scenes and heads of apostles carved on the pillars of its central crossing, while the decorative schemes of San Juan de Baños and others are strictly non-figurative, displaying only austere vegetal and geometric motifs in their capitals and string courses. The Arab conquest of 711 did not put an end to the building of churches in the peninsula, but only in the Christian kingdom of the Asturias do traces of the buildings of the next two centuries survive in any quantity. A particularly intensive campaign of church building took place in the reign of Alfonso III (866–910), and a number of these show traces of what would have been elaborate schemes of fresco decoration. Stone carvings in these buildings, however, are generally simpler and less well executed than in their Visigothic predecessors.

Above Daniel in the lion's den, on a capital from the 7th-century church of San Pedro de la Nave. The capital facing it across the nave depicts the Sacrifice of Abraham. Together they provide the finest extant examples of figurative carving from the Visigothic period.

Right The church of Santa Cristina de Lena, Asturias, has been dated, on not very secure grounds, to the mid 9th century. In the center of the chancel screen can be seen part of an earlier carved screen of Visigothic date, probably deriving from an earlier church on the site or in the vicinity.

Above Detail of a carved window screen from the church of San Juan de Baños, the only known Visigothic building of documented date. It was built by King Reccesuinth in 661 as a votive offering to St John the Baptist. A medicinal spring, encased within Visigothic stonework, is situated nearby.

Right This votive crown, now in the Museo Arquológico Nacional in Madrid, is amongst the finest surviving examples of Visigothic jewelry. It is one of eight crowns discovered in 1858, together with other items, in a field at Guarrazar near Toledo, the former Visigothic capital. Four more crowns were uncovered there in 1860. It is suggested that they were buried at the time of the Arab invasion. All of the crowns were votive offerings, intended for liturgical purposes, and the majority of them were of small dimensions. This large crown, 20.6 centimeters in diameter, bears the donor's name in pendant gold letters: RECCESVINTH REX OFFERET ("King Reccesuinth offers [this]"). Another such royal donation, a crown given by King Suinthila (621–631), was stolen in 1921. The body of the crown is of gold, set with garnets, pearls, sapphires and rock crystal.

The Visigoths ruled their possessions in Spain and southern France from Tolosa (Toulouse). When the Franks destroyed this kingom, overrunning the Visigothic lands in France in 507, Visigothic Spain became a protectorate of the Ostrogothic kingdom of Italy. Eventually the Spanish Visigoths broke away from Italy when Theudis assumed the title of king in 531. The new kingdom was far from stable, and in 552 the Roman emperor in the east, Justinian (527–565), was able to establish a small province of unknown size on the south coast of Spain, which lasted until 624. A united Visigothic state was only finally established in the peninsula by King Leovigild (569–586). He extinguished the Suevic kingdom of Gallaecia and established his capital at Toledo. This was to remain the center of the Visigothic kingdom until its fall to the Arabs in 711.

The Visigothic state

Just as Roman rule had not destroyed the older cultures of the peninsula, so Visigothic rule did not entirely efface Late Roman customs. The Visigoths, who ruled as a military elite, were far outnumbered by their subjects. In many ways the Visigoths used the Hispano-Romans much as the Romans had used their own subjects, retaining as much of the old Roman provincial administrative structure as possible. The Hispano-Roman nobility was left in charge of local day-to-day affairs, and were at least partially responsible for the collection of taxes on behalf of the central authority. The two populations remained distinct from each other in such things as dress, religious practice and the enjoyment of legal rights. In the case of religion, the Visigoths – unlike their Hispano-Roman subjects who believed in the Trinity – were Arian Christians, holding that the Son was not of the same substance as the Father, a doctrine that had divided the church since the 4th century. Legal distinctions were expressed in two law codes that adapted existing Roman law. The first, issued by Euric in 475 and subsequently amended by Leovigild, concerned the Visigoths themselves; the second, issued by Alaric II in 506, dealt with the rights of the Hispano-Romans.

The beginnings of the Visigothic period are recorded by the chronicler Hydatius, born in Galicia in c.400, who can be said to have been the father of Iberian historiography, as his work concentrates on events in the peninsula alone. The most outstanding intellectual figure of Visigothic Spain, however, was Isidore, bishop of Seville from c.600 to 635. A polymath, Isidore wrote numerous works of theology and history; his encyclopedic *Etymologia* long remained a standard reference work in medieval Europe. Isidore's vocation was that of a priest, and the Visigothic period marked a rise in the power of the church throughout the peninsula: the best account of life in Visigothic Spain, the *Lives of the Fathers of Mérida*, describing the late 6th century, depicts a society greatly affected by church matters. Though public building in general was neglected, ecclesiastical building was not. Large numbers of churches, including substantial cathedrals such as that at Mérida, were built in a distinct style, along with monasteries (four of which were constructed at Toledo alone) and public hospitals.

The conversion of King Reccared (586–601) from Arianism to Trinitarianism, at the Third Church Council of Toledo in 589, was a sign that the Visigothic and Hispano-Roman upper classes were drawing closer together. Reccared's reign also saw the disappearance of Visigothic dress and the beginnings of a unified legal system, a process that was completed in the reign of Reccesuinth (649–672) by the publication of the *Liber Iudiciorum* in 654. This is one of the finest achievements of the Visigothic period, assuring the survival of Roman legal principles as the basis of law while incorporating some elements of Germanic customary law. At about this time the old Roman provincial system was finally dismembered and replaced with a much more central system of rule.

Whether these changes would have eventually seen the emergence of a joint Gothic-Roman ruling class that would have guaranteed a stable political system is now impossible to judge. In 711 King Roderic (710–711) was defeated by an Arab army that had crossed the Strait of Gibraltar from North Africa, possibly at the invitation of a pretender to the Visigothic throne, bringing an end to Visigothic rule in Spain.

CONQUEST AND RECONQUEST 711–1480

The collapse of the Visigothic state

In late April 711, the Islamic general Tariq led a small force across the narrow strait that separates what is now Morocco from Spain to seize the rocky promontory of Gibraltar, the name of which derives from the Arabic *Jebel al-Tariq*, meaning the mount of Tariq. Though Tariq had been across to Spain in the previous year, we have no way of knowing whether his intention in 711 was to carry out any more than another rapid raid. Whatever the case, so rapid and emphatic was his success that his commander Musa ibn Nasayr, who was governor of Ifriqiya (Africa, the area approximating to present-day Tunisia), soon brought a larger army over to join him.

Roderic, who was at the time vying with another nobleman called Agila for control of the Visigothic kingdom, rushed south from yet another expedition to suppress Basque opposition in the north, but on 19 July was defeated in battle by Tariq at a place on the river Guadalete in the southwestern corner of Spain. After defeating another Visigothic army at Ecija, to the east of Seville, Tariq sent a light raiding party to look at the situation in Málaga, while he himself headed north to the former Visigothic capital, Toledo, capturing an undefended Córdoba on the way. Toledo itself fell in a similar manner, and Tariq proceeded northward to destroy attempts at Christian resistance in the Cantabrian and Asturian regions. It was only in 713 that he returned south to meet his supposed commander, Musa, who had come over to Spain in the summer of 712 and captured several towns himself.

In the course of the next three years, almost the whole of the Iberian peninsula, apart from the northern fringes on the Atlantic and Mediterranean coasts, fell to the Muslims. The future Spain and Portugal were thus absorbed into the rapidly growing world of Islam, which had already expanded from its place of origin among the nomadic peoples of Arabia in the early 7th century to include most of the Middle East and North Africa. Muslim Spain – known to the Arabs as al-Andalus (from which the name of Andalusia is derived) – was to be ruled by a series of governors

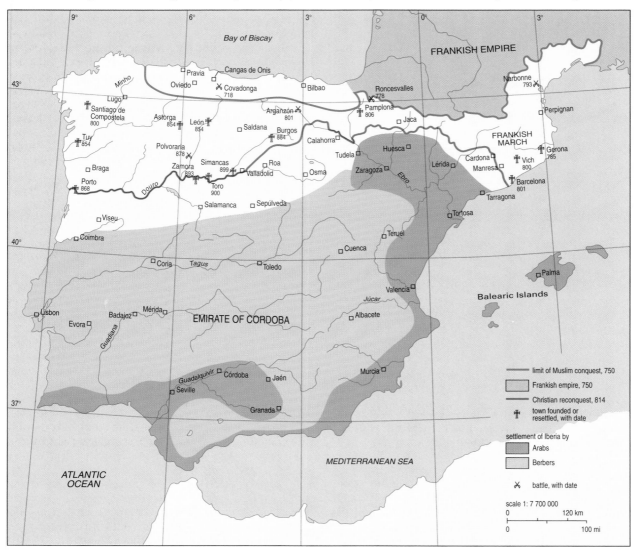

Christians and Muslims, 8th to 9th centuries

The Christian kingdom of Asturias, in the northwest of the peninsula, created after Pelayo's victory at the battle of Covadonga (718 or 722), was centered first on Cangas de Onis and then on Pravía and finally, from the 790s, on Oviedo. In the 9th century, the decline of the power of the Umayyad rulers of al-Andalus, who were facing an increasing number of revolts within their own territories, enabled the Asturians to expand south of the mountains. They founded new towns such as Burgos and resettled former Roman towns such as León, which become the capital of the kingdom under Ordoño II (913/4–923). Farther east, a brief and unsuccessful foray into the Ebro valley in 788 by the Frankish emperor Charlemagne was followed by the conquest of Barcelona in 801 and the establishment of Frankish frontier counties in what would become Catalonia. In the south, while the majority of the population, especially in the rural areas remained Christian until at least the early 11th century, the Arabs and Berbers turned what had begun as a military occupation into a genuine settlement. The Arabs tended to establish themselves in the richest and most fertile areas, such as the valleys of Guadalquivir and the Ebro, while the Berbers were relegated to the frontier districts in the center of the peninsula.

Above This 13th-century banner from Baeza in Andalusia depicts St Isidore, the 7th-century bishop of Seville, riding to battle with sword and episcopal cross in hand. The image is extraordinary in that the real Isidore had no martial associations whatsoever. However, from the time of Fernando I (1037–1065) he became increasingly venerated by the Leonese-Castilian royal house, and he was adopted as the personal patron saint of Alfonso IX of León (1188–1230). The latter's son, Fernando III of Castile (1217–52), gained control of Baeza in 1226. Isidore's cult as a warrior saint proved short-lived, but is testimony to the way that the Leonese and Castilian monarchies turned to the Visigothic period for symbols and images to support their contemporary aspirations.

Isabella, the Catholic Monarchs, brought an end to Muslim rule in the Iberian peninsula in January 1492, traditional accounts of the early days of Muslim conquest and Christian resistance had crystallized into established myth. As Ferdinand and Isabella's Italian courtier and chaplain, Peter Martyr d'Anghiera (1457–1526), told the sultan of Egypt in 1502, Spain had fallen because of internal treachery. According to this version of events, a certain count Julian had summoned Tariq from North Africa in order to help him revenge himself on King Roderic for some harm that the king had supposedly done to Julian's daughter. At some point in 718 or 719, a Visigothic noble, Pelayo, defeated Muslim forces at Covadonga high in the mountains of Asturias. In this minor skirmish – in which it was later said that the Christian women had helped their menfolk by throwing stones at the Muslim invaders – historians have traditionally seen the beginnings of the Christian "Reconquest" of Spain.

The initial impact of Islam

It is hard today to appreciate how small was the Muslim presence in the peninsula, particularly since the great Muslim monuments, such as the Alhambra of Granada or the Great Mosque at Córdoba have become so important a part of the tourist itinerary. The invaders were an ethnically mixed group who came from various parts of the Islamic world, including Arabia itself, Syria, Egypt and North Africa. As the history of Islamic Spain unfolded, conflict between the Arabs and their supporters on the one hand and the recently converted Berber peoples of North Africa on the other would come to undermine Muslim rule in much of the peninsula. At the outset, the Muslims were on foreign ground and were numerically at a disadvantage. In the decades before Tariq's invasion of Spain, however, a small and diverse group of Muslims had succeeded in overthrowing the Greco-Roman civilization of the Middle East and North Africa, though this seemed to many people at the time to be very much more sophisticated than their own. It looked, in the early part of the 8th century, as though the same had happened in Iberia.

Like the Visigoths, the Muslims governed the peninsula's Hispano-Roman population by making use of what remained of the basic institutions of the Roman state – the army, the governmental bureaucracy and the system of land taxation that provided most of the public revenues. This was not a new departure for Muslim invaders. The social structures of the nomadic Arabs among whom Muhammad (c.570–632) established the new religion of Islam proved ill suited to the task of governing the crowded, cosmopolitan Greco-Roman cities of the eastern Mediterranean and by the time Islam reached Spain, it had largely adopted their social and economic institutions. Because of their common heritage, these were broadly similar to the urban structures found by the Muslims in Spain. Consequently, the institutions of Muslim Spain remained much closer to those of the former Roman empire than did those of the Christian kingdoms that were coming into being north of the Pyrenees, where the Catholic church was increasingly the focus of political, social and religious allegiance.

Population figures are extremely difficult, if not impossible, to obtain from Islamic sources, because the compilers were not interested in such matters, but it seems clear that, at least until the 10th century, most of the population of al-Andalus remained Christian,

appointed by the spiritual and political leader of all Islam, the caliph ("leader of the faithful") of Damascus. In later usage, Muslim inhabitants of the Iberian peninsula were known as "Moors", from the Latin name for their province of northwestern Africa, Mauretania. In terms of Spanish and Portuguese history, though, this term is highly problematical.

Despite its inherent weaknesses, it is still hard to account for the apparently spontaneous collapse of the Visigothic state, It seems that, when it came to the point, almost no one was willing to fight for the Visigothic rulers. A lasting legacy from the centuries of Roman domination was a belief in strong central government, and so many of the largely Hispano-Roman population may have submitted to Muslim rule with little or no resistance. In addition, Jews had settled in Spain before the time of Christ and increased in numbers after the destruction of the Temple in Jerusalem in 70 AD, with the subsequent dispersion of Jews from the Roman province of Palestine. Under the Visigothic monarchy, they had been subjected to legal restrictions that, given the evident ineffectiveness of the secular authorities, were mainly enacted by the Catholic church, the chief agency through which the kings exercised power. Given that forced conversion, or else death, had been threatened by the church, it is hardly surprising that many Jews appear to have welcomed the Muslim invaders. As fellow monotheists, they even seem to have been entrusted by them with the duty of garrisoning the newly conquered cities.

The search for scapegoats who could be blamed for the Christian defeat began almost immediately and has gone on ever since. In the process of trying to identify the culprits, Spain and Portugal reinvented their history, forged an identity for themselves, and thus created many of the problems that were to beset them for centuries to come. By the time that Ferdinand and

The Great Mosque at Córdoba

Below Part of the fine mosaic decoration surrounding the *mihrab*, dating from the reign of al-Hakam II. Incorporated into the design are passages from the Qu'ran in gold lettering and a reference to al-Hakam. Like the *mihrab*, it was covered over after the Christian conquest, and so survived unscathed until brought to light in the 19th century.

In the early Islamic period, every major Arab town in Spain had one major mosque (*mezquita*) where all male members of the Muslim community were expected to come together to pray each Friday. As the size of the community grew, so the dimensions of the mosque had to be enlarged. (From the 9th century onward smaller local mosques were founded within the large cities as an alternative means of solving this problem.) Thus, the first mosque of Córdoba, traditionally said to have been built in one half of a church dedicated to St Vincent, was replaced by a new and more grandiose structure late in the reign of Abd al-Rahman I (756–788). This was expanded by an extension of almost equal size in the time of his great-grandson Abd al-Rahman II (822–852) and by yet another, even larger, section erected by al-Hakam II (961–976). This latter section is notable for the excellence of its mosaic decoration and for the dome, in the shape of a scallop shell, over the *mihrab* (the niche intended to indicate the direction of Mecca, and thus the way that worshipers should face while praying). A final, very substantial, extension of the building was undertaken by the *hajib*, or chamberlain, al-Mansur in 978/9, making it one of the largest sacred structures of Islam. After the Castilian conquest of Córdoba in 1236, a Gothic cathedral was built within the former mosque, and in the 1520s a larger and more obtrusive cathedral in Renaissance style was erected in the very center of the building.

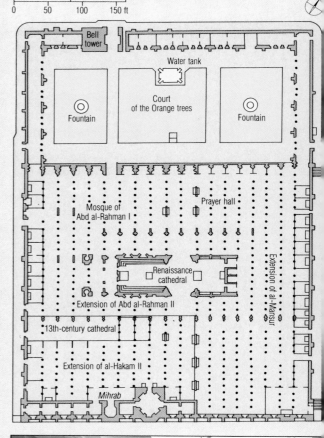

Below Plan of the mosque as it is today. A bell tower has replaced the minaret from which the *muezzin* called the faithful to prayer. Worshipers would ritually wash themselves in the courtyard before entering the prayer hall.

0   25   50 m
0   50   100   150 ft

Bell tower

Water tank

Court of the Orange trees

Fountain   Fountain

Mosque of Abd al-Rahman I

Prayer hall

Renaissance cathedral

Extension of Abd al-Rahman II

Extension of al-Mansur

13th-century cathedral

Extension of al-Hakam II

Mihrab

Above The dome of the *mihrab* was completed in 965. The mosaic decoration was influenced by the work of contemporary Byzantine mosaicists, and is similar to (if not quite as fine as) that of the late 10th-century mosaics in Haghia Sophia in Constantinople. Iran, Byzantium and Armenia have all been suggested as the source of the technique, using rib vaults, that was used to construct the dome.

Far left The unsympathetic construction of the Renaissance cathedral in the middle of the prayer hall infuriated Charles V. The open arches that gave access to the prayer hall were blocked up when the building was taken over by the Christians, making the interior darker than intended.

Left Perhaps the most famous feature of the Great Mosque is the system of double arches, supported on 850 marble columns, that divide the building into 19 aisles. This particular section belongs to the final extension built by al-Mansur.

Above Non-figurative patterns based on geometric and vegetal motifs are a feature of the rich decoration that surrounds a side door into the prayer hall. It dates from the time of al-Hakam II, and bears close similarity to the decorative scheme that is to be found in the audience chamber of the caliphs in the contemporary palace-city of Medina Azahara, about 8 kilometers west of Córdoba.

with a minority of Jews. Many Christians shared, to a greater or lesser extent, the way of life of their Muslim rulers. Controversy still surrounds the question of which term or terms should be used to describe these "arabicized" Christians, but the most common is "Mozarab", which derives from the Arabic word *musta'rib*, meaning one who has assimilated Arab customs. Some of them learned Arabic, and some – the *mawlas* or *muwallads* – even converted to Islam in order to join the multiethnic ruling group (one can hardly call it a class) that dominated religious and secular affairs. Nonetheless, a significant number of non-Muslims, both Christians and Jews, were associated with government, even after the establishment of a unified Muslim state in the early 10th century. When, in the 11th, 12th and 13th centuries, Christian settlers moved down from the north into central and southern Spain, they found many surviving Christian and Jewish communities.

The caliphate of Córdoba

When the Prophet Muhammad died in 632, he had made no spiritual provision for a succession, and his first four successors, who each took the title of caliph, seem successfully to have combined the spiritual and the political role of leadership. However, in mainstream Islam (later known as "Sunni") the political side became predominant when, in 661, the then governor of Damascus, Muawiyah, took the office of caliph and founded the hereditary Umayyad dynasty. In theory, at least, his descendants ruled all the territories of Islam, including the Muslim-held parts of Iberia, until the Umayyad rulers were overthrown in 750 by the Abbasid dynasty, which came from Baghdad. At this point, one of the Umayyads, Abd al-Rahman I (756–788), escaped to the west and set up what eventually became, in the 10th century, a new caliphate for western Islam in Spain, with its capital at Córdoba. Though its effective power was only to become a reality as late as 929, and was to last thereafter up to 1031, the Umayyads were regarded right from the start as a threat (and an insult and intrusion) by their Abbasid successors in Baghdad. Throughout the 8th and 9th centuries the Umayyads attempted to gain supremacy over the other local Muslim rulers in Spain, finding themselves in intermittent conflict with all of their Islamic neighbors at one time or another.

Despite the political confusion of al-Andalus, there was great prosperity, based to a large extent on a remarkable expansion of agriculture. The Arabs opened up new areas for cultivation by extending the use of irrigation in the peninsula: techniques such as the waterwheel and underground canals known as *qanats* were introduced from the east, along with a range of new crops such as rice, sorghum, cotton and sugar cane, as well as citrus and other fruits. They also imported the considerable mathematic and scientific knowledge they had inherited (and themselves added to) from the Greco-Roman intellectual tradition of the Middle East and North Africa, and were able to build upon the foundations left behind by the Romans and their Visigothic successors in the Iberian peninsula itself. They adorned the already existing towns of Spain with architectural monuments such as mosques and palaces in a style that combined the classical heritage with designs and techniques from farther east. Such buildings, together with the shaded, water-filled gardens of the Islamic tradition, were to be found throughout the peninsula, but those in and around the

fitna ("break-up") that divided the caliphate and by 1031 had destroyed it for ever. The collapse of what remained of Muslim unity in the Iberian peninsula began with the death of the mighty al-Mansur in 1002. Though the caliph, Hisham II, continued to rule in name until 1009, the Islamic state based in Córdoba began at this point to disintegrate. The trouble was caused partly by external intervention – mainly by Berbers from North Africa, and by Christians from the north of the peninsula – and partly by endemic weakness within the caliphate itself.

In al-Andalus, the primary focus of political allegiance was, of course, intended to be religious. This meant submission to Allah and the acceptance, by non-Muslims, of the political, social and cultural dominance of the Muslim elite, including the use of the Arabic language. Within the Muslim community (the *ulema*), status and priority were given to those families that could claim descent from the Prophet himself, or had played any role in his activities or in the later guardianship of the holy places in modern Saudi Arabia – Mecca and Medina. This clearly placed both non-Arab Muslims and Christians and Jews at a disadvantage. Generally, allegiance was given to one or other of the leading Arab families. In this way, large groupings that depended not on blood-ties but on personal, political and social links were formed; these were highly volatile, given that ethnic as well as ordinary political and dynastic conflicts were inevitably present. Thus, after 1008–09, the authority of the caliphate steadily declined, amid a welter of feuds, until its eventual fall in 1031, when al-Andalus dissolved into a collection of emirates, or petty kingdoms, known as *taifas* (pieces or parts).

The Christian north
Because the Islamic advance never succeeded in securing the whole of the Iberian peninsula, there was always a potential base for Christian attempts to regain the land lost to the Muslims. The period up to about 1040 saw the return of about a third of the peninsula to Christian rule. The starting point for this advance was a small area on the northern Cantabrian coast around Cangas de Onis, which fell into Christian hands in 722. In the 8th and 9th centuries, this developed into the kingdom of Asturias. In the western Pyrenees, the nucleus of what was to become the kingdom of Navarre was already discernible at this date, together with the nascent kingdom of Aragon farther to the east, around Jaca.

There was also Frankish influence in the region. In northeastern Spain, and forming the southwestern boundary border of the Frankish empire, was a collection of small Christian territories. During the late 8th and early 9th centuries, Charlemagne (742–814) – who had succeeded the Merovingian kings based in Paris and expanded the Frankish territories to include much of Germany and other parts of western Europe – annexed some of these northeastern Spanish lands. These were known thereafter as the "Frankish March" (borderlands), and created a kind of buffer zone between Christian Europe and Islamic Spain. Later they formed the nucleus of Catalonia, which with Aragon was to play an important role in the economic and cultural history of Spain in future centuries.

At about the same time that Charlemagne was setting a limit to Muslim power in the northeast, a crucial move began out of the Cantabrian mountains in the north and northwest onto the high land of the

caliph's capital of Córdoba itself, including the Great Mosque within the city and the palace of Medina Azhara just outside it, were of particular magnificence. The caliphate achieved its greatest political power during the rule of the chamberlain al-Mansur (976–1002) who assumed effective charge of government in the reign of the caliph Hisham II (976–1009). Al-Mansur, who presided over a considerable flourishing of Muslim culture, led some 50 campaigns against the Christian north. On one of these expeditions, in 997, he even stole the bells belonging to the great shrine of St James at Compostela and brought them back to the Great Mosque at Córdoba, which he was responsible for completing.

For all this achievement, the century-long history of the caliphate was one of conflict and infighting. There were many reasons for this, beyond the problem of ethnic division, already mentioned. The earliest traditions of Islam had held that religion and society could not be separated: the Qu'ran – the sacred writings revealed to Muhammad – and the earlier traditional commentaries upon it, assumed that religion must intervene in everyday life, or else it is meaningless. When the rulers of al-Andalus adopted the title of caliph, they were explicitly combining the religious with the political. However, their claim to exercise spiritual authority over western Islam (which was in any case disputed by the original holders of that office in Damascus and Baghdad) could not be enforced, even by the deployment of extensive military and economic resources. Though the Muslim rulers of the Maghreb states (modern Morocco, Tunisia and Algeria) were willing to send help to Iberian Islam at various periods and formed a common trading zone with the peninsula, they were perpetually divided among themselves and frequently caused or added to similar problems in al-Andalus itself.

The very nature of political ties throughout the Islamic world was a major contributory factor to the

Left An ivory casket made in 964 for the caliph al-Hakam II (961–976) as a present for his wife Subh, to mark the birth of their son, the future Hisham II. It is one of a number of surviving ivory caskets and boxes, probably made in the palace-city of Medina Azhara near Córdoba and dating from the late 10th century. Several of these bear inscriptions recording the date of their manufacture, and the names of the patrons who commissioned them. They represent one of the finest forms of the palace art of the late Umayyad state.

Right Depiction of a harvest from an illuminated manuscript of the *Commentary on the Book of Revelation*, written in the late 8th century by the Asturian abbot, Beatus of Liébana – a work that was very popular in Christian Spain and survives in many versions. This particular manuscript was made by a scribe called Facundus in 1047 for King Fernando I and Queen Sancha of Castile-León, and is one of the finest of the Beatus codices. The style shows some of the distinctive artistic traditions, such as the use of color and the dissolution of form, that had developed amongst the Mozarab communities of Spain. While the imagery is intended to be allegorical and apocalyptic, such details as the wine press seen at the bottom can help in the historical reconstruction of agricultural life in this period. The text in the picture refers to Revelations XIV.20 and reads: "Where the wine press is prepared outside the city, and the blood comes out of the wine press up to the bridles of the horses."

The expansion of the Christian kingdoms

To see the Reconquest as a ceaseless and ideologically motivated conflict between Christians and Muslims does less than justice to a complex set of relationships both at local level on the frontiers and more broadly between the various states. The gradual extension southward of the power of the Christian kingdoms of the north took place more as a series of bursts than as a continuous process. By the late 9th century Asturias had established itself in the northwest as far as the valley of the Douro – as much at the expense of local Christian Galician and Basque communities as of Arab rulers. In the later 11th and early 12th centuries the Leonese-Castilian successors of the Asturian kings imposed their authority south of the Guadarrama mountains, taking Toledo in 1085, while the Aragonese kings gained control of much of the Ebro valley with the capture of Huesca in 1096 and Zaragoza in 1118. The counterattacks of the two North African dynasties of the Almoravids and the Almohads put a stop to further territorial advance until the battle of Las Navas de Tolosa (1212) gave a decisive advantage to the Christian rulers. By the mid 13th century most of the south was in Castilian hands and Aragon had gained control of much of the Mediterranean coast. Only the Nasrid kingdom of Granada remained as a tributary state, until eliminated by Ferdinand and Isabella in 1492.

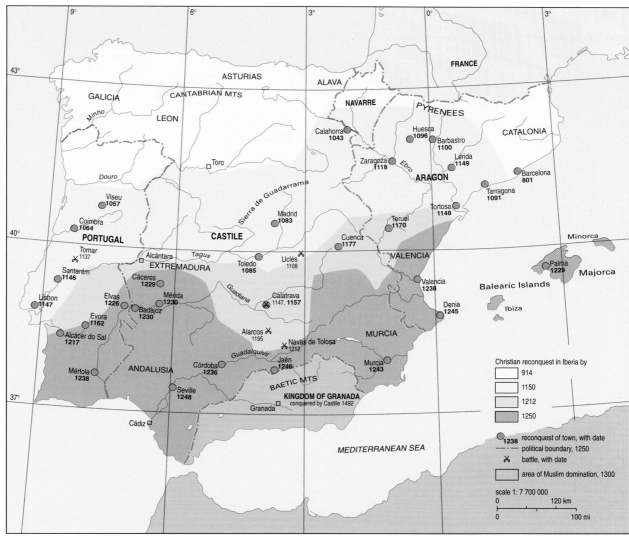

Christian reconquest in Iberia by
- 914
- 1150
- 1212
- 1250

1238 reconquest of town, with date
∙∙∙∙∙ political boundary, 1250
✕ battle, with date
area of Muslim domination, 1300

scale 1: 7 700 000
0 — 120 km
0 — 100 mi

northern *meseta*. It was this, above all, that made the further southward expansion of Christian rule into central Spain possible and, in the process, led to the development of the kingdoms of León and Castile. Both were clearly identifiable by the year 1000.

It is misleading at this early stage to talk of these early Christian groupings as "states" in the modern sense of the word. They were still largely "barbaric" kingdoms in which the descendants of Germanic invaders ruled with the help of what remained of the Roman infrastructure. Though their rulers and chroniclers (not to speak of later historians) saw themselves as the direct descendants of the Visigothic rulers of Spain, with a mission to restore the Christian state that had existed before 711, there was in fact no such link between these embryonic northern kingdoms and the earlier Visigothic state.

Furthermore, the Christian territories were at that stage insignificant when compared with their Islamic neighbor. Despite all its political, economic, social and religious problems, in the early medieval period al-Andalus was still by far the most sophisticated political entity in Europe west of Byzantium. It had inherited a rich land and strong institutions from the previous Roman rulers, including the power to raise large armies and pay for them by means of a tax on land. Nonetheless, the institutions and social formations that developed in the north of the peninsula before about 1000 were to be of great significance in the future. It is indeed arguable that the values of late medieval and early modern Iberian society – later transmitted to the overseas empires of Spain and Portugal – originated among the comparatively obscure nobles, peasants, traders and ecclesiastics who attempted to populate and settle the newly acquired lands in the north and center of the peninsula.

Iberian feudalism

Though no medieval ruler would have understood what was meant by the term if he had heard himself referred to as a "feudal monarch", the modern concept of feudalism as a bond between ruler and land-owning aristocracy as well as between landlord and tenant is useful in understanding the social, political and economic realities of the time. Feudal structures in most of Europe were based on the need to replace the departed or crumbling bureaucracy of the Roman empire, the lack of which deprived rulers of the ability systematically to tax landed wealth under the protection of a standing army. At the highest level, there was a desire to restore some kind of supranational authority through political structures such as the Frankish or Holy Roman Empire or by means of a strengthened papacy claiming for itself universal spiritual authority.

At a lower social level, the primary need was for physical protection. In the centuries up to 900, a tripartite notion of social "estates" or "orders" developed. These orders reflected the main preoccupations of the new societies that were being formed and divided people into "those who fought", "those who prayed", and "those who worked" – in other words, soldiers, churchmen and peasants. These divisions, which dominated western European society for centuries, had no recognized place for traders or for non-Christians, such as Jews and Muslims. While the church increasingly fought to secure and expand its rights against those of secular governments, it had nevertheless to form part of a society dominated by knights and kings in order to win economic support and protection. The warrior classes, in their turn, strengthened their hold over a formerly free peasantry and used their military muscle to secure dominance over whatever institutions may have existed.

In the centuries between the Muslim conquest and about 1050, Christian Spain conformed in many ways to the overall picture of European feudalism. It was precisely the religious imperative of resisting Islam, together with the very obvious need to give priority to military organization and action simply to achieve coexistence, even when the actual conquest of territory from Muslims was not a possibility, that shaped the later Christian kingdoms of the Iberian peninsula. The basic elements of a "feudal" society were in place from the very start. The earliest rulers, whether styling themselves "kings" (Asturias, León, Navarre, Aragon) or "counts" (Castile, Portugal, Barcelona), were essentially warrior-leaders who seized upon the ever-present threat of Muslim counterattack from the south to ensure that their rights, and those of their knights, were respected and that the church and the peasantry remained subservient.

The early kings of Asturias in particular shared the dream of many of their fellow rulers north of the Pyrenees that the old Roman imperial authority might be revived. Borrowing from the Carolingian emperors, they attempted to introduce the trappings of imperial power to their palace in Oviedo, constructing for themselves an elaborate royal mausoleum and other buildings that appear to have been modelled on those of Charlemagne's palace at Aachen. Thus they created an imperialistic concept of monarchy that greatly influenced the counts and kings of later periods, particularly those of what became, in the 15th century, the "crown of Castile", lasting into the so-called "Golden Age" of the 16th and 17th centuries.

A frontier land

In many ways, the conditions of the medieval Iberian peninsula resembled those of the 19th-century American West: between the cities of the Muslim south and the northern kingdoms was an extensive frontier zone lacking the clearly delineated boundaries of modern Europe. Though the population of Muslim Spain far outnumbered that of the Christian states, relatively few people lived in this zone. Consequently, as the Christians gradually moved southward in the 10th and 11th centuries, they were faced not with heavily populated towns and garrisons but with largely empty spaces. There was, moreover, a considerable passage of traffic to and fro across the boundaries between the Christian and Muslim territories. Those who failed to recognize the frontier as a real barrier not only included raiding and rustling parties, but also traders (legitimate or illegitimate), soldiers, refugees, prisoners, slaves, and the religious of both faiths.

Such a situation inevitably had its effect on the version of feudalism that grew up in the northern Christian states. There was remarkably little siege warfare or hand-to-hand fighting in this or any other phase of the Spanish Reconquest. Typically, a northern force would capture a center of population that had already been evacuated by its inhabitants and colonizers would then move in, who would proceed to exploit and defend their new possession. As in the American West in the 19th century, the representatives of the law and the church would arrive after the first settlers and would then try, often vainly, to restore order on their own terms. Before the 11th century, there was little building of stone castles as a means of defense, though watchtowers were often provided. Vigilance against enemies on the ground was the main requirement. There was consequently a need for a body of mounted fighting men who were able to respond quickly to an alarm. Without the presence of a peasantry to provide feudal rents and labor services these fighters had to support themselves through farming and trade – a combination of roles that did not at all correspond to the theory of three separate feudal orders that prevailed elsewhere in western Europe.

Such fighters came to be classed in the developing Castilian language as *caballeros villanos* – a term that has no equivalent elsewhere in Europe, and indicates the difficulty of applying general feudal terminology to the Iberian case. "*Caballero*" means "knight": that is, a soldier fighting on horseback, though not necessarily a nobleman. "*Villano*" on the other hand is an ambiguous word in Castilian meaning either a townsman (one living in a *villa*, or town in late Roman usage), or a "villein" or serf, someone bound to the soil (the term "villein" reflecting the earlier use of *villa* to mean the main house of a rural estate). In feudal terms, the description of a man as both a knight and a villein would seem to be an absolute contradiction in terms, but the special circumstances of the Spanish frontier made the double meaning quite plausible.

Consequently, though the status of knight had become generally equated in western Europe with that

Above The 11th-century fortress of Montemor-o-Velho, in the Mondego valley in the center of Portugal was built to defend Coimbra (captured from the Arabs by Fernando I of Castile-León in 1064) against attacks from the south. These were likely to come sweeping up the coastal plain. It is one of the numerous examples of military architecture dating from the 10th to 15th centuries to be found in most regions of Spain and Portugal, testifying to the problems both of open warfare and of local conflict that were endemic throughout the Middle Ages.

of a nobleman by the end of the 13th century, in the frontier towns of Christian Spain, knights still performed their basic function of fighting on horseback. The need to remain alert at all times for raiders and rustlers continued in the south as late as the 15th century. During the 1420s, the town council of Jerez de la Frontera (which, despite its name, had not actually been on the Christian–Muslim frontier since the 13th century) had its meetings periodically interrupted by reports of the arrival of Muslim raiders. The councillors would immediately run to their horses and ride off to seek revenge.

The Reconquest as a crusade

For the first four decades after the collapse of the caliphate of Córdoba, shortage of manpower means that there was little attempt from the Christian side to capitalize on Muslim weakness by direct military means. Instead the Christian rulers played the Muslim *taifas* off against each other by using the threat of war as a means of securing treaties and demanding cash

payments known as *parias* – a form of protection money. Then, in 1064, a small Aragonese-led military expedition (which included among its number a force from Aquitaine, on the other side of the Pyrenees) seized the Muslim-held town of Barbastro. Because it had received a specific papal blessing beforehand, this action has been described by some as a precursor of the crusading movement, predating by some 30 years the official "First Crusade" that was called by Pope Urban II in 1095 to free the holy places of the Near East from Muslim rule.

Whether or not a true crusade in the technical sense, the expedition against Barbastro marked an important change in the character of the warfare between Christians and Muslims in Spain. Increasing papal support for the Reconquest as part of the universal war against Islam substantially benefited the Christian rulers of Iberia by encouraging numbers of foreign knights to fight against the Muslims there with the aim of earning a crusading indulgence, or remission of all temporal punishment due for sins. Those who wished

Early Spanish Frescoes

About 2,000 Romanesque churches, dating from the 9th to the 12th centuries and representing one of the largest and most varied collections of such buildings anywhere in Europe, are preserved in the Pyrenean villages of northern Catalonia. The subsequent economic backwardness of these mountain communities meant that relatively few of the churches were rebuilt in the later Middle Ages and as a consequence a surprising number have preserved parts of their original fresco decoration. A number of the best examples have been removed to the Museum of Catalan Art in Barcelona where they are displayed in galleries that copy the design of the original churches. The quantity and good state of preservation of the frescoes have made it possible to study the different schools of fresco painters working in the region and to identify the artistic influences on them. Some examples show a high level of technical skill that points to sophisticated artistic patronage on the part of the Catalan church and local nobility.

Patronage of a more exalted kind can be seen in the best surviving frescoes from the kingdom of León-Castile – those that decorate the royal burial chamber (Pantheon of the Kings) attached to the west end of the church of St Isidore in León. This was dedicated by King Fernando I (1037–65) in 1063, but the extant frescoes date from the second half of the 12th century. They depict the major events of the Gospel narratives, together with images of the Apocalypse. There is also an agricultural calendar, showing the principal activities of the months. Few other Romanesque fresco cycles have been preserved in León-Castile. Those from St Isidore testify to the strong artistic influences from north of the Pyrenees that was being exerted on the kingdom in this period.

Above The vaulted ceiling of the Pantheon of the Kings in the church of St Isidore, León, is roughly 8 meters square in extent. It is covered by a uniform set of frescoes that fill every corner of space and probably date to the reign of Fernando II (1157–88). The painters of these frescoes incorporated a wealth of incident into the scenes they depicted, as is seen in the detail (*right*) from the ceiling showing the Annunciation to the shepherds. This gives an idea of the very high quality of their work. Neither the names nor the origins of the painters of these frescoes are known, but their art shows considerable indebtedness to the fresco-painting traditions of southwestern France.

Left This late 11th- or early 12th-century fresco, which shows Christ as Pantocrator (ruler over all) standing above the Virgin and Apostles, comes from the church of Sant Pau at Esterri de Cardós in northwestern Catalonia. It is now displayed in a specially constructed apse in the Museum of Catalan Art, Barcelona.

Below This depiction of a magnificent six-winged seraph with the figure of the prophet Isaiah on the right is part of a late 11th-century apse fresco from the church of Santa María de Esterri de Aneu, high in the Pyrenees. Though much damaged, the fresco painting in this church has been linked to the work of the artist responsible for the frescoes in the church of Sant Quirze at Pedret (now in the Museum of Catalan Art, Barcelona).

Below Another of the frescoes in the Museum of Catalan Art (originally in the nave of the church of Sant Juan in the Pyrenean village of Boì). Dating from the late 11th century, it is the work of an artist known as the Master of Boì and depicts the martyrdom of St Stephen. Here the finger of God is shown pointing down from the heavens toward the saint, who was the first Christian martyr.

to receive the spiritual benefits of the Crusade without actually fighting in it could pay a "Crusade tax" in return for a papal bull of indulgence. The cash thus raised was a useful supplement to royal revenues and, from the mid 13th century onwards, became a permanent part of the Spanish kings' income.

New military religious orders, in particular those of Santiago (St James), Calatrava and Alcántara, though there were many others, played an increasingly important role in the occupation and defense of the frontier. These groups of knights, who had not only gone through the ceremonies of knighthood but had also taken monastic vows, were a living embodiment of the crusading ideal as advocated by the papacy. They lived in barracks that were also monastic establishments and had taken the monastic vows of poverty, chastity and obedience. They were regarded by contemporary observers as a formidable fighting force. Over time, however, the receipt of massive donations to assist their work steadily reduced their military zeal and turned them instead into largely revenue-gathering (and spending) organizations.

Increased papal interest in the Iberian wars against Islam also hastened church reform in the peninsula. From about 1080 onward, monks, mainly from France, accompanied the knights of Europe into Spain. They used their influence to reform Iberian ecclesiastical institutions and bring them into line with those in northwestern Europe, especially France, by reducing lay control over churches and clerical patronage, enforcing celibacy among the clergy, and preventing clergy from buying their jobs. The Burgundian monastery of Cluny did particularly well from this connection. During the reign of Alfonso VI of Castile and León (c.1040-1109) a large part of the *parias* that were paid by Muslim rulers to forestall Christian attacks was passed to the monks of Cluny – a privilege they retained for some years thereafter, and which undoubtedly helped to furbish their magnificent abbey church, one of the finest Romanesque buildings of medieval Europe.

Nevertheless, the career of the Castilian adventurer Rodrigo Díaz de Vivar (c.1043–c.1099) makes it clear that pragmatism and personal gain had at least as great, if not greater, a part to play in the war against Islam as did crusading idealism. He is better known as El Cid – derived from the Spanish-Arabic *as-sid*, meaning "lord" – a name that he acquired in his lifetime. A native of Burgos in Castile, he was exiled by Alfonso VI after leading a military raid into Toledo, then under Alfonso's protection, in 1081. El Cid then offered his services to the Muslim ruler of Zaragoza, fighting both Christian and Arab opponents on his behalf. In 1094 he led a successful siege against the Muslim-held city of Valencia, and though he took possession of it in Alfonso's name, effectively became its independent ruler. Alfonso chose not to defend the city after El Cid's death, and it was reoccupied by the Almoravids in 1102, remaining in Muslim hands until 1238. By the time that El Cid's life, embellished with legendary deeds, came to be set down in the early 13th century in the epic poem *Cantar de Mío Cid* ("The Song of my Cid") – the earliest surviving major work written in vernacular Castilian – he had become elevated to the role of national and Christian hero.

The fall of Toledo

In 1085, Alfonso VI – benefiting from the new partnership between church and state – led a successful expedition to annex the *taifa* of Toledo. His force included not only troops from all over the Iberian peninsula but also foreign volunteers mainly, but not solely, from France. The capture of Toledo permanently changed Christian and Muslim perceptions of their respective roles in Iberian society. For the first time, a major town of Muslim Spain had fallen into the hands of a Christian army. The fact that many of those fighting on the Christian side were newcomers to the peninsula from northern Europe, filled with religious zeal for the expansion of Christendom at the expense of Islam, sharpened the religious aspect of the war.

It also increased the opportunity for French military and ecclesiastical involvement in Iberian affairs. A French monk was installed as the first archbishop of the restored see of Toledo, and similar appointments were made at this time to other sees in the north. As French influence increased in northern Spain, so did the importance of Santiago de Compostela as an international shrine. Growing numbers of French people settled along the pilgrim route (*camino de Santiago*) that led across northern Spain from the Pyrenees, and it was along this artery that the Romanesque style – seen in such buildings as the cathedral at Jaca, the church of St Isidore at León, and the cathedral of Compostela – penetrated into the peninsula in the 11th and 12th centuries. In the 13th century came the introduction of the new French Gothic style, which in Spain reached its greatest triumphs in the cathedrals of León, Burgos and Toledo itself.

In one sense, the capture of Toledo merely repeated the pattern of earlier Christian gains. A town was conquered and its surrounding territory subjugated afterward. Nevertheless, the cultural shock to the Christians who entered the city in 1085 must have been enormous. Toledo, lying amid good agricultural land and surrounded by market gardens, was very different from earlier conquests in the more sparsely populated lands farther north. In Toledo, the Castilians and their allies, both Iberian and foreign, found a complex and sophisticated city. Particularly startling to the Christian conquerors was the realization that not only were there communities of Christians and Jews

Above A woodcut illustration from an early printed edition of the *Crónica del Cid*, dated 1498. This was a prose recasting of the *Cantar de Mío Cid*, the epic poem of probably early 13th-century date, that offers a highly fictionalized account of the career of Rodrigo Díaz de Vivar (El Cid). The story illustrated here, in which El Cid's daughters are humiliated by their husbands, the heirs to the county of Carrión, is unhistorical. His two daughters actually made highly advantageous matches, marrying into the Navarrese and Catalan ruling families.

Right The magnificent Gothic cathedral at Burgos was begun in 1221, and consecrated in 1261. The immediate inspiration for it lay in some of the cathedrals of northern France and the Rhineland that were visited by Bishop Maurice of Burgos in the course of a diplomatic journey he made for Fernando III of Castile in 1219. The open spires on the two western towers were added in the 15th century.

living peaceably in Toledo under Muslim rule, but also that the former had adopted the Arabic language and culture, including modes of dress and styles of living that seemed to Christian eyes luxurious and decadent. Moreover, they appeared to have no great desire to learn the new dogmas of French feudalism or the ideas for church reform then being advanced by the papacy.

The discovery of this dynamic center of learning and intellectual exchange, which happened at a time when the cathedral schools of France and elsewhere were about to develop into universities, was to transform intellectual life north of the Pyrenees. When Toledo was captured by the Christians, western Europe was in fairly massive intellectual deficit in relation to the Muslim world. Most of the existing corpus of Greek and Roman science, mathematics and philosophy, preserved in the cities of the Near East, had been translated into Arabic, either in Damascus or Baghdad, by the 9th century. Islamic scholars brought to their study of these works an enthusiasm for scientific observation: in medicine, for example, Arab commentators added botanical, pharmacological and diagnostic information to the works of Hippocrates and Galen. The geographer al-Idrisi (1100–66), educated in Córdoba, used his own knowledge of the Mediterranean to fill out the works of the Roman geographers

Strabo and Ptolemy, then unknown in the west.

It was through contact with Muslims, mostly in Spain but also in Sicily and other parts of the eastern Mediterranean, that knowledge of classical learning was transmitted to the medieval (and modern) west. In the 12th century, Toledo became, along with other towns in Spain and southern France, an important center for the translation of scholarly texts (and poetry) from Arabic into Latin. Many of these works had originally been written in Greek, but the normal procedure at this time was for the Arabic text to be translated into the local language – Castilian, Catalan or southern French (Occitanian) for example – often by a Spanish Jew. The translator would then communicate this vernacular version to one of the schoolsmen of France, England or Italy, who would translate and distribute it in Latin, the universal academic language of the period. Thus the store of intellectual knowledge in western Europe was expanded in spectacular fashion. Not only did "pagan" Greek and Roman texts such as the works of Aristotle find their way into university syllabuses by this route; so, too, did the works of Jewish and Muslim scholars. In the mid 12th century, for example, the French Cluniac monk Peter the Venerable (c. 1092–1156) even commissioned a Latin translation of the Qu'ran.

Medieval Toledo

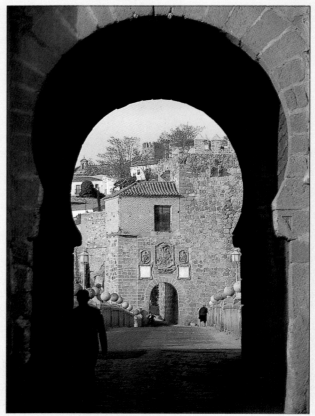

Surrounded on three sides by the river Tagus, Toledo occupies a naturally defensible site and has been continuously settled since the early Roman period. The former capital of the Visigothic kingdom, it was an important center of commerce and industry throughout the period of Arab rule (712–1085). Though the predominantly Christian population frequently rebelled against their Arab rulers in the south, they became thoroughly arabicized, not only speaking Arabic, but adopting Arab culture. A substantial Jewish community also existed in the city. After the collapse of the caliphate in 1031, the *taifa* kingdom of Toledo became increasingly dependent upon the rulers of León-Castile. Following its capture in 1085, it was immediately restored as a metropolitan see with primacy over the whole Spanish church: the archbishops soon became the most powerful figures in the city.

The churches built in Toledo after 1085 are among the best examples of Mudéjar architecture in Spain, showing the continued strength of Arab stylistic traditions among the Christian population. However, when work was started on a new cathedral in the mid 13th century, on the site of the city's former principal mosque, it was built in Gothic style. Only two of the city's medieval synagogues survive today, one of which was built by the Jewish treasurer of King Pedro the Cruel (1350–69). Such examples of *convivencia* were soon to vanish in the early 15th century as Christian attacks on the local Jewish population intensified.

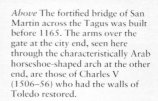

Above The fortified bridge of San Martin across the Tagus was built before 1165. The arms over the gate at the city end, seen here through the characteristically Arab horseshoe-shaped arch at the other end, are those of Charles V (1506–56) who had the walls of Toledo restored.

Left As the name suggests (*arrabal* means "suburb"), the church of Santiago del Arrabal stood outside the city wall when it was founded shortly after 1085. The mostly 13th-century building is a fine example of Mudéjar architecture. Its debt to Arab artistic influences can be seen in the window of the bell tower (dating from the 12th century), the blind arcading next to the transept window, and the south door. The grandiose New Bisagra gate in the background was erected by Charles V in the medieval wall that incorporated the suburb within the city confines to provide an imposing new entry into the city.

Right The church of Santa María la Blanca was originally a synagogue, built in the 12th century and restored in the 13th. It was seized by the Christian community and made into a church in 1405 as the result of an inflammatory sermon preached by St Vincent Ferrer.

Above This view of Toledo from the southeast clearly shows the strength of its defensive position built on a hill within a meander of the river Tagus. At the highest point of the city is the 16th-century Alcazar (the former royal citadel and palace) that occupies the site of earlier fortresses. To the left is the great Gothic cathedral, begun in 1227, a symbol of the church's powerful presence in the city after 1085.

Right This brick-built Mudéjar apse was added to a mosque, privately founded in 999/1000, when it was transformed into the church of Cristo de la Luz in the 12th century.

Muslim reform and counterattack

The Christian advances that culminated in the fall of Toledo were regarded by many in al-Andalus as a consequence of a falling away from the strictest standards of Islam. A reforming sect from North Africa known as the Almoravids was therefore invited by some of the *taifa* rulers into Spain with the aim of enforcing closer observance of religious law. A particular target of their condemnation was the apparently widespread cultivation of grapes to make wine – a practice that had no doubt been inherited from the Romans and Visigoths. For all their efforts, the Almoravids' reforms were seen as inadequate and in 1150 they were succeeded by a new wave of Islamic zealots, the Almohads, also from North Africa.

The Almohads' activities largely succeeded in bringing to an end the debates on religious and scientific questions between Muslim, Jewish and Christian scholars that, taking place in a climate of mutual respect if not agreement, were a feature of the "golden age" of *convivencia* (coexistence) of 12th-century Spain. Among the victims of their reforms was ibn Rushd (1126–98), whose commentaries on the works of Aristotle had brought him to the notice of medieval churchmen in the west, who knew him as Averroës. At one time court physician to the emir of Córdoba, ibn Rushd's works became suspect and he was forced into exile in Morocco in 1195. A similar fate had befallen the Jewish philosopher, physician and theologian Moses Maimonides (1135–1204), the foremost figure of medieval Judaism, who was also a native of Córdoba. The hostility of the Almohads forced him and his family to flee first to Morocco and then to Cairo.

In 1195 the Almohads won a great military victory over Christian forces at Alarcos, some way south of Toledo, but their triumph proved to be short-lived. In 1212, they were defeated by the armies of Castile and its allies in a battle at Las Navas de Tolosa in northeastern Andalusia, close to the mountain passes that admitted traffic and communications from the north. This battle proved to be a turning point in the Christian Reconquest of Spain, for it opened the way to the Guadalquivir valley and thus to the important Islamic cities of Córdoba and Seville.

A changing balance of power

Between the fall of Toledo in 1085 and the battle of Las Navas, almost a third of the peninsula had been recovered by Christian forces. Stone castles and fortified watchtowers – still such a feature of the Iberian landscape today – were built to defend these newly acquired territories, and town defenses were strengthened with outer walls. The political disarray that affected the small Muslim states of al-Andalus (even though the economy was still functioning quite well) in some ways resembled the situation in the Christian north in earlier centuries. But the major changes that had been taking place within the Christian kingdoms since the start of the Reconquest meant that they had now begun to match, in governmental and military terms, their feudal neighbors north of the Pyrenees. In the course of the century the old freelance, rather anarchic frontier societies of the north had been brought under the control of kings and seignorial magnates, and the political players for the rest of the medieval period - Castile-León, Portugal, Aragon-Barcelona, and Navarre – were now in place.

In the west, this had come about in the middle of the previous century when Afonso Henriques (1128–85)

began to extend the frontiers of the county of Portugal – at this time consisting of an area north of the Douro, and nominally under the control of Castile – southward. In 1147 Santarém and then Lisbon were captured from the Muslims, the latter with the help of a crusading army consisting of French, Flemish and Anglo-Norman soldiers, supposedly on their way to the Holy Land. In 1179 Afonso Henriques placed Portugal under the protection of the papacy, and in turn was recognized as king.

In the east of the peninsula, a new political entity had come into being with the betrothal in 1137 of Ramón Berenguer IV, count of Barcelona (1131–62), to Petronila, heiress of Aragon. In the previous half-century, the county of Barcelona had expanded to take on very much the shape that Catalonia has today. It had also established a loose hegemony over much of southern France and was already a trading power in the Mediterranean. Its cultural affinities with Provence were evident in the close links between the Catalan and Occitanian languages; unlike the other Christian kingdoms at this date, Barcelona possessed a written legal code. While Aragon-Barcelona was considerably smaller than Castile-León, it was nevertheless strong enough to pose an effective challenge to the latter's leadership of Christian Spain.

The Reconquest of Andalusia

The capture of Córdoba – the capital of the former caliphate – by Castile in 1236 seems to have happened largely by accident. The city was divided into two separate walled quarters, and a group of Christians – who appear to have been bandits from the area to the north of the city – were apparently let into its eastern, more industrial half by their coreligionists. The royal armies under Fernando III of Castile (1201–52) arrived later on the scene to take charge of the situation. As so often in earlier episodes of the Reconquest, almost no fighting took place, though it was some time before the western half of the city, containing the Great Mosque, the main markets and the former caliph's palace, fell to the Christians.

The pattern of occupation and settlement of Córdoba was similar to that of other towns conquered in the Guadalquivir valley in the mid 13th century, including Jaén (1246), Seville (1248) and Cádiz (1262). Initially, only the town itself was occupied. Most of the Muslim population left and was replaced by new Christian settlers. The occupying armies often contained foreigners, but they generally quickly cashed in the grants given them by the Castilian king and departed. Soon royal officials began to organize the redistribution of property, but this was not generally done until the surrounding countryside had been brought into Christian hands – usually by negotiation. While the towns were largely resettled by Christian colonists, in the countryside the political and ecclesiastical institutions of the north were imposed on a predominantly Muslim population, known as Mudéjars, who paid rent to their new Christian lords, but retained religious freedom.

In drawing up the settlements for the newly acquired lands and possessions in Andalusia – the details of which are known to us through documents called *repartimientos* – the crown of Castile (as the territories under Castilian rule were later to be known) attempted to apply the kind of ideas about monarchy and godly society that had become fashionable in Spain with the transformation of the Reconquest into a papal crusade. Urban and rural housing and land were allocated in accordance with conventional notions of the superiority of horse- over foot-soldiers, and the newly founded orders of Dominican and Franciscan friars were sent into the cities of Andalusia in preference to the monks of the older, more established Benedictine orders. While the latter lived in large

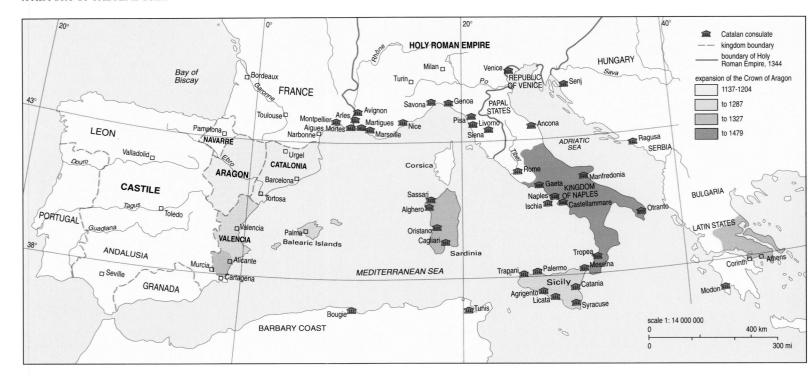

monastic estates in the countryside, the friars – who were committed to preaching the Christian faith and combating heresy – lived for the most part in small communities within the towns.

The system of agreement and coexistence in rural Andalusia fell apart in the early 1260s, when a series of revolts by inhabitants who had no wish to live under rulers of another religion made the Christian authorities conclude that expulsion of the Muslim population was the only answer. Thereafter, only small, urban communities of Muslims remained in these territories. They were generally engaged in artisan activity such as bricklaying and construction work, the leather trade and veterinary work. As craftsmen, they were responsible for a blending of Spanish and Arabic styles that is seen in the characteristic Mudéjar ornamentation of ceramics, metalwork and textiles and, in architecture, in the use of the red brick and tiers of blind arcading.

Paradoxically, the rural depopulation of southern Spain helped to bring the process of Reconquest to a halt by creating an acute shortage of labor to work the land. To rectify this situation, the nobles who had received grants of lands under the royal *repartimientos* attempted to attract manpower from the north. Their success was limited, but their efforts at recruitment nonetheless antagonized their northern neighbors. In the event, large areas of land in Andalusia that had previously been cultivated by Muslims went out of production after about 1260. In some places, they had still not been taken in hand again as late as the 19th century.

The expulsion from Christian territory of the bulk of the Muslim rural population had one other effect in that it led the Nasrid family (a political grouping hitherto unknown in al-Andalus) to move from Jaén to Granada. Here the Nasrids established what was a rarity in medieval Spain – a long-lasting state that enjoyed almost complete religious unity. The late medieval kingdom of Granada had the advantage of mountainous defenses and a population that, for the most part, chose to live there in order to experience the life of Islam. There were some Jews but few Christians,

apart from captives. Granada depended largely on trade through its Mediterranean ports of Málaga and Almería for its economic prosperity. It was only in the 1480s and 1490s, with the impetus of the crusade led by Ferdinand and Isabella, that this last Muslim redoubt fell to Christian attackers.

"A land of three religions"

Alfonso X of Castile (1252–84) took full advantage of Spain's growing contact with western Europe to absorb all the imperialistic notions of monarchy then current, particularly in Germany and France. In 1257 he even put himself forward as a candidate in the election of the Holy Roman Emperor. He saw himself as God's representative on earth, his country as a potential kingdom of heaven on earth, and his divinely inspired power as absolute. The problem for Alfonso and his advisers was that his leading subjects were still obstinately wedded to the earlier "feudal" notion that kings had to consult their nobles in military and political matters. When Alfonso attempted to introduce a seven-part law code (the *Siete Partidas*) embodying his ideas, the Castilian parliament, feeble though it was, rejected it. In the course of Alfonso's reign, social and political conflict increased. It seemed that only war against a common external enemy had earlier induced the Castilian nobles to accept the growth of royal power. The absence of hostilities brought about by the halting of the Reconquest in southern Andalusia plunged his subjects into squabbling and revolt. Only a century later was a more aggressive and effective ruler, Alfonso XI (1312–50), able to have the *Siete Partidas* enacted.

Despite his failure to become Holy Roman Emperor and his problems with his nobles, Alfonso X of Castile became known as Alfonso the Wise (*el Sabio*). This learned king published his own set of songs to the Virgin Mary (the *Cántigas de Santa Maria*), supervised the writing of a general historical chronicle of Spain, and produced books on such diverse subjects as chess and swearwords. Above all, however, Alfonso acquired his reputation for wisdom by means of his comparatively enlightened rule in cultural matters and

The formation of the Aragonese empire

When further Aragonese expansion within the Iberian peninsula was blocked by the Castilian conquest of Murcia in 1243, the kings took advantage of the opportunity afforded them by possession of Barcelona and the other ports of the Catalan seaboard to build up a navy and to involve themselves in wider Mediterranean politics. The conquest of the Balearic Islands was completed in 1287, but even more dramatic had been the Aragonese conquest of Sicily in 1282, following an invitation to intervene against its unpopular new Angevin ruler. The marriage of Pere III of Aragon (1276–85) to the heiress of the Hohenstaufen dynasty, the island's former rulers, led a junior branch of the Aragonese kings becoming independent kings of Sicily from 1283. Sardinia was added to the kingdom by conquest in 1324. The involvement in Greece of Catalan mercenaries to aid the Byzantine empire against the Turks led to the creation in 1311 of a duchy of Athens under a younger son of the king of Sicily. This only lasted until 1387. Commercially, too, Catalan naval power led to the establishment of a far-flung network of trading contacts, represented by the consulates set up by the city of Barcelona. The 15th century saw a rapid and severe decline in the Catalan mercantile economy, and also the extinction of the senior branch of the royal house in 1410. Renewed military expansion under the Trastamaran kings led to the conquest of the kingdom of Naples in 1443 by Alfonso V (1416–1458). On the latter's death the Aragonese "empire" was decisively divided, with Alfonso's brother Juan II (1458–1479) inheriting the kingdom of Aragon, while Alfonso's son Ferrante (1458–94) took the Italian possessions.

his concern to understand and represent all the peoples over whom he reigned: Christians, Jews and Muslims. This is not to say that the idea of reconquering the remaining Muslim territory in Spain was abandoned by him, or that he ceased to believe that the Christian religion was the only true one and would ultimately triumph. Nonetheless, later events in Castile and elsewhere in the peninsula would serve to highlight the merits of Alfonso's reign.

Up to now, the history of Iberian Jews had been largely overshadowed by the great battle being fought between Christianity and Islam. During the 13th century, however, the comparative "enlightenment" of the Spanish kings, coupled with the increasing influence of the papacy, brought longstanding tensions between Judaism and Christianity to the fore. In 1263, Alfonso X's neighbor, Jaume I of Aragon (1213–76), supervised a theological disputation in Barcelona between the Jewish rabbi and kabbalist Moshe ben Nachman (known to the west as Nahmanides, c. 1194–c. 1270) and a Christian convert from Judaism, Pau Cristià (Paul the Christian). Accounts of the discussion survive from both sides, and not surprisingly, each awarded itself the victory. The Barcelona disputation was, in fact, more like a trial of the Jews and of Judaism than a genuine religious dialog. Though Spain between 1000 and 1350 is sometimes represented as having been a "golden age" for Judaism, it was so only in the sense that the Iberian Jewish community – the largest in western Europe – was not, with some exceptions in Muslim-ruled areas in the 12th century, actively persecuted.

The Aragonese empire

The 13th century saw major changes of direction in the political and cultural interests of the crown of Aragon. Its links with southern France were severed when – under the guise of waging a papal war against heresy – the Capetian kings of France asserted their military authority over the counts of Toulouse and other ruling families (the Albigensian crusade, 1208–28). The culture of troubadour poetry and music that had flourished among the courts of Provence had spread to Aragon-Catalonia in the 12th century; the poetic tradition it inspired in turn influenced the compositions of Alfonso X of Castile. Within the peninsula itself, Jaume I captured the city and kingdom of Valencia in 1238, but was thwarted from making further advances against the Muslims by the Castilian occupation of Murcia. Furthermore, the Mudéjar population of Valencia – which was administered as a separate kingdom of the crown of Aragon, with its own laws and parliament – put up a fierce resistance to Christian rule in a series of revolts between 1247 and 1258.

Largely as a result of these developments, the energies of the Aragonese and Catalans became directed toward Italy and the eastern Mediterranean, where they were able to build on the extensive maritime interests already established by Catalan traders and sailors. The expulsion of the Muslims from Majorca by an Aragonese-Catalan army in 1229/30 was the first step in the establishment of a power base in the Mediterranean. Aragon's overseas ambitions were further realized when it assumed control of Sicily in 1283 and Sardinia in 1323. Later it acquired Naples as well (1442), leading to a lengthy and, in the eyes of many, ill-fated intervention in the affairs of Italy in the 15th and 16th centuries. The crown of Aragon showed remarkable cultural and political sophistication. The various territories ruled by the Aragonese kings functioned in a variety of languages and developed, in the 13th and 14th centuries, a strong parliamentary tradition that was to be a thorn in the flesh of the Spanish monarchy for many centuries to come.

Years of crisis

The Iberian peninsula seems largely to have escaped the famines that ravaged much of the rest of Europe in 1315–17, but it was very much affected by the Black Death – the bubonic plague that entered Europe from Asia in 1347. Spreading rapidly throughout the continent until 1351, it reached the peninsula quite late in its cycle. In most countries, the Black Death killed from a third to a half of the population. It used to be thought that, in Spain, only Catalonia suffered so badly. Now, however, it appears that losses in Castile, and even as far west as Portugal, were at least as high. The massive reduction of population led inevitably, in Spain and Portugal as elsewhere in Europe, to readjustments in social relations that mainly benefited the strong and prejudiced the weak, allowing rich or more enterprising peasants to gain advantage over their less fortunate neighbors.

The period between 1350 and the accession of Isabella to the throne of Castile in 1474 was a time of political, economic, social and religious crises in the Iberian peninsula. Civil war in Castile led to the murder in 1369 of Pedro the Cruel (1350–69) by his illegitimate half-brother who assumed the throne as Enrique II (1369–79), thereby founding the Trastamaran dynasty that was to last until the death of Ferdinand V (Ferdinand II of Aragon) in 1516. Border disputes between Castile and Aragon, which had been exacerbated by Aragon's intervention in Castile's civil war, only became less acrimonious when a Trastamaran prince was successfully placed on the throne of Aragon (Fernando I, 1412–16).

Right Detail of a 13th-century fresco, now in the Museum of Catalan Art in Barcelona, showing the siege and conquest of Palma de Majorca in 1229 by Jaume I of Aragon. The battle for the city was short but bloody. A typical banner of the Almohad period is seen here flying from one of the towers, and on another the Arab defenders are depicted using slings. Interestingly, this weapon is recorded as being a speciality of the Balearic islanders since the Roman period.

The Jews of Medieval Iberia

By about 1200, there were probably more than 200,000 Jews in the Iberian peninsula. This sizable population occupied a unique position astride the frontier between Christian and Muslim Spain and between the Latin and Catholic culture of medieval Europe and the Arab and Islamic culture of the Middle East. While Hebrew was used for religious worship and study, the Jews were equally adept in Arabic, Latin and the vernacular Romance languages of the peninsula, and their culture and scholarship reflected these influences. Their spiritual life showed great vitality too. However, throughout the medieval period the Jews had no territory of their own and had always to live under rulers of another faith who restricted their freedom. As the balance of power in the peninsula shifted from the Muslims to the Christians, Jews in the Christian kingdoms (though not in Muslim Granada) found themselves moving from a situation of relative toleration to one of subjection to increasingly hostile propaganda emanating from north of the Pyrenees: by 1300 they were required (at least in theory) to wear a distinctive badge. After a series of violent attacks in 1391, thousands converted to Christianity. Though Jewish scholars in the 15th century helped to compile the Alba Bible, their fate was by then already sealed; the remnant of Iberia's Jews were expelled from Spain in 1492 and from Portugal in 1497.

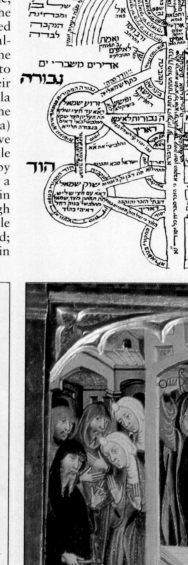

The rise of Portugal

There was also recurrent conflict with Portugal. The Portuguese advance into the Algarve, which had taken place after 1250, blocked Castile's ambitions to colonize this area from Andalusia, and in particular prevented it acquiring valuable ocean ports on the Atlantic coast. Tension continued, leading to the frequent building and refortification of frontier castles. When Fernão of Portugal (1367–83) died without an heir, Castile took advantage of the political crisis to invade, but was defeated at the battle of Aljubarrota (14 August 1385) by a much smaller force led by João de Avis (João I, 1385–1433), who had been elected king by the Cortes at Coimbra earlier in the year. The great monastery of Batalha (Battle) was founded to commemorate the victory, which left João firmly in control of the country. He further strengthened his position and international standing by marrying Philippa of Lancaster (1360–1415), granddaughter of Edward III of England (1327–77).

The success of the Avis dynasty was founded on close cooperation with the mercantile interests of Lisbon who had supported João's accession to power. Navigational and shipping skills acquired from the Muslims contributed to Portugal's rise as a maritime nation in the course of the 15th century. Much of its success in this direction was due to Prince Henry the Navigator (1394–1460), the youngest son of João I. He was able to use the rich resources of the Order of Christ, of which he was master, to sponsor exploratory and colonizing expeditions to the Canary Islands, Madeira, the Azores and Cape Verde Islands between 1419 and 1444, and by his death Portuguese sailors had explored the African coast as far as Sierra Leone. During the reign of Henry's nephew Afonso V (1438–81) a number of expeditions were made against North Africa, with mixed success, and Tangier was acquired in 1471.

Persecution and disorder

Since the mid 13th century Granada had been the only Muslim territory left in Spain. Through all the quarrels and fighting between the Christian states, the Nasrid rulers were able to keep well on the sidelines. Not so the Jewish community. During the civil war in Castile in the late 1360s, the Jewish population, particularly in Toledo, was attacked by the Trastamaran rebels. This was the shape of things to come, for the treatment of Jews came increasingly to serve as a barometer of the social climate of the Iberian kingdoms during the late Middle Ages. As Iberian chroniclers often pointed out, it was easy for Christians to attack Jews with impunity because they had no defenders, whereas if Muslims were attacked, there might be retaliation against Christians, either within the peninsula itself or living in Muslim lands.

In the midst of the severe social and economic problems that affected most of the peninsula in the early summer of 1391, a wave of anti-Semitic persecution was unleashed. It started when the inhabitants of Seville responded with unprecedented fervor and violence to what was most probably a conventional sermon preached against the Jews by the archdeacon of the nearby town of Ecija, Ferrán Martinez. His congregation immediately began looting the Jewish quarter and attacking its inhabitants. Anti-Jewish feeling spread throughout Andalusia and then moved north and east, eventually affecting every major Jewish community in Spain.

Above left Perhaps the most distinct contribution of medieval Spain to Judaism was the mystical movement known as the Kabbalah. First developed in 13th-century Catalonia, this attempted to link the various attributes of God as described in Scripture with the letters of the sacred text itself. These links were often represented in diagrammatic form, as here.

Above One of the last flowerings of the social and cultural coexistence (*convivencia*) of Jews, Christians and Muslims was the synagogue of the Tránsito in Toledo. Erected in the mid 14th century by Samuel ha-Levi with support from King Pedro the Cruel of Castile, it was built by Muslim craftsmen and is Islamic in architectural style.

Left By the time the synagogue was built, propaganda presenting Jews as the implacable enemies of Christians was widespread. This 14th-century Spanish illumination shows a number of Jews stealing the consecrated communion bread from a church to destroy it.

Far left The Alba Bible, commissioned in 1422 by a Christian patron Don Luis de Guzmán, is a rare 15th-century example of Jewish-Christian cooperation. This page shows Don Luis enthroned. At the bottom, he is seen receiving the manuscript from Rabbi Moses Arragel of Guadalajara, one of the Jewish scholars involved in its preparation.

Above A galleon in full sail, bearing the arms of the kingdom of Portugal, depicted on a 15th-century earthenware luster bowl. The continuing influence of Islamic decorative traditions can be seen in the highly stylized vegetal motifs around the rim. The Portuguese were to make enormous advances in navigation and seamanship in the course of the 15th century, in particular developing ships that were able to withstand the winds and currents of the Atlantic.

The authorities tried ineffectually to calm the situation, but most Jews took matters into their own hands. Those who refused to abandon their faith moved from the big cities, where the authorities had little control in situations of major violence, to smaller towns and villages, where the forces of law and order better matched the task. A third or more of Iberian Jews (that is, about 200,000) took the other option and converted to Christianity. They were to be followed by many others over the next three decades. The conversion of a large number of people in a short time was a unique phenomenon that would have major repercussions in the future.

At the time, and particularly after Isabella came to the throne of Castile in 1474, Jews and converted Jews (*conversos*) were made to appear central to every problem that afflicted Spain between 1391 and 1480. With hindsight, and set beside the genuine problems of the previous century, things do not seem to have been as desperate as contemporary observers believed. The international standing of the Spanish kingdoms was considerably raised by their efforts to help solve the Great Schism (1378–1417) – the split in the Catholic church that resulted in rival popes being established in Avignon and Rome.

Even during the civil war that convulsed Castile and Aragon for much of the 15th century, both kingdoms were growing steadily richer. While kings and nobles fought each other, artisans – and the few entrepreneurs able to overcome the prevailing feudal and crusading ethic that militated against them – were slowly building up the economy that was to form the basis, weak though it was, of the Spanish overseas empire of the 16th century. The problem, for both Spain and Portugal, was to be whether their generally meager agricultural resources would prove adequate to provide a strong enough economic base to support the worldwide expansion that was to follow.

The Altarpiece of St Vincent

1 St. Vincent   4 Dom João   7 Jew with Torah
2 Self portrait of Gonçalves   5 King Afonso V
3 Prince Henry the Navigator   6 Queen Isabel

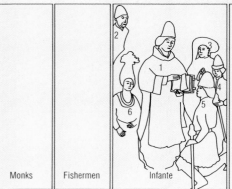

Monks | Fishermen | Infante | Archbishop | Knights | The relic

Nuno Gonçalves, court painter to Afonso V from c.1450–72, was the leading Portuguese artist of his time: Francisco de Holanda, writing in 1548, called him an "eagle of painting", worthy of comparison with such masters as Leonardo da Vinci and Michelangelo. That he is little known today is because most of his works were destroyed in the Lisbon earthquake of 1755. Indeed, for more than a century none at all were thought to have survived. Then in 1882 some dingy panels, suffering from neglect and over-painting, were discovered in the Convent of St Vincent in Lisbon, and in 1902 these were identified as the work of Gonçalves by the scholar José de Figueiredo, following years of painstaking study and restoration. At first it was believed that the panels belonged to an altarpiece of St Vincent painted by Gonçalves for the cathedral in Lisbon. However, many of the details differ from the description of the work provided by Francisco de Holanda, the sole source of all our information about the artist, and it is now thought that the surviving altarpiece is another work altogether. It reveals the mastery of composition, the richness of portraiture and the skilled use of color that make Gonçalves the equal of the great names of the Renaissance. There are no native precedents for his art. His style derives from Flemish and Burgundian painters and he was obviously influenced by Dieric Bouts (c. 1400–75) and Jan van Eyck (c.1395–c. 1441). The two center panels of the altarpiece both show the figure of St Vincent, the patron saint of Lisbon as well as the royal house of Portugal. He is surrounded by leading figures of the Portuguese court and church. These are clearly actual portraits, though there has been considerable debate about who is represented: many of Figueiredo's original identifications have since been questioned or supplemented. However, the figure kneeling before the saint on the so-called panel of the Infante is usually identified as Afonso V, and the boy behind him as his son, later João II. If correct, then the painting can be dated to c. 1465; it may have been commissioned by the king (nicknamed "Afonso the African") to commemorate his campaigns in Morocco of 1458–64, perhaps in fulfilment of a vow he had made to the saint.

Above The panels from left to right show the different orders of society. Religion is represented by the Cistercian monks of Alcobaça, workers by the Brotherhood of Fishermen and Navigators, monarchy by the royal court, the church by the archbishop and canons, and the military orders by the duke of Bragança and other participants in the African wars. The last panel shows the relics of St Vincent, which were housed in the Convent. The diagram gives the probable arrangement of the piece, though it is thought that a statue of St Vincent may originally have separated the two central panels.

Right The society ranked around the figure of St Vincent is one poised for the adventure of maritime discovery and overseas expansion that – foreshadowed in the moment of thanksgiving recorded here – was to come to fruition in the 16th century. As well as the king (5) and the infante Dom João (4 and *far left*), the Infante panel is believed to show Afonso's uncle, Henry the Navigator (3), in the black hat. Facing Afonso is his wife, Isabel (6). If these identifications are correct, the portraits of both Henry and Isabel are posthumous; by including them Afonso was perhaps seeking to acknowledge the part they had played in his and Portugal's success. The figure in the top lefthand corner is commonly identified as the artist himself (2).

Far right St Vincent was also the patron saint of the Brotherhood of Fishermen and Navigators. The fishermen's panel celebrates Portugal's association with the sea. The two figures in the top half are shown wrapped in their nets. Below them another fisherman is at prayer.

Left The inclusion of the Jew in the relic panel is enigmatic but, along with the portrait of a Muslim in another panel, hints at a spirit of tolerance in Afonso's court.

The Alhambra, Granada

The fortified palace-city of the Alhambra in the mountain kingdom of Granada is perhaps the best known monument of Islamic Spain. The area within its walls would once have been crowded with the houses, shops, workshops, mosques and baths of those who served the rulers of Granada, but today the only structures surviving from the Islamic period are the fortress at the western end of the site, parts of which date from the period of the Zirid dynasty (1013–90), and much of the palace complex built by the Nasrids, especially Yusuf I (1333–54) and Muhammad V (1354–59; 1362–91). Notable among these buildings are the council chamber (the Mexuar), the audience chamber (Hall of the Ambassadors), and the famous Court of the Myrtles and Court of the Lions, which formed part of the private residential quarters of the rulers and their extensive families. Towering over them all is the palace built by Charles V in the 16th century, whose interest in the Islamic structures was instrumental in their preservation.

1 Ruins of the Arab palaces
2 The Partal gardens
3 Tower of las Damas
4 Arab baths
5 Hall of the Kings
6 Hall of the Abencerrajes
7 Court of the Lions
8 Garden of Lindaraxa
9 Court of the Myrtles
10 Tower of the Comares
11 Hall of the Ambassadors
12 Golden Room
13 Mexuar
14 Palace of Charles V

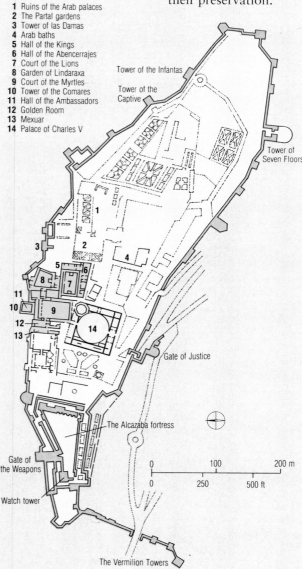

Above This vase, probably belonging to the 15th century, is made of glazed earthenware and painted with cobalt and luster. The central inscription wishes the owner prosperity and good luck. It is typical of the high-quality luxury wares produced in Granada during the Nasrid period, for use in the palaces or in noble households.

Left The site plan shows how little of the interior of the Islamic city has been preserved, apart from the buildings of the palace complex. The individual palaces, though adjacent to each other, did not form a single unit, but were used for different purposes and at different times of the year. A recreational summer place, the Generalife, was built on the hillside above and to the east of the city.

Left The name of the Alhambra means "red palace", from the color of its buildings. This view of the walled city was taken from the hill to its north, known as the Albaicín, probably the site of the earliest Islamic settlement in Granada. On the clifftop on the right are the formidable defenses of the Alcazaba, the main fortress, and on the left is the massive Tower of Comares, which housed the Hall of the Ambassadors - the setting for formal court activities such as the reception of envoys. Behind it is part of the palace of Charles V, built in the classical style of the Renaissance, with the mountains of the Sierra Nevada in the background.

Above The Court of Lions (named from the lions supporting the fountain) was the center of a palace built by Muhammad V as a place of recreation and informal entertainment for his family. The Hall of the Kings, probably the dining area for this palace, lies at the far end.

Far left Part of an early 14th-century wall painting, depicting a hunting scene, from the Tower of las Damas. It was painted for the Nasrids by Christian painters, as were three ceiling paintings on leather in the Hall of the Kings, which are associated with a group of painters working in the Palace of the Popes in Avignon.

Left The council chamber, or Mexuar, was begun by Isma'il I (1314–25), altered by Yusuf I and entirely reconstructed by Muhammad V. It served as the administrative and judicial center of the palace complex, and was the meeting place of the council of viziers.

THE CATHOLIC EMPIRE 1480–1670

The Catholic Monarchs and the rule of law

In 1469, five years before becoming queen of Castile, the infanta Isabella married her cousin Ferdinand, heir to the throne of Aragon. At first this seemed merely another dynastic alliance, a routine instrument of diplomacy. But the event was of great significance, for it marked the start of an unique political partnership, involving two of the three great kingdoms of the peninsula. With hindsight, it may be recognized that "Spain" was born, and evolved to maturity, from the historic association between Castile and Aragon. Yet this was far from being an inevitable process. Ferdinand II of Aragon (1479–1516; also Ferdinand V of Castile 1474–1516) and Isabella of Castile (1474–1504) did not set out to create a unified state, but rather sought to pool resources in order to achieve advantages for their respective kingdoms, which retained different legal and social institutions, different traditions, even different languages, right up to the 19th century.

One of the first objectives of the *Reyes Católicos* (the "Catholic Monarchs" – the title given to Ferdinand and Isabella by the Spanish Pope Alexander VI in 1496) was the imposition of law and order. Domestic peace was a natural longing after the years of civil war, but there was a strong religious, as well as political, motive behind their desire to obtain it. Isabella in particular regarded the salvation of souls through strict religious observance as a divine mission. It was only by increasing the power of the crown, and achieving physical security from enemies – especially non-Christians – that the Catholic Monarchs could hope to achieve full religious observance, instilling obedience and order where previously there had been chaos and internecine conflict. Consequently, they reformed the justice system by codifying the law, by strengthening the royal council (Castile's supreme court) and by establishing dependent tribunals (*chancillerías*) at Valladolid and Granada. In doing so, the Catholic Monarchs were obliged to confront the three most powerful groups in their lands: the church, the great nobility and the towns.

Of all their reforms, the establishment of the Inquisition was to have the most profound and enduring effects on Spanish history, especially on the process of unification. The Inquisition was founded in Seville in 1478–80, later acquiring jurisdiction throughout Castile and Aragon. Its original task was the supervision of those who had been converted to Christianity from the Jewish and Muslim communities – *conversos* and *moriscos* respectively – though later it concentrated on preventing abuses and relapses among "old" Christians. The Inquisition wielded great power. All appointments to it were made by the crown; its proceedings were secret and relied heavily on informants, while torture was often – though under strict conditions – used to extract confessions. Condemned heretics were burned at the enormously popular *auto de fé* (literally "act of faith") ceremonies, with their confiscated property being shared out between the crown, the Inquisition and the informants.

While it is impossible to defend the Inquisition's methods, which were dubious even by the standards of the time, it immunized Spain in advance against the Reformation. The cardinal-archbishop of Toledo, Francisco Jiménez (or Ximénez) de Cisneros (1436–1517), used the Inquisition to implement reforms among the clergy, making the Spanish church the least corrupt in Europe, and thus the least vulnerable to attack from the new Protestant heresies of the 16th century. In such interests it was even able, during Philip II's reign (1556–98), to proceed against the highest churchman in Spain, Bartolomé Carranza, Cardinal Archbishop of Toledo (1503–76). The Inquisition accordingly spared Spain the endless religious wars that, in France and Germany, were the cause of more, and more widespread, suffering than its own activities inflicted on Spaniards.

The elemental fear of heresy among ordinary citizens endowed the Inquisition with a status rare among departments of state – a genuine, enduring popularity at grass-roots level. However, it was more readily accepted in Castile than in Aragon, where its introduction was impeded by prolonged opposition, partly because its ruling council (the *Suprema*) was seen as an organ of Castilian government. Even at the end of the 16th century, the Inquisition could still inspire violent

Below The Casa de las Conchas ("House of the Shells") in Salamanca is perhaps the nearest thing to the ducal palaces of the Italian Renaissance to be found in Castile. Yet its bizarre adornment makes it unique. The original owner was so delighted to be made a knight of the Military Order of Santiago by the Catholic Monarchs that he employed the pilgrims' symbol of a shell as a decorative motif. The exterior is studded with carved shells, giving it an almost defensive appearance, like an enormous shield.

Right This magnificent *retablo*, or altarpiece, in Avila cathedral was painted by the greatest painter of the early Spanish Renaissance, Pedro Berruguete (d. 1504). Born in Valladolid, he is believed to have studied in Naples and in 1477 was known to have been working at the ducal palace at Urbino in central Italy. Both Flemish and Italian influences are to be seen in his works, but they are never imitative and display an impressive feeling for space and atmosphere. He was working in Avila at the time of his death, and it was there that he painted what is probably his masterpiece, the *retablo* in the convent of San Tomás (1499–1503). His son Alonso (c.1488–1561) studied with his father, but was to become better known as a sculptor in the Mannerist style, known for his portrayal of figures in spiritual torment or religious ecstasy. In later life he was responsible for embellishments to Toledo cathedral.

protest in Aragon when its activities conflicted with local laws and privileges (*fueros*). In general, however, religion – and the social influence of the church – contributed to Aragon and Castile's cohesion. Many prelates had been disloyal to the crown during the recurrent conflicts of the 15th century, but the church hierarchy was now brought under control. In part, this was achieved through royal intervention in church appointments, a procedure sanctioned by Pope Alexander VI. It is noteworthy that during the *comunero* uprising of 1520, when the towns of Castile and then Aragon rebelled against the government of

Charles V, only one bishop joined the rebels; he was in due course hanged from the battlements of the castle at Simancas.

Rome also agreed to the crown's takeover of the military-religious orders, the corporate owners of vast tracts of territory, especially in New Castile and Andalusia. Their political role had frequently aggravated civil disorder in the past, but royal control of the orders now enabled the Catholic Monarchs to tap a huge source of patronage and social prestige. This, in addition to the growing resources of the Inquisition, was to be crucial in bringing about the formation of a

Isabella – Patron of Learning

At the age of 31 – almost past middle life by the standards of the time – Isabella undertook the serious study of Latin and founded a grammar school within her court for the humanist education of the sons of the Castilian nobility. This sterling, if flawed, example of feminist initiative illustrates why Isabella became the most enduring inspiration of "Spain". Wife, mother, queen-regnant, warrior, scholar and devout believer, she seemed to be everything the Renaissance idealized. The propaganda image may have been overdone, but Isabella was certainly a leader of irrepressible energy and curiosity. From an early age she was friendly with the Mendozas, the family that almost single-handedly introduced humanist learning to Castile. The doyen of early Spanish humanists, the poet and Latinist Iñigo López de Mendoza, marquis of Santillana (1398–1458), had collected a huge personal library, and his two younger sons, respectively count of Tendilla and archbishop of Seville, became the trusted advisers of Ferdinand and Isabella in the 1470s. Both were avid for the new learning; the former introduced Italian scholars to court, whilst the latter founded the high-powered new university college of Vera Cruz in Valladolid – effectively the capital city of the Catholic Monarchs. Scholarship and the new technology of printing were duly mobilized in the service of the dynasty. During Isabella's reign movable-type presses were set up in most Castilian cities, many of them the result of a deliberate royal policy of inviting German technicians to settle there. Before her death, the 1,000th edition had appeared in Spain, and it is estimated that 50 percent of town-dwellers were able to read. Though most works were devotional, translations of classical authors and even imaginative literature in the vernacular also appeared under a royal licensing system introduced in the 1490s. Meanwhile, the queen took the lead in patronage, meeting and learning from men of ideas, and opening up her own mental horizons to the extent that she was able to share at least a part of Columbus' vision in 1492.

Left Though the scholar-monk in this woodcut seems to be presenting his book to Ferdinand rather than to Isabella, there is no doubt that the queen's interest in scholarship considerably exceeded that of her spouse. She personally supported the careers of young scholars brought to her attention by the Mendozas or by Cardinal Cisneros.

Above The new university of Alcalá was founded by Cisneros and built at his instructions by the architect Pedro de Gumiel at the turn of the 16th century. "The Complutense", as it was known, was transferred to Madrid in the 19th century, and Gumiel's superb facade, in the plateresque style, now houses a library and regional archive.

Right Among the teachers that Cisneros persuaded to Alcalá was the leading Spanish scholar of the day, Antonio de Nebrija, shown here in the center of a miniature from his *Institutiones Latinae*. Isabella took a great interest in his career after his return to Spain from Italy in 1473. Given the queen's encouragement of scholarship, it was fitting that Nebrija's daughter Doña Francisca should have become a professor at Alcalá, sharing the distinction of being the first woman to teach in a European university with Doña Lucía de Medrana of Salamanca.

Left The ultimate exemplar for all women was the Virgin Mother, and the Catholic Monarchs were often pictured (on one occasion with their children and bishops) in adoration of the Queen of Heaven and her Child. In this version, Isabella appears alone, rapt in contemplation while the angels sing and play. This illustration is from the queen's own Book of Hours – itself pictured on the *prie-dieu*.

military-bureaucratic nobility that was dependent on the crown.

Meanwhile, the Catholic Monarchs revived and extended the Castilian *hermandades*, or "brotherhoods", to deal with local disorder and organized crime. By suppressing dozens of private armies – often little more than gangs of outlaws controlled by the great nobles – they radically reduced the nobility's power to intervene in local politics. Both the economy and royal revenues of Castile benefited from the imposition of law and order: roads and bridges were built or rebuilt, the castles of unruly nobles were dismantled and customs posts were established to exploit the expansion of internal trade. In Aragon and Catalonia, however, royal authority remained relatively weak. Ferdinand wisely made no move to revoke the cherished *fueros* that, as king, he had sworn to observe. As a consequence, the nobles retained considerable powers and their depredations continued to afflict Aragonese society.

The officers of the *hermandades* were drawn from the minor nobility (*hidalgos*). This social group was almost unique in Europe, representing a numerous urban aristocracy that was partly derived from professional – or even mercantile – origins. Some *hidalgos* owned modest outlying estates, but equally often they had lost their links with the land. They formed an elite of city rulers (*togados*, or "toga-wearers") who shared power with the merchant class, and their relative independence of the higher nobility made such men very useful to the crown. As well as officering the *hermandades* they formed a lay rank in the Inquisition, bringing rewards and prestige to their families. During the 1480s, many were appointed as *corregidores* (full-time government officials) in the towns, with the duty of implementing royal decrees and presiding over town-council meetings. The *corregidores* played a critically important role in the 18 towns that sent representatives to the Castilian parliament, or Cortes. By allying with the *hidalgo* class, the Catholic Monarchs were able progressively to exclude the nobles from government, whilst acquiring an administration that was entirely dependent on royal favor.

1492 and the Last Crusade

When Ferdinand and Isabella came to their thrones, "Spain" was barely even a geographical expression. The glorious year of 1492 was to change that, putting Spain firmly on the map as a leading religious crusader and European power. Three momentous events took place in 1492: Boabdil (Abu Abd Allah; d. 1527) – the last Muslim king in Spain – surrendered Granada; the Inquisition moved against the Jews; and Christopher Columbus (1451–1506) made his historic landfall in the West Indies.

The Catholic Monarchs began the war against the Muslim kingdom of Granada in 1482 with an army that was largely not their own, paid for mainly by voluntary contributions from municipal and ecclesiastical sources. When it ended ten years later, they commanded a royal army and enjoyed a settled tax revenue granted them by the Cortes of Castile. The war was the first crusade against Muslim Spain since the fall of Seville in 1284, two centuries earlier. The pressures it placed on the political community could have sparked off a renewed bout of civil war; in fact, sustained campaigning against a common enemy had a unifying effect, especially as it was a joint venture between Castile and Aragon. Moreover, the political

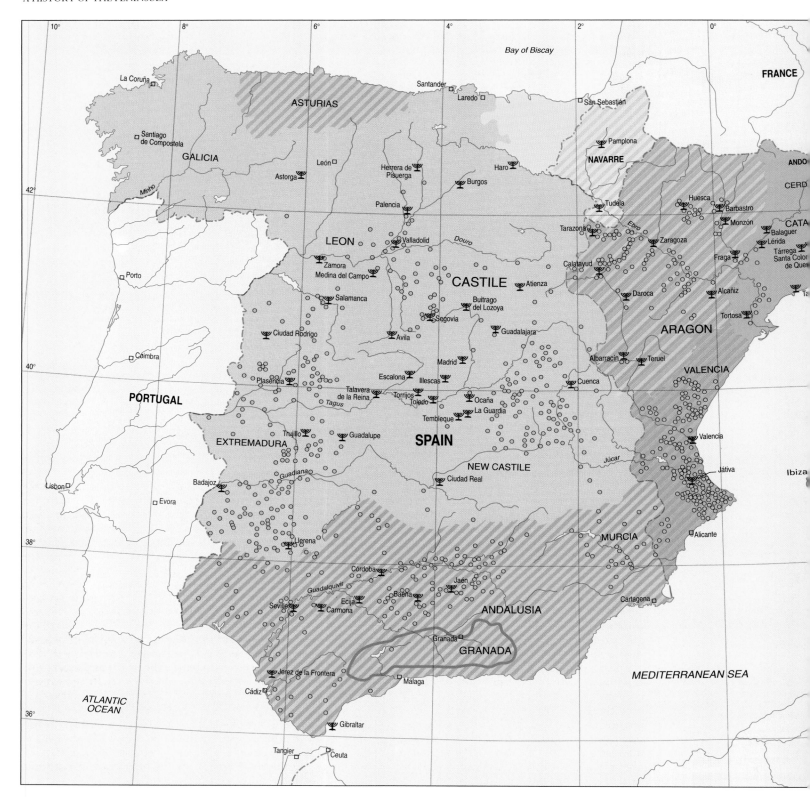

reforms of the late 1470s proved equal to the strain: they had consolidated and extended the institutions of government at both central and local levels. The Iberian achievements were beginning to make an impact on Christian Europe as a whole. The eventual reconquest of Granada in 1492 provided it with a much-needed triumph, coming as it did only 40 years after Constantinople (modern Istanbul) had fallen to the Muslim Turks. The war attracted hundreds of crusaders from outside the peninsula; its successful conclusion earned widespread praise.

The defeated Muslims in Spain were originally granted religious freedom and the right to emigrate in safety to Africa if they chose not to become subjects of the Catholic Monarchs. Within a short time, however, Cardinal Cisneros persuaded Isabella to enforce mass "conversions". Less than three months after the victory at Granada, the authority of the Inquisition was brought to bear against Spain's other non-Christian community. All Jews who refused to convert to Christianity – between 100,000 and 150,000 of them – were expelled from Spain, many of them crossing into Portugal. The expulsion was regarded inside and outside the peninsula as a triumph for the Catholic religion. Its chief effect, however, was to deprive Castile of some of its most economically important citizens.

The "Castilianization" of Spain, 1480–1600
Ladino or Sephardic – a blend of Hebrew and Castilian – was the language of Spain's urban-dwelling Jews before 1492, who carried it to Lisbon (and thence to Antwerp and Hamburg), North Africa, the eastern Mediterranean and the Balkans after they were expelled from Spain. *Moriscos*, speaking an Iberian form of Arabic, were restricted mainly to rural areas in the south and east of the peninsula. After the *morisco* revolt of 1569–71, however, their communities were forcibly

dominant language, c.1500

Arabic

Bable

Basque

Castilian

Catalan

Galego

Portuguese

boundaries, c.1500

town in Spain with large Jewish population, 1490

area of Morisco revolt, 1569-71

Morisco settlement in Spain, 1571-1609

scale 1: 4 500 000

0   120 km

0   80 mi

dispersed, mainly to New Castile and Extremadura, and by 1609 only 25,000 remained in the peninsula. Meanwhile, vernacular languages were losing ground to Castilian "Spanish", which had become the medium of political communication and literature, even for Catalans and Portuguese.

Above right A decoration from a prayer book displays the crowned initials of the Catholic Monarchs ("Fernando" and "Ysabel") on either side of a plumed helmet – an emblematic design that emphasizes their joint claim to rule.

The New World

In history's eyes, the crowning achievement of the year 1492 was the Atlantic voyage of the Genoese navigator Christopher Columbus. The consolidation of firm government at home allowed the crown of Castile for the first time to concentrate its resources on overseas expansion and to attempt to emulate the lead that Portugal had taken in maritime exploration. Now, after years of fruitless petitioning, Columbus finally persuaded Ferdinand and Isabella to sponsor his search for a westward route to India. In October 1492, after a journey of three months, he landed on an island in the Caribbean, probably San Salvador.

During the following century successive generations of *conquistadores* left the peninsula to conquer and colonize a huge empire in America. From the beginning there was tension with Portugal over these new territories. The Catholic Monarchs were able to call upon the influence of Alexander VI to protect their interests. In 1494 he was instrumental in bringing about the Treaty of Tordesillas, by which all land west of an imaginary line dividing the Atlantic just to the west of the Cape Verde Islands was assigned to Spain, and everything to the east of it to Portugal.

Typically, the *conquistadores* were land-hungry minor nobility from some of the most impoverished parts of Spain. They regarded the New World as a wild and hostile environment demanding to be tamed. Its raw materials – particularly its gold and silver – were there for the taking. The early *conquistadores* extracted all the wealth they could from the land and people, shipping it back to Spain. Isabella's insistence that Castile should have a monopoly of the American trade, and that it should be conducted through the port of Seville, was to lead to that city's rapid growth in the early 16th century.

Along with their quest for wealth and power, the Spanish came with a sense of mission to convert the Amerindian peoples. Even these otherwise ruthless and acquisitive conquerors believed implicitly that their work was assisted and rewarded by heaven in the cause of saving souls for Christ. Generally, therefore (if not invariably) they were open to the influence of the clergy. Dominican and Franciscan friars, who sometimes accompanied the invaders, did what they could to ameliorate the cruelties of defeat and exploitation, rapidly establishing missions as sites of peace and protection. Notable among them was the Dominican Bartolomé de Las Casas (1474–1566), who was fearless in debating the moral and legal problems arising from colonial rule. His efforts were to bear some fruit in the *Leyes Nuevas* ("New Laws") of 1542. Though all too often ignored, they did at least provide a framework of legal protection for the indigenous population – something no other colonizing nation was close to matching at that time. But no human agency could prevent the spread of European diseases among native populations that lacked genetic immunity and were made even more vulnerable to them by the socio-economic upheavals of conquest. A series of devastating epidemics drastically reduced the aboriginal population of Central America to perhaps one-tenth of its pre-Columbian size during the course of the 16th century.

In 1492, the Latinist and grammarian, Antonio de Nebrija (1444–1522), the foremost intellectual figure of the Renaissance in Spain, presented Isabella with the first printed grammar of the Castilian language. In this he made the far-sighted claim that "language is the greatest instrument of empire". Within a century, "España" (Spain) was familiar to all as the collective term for the Iberian territories under the rule of the

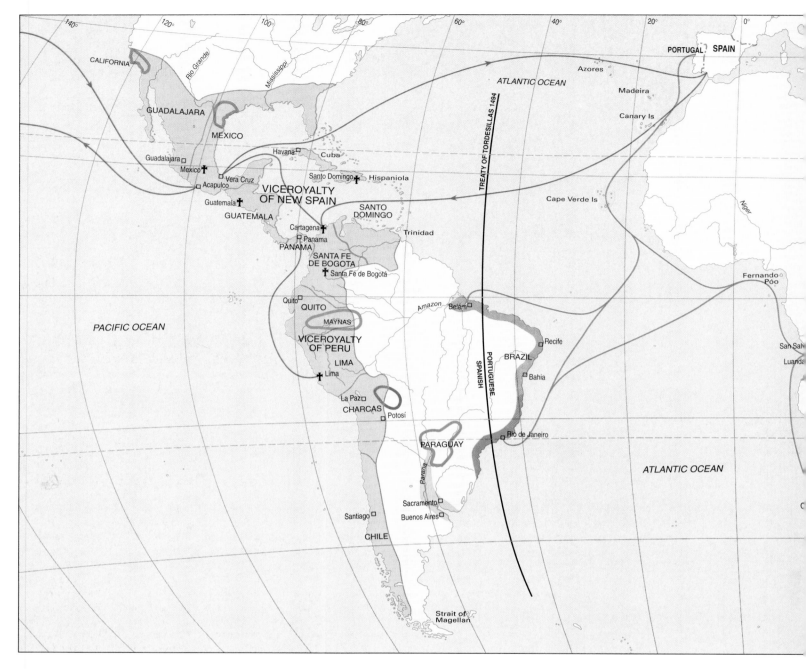

Spanish monarch, whose Castilian and Aragonese subjects distinguished themselves from others by the word *"españoles"* (Spaniards). Castilian became the preferred tongue for the majority of Aragonese. It was, in addition, the *lingua franca* of a huge overseas empire and was known and accepted throughout Europe as Spanish.

The legacy of joint kingship
By the time of Isabella's death in 1504, the Catholic Monarchs had succeeded in establishing royal power as the greatest authority in the land, far above that of any other corporation or group. But the two kingdoms were still far from being united: many important reforms, for example, applied only to Castile; Aragon's institutions remained largely unchanged. What was perhaps most significant about the achievement of the Catholic Monarchs was that their joint reign – which was based on a series of written agreements dividing specific responsibilities between them – lasted 35 years. This was long enough to allow powerful groups in both kingdoms to accustom themselves

to the regular routines of collaboration.

Isabella and Ferdinand had been married in Valladolid, a prosperous city of Old Castile set in a region of grain, viticulture and sheep-rearing. Though not a fixed capital, Valladolid remained their main center of power, one of many towns that flourished by exploiting the economic possibilities of the domestic peace they had created. In this respect, the Catholic Monarchs achieved what they had set out to do. They were less successful in another respect. At the beginning of their reign, they had prayed that God would give them a son to inherit both kingdoms. The succession seemed secure with the birth of their son, Juan, in 1477. When Juan died suddenly in 1497, followed by the death of his own posthumous son, politics were thrown back into confusion. The succession was unclear and the great nobles were not yet fully tamed. The survival of the emergent Spanish state was by no means certain.

Progress in Portugal
The history of Portugal as it moved from the 15th to the 16th century was also marked by struggle and

The Catholic world empire in the 16th century
In 1519–21 Ferdinand Magellan, a Portuguese sailing under the Castilian flag, discovered the route around South America and across the Pacific to the Philippines. He was killed there, but his ships continued their westward journey to Spain to complete the first circumnavigation of the globe. The Treaty of Zaragoza (1529) divided the Pacific between Spain and Portugal as the Treaty of Tordesillas had the Atlantic three decades earlier. During the 16th century two global empires emerged under the crowns of Iberia. Portugal concerned itself with trade: its small population was a bar to colonization, and settlement was confined to narrow coastal strips, fortified bases and trading posts (more than 50 by 1600). Only Castilians had right of entry to the "Spanish" empire in America. In the generation following Cortes' conquest of Mexico (1519–20), the whole of

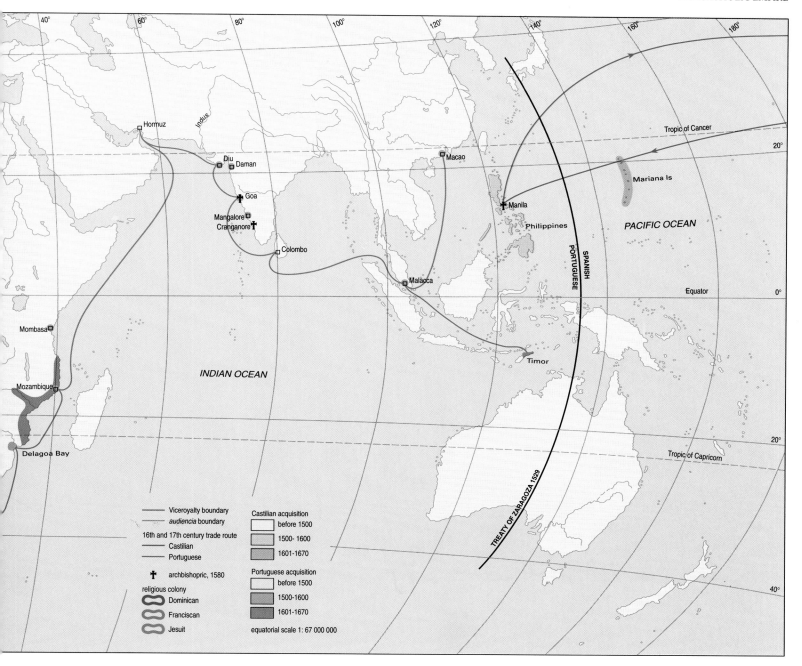

Viceroyalty boundary
audiencia boundary
16th and 17th century trade route
Castilian
Portuguese

✝ archbishopric, 1580
religious colony
Dominican
Franciscan
Jesuit

Castilian acquisition
before 1500
1500- 1600
1601-1670

Portuguese acquisition
before 1500
1500-1600
1601-1670

equatorial scale 1: 67 000 000

central America was settled to become the Viceroyalty of New Spain. After the discovery of vast silver reserves at Potosí in the 1540s, Peru – conquered by Pizarro in the early 1530s – became the senior Viceroyalty. Both were divided into administrative tribunals known as *audiencias*. Silver bullion was transported to Spain via a complex machinery of interlocking, synchronized voyages between Seville and Lima, with an extension to the Philippines. This "Indies road" lasted for nearly two centuries. In 1580 the two empires were united, but not merged, by Philip II. Both had in common a missionary purpose that carried Catholicism as far as Chile and Japan. In America, the Dominican and Franciscan orders staffed the parishes of the five archbishoprics, whilst the Jesuits worked in the frontier regions among the Amerindians. By 1600 their great missions were virtually autonomous republics within the *audiencias*.

accomplishment. Afonso V's acceptance of the union of the crowns of Castile and Aragon by the Treaty of Alcaçovas (1479) marked a turning point, for it meant abandoning his claim to the Castilian throne as the price for restoring peace. Afonso fell into a deep depression after this failure. He had already resolved to abdicate when he was overtaken by death in 1481.

No longer able to intervene in Castilian politics, Portugal's only possibilities for expansion now lay overseas. Yet even here there were limitations. At Alcaçovas, Portugal was forced to recognize Spanish possession of the Canary Islands in return for the Azores, Cape Verde Islands and Madeira and recognition of her own monopoly of the African mainland and eastward passages. Almost imperceptibly, the growing power of Castile-Aragon sucked Portugal into its orbit, first as the free collaboration of equals, but later with mounting signs of dependence and even of subordination.

João II (1481–95) was a determined and able monarch whose first aim – like that of the Catholic Monarchs – was to reclaim royal supremacy from an

increasingly unruly nobility. He immediately summoned the Cortes and demanded an oath of loyalty, which greatly displeased the more powerful nobles. At the same time he sought to extend the scope of royal justice while curtailing that of the nobles. But where Isabella and Ferdinand achieved their aims by winning political support and establishing meticulous legal procedures, João frequently enforced his demands at the point of a sword. His frantic persecution of his enemies actually annihilated several eminent families and weakened the ruling class. However, the net effect of his policies was little different from that of the Catholic Monarchs' more persuasive means. By the end of the 1480s the Portuguese crown had dramatically reduced the power of the nobility and was poised for great achievements.

Overseas exploration and its corollary, trade, received a new impetus under João II. Determined efforts were made to discover a searoute to India in order to gain control of the rich Arab trade in spices. By 1482 Portuguese explorers along the west coast of Africa had penetrated the Congo, and in 1487–88 an

Batalha

The great Dominican abbey of Santa Maria da Vitória (St Mary Victorious), also known simply as Batalha, stands in a valley about 160 kilometers north of Lisbon. It was founded in 1388 to commemorate the nearby battle of Aljubarrota. Here, three years before, the army of Castile had been decisively defeated by a smaller Portuguese force led by João I, thus ensuring Portugal's independence from Spain for the next two centuries. The abbey has been called the most magnificent architectural monument in Portugal: it is certainly a masterpiece, and contains some of the most significant examples of the Manueline style, the distinctively Portuguese form of decoration that marks the transition from Gothic to Renaissance architecture. The building was started in a flamboyant Gothic style reminiscent of some English cathedrals (João I was married to an English princess), and work continued on it for more than 150 years until abandoned in the middle of the 16th century. The Manueline design of the Unfinished Chapels was carried out during the reigns of Manuel I and his son João III. The abbey was declared a national monument in 1840; since 1921 it has housed the tomb of the Portuguese Unknown Soldier.

Below The Founder's Chapel, built between 1426 and 1434 from the designs of Master Huguet (probably an English or Irish architect) consists of a square chamber with an elaborate octagonal lantern supported on eight pillars. Below the star-vaulting are the effigies of King João I and his queen, Philippa of Lancaster; their tomb is supported by eight lions. Against the southern wall stand the tombs of João's four younger sons, including Prince Henry the Navigator. Three other kings are buried in the abbey: Duarte, Afonso V and João II.

Below The original design of the abbey, carried out by Afonso Domingues with the aid of Master Huguet, consisted of the church (3), the Founder's Chapel (1) and the Royal Cloister (5), with accompanying monastic buildings. The Unfinished Chapels (2) were planned as a mausoleum for King Duarte, and another cloister (6) was added in the reign of Afonso V.

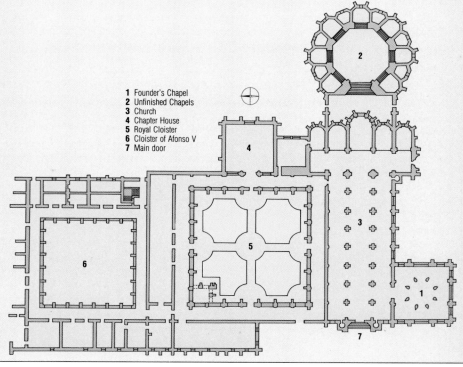

1 Founder's Chapel
2 Unfinished Chapels
3 Church
4 Chapter House
5 Royal Cloister
6 Cloister of Afonso V
7 Main door

expedition led by Bartolomeu Dias (c.1450–1500) succeeded in rounding the Cape of Good Hope to reach the coast of east Africa. Ten years later Vasco da Gama (c.1460–1524) followed the same route and continued eastward to reach the coast of India. This discovery of the direct searoute from Europe to Asia brought Portugal enormous profits in trade and laid the foundations of its overseas empire in the east.

Manuel "the Fortunate"

In 1490 the heir to the Portuguese throne, Afonso, fell from a horse and was killed. João II, "the Perfect Prince", died five years later to be succeeded by his cousin, Manuel I (1495–1521). The new king – who was nicknamed "the Fortunate" – inherited a firmly established monarchy and a growing colonial empire. Though no less jealous of his power than João, Manuel soothed troubled relations with the nobility by returning land and property to them. He strengthened the position of the crown by giving new or revised charters to the towns, taking over the mastership of the military orders and codifying the law, in this way passing administration into the hands of a professional class.

During Manuel's reign, overseas discovery was turned into conquest: there were more than 250 sailings from Lisbon to India alone. The round voyage took at least a year and a half on overcrowded and insanitary ships, and wrecks were frequent. Ships, castles and fortresses were built to protect the new overseas possessions and the valuable trade they produced – spices from the east, gold (and later slaves) from Africa, sugar from Madeira, São Tomé and, eventually, Brazil. At home, the new-found self-confidence of Portuguese society was reflected in the highly ornate Manueline style of architecture, which is found in the monasteries of Batalha and Tomar and in the Belém tower at the mouth of the Lisbon river. Like the contemporary plateresque style in Spain, it imaginatively fused Arab and Christian details to create a robust style all its own; some have even seen Indian influences in its exuberant decoration.

Manuel did not lose hope of uniting the whole of the Iberian Peninsula under the Avis dynasty, and married three times into the Castilian royal line in his unsuccessful quest to do so. His first wife, Isabella, was the eldest daughter of Ferdinand and Isabella (Manuel subsequently married her sister Maria following Isabella's death in 1498). As a condition of his first marriage, the Catholic Monarchs demanded the expulsion of Jews from Portugal – many of whom had previously been expelled from Spain in 1492. In October 1497, the Jews – as in Spain, intellectually and economically important members of the community – were assembled at Lisbon for embarkation. Some were forcibly converted and thus were prohibited from leaving Portugal; others who resisted were allowed to leave. The converts, or "New Christians", were useful to, and protected by, the crown, but generally they were regarded with suspicion and prejudice; very many were killed during anti-Jewish riots in Lisbon in 1506.

A precarious inheritance

After the death of Isabella of Castile in 1504, Ferdinand continued as ruler of Aragon; their eldest surviving daughter, Juana, succeeded to the crown of Castile. In 1496 she had married Philip, son of the emperor Maximilian I and – through his mother Mary

Above The main door of the church shows a delight in Gothic detail: figures of saints and prophets are interspersed with angels praying, singing or playing musical instruments, each standing on the elaborate canopy of the figure beneath.

Above left More exuberant is the decoration of the Royal Cloister, seen here from the Chapter House. The design of the arcading includes briar-branches and armillary spheres as well as the cross of Prince Henry's Order of Christ and lotos-blossoms, presumably symbolizing Portugal's missionary work in India.

Left The great Manueline doorway into the Unfinished Chapels is almost oriental in style: the convoluted tracery based on vegetal motifs clearly displays the influence of Moorish design. This elaboration was not to everyone's taste: the English novelist William Beckford visited the abbey in 1794, and wrote scathingly of "Dom Emanuel's scollops and twistifications".

Right The Complutensian Polyglot Bible was produced at the university of Alcalá de Henares (the Roman name for which was Complutum) under the sponsorship of Cardinal Cisneros between 1514 and 1517. A work of outstanding scholarship and academic collaboration, it exploited the new technology of printing by displaying parallel texts of the Pentateuch (the first five books of the Old Testament) in Hebrew, Aramaic, Greek and Latin; the rest of the Old Testament in Hebrew, Greek and Latin; and the New Testament in Greek and Latin. Shown here is a page from the book of Jeremiah, with the Greek text on the left, the Latin in the center, and the Hebrew on the right.

of Burgundy – ruler of the Netherlands. Doubts about Juana's mental stability meant that Isabella in her will had ensured that Ferdinand should act as regent in Castile until Juana's son (the future Charles V), born in 1500, achieved his majority. Many Castilian grandees, who resented having to accept the rule of an Aragonese regent, enthusiastically backed Philip's claim to the throne and Ferdinand was forced to withdraw. Philip I of Castile (1504–06) died shortly after arriving in the kingdom. Though his widow was clearly unfit to rule, the grandees opposed the reintroduction of Ferdinand's authority. By decrees issued at Toro, Zamora, in 1505, Juana had relinquished the controls on noble property-holding and legal inheritance introduced by Isabella. Private armies reappeared; many towns reacted by arming themselves.

Meanwhile, Ferdinand took steps to deny control of Aragon to the Habsburgs by marrying a French princess, Germaine de Foix. When she became pregnant in 1508, the unitary succession and thus the political reality of a "united" Spain was once more thrown into uncertainty. However, her son survived for less than a day. This, and Juana's determination not to remarry, meant that only Ferdinand's presence and the succession of the infante Charles could guarantee order in Castile. In 1507, at the request of the Cortes, Ferdinand returned as regent and lost no time in suppressing the few nobles who opposed the arrangement. In 1510 the Cortes gave him powers to maintain a modest professional army, which he used to conquer the kingdom of Navarre in 1512, a largely Basque-speaking region allied to France; the part of the kingdom north of the Pyrenees remained independent. It was the first territorial gain within the peninsula since the fall of Granada, and restored much of the prestige of the Castile-Aragon alliance.

Religion, culture and learning

Contemporary observers, for the most part, did not regard the years of danger and dispute after Isabella's death as a crisis in the development of a united Spain, but as a reversion to a more normal state of affairs. Yet some people had a vague awareness of Spain – or the Spanish ruling dynasty – as a desirable, emergent political entity and worked to preserve the integrity of monarchical authority *per se*. The most important of these figures was Cardinal Cisneros, the veteran archbishop of Toledo, the largest and richest diocese of Castile. A minor noble who became a Franciscan, Cisneros combined the best qualities of his calling and era – the drive for simplicity of the mendicant orders, the instinct for statesmanship of the higher clergy, and the amplified attitude to learning of the Renaissance church. As a young man he ministered in the Maghreb; in middle age he reformed his own religious order; in old age he answered the call to government, becoming Isabella's closest associate in reform. Subsequently, as Ferdinand's minister in Castile, he governed even-handedly but firmly to preserve reform and royal authority.

Cisneros was a scholar and patron of scholars whose life work forms a link between the intellectual currents of medieval Spain and the humanist, critical approach of the Italian Renaissance. He himself founded the University of Alcalá de Henares, near Madrid. Here, at Cisneros' own expense, the Polyglot Bible, a collaboration between Hebrew, Greek and Latin scholars, and the finest achievement of early Spanish Renaissance scholarship and printing tech-

nology, was produced; it was the last grand gesture of the spirit of *convivencia*. Yet it was something of a paradox that Cisneros was also Inquisitor-General, responsible for imposing religious orthodoxy; in this capacity, he supervised the reform of the Castilian church, introducing many improvements that anticipated the reforms of the Council of Trent (1545–63), called to define Catholic teaching and reform church practice in response to the growth of Protestantism in northern Europe.

Such activities created an atmosphere that produced some of the most intellectually formidable and politically dynamic clerics in early 16th-century Europe: humanist thinkers such as Juan de Valdés (1490–1541) and Juan Luis Vives (1492–1546), the student and colleague of Erasmus of Rotterdam (1467–1536); lawyers and social critics such as Bartolomé de las Casas; and organizational innovators such as Ignatius Loyola (1491–1556), the soldier turned ascetic and theologian who founded the Society of Jesus (the Jesuits) in 1539. The Jesuit order, though influenced in some respects by Italian models, owed little to Renaissance influence. Loyola himself was from Navarre – a region of Spain that even today has a reputation as the most fanatically Catholic – and after his "conversion" went to be taught at the scholastic-dominated university of the Sorbonne in Paris. His disciples were associated with an ascetic movement of reform inside the church and evangelical reconversion outside it. The order's dynamic was utter dedication and discipline; but so profuse was its development that by the third quarter of the 16th century it had taken Spanish approaches to Catholic practice to almost

Left Built in 1515–21, the Belém Tower, guarding the entrance to the port of Lisbon, is one of the best-known examples of Manueline architecture. It has come to symbolize not only the city itself, but the great age of Portuguese discovery. Its architect, Francisco Arruda, had traveled in North Africa and it incorporates features of Moorish design, such as the balconied windows; the crowned cupolas are Byzantine in inspiration.

every part of the European mainland, and by the time of the second session of the reforming Council of Trent (1560–63), Jesuit theologians came near to dominating the Catholic church's major debates on dogmatic revision and refinement.

The power-house of the Spanish "Renaissance" was Salamanca university, which was, to some extent at least, a medium of Florentine humanism and artistic tastes. Its most famous professor was Antonio de Nebrija, an outstanding advocate of humanism, who attracted several luminaries to Spain from Italy. These he placed in key university chairs as well as in tutorships at court. The Salamanca curriculum was liberal and "advanced" by any standards in this period, a tendency that reached its apogee in the period of the philosopher Luis de León (1537–91). The university's new buildings, like those of new foundations at Valladolid and Alcalá de Henares, were distinguished indigenous versions of the Tuscan vernacular. Yet Jesuits and Dominicans – often divided in other matters – were united in their suspicion of the anticlerical aspects of humanism. The latter order was powerful at Salamanca and other academic centers (and, of course, staffed the Inquisition). The independent critical tendencies represented by Erasmus – whose influence in the universities was greater than that of any Italian thinker, partly owing to Castile's growing links with the Low Countries – were seen as especially dangerous, and were eventually rooted out. For this and other reasons humanistic learning and artistic aspiration in Spain were to remain within the bosom of the Catholic church to a degree that was not evident in Italy or even in France. Thus, the "Golden Age" of music, writing and painting that was being forged in the middle of the 16th century was inspired by intense religious conviction and closely nurtured by the institutions of the church itself. This may not have encouraged the development of a pluralistic intellectual society but it certainly brought immense reserves of strength to Spanish Catholicism.

Over 20 universities were founded in Castile in the course of the 16th century. They developed as training grounds for bureaucrats as well as scholars. Graduates (*letrados*) increasingly staffed the burgeoning civil service, excluding the higher nobility in the process. In the 1520s, Francisco de los Cobos (c. 1477–1547), a protegé of Cisneros and a small-town *hidalgo* from Andalusia, rose steadily to become head of the council of Castile. His career encapsulated the alliance that was being forged between the lesser nobility and the crown, of which the council of Castile was the main political manifestation.

Expansion by war and diplomacy

Though often supported by luck, Ferdinand's outstanding gifts as a politician were evident as much in the international as in the domestic area. He acquired status and recognition in Europe by marrying his daughters into the royal houses of Burgundy, Portugal and England. The alliance with Castile by and large strengthened his rule in Aragon, at least to the extent that it improved the crown's position in relation to its traditional opponents – the feudal nobility and the commercial interests of Catalonia. However, Aragon's privileges (*fueros*) obliged any ruler to proceed by negotiation, and Ferdinand was careful not to overplay his hand by threatening his opponents with the military strength of Castile. Once the war with Granada was concluded, it was outside the peninsula

that his enlarged military reserves were mobilized.

Sardinia and Sicily were all that remained of the once extensive Aragonese empire in the Mediterranean, but in 1493 Charles VIII of France (1483–98) – planning an invasion of Italy – agreed to return Roussillon, north of the Pyrenees (lost during the Catalan civil wars of the 1460s), to Aragon in return for protection on his southern flank. A year later, however, Ferdinand did not hesitate to answer the Pope's appeal for assistance against France in Italy. During the subsequent campaigns, the army of Castile-Aragon was molded into Europe's most efficient fighting force by the "Great Captain", Gonsalvo Fernandez de Córdoba (1453–1515). The reward for Aragon's intervention was the huge kingdom of Naples, which was acquired in 1503. The message of the *tercios* – Spanish regiments – and of Spain itself was carried at the point of a pike the length of the Italian peninsula, to be halted only by the French victory at Marignano in 1515.

Ferdinand ruled Castile as regent until his death

Above The Catholic Monarchs, as joint patrons of the new learning in Spain, appear side by side on the main facade of the university of Salamanca completed in 1529: above them are the crowned arms of the emperor Charles V; at the top, the pope is seated on his throne. The decorative scheme is a fine example of early plateresque, the 16th-century Spanish style that is noted for its heavy and intricate surface ornamentation embellished with heraldic escutcheons and other devices. Literally meaning "silversmith-like", it was influenced both by the Italian Renaissance and the Manueline style.

early in 1516. In typical medieval fashion he tried to cover all eventualities by insisting on custody of his younger Habsburg grandson and namesake, whom he kept in Aragon. But in his testament he formally bequeathed Aragon not to his elder grandson, Charles of Habsburg, but to the lineal heir, Queen Juana, giving his illegitimate son, Alonso, the regency. Even at the last gasp, one of the alleged founders of Spain was fundamentally uncertain about the nature and future of what he had created.

Charles I – an uneasy succession

Charles of Habsburg, heir-apparent to the Castilian throne, remained in his native Netherlands during Ferdinand's regency, though he came of age in 1514. Soon after Ferdinand's death two years later, Charles – now Charles I of Spain (1516–56) – arrived in Spain for the first time, landing on the coast of Asturias. The death of Cisneros at this time deprived the new king of an experienced adviser. However, the king's tutor, the theologian Adrian of Utrecht (1459–1523), had been sent in advance from the Netherlands to liaise with Cisneros and Francisco de los Cobos, ensuring continuity with the previous reign. Charles was greeted with enthusiasm by both aristocratic and urban interests in Castile and Aragon, and the Cortes of both kingdoms gathered to swear loyalty.

This promising beginning was soon spoiled by a series of blunders. Charles' Walloon advisers were rewarded for their services with offices acquired at the expense of the existing establishment. Bad feeling was aggravated by the demand for funds to procure Charles' success in the imperial election that followed Maximilian I's death in 1519. Duly elected as the Emperor Charles V, his new responsibilities soon required his presence in Germany. Before taking ship in 1520 Charles convened a Cortes at Santiago at short notice: delegates were bullied into accepting huge increases in Castilian taxation, yet nothing was done to address grievances that were already causing disturbance in the constituencies. As the new king abandoned Spain, many feared they were passing into an era of absentee rule and exploitation.

Resentment exploded into rebellion. The *comunero* revolt began in Toledo, where the archbishopric, the fountainhead of patronage, had been given to the nephew of one of Charles' Walloon ministers, emphasizing the domination of government by foreigners. The revolt spread rapidly from town to town. There was resentment at the plunder of office, anger at the taxes imposed for use abroad, and exasperation amongst communities that expected the regular presence of their ruler. Yet the rebellion was not simply the expression of chauvinistic outrage; it was marked by bitter disputes between local factions.

The *corregidores* were generally unable to contain the rebellion. Nevertheless, the influence of loyal *hidalgos* prevented it from taking hold in some towns, such as Burgos, Palencia and Valladolid. Happily for Charles, he had left his most able minister, Adrian of Utrecht, as regent. Adrian adroitly granted concessions to the grandees, and when the rebellion began to take on an antiaristocratic character was able to mobilize their support to defeat the rebel army at Villalar in 1521. Meanwhile, in Valencia, economic and political unrest sparked off a further revolt. The *germania* ("brotherhood") rebellion was a desultory war between rebel bands based on artisan guilds on the one hand and their bourgeois-aristocratic masters on the other. From Valencia it spread to Majorca before it was eventually suppressed in 1522.

Peace and stability in Spain

Charles returned to Spain as the rebellions were collapsing. This time he stayed for over seven years, accustoming himself to Spain and building up reserves of goodwill. He and his advisers – the chancellor, Mercurino Gattinara (1465–1530), and the secretary, Francisco de los Cobos (Adrian of Utrecht had by now been elected Pope Adrian VI) – constructed a conciliar system of government, establishing first a council of state (1522) to supervise and coordinate the affairs of the various Spanish kingdoms, and then a finance council (1527). As the royal service expanded, the *hidalgo-letrado* class was the main beneficiary.

By 1529, the progress that Charles had made in Spain enabled him to return to his other obligations in Europe. In his absence, effective government was maintained by de los Cobos, along with Charles' Portuguese wife Isabel (1503–39), sister of João III, and later his son Philip (b. 1527). Though Charles demanded more and more Castilian revenue – taxation increased tenfold in the 1530s alone – there seems to have been little protest. It has been said that under Charles V – who spent only 16 of his 40 years' reign in Spain – "the country had almost no internal history". After the unrest of 1521, there was only a beneficent internal peace.

Below A Habsburg family portrait, probably dating from the third decade of the 16th century, depicts the Holy Roman Emperor Maximilian I (d. 1519) – on the left – with his immediate descendants. It presents the main figures in the Habsburg takeover of Castile and Aragon after the death of the last Trastámara monarch, Ferdinand, in 1516. Facing Maximilian is his son Philip (*El Guapo* – "the Handsome"), whose marriage to Ferdinand and Isabella's daughter Juana (*La Loca* – "the Mad") produced both Charles V (bottom center) and Ferdinand (bottom left), his Spanish-reared brother to whom he assigned the Holy Roman Empire in 1556. Their father is given here the unambiguous title "Philip I, King of Spain", increasing the likelihood that the written identifications of the subjects of the painting were added some years after its completion.

MAXIMILIANVS I IMP. ARCHIDVX AVSTRIÆ DVX BVRGVNDIÆ

PHILIPPVS HISP. REX.I. ARCHIDVX AVSTRIÆ

MARIA DVCISSA BVRGVNDIÆ MAX: VXOR.

FERDINANDVS. I. IMP. ARCHIDVX AVSTRIÆ

CAROLVS.V. IMP. ARCHIDVX AVSTRIÆ

LVDOVICVS REX HVNG. MASA

The Escorial

Below right The huge church of St Lawrence, dominated by its Italianate domes, rises above the austere walls of the monastery-palace. The shelf of land on which it stands was partly carved out by the quarrying of iron ore, and the name of the Escorial derives from the Castilian word for the industrial waste that littered the place before work began on the building.

Right At the opposite end of the complex from the church, above the modest entrance, is the library. To these vast rooms were brought printed books in vernacular languages from all parts of Europe. The library is notably secular for its day and place. The Italian painter and sculptor Peregrino Tibaldi (1527–96) was responsible for the decoration of the ceilings, which celebrate the liberal arts. Matronly figures personify Grammar, Arithmetic, Astronomy and so on, reflecting the breadth of intellectual interests at court. Many international artists, including the painters Titian and El Greco, contributed to the interior decoration of the Escorial.

Below Shortly before Philip's death, though not completed until 1654, work began on the construction of a many-chambered mausoleum beneath the church. Members of Spain's royal dynasties, starting with Charles V, are interred here.

The popular image of Philip II is of a sedentary monarch who spent his time plotting to rule the world from his mountain fastness of the Escorial deep in the heart of Spain. Yet for most of his life he was extremely active. Present (and nominally in command) at the crushing defeat of the French at St Quentin (1557), he was inspired to give thanks to God for the victory by building a church of unparalleled grandeur and dedicating it to St Lawrence, on whose feastday the battle had been fought. And it was during one of his regular hunting trips – an exercise equally as rigorous and often as dangerous as war – that Philip discovered the perfect site for his foundation: on a south-facing spur of the Guadarrama hills about 40 kilometers north of Madrid. Here, between 1563 and 1584, the construction of San Lorenzo de El Escorial took place – described by the chronicler José de Sigüenza as "an unbelievable conjunction of planning, labor, direction, noise, skill, fabulous wealth and universal creativity". To Philip's original scheme for a church alone were added major new provisions for a royal palace and a monastery, and the Escorial eventually developed into a multi-purpose complex of buildings, unique among royal palaces – a place for prayer and contemplation, for administration, for rest after hunting, where Philip's vast collections of books, manuscripts, paintings and holy relics could be stored, and the bones of his ancestors laid to rest. Above all, it was the headquarters of a European hegemony that was not merely political and military: a multi-faceted symbol of Spanish civilization.

The growth of centralized royal administration during these years was in part a response to an expanding economy. Agriculture improved in several areas. Large parts of the south were opened up for the cultivation of vines (forbidden by the Muslims) and olives to meet rising American and European demand. Rice, originally introduced to the peninsula by the Muslims, was established as a plantation crop in Valencia. The replacement of the ox by the mule as a draft animal, though it had some drawbacks, helped to improve grain production and increase farming profits. By the mid 16th century the country supported nearly 5 million sheep. Spanish Merino wool was the most sought-after in Europe, with the result that the domestic woolen industry found prices of its raw material being pushed up. Nevertheless, flourishing manufacturing centers grew up around Segovia and Toledo. In addition to wool, Spain's principal exports were salt (from the largest deposits in Europe), leather, silk, and other luxury goods.

The continuing buoyancy of the Atlantic trade continued to fuel Seville's growth, and the ports of Santander and Bilbao also expanded at this time through commerce, shipbuilding and a growing fishing industry. In the heartland of Castile – traditionally regarded as Spain's least businesslike region – Europe's most intensive trade fairs were operating at Medina del Campo and Burgos. By mid-century, Castile's economy was strongly linked to that of northern Europe via the great entrepot of Antwerp in the Netherlands, while Aragon benefited by its connections with Italy. Economically, culturally and politically, Spain had become an integral part of the wider European community, as well as managing its expanding empire across the Atlantic. This was palpably a golden age, with amazing mineral wealth arriving annually from America, wide fields of grain enriching the interior, and huge profits from the sheep-rearing industry. Little wonder that Spain's most prominent symbol was that of the Golden Fleece, Charles V's elite order of knighthood, which united both his Spanish and his Burgundian subjects.

War in Europe

Outside Spain, Charles V's uniquely extensive collection of territories and rights, gained mainly by diplomatic foresight, had to be defended constantly by war. In addition, Charles was very conscious of his privileges and responsibilities as the Christian leader of temporal Europe. A soldier-emperor in the epic mold, he responded with vigor (in youth with eagerness) to each and every challenge. The expansion of Habsburg power was particularly threatening to France. Charles controlled not only Spain on the Pyrenean border, but also Lombardy to the southeast of France and Burgundy on its northern and eastern borders. Franco-Spanish competition had already emerged in Ferdinand's reign in the wars in Italy and in the skirmishes over Navarre and other enclaves in the Pyrenean borderlands, from which Spain seemed to be emerging with the big prizes. It was now sharpened by the dynastic – and personal – rivalry between Charles and Francis I (1515–47), France's equally bellicose king. Europe's third great ruler at this time, Henry VIII of England (1509–47), was traditionally opposed to France and, furthermore, was drawn into Charles' camp through his marriage to the emperor's aunt, Catherine of Aragon (1485–1536), youngest daughter of Ferdinand and Isabella.

Francis was encouraged in his constant attempts to weaken Habsburg power by two coincident phenomena: the first major split in the religious fabric of Europe, the Lutheran Reformation, and a surge in the power and ambition of the Ottoman Turks. Though himself strictly orthodox in religion, Francis offered political comfort and financial help to the dissident princes of Germany when they came under pressure from Charles V to disavow Luther's reform movement in the 1520s. Simultaneously, the Ottoman offensive under the Sultan Suleiman I (the Magnificent, 1520–66) reached a fearful culmination with the defeat of the Habsburg-Hungarian forces at Mohács (1526), after which huge tracts of eastern and southeastern Europe fell into Muslim hands. The scale of Charles' military commitment was now vast and unprecedented. Struggling to hold the landward line in the east, Charles was also called upon to stem the tide of Turkish advance in the Mediterranean. His triumph at Tunis in 1535 – in a campaign that was the prototype of the combined operations expedition for which Spanish power was to become celebrated – intensified demands upon the resources of Charles' lands and subjects, above all, in Spain.

The rivalry between Charles and Francis dated back to the imperial election of 1519, when both had stood as candidates. In 1525, Francis I was defeated by Charles' Spanish *tercios* at the battle of Pavia in Italy and held prisoner in the town of Madrid, deep in the heart of Castile; his release was only secured on payment of a large ransom and promises to behave himself. The enmity between the two kings thus engendered bore fruit in Francis' decision to make the royal shipyards at Toulon available for the refitting of the Ottoman fleet: Spain would derive political capital from this action for generations to come. In 1541, the emperor prepared another expedition against Algiers, Suleiman's main Arab ally, whose ships constantly raided the Spanish coast. Charles scraped resources together and mobilized some of the greatest commanders of the age including the duke of Alba (1507–82), the Genoese captain Andrea Doria (1466–1560), and even the conqueror of Mexico Hernán Cortés (1485–1547), making a dramatic final comeback – but met with utter disaster. This bloody humiliation was laid by Charles at Francis' door, and though his enemy died in 1547, France was also blamed for the emperor's political frustration and military overthrow by the rebel Lutheran league in Germany (1552). Like Francis to Henry II of France (1547–59), Charles handed on this vendetta as a legacy to his main heir, Philip II of Spain (1556–98).

Philip II: transition and transformation

In 1556, Charles V took the momentous decision to abdicate as king of Castile and Aragon in favor of Philip. He also resigned the Holy Roman Empire to his brother, Ferdinand. In so doing, he admitted that his European empire was a practical impossibility. Instead, Charles envisaged a fraternal division of leadership between two branches of the Habsburg dynasty: a dual monarchy that would operate somewhat like Aragon-Castile but on a much larger scale. He therefore insisted that the Netherlands, other parts of Burgundy and the duchy of Milan should go to Philip rather than be absorbed into the German patrimony of the Holy Roman Empire. He wanted to maintain the strategic bridle on France that unitary control of the surrounding lands guaranteed, but his plans

The Spanish Mystics

The mystical movement that flourished in 16th-century Spain was essentially Castilian: its main practitioners were priests and religious who were usually attached to one of the great universities or religious houses of Castile; their writings – in Castilian – are suffused with references to the landscape and climate of the *meseta*. Yet though their work proved difficult to export, it was not elitist in content, intention or origin. Indeed, the prominent characteristic of the Spanish Mystics was that their speculations blended several strains of Renaissance thought and writing - the secular humanism of the Florentine school and of Erasmus on the one hand, with the profound mysticism of the 15th-century Netherlands and indigenous features of reformist Catholicism in the tradition of Cardinal Cisneros on the other. Hugely influential was Luis de León of the university of Salamanca – an innovative teacher, theologian and poet. The movement's greatest luminaries were Teresa of Avila and John of the Cross, who in their poetic addresses to the Godhead transmuted the profane lyricism of Renaissance writers like Garcilaso de la Vega into a species of religious ecstasy. A type of mysticism of a more severely practical kind drove the career of Ignatius Loyola, a hard-bitten Basque and former soldier who founded the Society of Jesus. So conscious was the next generation of Spain's spiritual achievement that all three were canonized together in 1622, an occasion marked by Philip IV with a week-long fiesta in Madrid.

Ignatius' message was missionary and active. His *Spiritual Exercises* (1521–48), which became in effect the rule book of the Jesuits, were meant – as their title implies – to prepare and train the body along with the mind. Formulative in his life was a period spent in retreat from the world in a cave at Manresa, an episode portrayed (*below*) by Domínguez Martínez (1688–1749) in the mawkishly pious style of the Spanish baroque. While Teresa of Avila and John of the Cross, writing in the second half of the 16th century, drew on the earlier period of intellectual experiment that had nurtured Loyola, their works were metaphysical and contemplative. Yet Teresa reformed an order – the Carmelites – and her life shows that women could exert seminal influence in the Catholic world. For centuries images like this statue (*right*) inspired women with aspirations to writing. Her prose is highly readable – as she used human love and compassion as a metaphor for the ideal relationships between the soul and its creator, so she brought into her style everyday objects and expressions, including jokes. The poetry of John of the Cross, her close colleague and friend, was seen as more difficult, even in his own day. Shown here (*below left*) is the frontispiece to the 1649 edition of his works.

Escorial, in the foothills of the Guadarrama mountains north of Madrid. At once palace, monastery, administrative center and fortress, the Escorial symbolized the triple alliance of crown, church and armed forces that were the instruments of Spain's greatness. A fixed court came into existence; most of the grandees were obliged to attend on the king at Madrid to obtain the honors and preferment that were essential to their lifestyles.

Popular pastimes and court culture

Philip II was no intellectual, but youthful travels in Italy and the Netherlands had evoked a lifelong interest in the arts. Throughout Europe, royal patronage was stimulating a specifically courtly culture, opening a gap between popular and aristocratic entertainments. The evolution of popular into high culture occurred alongside the struggle of secular themes to emerge from a religious context, but both processes were immensely slow. Painting – perhaps the most courtly of the arts – was Philip's main enthusiasm. He inherited his father's regard for Titian (d. 1576), arguably the most obviously secular master of the late Renaissance, whose refined sensualism appealed to the king and who duly painted him as a refined sensualist. By contrast, the king was repelled by the ascetic, convoluted style of the Roman-trained Cretan, Domenikos Theotokopoulis, known as El Greco (1548–1625). Despite his failure at court, El Greco found strong support among the religious and noble society at Toledo, where he settled.

Most significant, perhaps, was Philip's fascination for the allegories of Hieronymous Bosch (d. 1516), the Flemish artist whose fleshly horrors convey rigorous Christian instruction. Whilst Titian and other Italian influences crucially molded early Spanish schools of painting, it was the religious mysticism of the Netherlands that most enriched Spanish speculative thought and poetry at this time. This is most apparent in the works of the Carmelite nun Teresa of Avila (Teresa de Jesús, 1515–82) and her friend and contemporary, John of the Cross (Juan de la Cruz, 1542–91), both of whom were later canonized. In their intense lyrics, physical and metaphysical feelings subsist in parallel: "popular" romance in harness with religion.

A similar dualism is present in the music of the period, especially that of Tomás Luis de Victoria (c. 1548–1611). He exploited the relaxation of church regulations to produce even more sensually beautiful liturgical settings than those of his Italian mentor, Palestrina (c.1525–1594). Even before Victoria, an entirely native culture had produced Antonio de Cabezón (1510–66), who brought variation (*diferencias*) to its first great European flowering in his compositions for the keyboard. Outside the churches, the romances and *canciones* (ballads) of the countryside were captured and adapted by composers such as Luis Milán (c.1500–1561), who used them to set verses by city poets. Accordingly, popular music permeated the worlds of theater and literature; in the next generation, the greatest of all the Golden Age novels, *Don Quixote*, was to be littered with well-known musical references.

Artistic activity was stimulated not only by royal example and the creation of a fixed court, but also by the increasing generosity of church patronage; the mainspring of both was American silver. In the world outside the great palaces and fashionable churches, popular entertainments remained a vital force. Many

also recognized the political and maritime gifts of his Iberian subjects, and the cultural links that bound them to the Netherlands. But another factor had even more importance for Charles. He regarded as his greatest failure his inability to prevent the spread of Protestantism in Europe. In life, Charles had been a selfish dynast, but in the face of death he wanted to make his peace with God. Just as he wished to do penance by living out his remaining days in the humble retreat of a Spanish monastery, so he hoped that Philip's inheritance, free of heretical stain, would be pleasing in the sight of God.

While Charles made the painful journey to his last home at the monastery of Yuste in the countryside of Extremadura, Philip II stayed in the Netherlands to settle his affairs. This included defeating the French in the best tradition of the warrior-emperor at the battle of St Quentin (1557). By the time he returned to Spain in 1559, both his father and his childless second wife, Mary I of England (1553–58), were dead. Few monarchs have marked a reign with a personal stamp as quickly as Philip II. Conscious of both his Catholic and his Habsburg heritage, he was above all a king of Spain, more particularly of Castile. His most significant early gesture was to establish a permanent site of government in Madrid (1561). His choice revealed a sense of mission: the new capital was near the exact geographical center of the peninsula. Soon afterward he began to construct his permanent residence, the

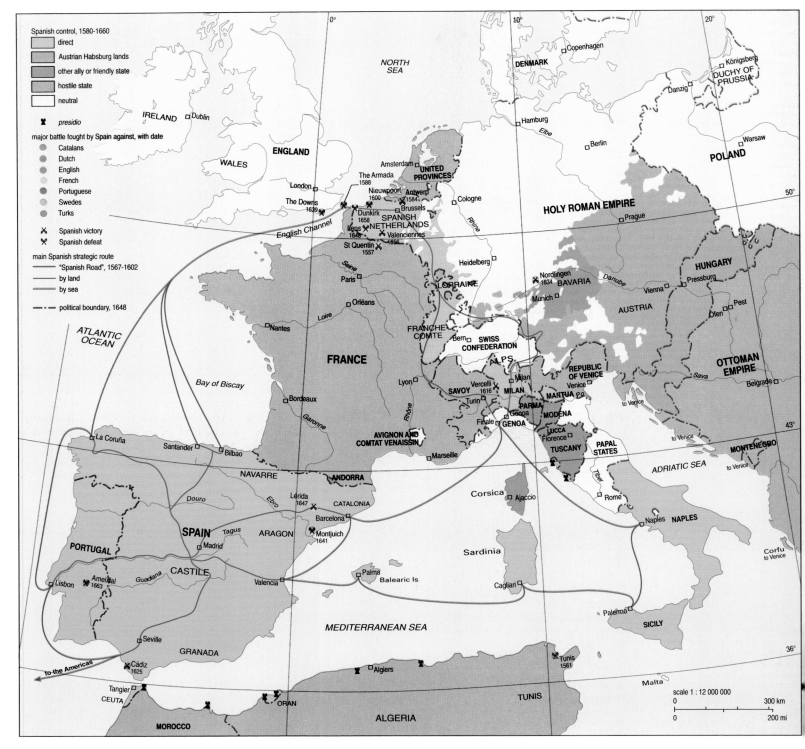

Spanish control, 1580-1660
- direct
- Austrian Habsburg lands
- other ally or friendly state
- hostile state
- neutral

✗ *presidio*

major battle fought by Spain against, with date
- Catalans
- Dutch
- English
- French
- Portuguese
- Swedes
- Turks

✗ Spanish victory
✗ Spanish defeat

main Spanish strategic route
— "Spanish Road", 1567-1602
— by land
— by sea

--- political boundary, 1648

of these derived largely from religious celebration, especially the rapidly developing genre of drama. Here, the pioneer was the Portuguese court poet Gil Vicente (c. 1465–c. 1536), who left 44 extant plays, including 11 wholly (and another 17 partly) in Castilian; these were to have a major influence on the development of the Spanish stage. But though it was later to become a courtly art form, at the time of Philip II's accession to the throne drama still belonged to the city streets. Tavern yards and courtyards were used as makeshift arenas (*corrales*) for spectacles in which popular songs and dances were spontaneously included. One performance alone could be watched by a thousand or more paying customers. During Philip's reign, the traditional *autos* (literally, "acts") with religious themes began to be supplemented with more

secular plays (*comedias*) with historical plots.

Even more explosive was the development of the genuinely "popular" oral tradition of story-telling – in which humorous tales and gossip were interlaced, usually with a moral attached – into the picaresque novel. The first and most famous collection of picaresque tales, *The Life of Lazarillo de Tormes*, published in 1554, relates episodes in the life of a boy born in downtown Salamanca who rises to become town-crier. This rags-to-riches story was to set the stage for the astonishing era of vividly documented social and cultural interaction of Spain's Golden Age.

Renewal of the holy war
International affairs dominated Philip's reign. At the outset, Spain faced three challenges: the unfinished

Right The German artist Christof Weiditz, who visited Spain in 1529, became fascinated by the *moriscos* of the peninsula, still very numerous in Granada at this time. Though the *moriscos* were officially Catholic, there was considerable toleration, especially in remote areas, and many practiced their religion in secret. Weiditz made a series of sketches showing *moriscos* in Muslim attire, which they were still free to wear. However, growing fears of links between the *morisco* communities and the Ottoman Turks and their North African allies led to greater restrictions. Muslim dress was banned in 1568, the year before the *moriscos* of Granada rose in revolt against Castilian rule.

flowed around the "traffic island" of France. So long as France was weak it worked efficiently, but the ending of the French religious wars and the growing strength of Bourbon government revealed the system's vulnerability: Savoy was able to gain a precarious neutrality by playing one power off against the other, thereby obliging Spain to establish a longer and more dangerous route through the Alps after 1602. The system's power-axis was Madrid–Milan–Brussels, and it needed constant maintenance by teams of diplomatic, military and financial agents at all key points in between. The fleets of the "Barbary States" of North Africa always threatened the safety of the Mediterranean route, despite the construction of *presidios* (coastal fortresses). During the Thirty Years War (1618–48) troops and equipment from Spain, Sicily and Naples were assembled in Milan before being sent on to fight in Germany, France or the Netherlands. The physical location of most of Spain's crucial battles in this period illustrates the geographically schematic nature of its struggle for power.

war against France, the encroachment of Protestantism, and the expansion of Ottoman power. Peace with France was achieved with the Treaty of Cateau-Cambrésis (1559), which confirmed Spanish control in Italy and left the frontier with the Netherlands intact: France was subsequently paralyzed by a long succession of civil wars, lasting until 1595. The threat of Protestant heresy being imported into Spain was also swiftly dealt with. In an atmosphere of popular frenzy, the Inquisition cauterized several proto-Protestant cells, notably at an *auto de fé* in Valladolid, attended by Philip in his first public engagement as king. The third challenge was less easy to confront. Ottoman power in the Mediterranean came dangerously close in 1558 when a Turkish fleet – more the size of an invasion force than a raiding party – landed at Minorca, destroying Ciudadela, plundering the island and carrying off thousands of Philip's subjects. Suddenly, Spain found itself in the front line of a new Islamic holy war.

Philip's reaction was ill-considered. Forgetting his father's disastrous misadventure at Algiers (1541), he hastily launched an expedition to capture and fortify Djerba, near the Tunisian base of Turkey's main Arab ally. The idea was sound – to close off the western Mediterranean – but the result was a humiliating defeat, though Philip learned his lesson from it and in future prepared every operation with meticulous thoroughness. The 1560s were dedicated to reversing the Turkish tide. The focal point was Malta, which was besieged by Muslim forces in May 1565. An extended campaign to save the island followed, using the financial and manpower reserves of Castile and the maritime expertise of Catalonia and Valencia. If the Ottoman Turks had gained Malta, they would have turned their attention to Aragon's Mediterranean pos-

sessions, Sicily and Naples. Thus, these kingdoms contributed to the building of a great galley-fleet. By the 1570s, Philip had over 100 galleys in the Spanish fleet alone; Malta had been saved, and a "Holy League" between Spain, the papacy and Venice been constructed. The Holy League's stunning naval victory over the Ottoman fleet at Lepanto (1571) was the last great glory of Christendom – more than half paid for by Spain, and won primarily by Spanish arms.

During the final stages of this campaign, Spain had to cope with a sudden attack in the flank. In 1569, the *moriscos* of Granada, centered on the remote Alpujarras mountains, launched an uprising. Local authority reeled. Arab reinforcements began to cross the Strait of Gibraltar and a full-scale civil war spread across Andalusia. Philip went to Córdoba to supervise operations, appointing his illegitimate half-brother Don Juan of Austria (1547–78) as commander. It was not until 1571, after great cost and effort, that the resistance was overcome. Some Spaniards vociferously demanded the deportation of all *moriscos* from the peninsula, but others criticized the methods of mass conversion, demanding a coherent policy of assimilation. A compromise emerged: the *moriscos* were uprooted and distributed among the towns of Castile. About 80,000 were resettled in the marches of New Castile – from where many of their forebears had fled to Granada as refugees during the Reconquest. The *moriscos* were now trapped in watchful Christian communities, often indentured to Christian masters and, above all, isolated from their coreligionists in North Africa. Against the background of this new victory over the Muslims, the celebrations over Lepanto had a dual significance, marking the profound relief and gratitude of Catholic Spain.

Dynastic difficulties

Though Ciudadela, Djerba – even Algiers – had been avenged, Philip himself was not in triumphal mood. Lepanto was not followed up with further victories against the Muslims, and the king was in grave difficulties at home. None of his father's ministers had gained his confidence; in any case – heeding Charles' own advice – Philip was determined never to allow even successful ministers to gain too much power. Since he regularly deflated the ambitions of his ministers, Philip could ensure continuity in government only by doing everything himself. Fortunately, Philip's character was suited to the task of managing a world empire. But his curiosity was encumbered by pedantry, leading him to devote attention to small, even trivial, issues, sometimes to the detriment of important ones.

The king's natural distrust was exacerbated by the behavior of his son. The infante Carlos (1545) had exhibited worrying character defects even before an accidental blow to his head drove him obviously insane. His vicious outbursts poisoned the atmosphere at court, interfering with the proper despatch of business. When Don Carlos plotted against his life, Philip was forced to arrest his son for treason – a responsibility he discharged in person. The prince later died under house confinement (1568).

Crisis in the Netherlands

Despite three marriages, the death of Carlos left Philip bereft of a male heir. Dynastic crisis, and the emergency in relations with the Muslim world, turned his attention away from a problem that at first seemed

The Portuguese Navigators

The enthusiasm for maritime adventure that led Portuguese seamen to find the way around Africa to India and opened the route to the Far East was largely inspired by one man: Prince Henry, known as "the Navigator". His reasons for devoting the resources of the knightly Order of Christ to the encouragement of Portuguese navigation and exploration appear to have been mixed: while appreciating the importance of trade and colonization, he seems also to have nurtured the ambition of a Portuguese-led crusade against Islam, and hoped his explorers would find Prester John, the mythical Christian priest-king whose empire was reputed to lie beyond the Nile. Henry himself traveled no farther than Tangier, and at the time of his death Portuguese sailors had only reached as far as the coast of Sierra Leone. But it was his example that led João II, and after him Manuel I, to sponsor the voyages of Bartolomeu Dias to the Cape of Good Hope (1488), Vasco da Gama to India (1497–99), and Pedro Alvares Cabral across the Atlantic to Brazil (1500). After the Treaty of Tordesillas (1494) had granted Portugal exclusive rights in the East, her sailors and traders explored the Spice Islands, China and Japan, followed closely by missionaries. By 1600 the Portuguese had founded a trading-post at Macao, and secured a monopoly of the Japanese trade.

Right Prince Henry stands at the head of a throng of Portuguese navigators on the Monument to the Discoveries in Lisbon, erected in 1960 to commemorate the quincentennial of his death. He holds a model ship; among the other idealized portrait-sculptures is the figure of Manuel I with his emblem, the armillary sphere.

Below Portugal produced many skilled map-makers; their *roteiros* (pilot-books) had long been highly prized (Columbus has been accused of using a stolen *roteiro* on his 1492 voyage to America), and their portolans, or navigational charts of coastlines, were also much in demand. This splendid world map, with winds blowing from the four corners of the globe, belongs to an atlas that was made by Lopo Homem in 1519.

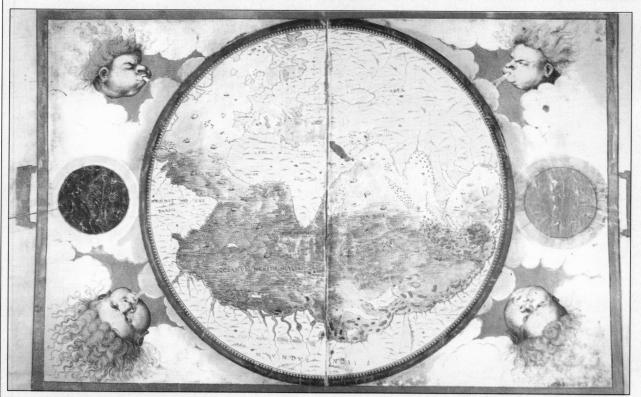

Above The voyages of discovery had great influence on the Manueline style of architectural decoration, as this astonishing window from the Convent of Christ at Tomar shows. The whole design is supported on the bust of a sea-captain and consists of a profusion of marine objects, including ropes and cables, seaweed, coral and anchor-chains, all crowned with the cross of Prince Henry's Order of Christ.

Top By the end of the 16th century Portuguese ships had become a familiar sight in Japan. A local artist has pictured one on this painted screen.

Right The sea-route to Asia was first established by Vasco da Gama. His pioneering voyage round the Cape of Good Hope to the coast of India and back lasted more than two years.

DOM VASCO DA GAMA CONDE ALMIRANE QVE FOIO
PRIMEIRO Q̃ DOREINO VEIO CÕTITOLODE VIZOREI
O: 6: G DA ÍMDIA

relatively minor, but which was to become the bane of Spain: the Netherlands. Philip had left his illegitimate half-sister, Margaret of Parma (1522–86), as governor in Brussels. She was capable and industrious but lacked personal royal authority and was overwhelmed by the sheer complexity of her task. Consensus among the local nobility broke down, with men who had been highly valued by Philip in earlier years, such as William of Orange (1533–82) and the count of Egmont (1522–68), turning against him. The spread of Calvinism among the crowded commercial towns of the Low Countries quickly bred distrust of Catholic rulers. Resentment over high taxation turned distrust into a popular hatred of Spain. When the Inquisition made a series of heavy-handed investigations, protests started, organized by the aggrieved nobles, in which churches were desecrated and holy images destroyed. Such flagrant challenges to authority and religion obliged Philip belatedly to tackle the problem. A new governor was appointed – the daunting duke of Alba (1507–82), a Spanish general and strict disciplinarian, who crushed the rebellions with great brutality. In 1572, when it seemed that order had been restored, a major resistance movement began in the northern Netherlands. When it spread rapidly among the fishing communities of Holland and Zeeland, Alba reacted more violently than ever by instigating the massacre of Haarlem (1573).

Ruling at such a distance, and alternating compromise with repression, was a recipe for failure in the Netherlands. Despite the creation of a system of military communication – the transalpine "Spanish Road" from Italy, and the sea-route through the English Channel from Spain – financed by loans from international money lenders, sufficient resources could never be mobilized to suppress the rebellion. Thousands of citizens of Bruges, Ghent and Antwerp in the southern Netherlands escaped religious persecution or taxation by fleeing to Amsterdam and Utrecht in the north. Capital, industrial skills and commercial expertise drained away from the supposedly "obedient" southern provinces. Antwerp, cut off from the sea by the military situation, fell into decline, and the lines of economic cooperation between Spain and the Netherlands withered away. In 1575, the level and range of its commitments forced the crown to declare a bankruptcy. Four years later, the rebels, led by Holland and Zeeland and under the nominal rule of William of Orange, formed the Union of Utrecht, which, after many vicissitudes, survived as the basis of an independent Dutch state.

The prize of Portugal

Through frustrated in northern Europe, Philip was on the verge of a major gain in the south. In 1581, he achieved the cherished dream of the Habsburg dynasty by adding Portugal to his possessions. He could not have gained his prize at a more auspicious time. Portugal had continued to prosper after the death of Manuel I (1521). By the Treaty of Zaragoza (1529), Spain and Portugal settled remaining disputes over colonial rights. João III (1521–57) made the decision to occupy Brazil in the following year, granting huge tracts of coastal land to Portuguese settlers. Colonial trade produced enormous riches, much of which accrued directly to the crown through monopoly rights. Apart from building bigger ships or sending larger fleets to the East Indies, there was little outlet for investment. Consequently, architecture and the arts

flourished, with Lisbon becoming one of the greatest cities of Europe.

Not surprisingly, the Portuguese excelled in map and chart-making, and in other branches of navigational science. The renowned cosmographer and mathematician Pedro Nunes (c.1502–78) was responsible for developing the astrolabe as a precision instrument. The age of discovery stimulated a rich literary tradition, ranging from botanical treatises on the plants of India to tales of adventure such as the *Peregrinação* (*Pilgrimage*) of Fernão Mendes Pinto (c.1510–83). Recounting his life as a merchant and sailor in China and the east, it is an exuberant mixture of satire, social observation and fantasy. Most famous of all is Luís de Camões (1524–80). A member of the old impoverished aristocracy, Camões was well educated in classical learning and philosophy. As a young man he embarked on a military career and acquired a reputation for wild living – pardoned in 1553 by the king for his part in a street brawl, he set sail for India and subsequently spent 17 years in the east, returning to Portugal in 1570. His epic poem *Os Lusíadas* (*The Lusiads*, a reference to Portugal's Roman name of Lusitania) was published two years later. Recounting the voyages of Vasco da Gama, the poem is a rich celebration of Portuguese history and seafaring, in which allusions to classical learning and mythology are balanced with realistic description of storms, battles and sensual love. It is the most famous of Camões' works (he also wrote plays and lyrical verses) and remains an enduring symbol of Portuguese nationalism.

Spanish influence in Portugal increased during the reign of João III, a diffident and pious man who was dominated by his Castilian wife, Catherine (1507–78), the sister of Charles V. Encouraged by Catherine and his zealous brother, Henrique, Cardinal-archbishop of Evora (1512–80), João gained papal consent to establish the Inquisition in Portugal in 1536. The first *auto-da-fé* was held in 1540, the same year in which the Society of Jesus appeared in Portugal. The

Jesuits soon gained control of Portuguese education and also earned great prestige and influence through their missionizing work in the Portuguese colonies, building on the achievements of St Francis Xavier (1506–52), one of Loyola's earliest followers, who led a mission to Goa on the west coast of India.

Lisbon – the nerve center of the empire and the political and cultural capital of the country – grew at a rapid pace, reaching a population of about 100,000 by 1557. Slaves from the colonies accounted for some 10 percent of the population, while many other inhabitants were emigrants from the countryside who had been attracted by reports of great wealth. Widespread rural depopulation caused a serious shortage of agricultural labor, while the large estates were hopelessly mismanaged by their absentee landlords. Consequently, the country could not produce enough food and was obliged to import meat, grain and dairy products. The paradox of boundless wealth at court and increasing stagnation in the regions seriously weakened the country's economic and political viability over the centuries.

African disaster

Of João III's ten children, only one survived childhood: his namesake, who married Juana, the daughter of Charles V, and died in 1554. Juana gave birth to a son, Sebastião, just a few days after she was widowed. The king himself died three years later, and the throne passed to the infante Sebastião – *o Desejado*, "the Desired One" (1557–78). The young king, who grew up surrounded by priestly tutors and steeped in chivalric reading, became obsessed with the idea of a crusade. Fanatically religious and highly stubborn, he was convinced that God had chosen him to liberate Jerusalem. In June 1578, at the age of 24, Sebastião sailed for Morocco determined to fight his way to the Holy Land. He was accompanied by a largely reluctant army of some 16,000 men, including virtually the whole adult male membership of the Portuguese nobility. On 4 August, about half the army, along with their king, were killed at El-Ksar-el-Kebir (Alcácar-Quibir). It was more a massacre than a battle; thousands more were taken prisoner and only a few hundred escaped.

Portugal was shattered by the defeat. Alive, Sebastião had been widely regarded as boastful and inept; his death elevated him to a national hero. Myths abounded, with many Portuguese preferring to believe that the king was still alive and would one day lead the nation to victory rather than accept the consequences of defeat. The Spanish claim to the vacant throne immediately threatened Portugal's cherished independence. In a desperate attempt to forestall the inevitable Sebastião was succeeded by his aged uncle, the cardinal and Inquisitor-General, Henrique (1578–80). Though he was released by Rome from his vows of chastity, the old man died before he could convert his dispensation into a successor, leaving Philip II of Spain as the only serious candidate. Dom António (1531–95), the illegitimate son of a brother of João III, gained some support, but Philip's offer to pay the huge ransom Morocco demanded for its Portuguese prisoners gradually shifted opinion in his favor.

Peninsular unity and the war with England

Philip rapidly made good his claim to Portugal. In a textbook operation, the duke of Alba marched on Lisbon, while a fleet commanded by the marquis of Santa

Cruz (1526–88) blockaded the mouth of the river Tagus. Dom António was forced to flee as the Spanish troops entered Lisbon. With order restored, Philip traveled to Lisbon, convening a Cortes at nearby Tomar where he swore to observe the rights and privileges of his new subjects. He would retain existing officials, appoint Portuguese to vacant posts, and hold Cortes in Portugal. Justice, the currency and military organization would remain autonomous. In return, Philip gained the substantial income of the defunct Avis dynasty and maritime resources that included 12 huge war galleons. The prestige of Portugal's empire now belonged to Spain; in the same year, a new Spanish colony in the Pacific was inaugurated and was given an appropriate name – the Philippines. Spain's Catholic monarchy and empire now stretched across the whole of the known world.

Strengthened by his new possession, Philip could adopt a more comprehensive approach to the situation in the Netherlands. By 1583, his new governor and nephew, Alexander Farnese, duke of Parma (1545–92), had begun to reassert Spanish control there. Basing his plans on improved relations with the southern provinces, Parma began the reconquest of

The Spanish Armada

Philip II's sending of a great fleet (or *Armada*) against England in 1588 formed part of a larger "enterprise": it was intended to join up with and assist an invasion force from Flanders led by the duke of Parma. The fleet that left La Coruña in July under the command of the duke of Medina-Sidonia (1550–1619) consisted of more than 130 vessels, nearly 20,000 soldiers and 10,000 sailors – the largest ever seen in the waters of northern Europe. Nevertheless, despite more than two years' planning, both the fleet and the plan of campaign had serious deficiencies. Several squadrons were technically ill-equipped and undermanned; furthermore, the coastal topography on both sides of the English Channel precluded the possibility of galleons being able to protect troop-carrying barges from enemy warships. Philip, who knew the Netherlands well, must have been aware of this fact, but it is also fair to say that his expedition was in many ways a venture into the unknown – the encounter that took place off Gravelines on 9 August was the first artillery battle ever fought between massed warships. Yet, as one Spanish captain put it, the Armada sailed "in the confident hope of a miracle" – after all, God had led Columbus to the New World and enabled Cortés with a few men and horses to overthrow an immense empire. Philip and his subjects had done all that was humanly possible to bring success to the crusade. In the event, the Spanish fleet came off worse in the confrontation, but a shift in the wind allowed the Armada to break away into the North Sea. Only about 80 ships weathered a fearsome summer storm to make their way round the British Isles and back to Spain.

Right This portrait shows Philip II, "Master of the Armada", accoutered for war and in an attitude of command. One hand rests on his sword, the other grasps the general's baton; around his neck hangs the supreme emblem of chivalry – the Order of the Golden Fleece. It was painted at the time that Philip, by virtue of his marriage to Mary Tudor, was king of England as well as Spain. This frustrated alliance is curiously represented by one of the siege guns (*below right*) recovered from the wreck of the Armada galleon *La Trinidad Valencera*, which lies off the northernmost point of Ireland. The gun, which was intended to support the invasion force in the event of a successful landing, bears its date of casting – 1556 – and the quartered arms of England and Spain.

Below Depicted on the Greenwich Cartoon is one of the Armada galleases. The role of these oared vessels has recently been reevaluated. The remarkable series of charts (*far right*) commissioned from Robert Adams by Admiral Howard, the victorious English commander, show that their function was to maintain the fleet's impregnable crescent formation by harrying stragglers and nudging wanderers into line. In the phase of the campaign shown here, the English fleet, sailing out of Plymouth, has outflanked the Armada to take up a position to its rear.

Right The printed list sets out the Armada's total resources squadron by squadron – the number and tonnage of ships, their strength in soldiers and crew, the amount of artillery, powder and shot carried. Near the bottom of the muster are registered over 2,000 galley-slaves (*gente de remo*) who were distributed amongst the galleys and galleases.

SVMARIO GENERAL DE TODA EL ARMADA.

	Numero d'Nauios	Toneladas	Géte d'guerra	Géte d'mar	Numero d'todos	Piecas de artilleria	Peloteria	Poluora	Plomo quí tales	Cuerda quí tales
Armada de Galeones de Portugal.	12	7.737	3.330	1.293	4.623	347	18450	789	186	150
Armada de Vizcaya de que es General Iuan Martinez de Ricalde.	14	6.567	1.937	863	2.800	238	11.900	477	140	87
Galeones de la Armada de Castilla.	16	8.714	2.458	1.719	4171	384	23.040	710	290	309
Armada de naues del Andaluzia.	11	8.762	2.325	780	3.105	240	10.200	415	63	119
Armada de naos de la Prouincia de Guipuscua.	14	6.991	1992	616	2.608	247	12.150	518	139	109
Armada de naos leuantiscas.	10	7.705	2.780	767	3523	280	14000	584	177	141
Armada de Vrcas.	23	10271	3121	608	3729	384	19.200	258	142	215
Pataches y zabras.	22	1.221	479	574	1.093	91	4550	66	20	13
Galeaças de Napoles.	4	873		468	1.341	200	10.000	498	61	88
Galeras.	4			362	362	20	1.200	60	20	20
	130	57.868	19295	8050	27365	2.431	123790	4.575	1.232	1.151

Gente de remo.

En las Galeaças.	1.200.
En las Galeras.	888.
	2.088.

De mas de la dicha poluora se lleua de respecto para si se ofreciere alguna bateria 600. qs. — 600.

5.175

Por manera que ay en la dicha armada, segun parece por este sumario, ciento y treynta nauios, que tienen cincuenta y siete mil ochocientos y sessenta y ocho toneladas, y diez y nueue mil dozientos y nouenta y cinco soldados de Infanteria, y ocho mil y cincuenta y dos hombres de mar, que todos hazen, veyntisiete mil trezientas y setenta y cinco personas, y dos mil y ochenta y ocho remeros, y dos mil y quatrocientas y treynta y vna piecas de artilleria, las mil quatrocientas y nouenta y siete de bronze, de todas suertes en que ay muchos cañones, y medios cañones, culebrinas, y medias culebrinas, y cañones pedreros, y las nouecientas y treynta y quatro restantes de hierro colado de todos calibos, y ciento y veyntitres mil cien y dozientos y treynta y ocho de plomo, y mil ciento y cincuenta y vn quintales de cuerda: y los generos de los nauios son en esta manera.

the north, progressing at the rate of two or three key citadels a year. However, in 1585, Queen Elizabeth I of England (1558–1603), worried by the prospect of outright Spanish victory, sent an expeditionary force to the aid of the Dutch. In that same year Sir Francis Drake (c. 1540–96), with a fleet that included two royal warships and a force of 1,500 soldiers, made an unprovoked landing in Galicia and sacked the town of Vigo. The challenge could not be ignored; open war was inevitable, and waited only on Philip's meticulous preparation.

In 1588, the Spanish Armada – a magnificent symbol of the Spanish monarchy at the height of its power – set sail to invade England. Never before had one great fleet of gun-bearing sailing ships been sent to fight against another in enemy waters. But the result was disaster. The "enterprise of England" cost Philip a whole year's revenue and irreplaceable losses of ships and men. Yet far from marking the collapse of Spanish maritime power, its failure stimulated Philip to build a modern navy to replace it. When he died in 1598, Spain was still locked in combat with England.

The Spanish achievement in crisis

Spain's economy and population had been expanding for more than a century to reach some 8 million by the end of Philip's reign. Castile had some 30 towns of more than 10,000 inhabitants, compared to England's three. This thriving society produced the first schools of economic and political theory at universities such as Salamanca, where the ideas of the Polish astronomer Copernicus (1473–1543) and other advanced thinkers were on the syllabus. In many areas of study, Spain was ahead of its rivals. Not surprisingly, these were linked to the management of a world empire – cosmology, navigation and cartography. Castile was also the scene of important developments in social science theory and practice. Municipal authorities collaborated with the church to provide a range of social services for the poor and the sick, from which even minority groups, such as *moriscos* and gypsies, often benefited.

Philip II was no absolute despot. He ruled by right but also by consensus. Like Elizabeth I, he had to bargain with parliaments for tax concessions, but he also had to operate within the limits laid down by hundreds of *fueros*. The sight of subjects kneeling as the monarch passed – as the English did before Queen Elizabeth – would have been abhorrent to Spaniards, while the idea of the divine right of kings was blasphemous to contemporary Spanish political theorists, who rigorously defended constitutional principles. Under Philip, Spain had become the first bureaucratic world empire, with sophisticated information systems, a civil service of unprecedented size and professional standards, and the largest and most efficient armed forces since those of imperial Rome.

Nevertheless – despite the many achievements of his reign – Philip left so many problems that his death is often regarded as the beginning of Spain's notorious decline from greatness. If not yet in decline, Spain certainly suffered recurrent problems in society, economy, government and finance. Little of this was Philip's fault, and his successors were helpless to restore the situation. Spain's geophysical makeup, especially the restricted extent and poor capacity of its fertile land, meant that it was unable to maintain the population levels reached in the 16th century, let alone expand them to the proportions that were necessary

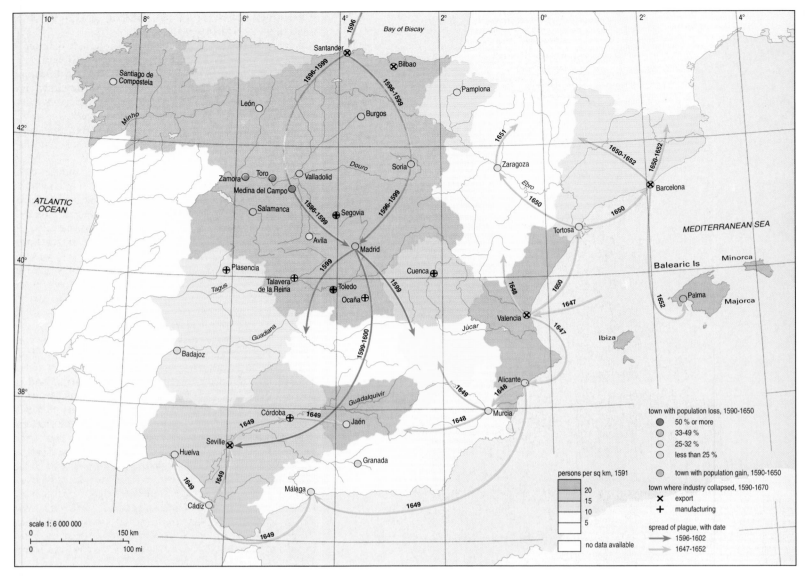

for successful competition in the 17th century. Furthermore, in the last quarter of the 16th century, climatic changes adversely affected the peninsula's agriculture, which was precarious at the best of times. Population growth slowed down; Spain became a food importer even before the widespread harvest failure of the mid-1590s. Four years of famine (1591–94) were followed by five of plague (1596–1600). These disasters reduced the population by some 10 percent, inaugurating a cycle of subsistence crisis and epidemic that continued to 1680.

Meanwhile, the absolute political imperative of defending the Catholic empire was a drain on dwindling resources. The crown's defense of its interests in northern Europe produced a relentless escalation of taxation, especially in the years after the Armada. The constitutional independence of the Spanish kingdoms precluded the possibility of augmenting revenues from non-Castilian sources. Consequently, the main burden of defense fell on a crisis-torn Castile that was increasingly unable to support it.

In principle, Philip recognized the need to reduce the pressures of war. The difficulty lay in making a "conscientious peace": achieving diplomatic compromises without unacceptable losses in religious leadership, territory or international reputation. In 1598, the year of his death, Philip II accepted a peace with Henry IV of France (1589–1610).

A satellite king

Philip III (1598–1621), had little of his father's spirit or talents. For a time he attempted – with some success – to sort out the confusion in government that his father's final illness had left, and continued the search for peace by signing treaties with England (1604) and the rebel Dutch (1609) – though the latter was a 12-year truce that did not actually concede independence. Nevertheless, many Spaniards felt that the Truce of Antwerp had not been a conscientious peace – a view that the king himself eventually came to share.

After this initial flurry of activity, Philip III retired from direct rule. This was made possible by Francisco de Sandoval, duke of Lerma (1553–1625), the royal favorite (*valido*) to whom the king delegated the regular exercise of power. Until about 1612, Philip trusted Lerma unreservedly. The king was a morose personality, and was obsessively dependent on the consolations of religion and on the support of his wife, Margarita (1584–1611), as well as that of Lerma. He sought escape from the problems of death, salvation and government in hunting, a popular palliative among Iberian rulers.

Though he created a splendid baroque court in Madrid, which was much improved architecturally during his reign, Philip spent relatively little time in the city. For some years he actually moved the capital to Valladolid, mainly to please Lerma, whose estates and

Economic recession, 1590–1650
Evidence of economic recession in the early 17th century is overwhelming. The process began with a series of harvest failures in Castile in the early 1590s. Population growth, already slowing down, was abruptly halted; refugees flocked into the towns from the starving countryside. In 1596 plague broke out in Santander and spread into the interior; by 1602 500,000 – one in twelve of the population – had died in Castile, and thousands more emigrated to the Americas. Agriculture collapsed, confirming Castile's longterm dependence on imported grain. Fishing, manufacture and export trades - already disrupted by the war in the Netherlands – were further affected by a catastrophic royal bankruptcy in 1596. Soaring costs were aggravated by rampant monetary inflation and (especially in 1620–40) an oppressive tax regime, causing industrial collapse: sheep-farming and certain strategic enterprises such as shipbuilding, mining and metallurgy – given a degree of government protection – managed to survive. Further epidemics in mid century reversed the effects of short-term demographic recovery.

Above Francisco de Sandóval y Rojas, duke of Lerma, was the originator of the office of *valido* (royal favorite and chief minister) under Philip III. He amassed an unprecedented fortune through patronage and what would today be regarded as peculation, but when his political luck changed, he escaped retribution by accepting a cardinal's hat from the pope. This sculpture - by Pompeo Leoni (1533–1608), the Italian sculptor and medallist who made his home in Madrid after 1556 – is in gilded bronze. It closely resembles the figures of the Habsburg royal family that the same artist made for the chapel of the Escorial.

governing together, they were able to restore much of the Habsburgs' lost prestige.

It was the war against the Dutch – which reached a climax with the prolonged and bloody siege of Ostend in 1602–4 – that helped to provoke the first financial crisis of the reign. The crippling cost of the campaign obliged Madrid to revise its finances. A major new tax, the *millones*, had recently been introduced, but failed to produce the expected returns. The crown was desperate for extra-parliamentary revenue, since this would circumvent the Cortes' ability to obstruct new taxation or use it as a bargaining lever for further concessions. The government's solution was to debase the coinage through the issue of an alloy currency (*vellón*). Though extremely profitable to the exchequer, the *vellón* wreaked havoc with industry and commerce. It is possible that, without this blow, the commercial and manufacturing sectors would have recovered from the depressions caused by war and crown bankruptcies. As it was, high wages and monetary inflation suffocated business. In 1607 a dramatic fall in silver imports from America forced the government to declare yet another bankruptcy.

Nevertheless, shortage of cash was not the principal reason for seeking an end to the conflict in the Netherlands. More important was the fear that Henry IV of France, allied with the Dutch and the Turks, and in secret league with the Iberian *moriscos*, was about to declare war – a fear that was ended only by Henry's assassination in 1610. These suspicions meant that the long-avoided decision to expel the Moors from the peninsula was finally taken. The mass deportation took place in 1609–14, using many men and ships released from the northern fronts by the Truce of Antwerp. An act of ethnic cleansing that definitively solved Iberia's religious and racial problems, the expulsion was greeted unanimously by Spaniards as Philip III's greatest achievement, its glory transcending the fact that Spain had lost over 300,000 citizens. Mounting dissatisfaction with the Dutch truce and the growth of opposition to Lerma forced Philip to dismiss his favorite in 1618 and power passed to a faction dedicated to reform led by Baltasar de Zúñiga (?1561–1622) and his nephew Gaspar de Guzmán, count of Olivares (1587–1645), who were tutor and household governor to the king's son.

Intellect and imagination

For all its domestic misery and foreign failure, Philip III's Spain witnessed a triumph of the intellect. The joint activities of court and church generated a veritable explosion of literary activity. Works of history, philosophy, economics, politics, poetry, drama poured from the printing presses of Spain's cities. The links between religion, politics and literature were profound. Many writers were in holy orders, some were university professors, most sought government employment. Tirso de Molina, author of the first dramatic treatment of the Don Juan legend, was in reality the Mercedarian friar Gabriel Télluz (c. 1584–1648). Miguel de Cervantes (1547–1616), the author of *Don Quixote*, was a veteran of Lepanto – he lost his left hand in combat – and had helped to organize the Armada. Lope de Vega (1562–1635), the most prolific dramatist in history with 1,800 plays to his name, 431 of which are extant, actually sailed in the Armada. Another novelist, Mateo Alemán (1547–1610) was for a time manager of the royal mercury mines at Almadén, where convicts slaved in conditions that

connections lay nearby. Lerma had no more interest than his master in matters of state, being as concerned with the affairs of this world as the king was with those of the next. His principal interest lay in controlling patronage. He amassed great wealth through Philip's direct grants of lands and titles and creamed off the profits of an extended system of clientage. Lerma ruled through a "family" of relatives and lieutenants who were appointed to the major posts of church and state. He retained the senior household offices for himself, through which he supervised access to the king, and was powerful enough to hold off several challenges, including one in 1608 that was backed by the queen. Though unsuccessful, this exposed the corruption of the king's senior aides and dented Philip's confidence.

The conciliar system of government had reached an advanced state of autonomy, and despite – or because of – the indifference of king and *valido*, the business of government ticked over smoothly. Indeed, though plunged in socio-economic crisis and presided over by a royal recluse and an incompetent favorite, Spain arguably attained its greatest European status during these years. The key outposts of Naples and Milan were in the hands of capable governors trained under Philip II. In the southern Netherlands Philip II's daughter Isabel (1566–1633) had joint sovereignty with her husband and cousin Albert (1559–1621);

The Role of the Plaza Mayor

During the long domestic peace that lasted from about 1520 to 1640 aspects of urban construction were developed in Castile that gave attention to planning and function as well as beauty and magnificence. Central to this process was the *Plaza Mayor*, or grand square. Unike the *piazzas* of central Italy, the Spanish *plazas* are usually unitary in design, being the work of a single architect, and are nearly always rectilinear in shape. They differ also in the use of colonnades to support a projecting floor of the lateral buildings. These provided spaces sheltered from the sun and rain where business could be conducted in comfort and perishable goods safely displayed. Above them were the ranks of balconies where more private observation and transaction could take place: these are perhaps the origin of theater boxes, with their notorious dual function of privacy and public display. In cases where a *plaza* has been laid out in front of a cathedral or shares space with a town hall (*ayuntamiento*), however, it may appear closer to Italian examples.

The *plaza mayor* provided a focus for local pride and civic splendor. On feast days its paved open space was used for religious processions, and sometimes it became the site for *autos de fé* held by regional tribunals of the Inquisition. Here also the *hermandades* received rudimentary military and equestrian training. The earliest *plaza mayor* was constructed in Valladolid at the instigation of Philip II, whose birthplace it was. The *Plaza Mayor* of Salamanca is renowned for its classical proportions, embellished in the purest style of the Spanish Renaissance, while that of Madrid is easily the largest and grandest in Spain.

Above Philip III is seen here entering the great *Plaza Mayor* of Madrid, which was built on his orders. He was born in Madrid, but spent much of his time away from the city, even transferring his capital to Valladolid from 1601 to 1606. It took a long and costly campaign to persuade the king to return the court to Madrid and the square, officially opened in 1620, shortly before his death, may be regarded as a symbol of the city's final establishment as the capital of Spain.

Below The new *plaza* provided a notable arena for court spectacles such as chivalric squadron-jousts and other mock-combats, and above all for the frequent bullfights (*corridas de toros*) held to celebrate religious feast days, royal occasions and military triumphs.

Below This painting by Francisco Rizi shows the last *auto de fé* to be held in Madrid's *Plaza Mayor* in 1683, which was attended by the religion-obsessed Carlos II and his queen as part of their sacrosanct duty. None of the condemned was actually burned on this occasion. The *auto de fé* was in fact a very rare event in the capital, and even then did not always take place in the *Plaza Mayor*: the notorious burning, in 1632, of five "new Christians" who had allegedly relapsed into Judaism was held some distance away, near the huge triumphal arch later erected by Carlos III. But the *Plaza Mayor* was the scene of other judicial horrors, such as the execution in 1621 of the disgraced (and certainly corrupt) minister, Rodrigo Calderon, which attracted an enormous crowd.

Above In this aerial view the large open, rectilinear space of Madrid's *Plaza Mayor* contrasts strikingly with the surrounding canyon-like streets. The square was restored and improved in the late 18th century, and it was at this time that Philip III's equestrian statue was appropriately installed in the center. During the riots that accompanied the overthrow of the monarchy in 1931 the statue was pulled down and damaged. Its re-installation meant that Spain preserved at least one memorial to an otherwise unmemorable monarch.

Right Madrid's *Plaza Mayor*, like those of other towns, is still the scene of busy social activity. People meet to talk, eat and drink in bars and cafés (those in the center of the square being mostly the preserve of tourists), and also to enjoy open-air theater, concerts, art exhibitions and book fairs. On Sunday mornings, many come to the colonnades to browse among the stalls of stamp- and coin-specialists. At night the *tuna* bands – wearing a peculiar garb based on the student dress of the original groups – serenade the crowds with "traditional" Castilian music and *zarzuela* medleys.

were worse than those endured on the oar-benches of the galleys. Better connected writers received sinecure appointments in the royal households, such as the dramatist Juan Ruíz de Alarcón (1580–1639) and the economist Pedro de Navarrete (1574–1633), among literally hundreds of others.

Great nobles were also beginning to value the social cachet and political advantage of having a skilled writer among their entourage. Minor vendettas and even major political issues were fought out not only by the sword, but through printed squibs and posters. Francisco de Quevedo (1580–1645), secretary and hired hack to the duke of Osuna, was also a feared swordsman. Osuna's enemy, the count of Villamediana, was himself a satirical poet, dramatist and noted exponent of the duel.

Under these circumstances, it is not surprising that political and social comment became the stuff of literature, though many books still concerned themselves with religious themes. Of nearly 1,000 authors identified in the period 1500–1700, over 400 published on some aspect of religion. During the mid 16th century, the long-running dispute between the Jesuit Luis de Molina (1535–1600) and his Dominican opponents over the role of divine grace in salvation was followed closely by thousands of readers. Another Jesuit, Juan de Mariana (1536–1624), completed the first major history of Spain in 1595. By this time, literacy was commonplace among the upper classes; in society as a whole, about a third of the population could read.

Though some earlier Spanish writers had made reputations outside the country, it was Cervantes' novel *Don Quixote de la Mancha* (Part I, 1605; Part II, 1615) that captured the imagination of Europe. The adventures of an idealistic, poverty-stricken minor *hidalgo* whose wits have been turned by reading too much pulp chivalric fiction could only have been written in a society where literature and literacy were increasing in importance. The novel's combination of psychological observation and mordant social comment prefigure the modern novel, while its treatment of universal, eternal themes make it one of the finest early examples of its genre. Cervantes explores the difference between appearance and reality in the witty interplay between the dreamy, self-deluded knight and his shrewd and self-seeking servant, Sancho Panza. Similarly, on the stage, the comic role of a witty servant or naive peasant who punctures the pretensions of the sophisticated townsfolk was immensely popular in 17th-century Spain.

Cervantes was intellectually close to the *arbitristas* – a school of writers who advocated socio-economic reform – because his nostalgia for the great deeds of the past was sharpened by an awareness of present failings. A few years before the publication of *Don Quixote*, the economist González de Cellorigo (?1565–?1615) commented that Spain was "a society of enchanted beings, existing outside the natural order of things". These words exactly capture the spirit of *Don Quixote*, and Cervantes' own deep concern over the condition of his country. Yet it is possible to exaggerate the mood of disillusion (*desengaño*) that frequently descended on Spain after the 1580s. Like many fine satirists, Cervantes was a moralist and patriot. He believed in the greatness of Spain, the truth of its religion and the destiny of its people. The *arbitristas*, too, were incurable optimists – some of them as fantastically so as Don Quixote – who worked to bring about the restoration of Spain's greatness. As

clerics, they believed that through moral as well as practical reform, Spain could earn the return of divine assistance in all its enterprises.

Olivares and reform

A new reign and a new government were preparing to meet the challenge. Philip III left three sons, Queen Margarita having produced eight healthy children in only 12 years of marriage. This was a record for the Habsburg dynasty – paradoxical since Spain's population was otherwise in precipitous decline, and bizarre in contrast to the king's inertia in other affairs of state. The new king, Philip IV (1621–65), a teenager, was as worldly as his father was pious, but differed also in being intelligent and in having been prepared for government, though the latter was not to his natural taste. Yet he knuckled down to the work of kingship, seeking to emulate the methods of his grandfather, Philip II. Again in contrast to his father, he was fortunate in his chief adviser. From the age of 14 to nearly 40, Philip's personality was molded by the count of Olivares, the greatest statesman produced by Spain during its era as a world power. A mature mind and steady hand were undoubtedly needed. This was the only long reign of a major Spanish monarch to be wholly occupied by war. The Thirty Years War (1618–48), the conflict between Protestants and Catholics that started in Germany and gradually became a European war, had already begun at Philip's accession. For Spain, it was to develop into a continuous series of conflicts lasting 50 years and ending only after Philip's death.

In the latter years of Philip III's reign Olivares' uncle, Baltasar de Zúñiga, had initiated a veritable revolution in government, refusing in 1621 to renew the Truce of Antwerp on the original terms, which the new regime regarded as unacceptable, and initiating a thorough reform of government and finance in order to equip Spain for economic renewal at home and success abroad. It was this last strand of reform that Olivares took up most earnestly when he succeeded his uncle as chief minister in 1622. Strenuously though he denied it, Olivares too was a *valido* who, like Lerma, built up a power base in court and government. He controlled patronage and had exclusive influence over the monarch. He impressed Philip with a profound sense of royal responsibility, yet himself aspired to be indispensable in government. In contrast to Lerma, however, Olivares did not seek power in order to enrich himself, but rather to glorify the monarch and the monarchy and to restore their all-important *reputación* (reputation). The association of king and minister developed into a partnership in which Olivares led in terms of ideas and dynamism, but the king contributed sharp reminders of his own sovereign will.

Olivares was the first statesman of European stature to come to power with a ready-made program for reform. He was not responsible for the ideas themselves, nor the initial impetus to reform, but his genius lay in the force of his advocacy, analytical grasp and political vision. His main influences were the writings of the *arbitristas*, but he also wanted to emulate the successful innovations of Spain's enemies, particularly the Dutch. He had two main objectives. The first was to make Philip "truly king of Spain", rather than the ruler of a dozen diverse patrimonies, in order to relieve pressure on Castile by spreading tax burdens. The second was "to turn Spaniards into businessmen". This would be done by consolidating government bonds

(*juros*) into a sinking fund to attract domestic capital, establishing a central bank to supply credit to government at lower rates than the private Genoese bankers, and investing in commerce and industry. Above all, the chaotic fiscal system would be abolished and replaced by a single tax (*medio universal*).

By the mid 1620s, progress had been made in all these directions, and the situation seemed promising. In 1624, Olivares proposed a "Union of Arms" that would create a reserve army paid for by all the Spanish dominions in proportion to their resources. The scheme was universally unpopular outside Castile because it infringed ancient liberties and was rightly interpreted as an attempt to reduce local autonomy. In the upshot, few of Olivares' reforms were ever fully achieved, with resistance from vested interests forcing him to compromise time and time again.

Success abroad, crisis at home
The early years of Philip's reign saw a spectacular series of victories. In 1625 alone, France was beaten in northern Italy; Breda, the family seat of the rebel

princes of Orange, was captured; the Dutch fishing fleet was destroyed; a Dutch invasion of Brazil was repulsed by a joint Portuguese-Castilian expedition; and a huge Anglo-Dutch task force sent to attack Cádiz was routed by the local Andalusian militia. In 1626, France sued for peace, and four years later, his navy outmaneuvered, Charles I of England (1625–49) also backed down. Meanwhile, the Dutch, assailed by land and sea, were considering major concessions in order to gain peace. Olivares claimed that even Philip II's achievements had been surpassed, and poets, dramatists and painters were commissioned to celebrate the splendors of Spanish arms.

The early triumphs were overshadowed by domestic crisis. Though other European communities suffered mortalities and economic slumps during the 17th century, those that assailed Castile were the most frequent, the most severe and the longest lasting. Agriculture lacked the flexibility and resilience to withstand adverse conditions. Hardly a generation after the first great subsistence crisis, another struck the central regions in the mid-1620s. Long winters that diminished harvest yields were followed by widespread flooding of fertile lands. Dearth stalked the countryside; provincial towns such as Salamanca and Medina del Campo were in the grip of famine. Local outbreaks of viral diseases made further inroads into the population. While Spanish infantrymen starved in their billets at the siege of Breda, their wives and children starved in their hovels at home. Refugees crowded into Madrid, which attained its highest population of the Habsburg era – perhaps as many as 300,000 people. Not surprisingly, in 1630 the capital's extensive food-requisition system broke down, and its people starved.

Spain had always been deficient in certain resources essential for empire: it lacked enough fertile land for food production, forestry for shipbuilding, and a solid population base for labor and defense. The crisis of 1627–31 decisively depleted its reserves. Economic depression hardened the determination of Castilian landowners to resist reform. With the war budget going out of control and another bankruptcy declared in 1627, Olivares was forced to compromise. He exploited the occasion to reorganize the government's funding for war by negotiating improved arrangements with a group of Christianized Portuguese Jews.

Opportunism was again in evidence – this time calamitously – when Olivares intervened in Italy in 1628. His action allowed France to invade Lombardy on the pretext of defending liberty, and the Spanish suffered serious losses in the fighting that followed. In the same year, the annual American treasure fleet was lost – for the first time – to enemy action, falling into Dutch hands at Matanzas in Cuba. With his credit exhausted, his people starving, his forces in retreat in Italy, Flanders and the Atlantic, Philip's confidence in Olivares was undermined. The minister was in disgrace for much of 1629, but the king knew that no other candidate could bring his degree of commitment to the business of government.

Culture and propaganda
The Olivares regime was perhaps the first in Europe to use the arts as a means of overt propaganda. This was a response to the frenetic atmosphere of war and the crisis in Madrid: "unless we succeed, here go nation, here go king, queen and everything else besides", as Olivares put it when declaring war on France in 1635.

The Art of Velázquez

The meteoric career of Diego Velázquez, who rose from humble origins in Seville to become the greatest painter of 17th-century Spain, is perennially fascinating. Appointed chief court-painter by the age of 24, his affectation of the grander denomination of Diego de Velázquez y Silva (his maternal surname being a tenuous link with gentlemanly Portuguese antecedents) was not mere self-indulgence. Like his contemporaries Rubens and Van Dyke, he occupied a dynamic phase in the process that transformed the artist from servant-craftsman to a species of nobility. In this, his lifelong personal friendship with King Philip IV, who himself aspired to be a painter, was of crucial importance. In the end, the demands of his royal patron helped to end his life. In 1659, following the Peace of the Pyrenees, Velázquez was entrusted with stage-managing the

meeting between Philip and the French king Louis XIV. He splendidly succeeded in outshining anything the Sun-King could offer, but the stress and effort involved precipitated his death a year later.

Velázquez' work displays an amazing variety of style and subject-matter. Though trained (like all his peers) as a religious artist, over the years this became the least important of his interests, and he preferred instead the recreation of themes from classical mythology. His affection for the so-called "genre" style – direct observation of the obscure society from which he sprang – never flagged, and he constantly exhibits penetrating honesty and compassion. At the other end of the scale he was the most accomplished portraitist of the baroque court, able to reflect genuine magnificance and fallible humanity on the same canvas.

Right The 1630s were the high point of the Habsburg passion for hunting the wild animals – wolf, deer and the dangerous tusked boar (*jabali*) – that inhabited the sierras around Madrid. Several consecutive days might be spent in the chase, necessitating the building of large hunting lodges, the walls of which were hung with appropriate scenes. It was for one of these that Velázquez painted this portrait of Philip IV – one of between 15 and 20 that are extant. Almost resembling a casually posed snapshot, it is nearly identical to another contemporary study of the king, and also to others of his brother Don Fernando (1609–41) and his son and heir, the infante Baltasar Carlos (1629–46).

Left Before the accession to the throne of Philip IV in 1621, Seville was the center of devotion to the Immaculate Conception – the belief that Mary, mother of Christ, had been born without stain of Original Sin. In 1617, after strong Spanish lobbying, the pope conceded that such belief was permissible – but not obligatory – among Catholics. Velázquez' own homage to the cult possibly celebrates this event and is the most serene product of his apprenticeship in religious modes. It was certainly the progenitor of thousands of imitations. The model is totally convincing as a simple, unaffected peasant girl. She might have been a servant in the house of his Seville patron, though some believe her to be Velázquez' wife, daughter of his teacher Pacheco. The figure combines a sculptural gravity with lightness of appearance. The rather gloomy and formal landscape is over-crowded with emblematic allusions to the cult of the Virgin.

Left This is Velázquez' earliest dated painting (1618) and is typical of his achievement in the comparatively short time he carried out his profession in his home town. The scene seems to represent an episode from a contemporary picaresque novel, *Guzmán de Alfarache* by the Sevillan writer, Mateo Alemán. The term *bodegón* (which later came to mean "still life" studies of inanimate objects) is still sometimes used to describe these paintings, which give such prominence to "props". The utensils on display seem to recur in several contemporary works, as do the human models of the old women and the boy. This indicates a residual tendency to the exercise, whilst the heavy use of *chiaroscuro* suggests the influence of Caravaggio, which came to Seville via Spanish-dominated Naples.

Right Las Meninas (The Handmaidens), painted in the mid 1650s, is the most famous of Velázquez' court portraits, and his most celebrated achievement. As in so many canvasses, Velázquez captures an interruption to a complicated and larger-scale event, for as he works on a huge double-portrait of the king and his second consort, Mariana, their only child, the infanta Margarita, appears to show off a new dress – perhaps on her birthday. The royal couple themselves are reflected toward our eyes (and their own) in the mirror that stands at the back of the artist's studio. Some experts have considered *Las Meninas* the single greatest painting of all time. Pablo Picasso painted no fewer than 40 variations, and it has been the subject of famous poems, novels and even a feature film.

As it happened, the king's favorite intellectual diversions were painting and the theater, both easily turned to serve political interests. In 1623, Diego de Velázquez (1599–1660) – like Olivares a native of Seville and discovered there by him – became the main royal portraitist. Velázquez' early studies of king and favorite convey the desired impressions of serious endeavor, authority and achievement, without ostentation or pomposity. His example was followed by dozens of other painters who flocked to Madrid, where a lively art market sprang up. Velázquez was the true founder of a Spanish school; though several of his contemporaries, such as Francisco Zurburán (1598–1662) and Bartolomé Murillo (1618–82), had exquisite special gifts and achieved greater fame outside Spain, only Velázquez was equal to the task of conveying to the world the images of an imperial capital at its apogee. These decades were the climax of the

Above Velázquez' *Surrender of Breda* – one of the greatest war scenes ever painted – immortalizes a moment in 1625 when the Spanish commander in the Netherlands, the Genoese Ambrigio Spínola (1571–1630), has just dismounted to accept the keys of the city of Breda from the Dutch leader and descendant of William the Silent, Justin of Nassau.

European baroque court, a glittering phenomenon that expressed itself in the assertive language of counter-reformation Catholicism. In architecture, sculpture and music Rome – and the Jesuit order – took the lead in developing its triumphal, richly embellished style, but in painting its most gifted exponent was the Antwerper Peter Paul Rubens (1573–1640), subject, friend and adviser to Philip IV.

Theater had been drifting into the royal orbit for some time, becoming increasingly lavish in the process, using elaborate plots, costume and settings. The leading dramatist of the day, the accomplished Pedro Calderón de la Barca (1600–81), frequently communicated a patriotic message in his plays. Painting and the theater came together in the great project for a new palace, the Buen Retiro, that went forward in the 1630s. The building was designed as a royal showcase for the benefit of political opponents, faint-hearted patriots and foreign visitors. Its main hall displayed the escutcheons of Philip IV's numerous dominions – literally a union of arms – and 12 enormous paintings of Spain's recent military and naval victories. Velázquez contributed "The Surrender of Breda" ("Las Lanzas"), a subject that had earlier been treated on the stage by Calderón. In another wing of the palace was the new Coliseo, Spain's first permanent purpose-built theater, and the scene of many allegorical presentations in praise of a great king and his wise favorite. Another dimension of brilliant self-display lay in the organization of great outdoor spectacles, many of them held in the environs of the palace – bullfights and boar-runs, squadron-jousts and mock battles, marches and processions – that dazzled the immense public that turned out to watch.

In painting, architecture and decoration, the baroque style swept all before it. Hundreds of parish churches and other religious foundations – especially in the towns – were built or rebuilt in modes derived from the original Jesuit church in Rome (the *Gèsu*, 1562), many of them combining a restrained, noble, often severe exterior with a surprising and sometimes riotously ornate interior decoration. The genre came to be oppressive and rather tortured in the later part of the century, but in the earlier was often joyous and liberating. Above all, the representational arts celebrated an amazing plasticity – an emphasis on movement that seems essentially musical.

Dictatorship, war and rebellion

During the 1630s the Spanish monarchy was sucked into a spiral of conflict unprecedented in its intensity. Olivares, determined to prepare for a showdown with France, constantly extended the king's prerogative to impose tax contributions on every sector of society. The new offensive began with further sensational victories, culminating in 1634 with the destruction of the Swedish army at Nördlingen in Bavaria. Full-scale war with France began, but Olivares' plans to disable the enemy by simultaneous attacks on three different parts of France misfired. Spain was soon in retreat, and in 1639–40 there were punishing naval defeats by the Dutch. By now, all attempt at reform abandoned, Olivares was frantically raising funds from every conceivable source to feed the war machine. He muzzled the Cortes, beat the councils of state into submission, plundered the wealth of the court aristocracy, offended many powerful grandee families and alienated the church. Moreover, other basic divisions, plastered over by the Habsburgs' cohesive rule and

Castile's wealth from the colonies, now reopened under the pressures of war on five fronts.

The association of Castile with the other kingdoms was still based on respect and a loose rein of central government. The balance of power was delicate: in 1631, for example, the Basques protested violently against a scheme for tax on salt. Aragon and Valencia compromised over the Union of Arms, despite the threat to their *fueros*, but Catalonia refused to budge. For Olivares, the reputation of the crown and the demands of the greater community were paramount: "the devil take the constitutions", as he put it. For the patriarchs of Barcelona, Spain itself was conditional on the maintenance of the constitutions. Olivares tried to coerce Catalonia into acceptance by sending troops to the border. The depredations of the soldiers gave the local peasantry common cause with the magistrates of Barcelona, even though the maintenance of the magistrates' caste privileges – what the *fueros* actually represented – was not usually in their interests. In June 1640, bloody insurrection in Barcelona turned into full-scale rebellion throughout Catalonia.

Portuguese independence

Portugal's three Spanish kings from 1580–1640 first respected, then neglected, and finally ignored, the undertakings given at Tomar to observe the rights and privileges of the Portuguese. Philip II meticulously kept his promises. He remained in Portugal for three years, making arrangements for his new kingdom and quelling rebellious islands in the Azores that had declared for the pretender to the Portuguese throne, António. He finally departed in February 1583 after appointing a governor, his nephew Albert of Austria (1559–1621), and three Portuguese advisers. Though Philip II promoted institutional links between Spain

Right Francisco de Zurburán - one of the astonishing school of artists active in the reign of Philip IV – is best remembered for his paintings of scenes from religious life. His portrait of Saint Margaret – looking as if she is on her way to market – is typical of his disarmingly domesticized studies of saints and martyrs.

and Portugal, especially by increasing the influence of the Inquisition and the Jesuit order, he continued throughout his reign to appoint Portuguese to high office, as he had promised.

The union between Portugal and Spain was initially a mutually convenient and largely productive arrangement. Until 1630, the balance of defense expenditure was in Portugal's favor, and the Habsburgs appointed distinguished and gifted viceroys, who reduced court expenditure and slowed the unhealthy growth of Lisbon to the benefit of the provinces. Neglected land was brought into production and farmers were freed from some of their obligations to the nobility. In contrast to other regions of the peninsula – notably Castile itself – Portugal's population rose by over 10 percent between 1580 and 1640. But Portuguese discontent with the union grew over time. Domestic peace was punctuated by regular disturbances, often inspired by "reappearances" of Sebastião, impersonated by ingenious imposters.

Though Portugal's economy remained buoyant, the

he extended the ban to the Dutch. In consequence, the Dutch began to make their own voyages to the east, establishing the Dutch East India Company in 1602 and gradually taking over the Portuguese monopoly of the spice trade. However, the loss of eastern trade was not as serious as it would have been in the early 16th century, for from the 1550s the Portuguese economy was increasingly sustained by wealth from another source, the sugar plantations of Brazil. During Philip III's reign the Dutch began to aspire to this area also, forming the West India Company which preyed on Iberian shipping and finally seized Bahia, the capital of Brazil, and surrounding sugar plantations. A joint Spanish-Portuguese expedition drove the invaders out in 1625.

Philip III failed to hold a Cortes in Portugal on his accession in 1598. He caused further offence by appointing Spaniards to important posts and visited the country only once, toward the end of his reign. A scheme of Lerma's to raise much-needed revenue by selling privileges to Portugal's New Christians

Below Velázquez' painting of *The Riding School* shows the young heir to the throne, Prince Baltasar Carlos (1629–46), being instructed in the equestrian arts. On the right, Olivares is handing a lance to a teacher – perhaps in order to pass it to his pupil – whilst the boy's proud parents look on from a balcony in the background. In a copy made in the artist's studio after Olivares' fall from power (*below left*), he has been painted out of the picture – surely deliberately. The act is reminiscent of the removal of Leon Trotsky from Lenin's side in edited versions of photographs of the Bolshevik Revolution issued during Stalin's dictatorship.

country largely failed to share in the intellectual and artistic efflorescence that was such an outstanding feature of Spain at this time. Part of the reason was that wealth was more evenly distributed than before, while the arts had not yet become an arena of patronage for the middle classes, whether urban or rural. But the removal of the royal house of Avis – previously a munificent central source of patronage – also took its toll, as did the drastic fall in the number of aristocratic families and palaces following the disastrous slaughter of El-Ksar-el-Kebir. Other Portuguese nobles gravitated toward the delights and honors furnished by the Madrid court and service to the Spanish monarchy. Furthermore, by the 1620s Portuguese writers were abandoning their native tongue and resorting to the use of Castilian.

Spain's foreign policy had serious consequences for Portuguese trade. After the defeat of the Armada, Philip II closed Portuguese ports to all English ships, thereby depriving Portugal of valuable trade. In 1594,

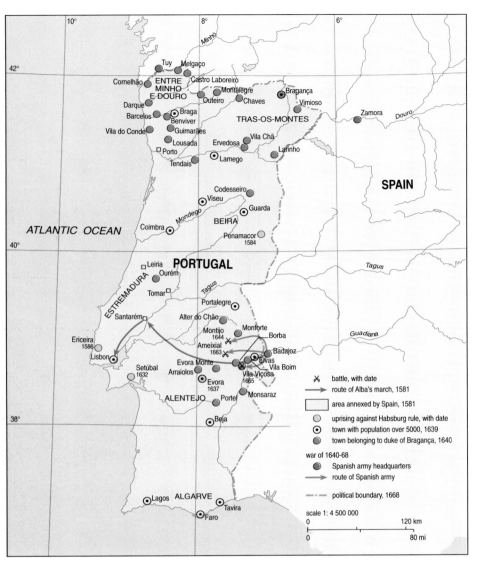

in the 1650s, João mortgaged the wealth of the country in his search for allies. In 1654 he secured a crucial treaty with the English Protectorate of Oliver Cromwell (1653–58). From this time on England became Portugal's firmest ally, a situation that brought economic and strategic benefits to both countries. In 1662, after the restoration of the monarchy, Charles II of England (1660–85) made a dynastic alliance with Portugal by marrying João's daughter, Catherine of Bragança (1638–1705). In return for a huge dowry, which included the cession of Bombay and Tangier to England, he sent English troops to help the Portuguese to victory over the Spanish (1663–65).

Decline and disillusion

The Catalan and Portuguese rebellions meant the end of the road for Olivares. Most of the Castilian ruling class had withdrawn their support. Only his own dependents – some able ministers among them – continued to back him. To Philip IV's dismay, the basis of government – which he had hoped to extend, incorporating talent from every part of the monarchy – had shrunk to a faction even smaller than Lerma's. After the Catalans had defeated the army sent to quell them, placing themselves under French rule rather than surrender, Philip insisted on taking personal command in Catalonia. He was literally in the saddle, while Olivares, once a superb horseman but now too fat and ill to ride, was carried around in his train. With Olivares away from Madrid, his faction split. The king finally dismissed him early in 1643.

French troops remained in Catalonia until 1659 when the Treaty of the Pyrenees, by which Roussillon was permanently ceded to France, marked the final collapse of the revolt. Many Catalans actually welcomed the peace, having found France an even less desirable master than Castile – which immediately restored all Catalonia's privileges. The turning point in the Portuguese war was the Spanish defeat at Ameixial (1663), but for Philip, a peace that conceded Portuguese independence quite simply meant eternal damnation. Thus he carried on a struggle that had bled Castile dry and indirectly ruined Spain's capacity to defend any other frontier. During the conflict, the population of Spain reached its lowest ebb, as did the flow of silver from America. Philip died amidst the resentful indifference of his people in September 1665, a few weeks after his last army of reconquest was smashed at Vila Viçosa.

Philip's will made his widow Mariana (1634–96) regent for their son Carlos (b.1661). She accepted Portugal's independence. Her hand was forced by the English, whose help was necessary to prevent Louis XIV of France (1643–1715) annexing the Spanish Netherlands. A further price of English support was recognition of their occupation of Jamaica (1667–70). Spain's rivals were now marauding freely in the Caribbean; in 1670 the Welsh adventurer Henry Morgan (1635–88) captured and sacked Panama, the central fortress of Spain's global communications. Ministers of Charles II of England plotted a deal with Louis XIV in which France would inherit all Spain's territories, while England would take over – at the stroke of a pen – the whole Atlantic empire. Though the plot came to nothing, it indicated the extent to which Spain had lost its international standing. With Philip IV's death, the Catholic empire initiated by Ferdinand and Isabella and completed by Philip II was effectively defunct.

Portugal under the Habsburgs
The duke of Alba's campaign to enforce Philip II's claim to the Portuguese throne in 1580 met with little resistance. Philip undertook to respect Portugal's rights, and for the first 20 years of Habsburg rule, Portugal enjoyed stability and relative prosperity. However, the 1609 truce with the Dutch led to increased competition from the Dutch East India Company in Asia, disrupting Portugal's trade with the Spice Islands and India. After 1621, Portugal – along with the other Spanish kingdoms – was called upon to make ever greater contributions to the renewed war in the Netherlands. Though Castile shared the costs of defending Brazil, the Portuguese regarded this as arising from self-interest: the Habsburgs allowed Portugal's Asian interests to decline. Discontent grew, leading to outright rebellion in 1640. The Portuguese claimant to the throne, the powerful duke of Bragança, headed the war of secession and Portuguese independence was assured by a series of victories. At the same time, the Portuguese succeeded in ejecting the Dutch from Brazil, much of which had been forcibly occupied since 1630.

aroused deep opposition from the Portuguese. Eventually all the privileges granted to New Christians were revoked, though not before substantial sums of money had been paid to Castile.

Portuguese discontent turned to outright rebellion during Philip IV's reign. Olivares' reforms directly contravened the Tomar agreement, leading to inconsequential uprisings against the Spanish in 1634 and 1637. The final straw came in 1640 when Olivares demanded Portuguese money and troops to fight the equally discontented Catalans. A group of conspirators persuaded the duke of Bragança, Portugal's wealthiest and most influential noble, to revive a dormant claim to the throne. A coup was launched and the duke was declared King João IV (1640–56) on 1 December 1640 in Lisbon. Though Portugal dates its independence from this moment, the fact was by no means assured. Philip IV was humiliated by the loss of the territory gained by his hero, Philip II, and dedicated the rest of his life to the recovery of Portugal. The result was a war of attrition that lasted almost 30 years. As a consequence, lands lying on both sides of the Portuguese-Castilian frontier were reduced to a virtual desert.

João was sustained by occasional French assistance, but his military resources were stretched to the limit by an extended campaign to defend Brazil from further Dutch depredations. Faced with the prospect of Spanish invasion once the Catalan revolt petered out

DYNASTICISM AND PRAGMATISM 1670–1812

The Habsburgs fade away

Philip IV's successor, Carlos II (1665–1700), the last of the Habsburg kings of Spain, was the end result of three consecutive quasi-incestuous marriages. He was chronically unhealthy: his grotesquely enlarged Habsburg jaw and tongue meant that he could not chew and thus properly digest his food, and in adolescence his immune system deteriorated to the point where any virus attack made him seriously ill. Whenever the doctors permitted him to leave his bed, Carlos preferred to spend time on his knees before the altar rather than in his study working. In such circumstances, a stunted body and mind are not surprising, but Carlos was not the catatonic idiot sometimes portrayed. By the time his illegitimate half-brother Don Juan José (1629–79) died, it was clear that Carlos would never father children and would thus be the last of his line. The Austrian Habsburgs expected imminently to claim the Spanish patrimony, but were constantly disappointed. Confounding all expectations, Carlos' reign lasted 35 years, above the European norm for the period, and he saw off many of those who had predicted his early demise, including his first wife, Marie Louise of Orléans (1662–89). But though Carlos was mostly in possession of his senses until the later stages of his life and was sometimes capable of intervening in government, he was never capable of giving sustained attention to it. Above all, he was easily swayed by any strong personality who could gain regular access to his presence.

Philip IV had tried to safeguard his son's interests by giving his widow Mariana executive powers in collaboration with a nominated junta. Mariana, however, was uncomfortable chairing a committee of powerful grandees, and resorted instead to the counsel of her Austrian Jesuit confessor, Everard Nithard (1607–81). The first foreigner to govern Spain since the early 16th century, Nithard was widely unpopular. In the face of threats of violent intervention from Don Juan José, Nithard was dismissed and sent into exile in 1669. After a brief interlude he was succeeded by a young Andalusian adventurer, Fernando de Valenzuela (1630–92), a very different character from Nithard, who succeeded in captivating Mariana and – for a time – Carlos.

Valenzuela was an insignificant figure compared with previous favorites such as Lerma, but since Mariana controlled the king, nobody could impede Valenzuela's rise to fame (or, at least, notoriety) and riches. When, in 1677, he finally overstepped the mark in his relations with the court nobility, they were reluctantly compelled to call upon Don Juan José. On reaching his fourteenth birthday in November 1675, the young king had attempted to have Don Juan José made chief minister, but had been forestalled by his mother. Now Don Juan José demanded nothing less than supreme power as his price for restoring political credibility. All was to come to nothing, however: Don Juan José died of a disabling illness only two years later.

For a short and unique period in its history, Spain

was now governed by members of the traditional aristocracy. Acting on the advice of his mother and his Francophile first wife, Carlos successively appointed two ministers – the duke of Medinaceli from 1680–85, and the count of Oropesa from 1685–91 – both of whom competently managed the monarchy's affairs. During the final decade of his reign, and of the century, Carlos was heavily influenced by his second queen, Maria Anna of Neuberg (1667–1740) who was the leading agent of the Austrian interest in Spain. Political power devolved to the regions in the persons of major grandee landowners, such as the Velasco family in Old Castile and the Enríquez family in Andalusia, who acted as lieutenants-general. The council of state was dominated by the duke of Montalto, "ruler" of New Castile, from 1691–96 – but the reality was that central government had virtually ceased to exist, with the result that the city and the court of Madrid

Above Claudio Coello (1561–1627) was the chief royal painter in the generation after Velázquez. Despite the strong influence of the latter's late work, Coello developed a personal style, if a rather gloomy one. His most celebrated work, *The Sacred Image*, shows Carlos II kneeling before the consecrated host – the moment that is at the center of Catholic ritual. Even military triumph is subsumed in worship: the references to Velázquez' *The Surrender of Breda* are unmistakable in the suite of courtiers grouped behind him and in the background range of candles. In the Escorial chapel today the tourist can see a larger-than-life-size reproduction (as well as the original), which winds down to reveal, in exact perspective, the actual physical setting of the scene depicted.

temporarily lost much of its political importance. Outraged citizens, whose economic well-being was adversely affected by the loss of status and price subsidies, expressed their disillusionment with the Habsburgs in a series of riots.

The nature of government
For all that Mariana, a Habsburg by birth as well as marriage, represented the legitimate authority of the dynasty, the factional politics of Carlos' reign demonstrated that during a minority Spain could not be governed without at least the complaisance of the grandees. These belonged to about 40 elite families (reduceable to perhaps a dozen interconnected interests) who traced their descent from medieval times, but despite their regional power and court magnificence, many were bankrupt, and depended heavily on the patronage and legal protection of the crown for their survival. Divided by historic but nonetheless bitter vendettas, the grandees had come closest to group action over the removal of Olivares in 1643. To them, any royal favorite was automatically suspect, and Mariana's particular choices were, to say the least, unfortunate: a haughty foreign priest and a rampantly ambitious upstart who, by demanding ever-greater rewards, threatened to deprive the grandees of lucrative posts that they regarded as theirs by hereditary right. The fact that in 1677 a majority of grandees pledged support for Don Juan José, whom they disliked and suspected, indicated their desperation. In fact, within a year of his takeover, many nobles had expressed remorse for their action and secretly made their peace with Mariana.

Between 1677 and 1691, Spain's aristocratic government tentatively experimented with reforms similar to those of Olivares 50 years earlier. Don Juan José

started the process by reducing tax burdens, especially on the poor of Madrid, and commissioning a junta to report on the state of commerce (1679). His successors performed the immensely difficult task of stabilizing the currency, and began to investigate the church with the aim of reducing the number of vocations. The tendency toward the regional devolution of political power – initiated by Juan José who demanded a free hand as viceroy of Aragon after 1669 – would have been less to Olivares' taste. The reforms themselves were marginal, and certainly did not form part of any clear program for change. All the same, the willingness to intervene in the life of the nation in areas distinct from war – even where it might challenge the immemorial privileges of the corporations – represented a decisive step toward the more thoroughgoing reformism of the next century.

Collectively, the grandees had no common political ideology, but most were united in the desire to maintain the Catholic empire intact. They opposed the loss of Portugal, and were keen to reject both French attempts to dominate the Low Countries and Anglo-Dutch ambitions to plunder the Americas. Carlos II himself agreed with these sentiments, reacting over and over again with defensive campaigning when Louis XIV of France – scheming through military might and political machination to win for France the Spanish inheritance on the death of the childless Carlos II – attempted prematurely to seize parts of it. Louis had already captured the standard of *reputación* – which the French called *la gloire* – from Spain to become the darling of Catholic Europe, while lack of funds forced Carlos to shelter behind the protection of armies and fleets hired from Protestant England, Holland and Sweden.

Economy and society
The lowest point of Spain's 17th-century economic depression was reached in the 1650s. However, some regions had already started on the road to recovery a generation earlier. For example, agricultural productivity and population levels had begun to rise in the northern coastal regions, despite the prolonged demands of wars against Catalonia and Portugal, and Bilbao had already embarked on its great age of commercial growth. Even some of the previously blighted towns of León and Old Castile were making small gains in the 1640s. Recovery was far more spectacular on the Mediterranean coast, particularly in Catalonia. After the reconciliation between Catalonia and Castile, initiated by Philip IV and completed by Don Juan José in the 1650s, a dynamic phase of commercial and industrial development was instigated in Barcelona and Tarragona, and agricultural productivity, boosted by the introduction of new crops such as maize from central America and of new techniques, also rose. Between 1650 and 1700 Catalonia's population leapt from less than 250,000 to over 400,000. In the 1690s, a Catalan bank became the first native broker to the crown for more than a century.

However, such economic growth was mainly restricted to the peripheries of the country. The agrarian heartland continued to stagnate, while the once-flourishing textile and metallurgical industries of cities such as Cuenca, Segovia and Toledo almost completely collapsed during the 1670s. Much of the following decade was disastrous: the southwest was hit by crop failure and famine, followed by widespread epidemics of influenza and typhus. When, in 1684, the

English diarist Samuel Pepys (1633–1703) spent a week in Seville in a continuous downpour, the capital of Andalusia appeared to him the most poverty-stricken and miserable place in Christendom. By the end of the century Atlantic trade was beginning to improve, silver imports were buoyant and foreign entrepreneurs were flocking to the ports, but the recovery was tenuous and limited. On the death of Carlos II the Habsburgs would leave Spain no more and no less prosperous than they had found it. However, this would prove nowhere near adequate for the altered circumstances of the 18th century.

The effects of empire

Throughout the 17th century, the Spanish continued to explore and colonize the Americas, expanding northward from Mexico into Texas and California and southward into Chile and the River Plate basin. Colonists were in high demand, the more so because local Amerindian populations were often decimated by the introduction of diseases to which they had no immunity. Emigration was officially allowed to take place at the rate of about 2,000 people a year, but it is highly probable that many more left Spain clandestinely, particularly during the worst periods of economic depression. Since most emigrants were mature males, the Spanish population failed to rise.

The effects of the American discoveries on Spanish society and culture were very gradual; indeed, for most ordinary people, excluded from a share in colonial wealth and uninterested in its challenges to knowledge, the impact of America was almost negligible: only a few imports such as maize had any lasting or substantial effect. While it is true that many Castilian words have their origins in otherwise defunct Amerindian languages, the contribution of the colonies was to be found mostly in specialist works of navigation, cartography, botany and anthropology. Real or pretended descendants of the last Aztec emperor, Montezuma, occasionally presented themselves at court, exotically attired and seeking handouts. A more substantial figure, Garcilaso de la Vega (1540–1616), the son of a Peruvian noblewoman and a celebrated *conquistador*, achieved fame as a chronicler in Castilian of the culture and history of his native lands. Yet, despite the prolonged academic debate over the nature of "the Indians" in the 16th century, the first literary treatment of an American theme was a play by Lope de Vega, *Brasil Restituido* (1625), produced to celebrate the victory over the Dutch that prevented them from annexing Bahia.

The effects of empire were most powerfully felt in Andalusia, whose economy was both shaped and sustained by American demand. Though the major commercial collapse of the 1640s began the process whereby Seville eventually lost its monopoly of American trade to Cádiz, Andalusian culture continued to reflect the long and fruitful connection with the American colonies. The indigenous music of Andalusia – which we now know as flamenco – was strongly influenced by dance rhythms imported from Hispaniola and Cuba. These seeped into both popular songs and the music of the court. It was during the second half of the 17th century that the Spanish lute evolved into the familiar guitar. The first great exponent of the new instrument, Gaspar Sanz (c. 1640–c. 1690), transformed Latin-American dance rhythms into music acceptable in the salon. In Madrid, Sanz gave guitar lessons to both Don Juan José and the English ambas-

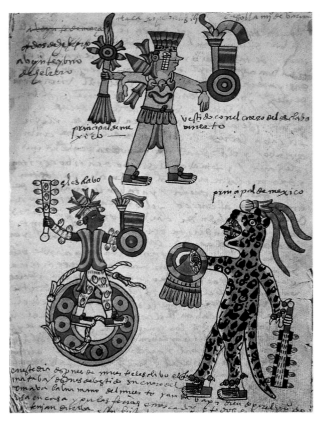

Left Though the Spanish conquerors of Mexico were impressed by the exotic glamor and wealth that surrounded Montezuma, they shrank in horror from the Aztecs' religion and customs. The Spanish writer who has annotated this post-Columbian Aztec manuscript depicting magical rites explains that the figure at the top, a leader or chieftain, is wearing the flayed skin of the slave pictured below him; the figure on the right has donned the skin of a jaguar to perform a wardance.

sador, Lord Sandwich. On his journeys through Italy he passed the new rhythms into the mainstream of European music, with the result that the refined musical repertoire of the enlightened European courts of the 18th century included such forms as the chaconne, pavane and folla, all of which had their origins in the everyday entertainment of the pre-Columbian Caribs.

Questions of succession

In Portugal, the future of the restored Bragança dynasty was finally assured when Spain recognized the country's independence in 1668. On João IV's death his widow acted as regent for the weak-minded Afonso VI (b. 1643; reigned 1656–83) until 1662. Like Carlos II of Spain, Afonso was also weak in body, vulnerable to court intrigue, and childless. The scheming courts of both kings were much preoccupied with securing the succession of their royal houses. From 1662, the count of Castelo Melhor (1636–1720) governed capably on Afonso's behalf, but was removed in 1667 as the result of an intrigue between Afonso's French wife, Maria Francisca of Savoy-Nemours (1646–83), and his brother Pedro (b.1648).

With Castelo Melhor out of the way, Afonso was at the mercy of the court. Maria Francisca locked herself in a convent, asking for an annulment of her marriage and to be allowed to return to France – together with her large dowry. Alarmed advisers persuaded Afonso to stand down in favor of his brother in order to secure the royal succession. The unfortunate king became a virtual prisoner almost as soon as he had signed the agreement that made his brother prince regent. In January 1668 the three estates of the Portuguese Cortes at Lisbon supported Afonso's removal but asked that Maria Francisca should stay "both for the great love these realms bear to her great virtues and for the necessity of succession" – though the threat of having to repay her dowry may have more powerfully influenced their wish for her to remain.

Above For most of the 17th century, Spanish music remained highly conservative and church-based. Not until late in the reign of Carlos II did signs of innovation, and even daring, begin to appear in stage works and other secular forms of entertainment drawing on popular dance and song: Gaspar Sanz, in particular, popularized the new instrument of the guitar. This painting, of a court musician earlier in the century who is providing the continuo accompaniment to a church choir, may represent either Mateo Romero, Philip IV's *maestro de capella*, or his organ-master, Mateo de Avila.

Once Afonso's marriage was annulled, Pedro promptly married Maria Francisca. The Portuguese succession was duly secured with the birth of their daughter Isabel in 1669. In the same year, Afonso, previously confined to his rooms in Lisbon, was shipped to the Azores. However, after the discovery of a plot to restore him in 1674, he was brought back to Portugal to live out the rest of his days a miserable prisoner in the royal palace at Sintra. On his death in 1683, his brother finally became King Pedro II (1683–1706). Maria Francisca died three months later, and in 1687 Pedro married again. His second wife succeeded in producing a male heir, the future João V, in 1689 and had four more children before her death in 1699. In 1697 the Cortes was called simply to recognize João as heir to the throne. Thereafter it was not called again: the age of Portuguese absolutism had begun.

The final years of Carlos II's reign were feverishly occupied with the disputed succession to the Spanish throne. The vacancy was of as much moment outside Spain as within it, for other European states saw it as an opportunity to extend their powers, or at least to share in the possible partition of the Spanish empire. After the death of Don Juan José – the favored candidate of England and the Netherlands, who were equally opposed to any extension of French or Austrian power – the two remaining candidates were the Bourbon Philip of Anjou (1683–1746), the teenage grandson of Louis XIV of France, and the Habsburg Archduke Charles of Austria (1685–1740), second son of the Holy Roman Emperor Leopold I (1640–1705). After a lifetime's resistance to the pretensions of the French, Carlos finally capitulated and left his entire inheritance to Philip of Anjou. His decision was made for sound reasons. Philip's claim was legally little worse than that of Archduke Charles, while France, through its great military strength and geographical proximity to Spain, was better equipped to prevent the breakup of the Spanish possessions in Europe, and preserve the integrity of the empire, than was Austria. Carlos was under no illusions; he knew that the succession would be fiercely contested by whichever side had been overlooked.

European war

Carlos died in November 1700. Philip was immediately proclaimed king of Spain in Versailles, crossing over the Pyrenees shortly afterward to take possession of his new throne as Philip V of Spain (1700–46). His *camarilla* (cabinet) of French advisers rapidly depleted the fund of goodwill toward him; Spain's ruling class, in particular, had expected an alliance of equals, not an outright takeover by their old adversaries.

Louis XIV, however, regarded Bourbon Spain as an extension of France, to be ruled indirectly from Versailles for France's political and commercial benefit: he refused to exclude Philip from the line of succession to the French throne. The threat posed by his expansionist ambitions drew much of western Europe into the ensuing War of the Spanish Succession (1701–13), fought principally in Germany, the Low Countries and Italy. At first, Portugal tried to remain neutral in the conflict, though when the Grand Alliance of England, Austria and the Netherlands declared war on France, Pedro II was forced to reconsider his position. By the Methuen Treaty (1703), Portugal adhered to the Grand Alliance in return for British and Dutch guarantees to defend the country against French attack. The treaty also established the exchange of port wine for British textiles that was to become the basis of Portuguese-British trade.

In Spain, Castile remained loyal to its new king. Catalonia, on the other hand, was deeply wary of the centralist policies of the Bourbons. When the Grand Alliance landed armies in Portugal and Catalonia, threatening the Bourbon-held center of the peninsula from both flanks, Philip despatched troops of his own, marching them through Aragon to reach Catalonia. At this blatant violation of its ancient *fueros*, Aragon defected to the Austrian side. Though other Spanish regions rallied to Philip, only French arms could keep him on his throne: Castile had exhausted its military resources. In return for military aid, Louis XIV expected to be arbiter of Spanish Bourbon policy, both at home and abroad.

In the early years of his reign, Philip V was influenced in political matters by his wife, Maria Luisa of Savoy (1688–1714). She was manipulated by her chief confidante, the redoubtable French princess des Ursins (1642–1722), who in turn was advised by the French ambassador, Jean-Jacques Amelot (1689–1749), a dynamic careerist of lowly origins. All three were directly controlled by Louis XIV. Louis attributed much of his success in France to his reduction of the French nobility to a purely decorative political role and, by contrast, considered that the pitiful decadence of the Habsburgs had been caused by their failure to do the same. His first aim, therefore, was to provide Spain with an efficient, centralized administration along French lines. This meant nothing less than a social-political revolution – at least at the top – to exclude the traditional aristocracy from government and create a new governing class. In fact, Spain's nobility had only recently achieved real power, in Carlos II's reign, and from their viewpoint this was merely a belated restoration of the proper order of things. Previously, under active autocrats such as Philip II and

Philip IV, they had exercised their rights of advice and consent in only a limited and intermittent fashion through membership of the royal councils. These bodies were anathema to Louis XIV, who believed that their cumbersome post-medieval procedures were incompatible with efficient government.

The principal architects of reform, besides Amelot, were Jean-Henri-Louis Orry (1652–1719), who was an inspired finance minister, and Melchor de Macanaz (1670–1760), a Spanish lawyer. The grandees were blatantly humiliated by Amelot's political reforms, which suppressed the councils and replaced them with a cabinet of secretaries directly responsible to the king. Yet, at the same time, the grandees were expected to pay the huge tax contributions designed by Orry to fund the war effort. Understandably, their loyalty wavered. When Archduke Charles landed in Barcelona in 1705, several dozen grandees slipped away to join him, including the Admiral of Castile, the dukes of Infantado and Medinaceli, and the count of Oropesa. These men contributed little to the Habsburg cause apart from the luster of their names; in fact their defection unintentionally contributed to Philip's cause. Though Philip wisely refrained from outright confiscation of their palaces and estates, he was enabled by their absence to draw freely on their wealth at several critical points in the conflict.

The fortunes of battle oscillated wildly. On two occasions, the forces of the Grand Alliance entered Madrid and proclaimed the restoration of the Habsburgs, but were subsequently forced to withdraw. Even after Philip's victory over Aragon at the battle of Almansa in 1707, often regarded as the turning-point in the war, Catalonia continued to wage a tenacious struggle against the Franco-Castilian armies. The Catalian repulse of one incursion on 11 September 1711 is still celebrated as the national festival of Catalonia (La Diada). However, the real turning point in the war was not military but political (and accidental): the death of the Holy Roman Emperor Joseph I (1678–1711). He was succeeded by his brother, Archduke Charles, who now ruled as the Emperor Charles VI, an event that completely altered the international situation. For Britain and Holland, a Europe dominated by Austria was only a slightly lesser evil than one dominated by France. They withdrew their support for Charles' Spanish claim, leaving Catalonia bereft of allies. Philip V's armies closed in and reduced its defenses to rubble, despite ferocious resistance.

Regional opposition to the centralizing policies of Madrid was to be a recurrent theme in Spanish history. Yet despite the tragic crushing of Catalonia, the war was not fundamentally inspired by internal differences – the peninsula became the arena for political struggles that had their origins in the far-off courts of Europe. Whereas the Spanish had once sent their feared *tercios* tramping across Europe, Europe's soldiery now bivouacked in the ruined castles of Castile. By the Peace of Utrecht (1713), Philip V retained all of metropolitan Spain on condition that he renounced his rights to the French crown and divested Spain of its European possessions. France consolidated earlier gains in Franche-Comté and Alsace, Austria acquired the Spanish Netherlands and Luxembourg, Milan, Sardinia and Naples, while Britain gained a foothold in the Mediterranean with the vital strategic bases of Gibraltar and Minorca. Though Philip and his successors refused to accept it, Spanish hegemony in Europe was well and truly a thing of the past.

Above This portrait of the founder of the Spanish Bourbon line, Philip V, is a suitable compromise between French and Spanish styles of royal portraiture. It is by the French painter Hyacinthe Rigaud (1659–1743), who made many ostentatious studies of Louis XIV. By contrast, the new king of Spain appears in the modest black garb and almost clerical collar of his Habsburg predecessors, so different from the French style, yet his physical stance is assertive and lively, as befitted his nickname, *El Animoso*.

The Nueva Planta

Philip V and his ministers had been infuriated by Aragon's rebellion against central authority. When the rebels were defeated at Almansa in 1707, Philip took advantage of his victory to suppress the *fueros* that had caused so much trouble to Madrid governments. He abolished the provincial assemblies, decreeing that the kingdoms of Aragon and Valencia would henceforth be ruled on the same footing as Castile (where the Cortes, which had not been called since 1665, was already effectively defunct). In 1716, with Catalonia prostrate at his feet, Philip pressed his advantage to publish the *Nueva Planta* ("new foundation") of government, abolishing economic and legal distinctions between Castile and its defeated neighbors. To provide a general framework, the French system of royal *intendants* (officers appointed to oversee the conduct of local officials) was introduced to all parts of Spain, with hundreds of Castilian functionaries moving into municipal and local government in the reconquered provinces. They were able to arbitrate in military as well as fiscal matters, and thus were much more powerful than the old Castilian officials, the *corregidores*.

Spain had become – theoretically at least – a unitary state governed from Madrid. However, while the *Nueva Planta* went a long way toward achieving the centralization that was considered essential for the restoration of Spanish power and prosperity, it fell short of abolishing the kingdoms and annexing them to Castile: in the strict constitutional sense there was still no "king of Spain". Moreover, when the abolition of economic boundaries was extended to the Basque Country and Navarre in 1720, popular opposition was so fierce that Philip was obliged to give way. The so-called "exempted provinces" retained their own customs-posts and other fiscal rights until the 1870s, becoming bastions of anticentralist feeling. The destruction of local liberties was bitterly resented by contemporary and subsequent generations of Catalans. Yet without the *Nueva Planta*, it is doubtful whether Catalonia could have achieved the economic growth that it did, for integration opened up large new markets both within Spain and in America.

In 1714, after the death of Maria Luisa, Philip took as his second wife the strong-willed Isabella Farnese of Parma (1692–1766). Even before then, the links between Versailles and Madrid were breaking down. As French influence on the new regime grew steadily weaker, so did the motivation for radical reform. One victim of this change of direction was Macanaz, who was condemned by the Inquisition and imprisoned. In earlier days, Philip's high spirits and energy had earned him the nickname of *El Animoso* ("the lively"), but as his reign progressed he became less and less active and – especially in the last 20 years – was overtaken by hypochondria, religious mania and general torpor. In 1724 he actually abdicated (at the age of 40) in favor of his eldest son, who was duly proclaimed king of Spain as Luis I. After a comic-opera reign lasting less than 8 months, the new king fell victim to smallpox, and Philip was reluctantly persuaded to assume the crown again.

Philip was always content to leave the business of government to Isabella, who became the most powerful influence on the selection of ministers. Her favorite was the Italian cardinal Giulio Alberoni (1664–1752), who had helped to negotiate her marriage to Philip. He was aided by an energetic team of ministers from a variety of national backgrounds, but mostly trained under the formidable Orry. Early Bourbon government was fluid and pragmatic, perhaps in reaction to the perceived rigidity of the Habsburg system. Changes in procedure made by one minister were, as often as not, set aside by his successor. The titles and functions of government officials changed so frequently that government policy seemed driven by the desire to strengthen the ephemeral position of one particular figure rather than to put through a coherent plan of reform. For the entire 18th century, there was no recognized "chief minister", though for long periods the preponderant influence of a single adviser can be detected. Alberoni himself never held any formal post in government, though he acted as chief executive. Secretaries of state who enjoyed royal favor were allowed to cut across spheres of government in terms of influence or even initiative. Early ministers such as Melchor de Macanaz and José Patiño (1667–1736) – both of whom had the benefit of experience as regional *intendants* – introduced a new level of professionalism and responsibility into the work of government. Though they could not resolve some longstanding problems, in particular the antiquated tax system, they provided the atmosphere in which Spain recovered from the ravages of war.

Dynastic ambitions and the Mediterranean

The Peace of Utrecht had stripped the Spanish monarchy of much of its former power in international affairs. Philip, who had accepted the terms of the treaty under duress, remained convinced of his inalienable moral right to revise them, by force if necessary; as a result his reign was punctuated by intermittent wars and continual changes of allegiance. The religious imperatives that had driven Spanish expansionism during the previous century were fading as a motive for political action. In Bourbon Spain, statehood and dynastic ambition replaced crusading zeal as the new, but equally powerful, motive for territorial acquisition.

Spain's aggressive policy in Italy was largely dictated by Isabella. She had a growing family to place – Spain was reserved for her husband's children by his first wife – and schemed tirelessly to gain Italian kingdoms and principalities for her sons. It could be argued that southern Italy, having been associated with Aragon for so long, was as much "Spanish" as "Italian"; it certainly had no historical or cultural affiliation with its new ruler, Austria. In any case, Philip actively supported the Italian policy, if he was not its prime mover. The king was a veteran of the hard-fought Italian campaigns of the War of Spanish Succession and, in middle age, seemed able to rouse himself from torpor only by the drives of sex and war – apparently in that order.

Alberoni initiated the new phase of foreign policy in 1717 with naval expeditions that conquered Sardinia and made a decisive landing in Sicily. However, the major obstacle to Spanish recovery in Europe became immediately obvious. No adjustment to the arrangements of the Peace of Utrecht could be made without the acquiescence of Britain. British possession of Gibraltar and Minorca, and the superiority of its navy, had turned the western Mediterranean into a "British lake". This point was firmly made when the British destroyed Alberoni's new fleet in a single day's work at Cape Passaro in 1718. Spain scored a remarkable victory against an attacking British fleet at Cartagena in 1741, but this was exceptional.

War, economy and society

In pursuing any active policy abroad, Spain had two alternatives: to collaborate with France – inevitably in a junior capacity – giving the combined fleets a fighting chance of defeating or neutralizing the British navy; or to try to challenge Britain alone. The Bourbon government vacillated between these strategies, but worked with energy and consistency to establish an effective navy. This objective was so important that it conditioned economic and fiscal, as well as military, policy. The resources of the state continued to be expended largely on warfare; as under the Habsburgs, international relations not only dictated the pace of domestic political events but also provided the main

Below A series of 18th-century decorative tiles from Catalonia illustrate scenes from the daily life of the countryside and depict everyday crafts such as barrel-making and basket-weaving.

Above João V built his marble palace-monastery at Mafra in imitation of the Escorial. The entrance to the church stands at the center of its western facade, which is 244 meters long. The vast rectangular block is a monument to the wealth that flowed into Portugal from the goldmines of Brazil in the early 18th century. Its scale is overwhelming; its greatest glory the rococo library that is filled with thousands of volumes. The French philosopher Voltaire nevertheless poured rationalist scorn on the project.

meseta recovered much of their lost prosperity. By mid-century an articulate middle class, increasingly independent of the local nobility and the influence of the clergy, was beginning to emerge from among families engaged in trade and in the professions, particularly law. In major ports such as Bilbao and Barcelona, the merchants' guilds not only expanded commercial opportunities but also began to influence culture and education. Such groups often formed local branches of a national organization, the Economic Society of Friends of the Nation, which fostered growth in many areas of enterprise and education.

Peace and prosperity

The Portuguese economy had already begun to recover from the strain of wars with Spain during the reign of Pedro II. His finance minister, the count of Ericeira (1632–90), took measures to control spending and built up national industries in glass, textiles and salt production. After Ericeira's death, the need for such economic prudence was swept away by the discovery of large gold deposits in the *Minas Gerais* (General Mines) of Brazil. Brazilian gold and, after 1728, diamonds funded an era of great prosperity in Portugal, bringing its rulers vast revenues and absolute independence of parliaments and domestic taxes. The aristocracy did nothing to restrain the growth of royal power, contenting themselves instead with petty intrigues and diplomatic appointments and honors. Furthermore, the country's strongly developing alliance with Britain, enshrined in the Methuen Treaty, gave Portugal military security that virtually guaranteed peace along with prosperity.

Unlike Spain, regional separation was never a strong force in Portugal, and João V (1706–50), Pedro's successor, was in the fortunate position of being an absolute ruler who was both rich and universally accepted. He modeled his court on that of Louis XIV of France, though – in contrast to Louis – João was a reserved, docile man who, while not without vanity, was content to rule peaceably at home and raise monuments to God and the Bragança dynasty. He did not expect his services to the church to go unrewarded by the papacy, however. In 1716 the archbishop of Lisbon was made a patriarch and – after much engineering and a short break with Rome – a cardinal. João himself was given the title "Most Faithful Majesty" in recognition of the Portuguese contribution to the defeat of the Muslim Turks at the battle of Matapan (1717).

As a result of Portugal's alliance with Austria during the War of the Spanish Succession, João had married Maria Ana of Austria (1683–1754) in 1708. When their son died at the age of two, João vowed to build a great monastery to rival the Escorial in Spain if God would grant him an heir. In 1712 he selected Mafra in the countryside northwest of Lisbon as the site; a baby, a daughter, was born two years later. Work on this magnificent project, which – like the Escorial – incorporated a palace as well as a monastery and church, finally began in 1717 and took 18 years to complete. The construction absorbed enormous amounts of money, and workmen often went unpaid for months at a time. The rooms, numbering more than a thousand, were lavishly furnished. Formal gardens surrounded the splendid baroque edifice.

The king's largesse was not restricted to religious endowments. He also rebuilt in ornate style the library at the university of Coimbra and founded a Royal

engine for social and economic change.

The wars of the Bourbons, however, were less prolonged, intense and extensive than those of the Habsburgs. Partly for this reason, the economy was better able to withstand the cost of war, and, indeed, staged something of a recovery. The pro-Habsburg grandees were not allowed to return from exile until the mid 1720s, and in the meantime the crown had allowed thousands of tenancies to be granted, which brought good land (much of it previously reserved for hunting) under the plow. The phased abolition of privileges held by the powerful sheep-farmers' guild, the *Mesta*, though not completed until later in the century, also increased the amount of land under cultivation. On the periphery of the cereal lands of the *meseta* a great diversity of crops such as rice, maize and citrus fruits were grown, and livestock farming was increased. By the 1720s, Spain was self-sufficient in foodstuffs for the first time in well over a century. Nevertheless, the countryside was still the scene of great poverty, especially in Andalusia.

The abolition of customs barriers (the *puertos secos*, or "dry ports") within Castile and between Castile, Catalonia, Aragon and Valencia boosted economic recovery by opening up new internal markets. As a result, the great market towns of the central

Academy of History. During his reign major collections of Portuguese grammar, poetry and history appeared, and the Portuguese were encouraged to go abroad to study. New hospitals and factories were built at this time, but the most impressive engineering feat of all was the construction of the Aqueduct of Free Waters. Commissioned by the city fathers of Lisbon between 1732 and 1748 to carry drinking water from the hills outside the city, it contained 109 arches and was 18.5 kilometers long. Many of the capital's street fountains also date from this period.

The *castrato* and the *catastro*

In Spain, the reign of Philip V's son, Fernando VI (1746–59), also brought a period of stability. In 1748 the treaty of Aix-la-Chapelle ended the war of the Austrian Succession (1740–48) and strengthened Spain's position in Italy. In any case, Fernando took none of his father's pleasure in war. He married Barbara of Bragança (1711–58), João V's daughter, and shared his Portuguese queen's love of the arts, particularly music. The celebrated operatic *castrato*, Carlo Farinelli (1705–82), possessor of what was widely regarded as the most beautiful singing voice ever heard, was the inseparable companion of the Spanish king and queen. It was his patronage as much as theirs that stimulated a superb national revival in music. Barbara of Bragança was an accomplished musician and friend of Domenico Scarlatti (1685–1757), the Neapolitan-born composer. He accompanied her from Lisbon to Madrid and wrote most of his keyboard sonatas for her. They were among the most advanced music of their time, incorporating popular dance rhythms and even adapting the sound of the guitar to the harpsichord. Scarlatti's pupil, the Catalan Antonio Soler (1729–83), took these developments even farther, providing a link between the Spanish baroque and classical periods in music.

Fernando – lacking intelligence and public poise – had no interest in the business of government. Nevertheless his reign gave Spain a beneficent decade of peace. In this climate his minister the marquis of Ensenada (1702–81), launched a series of reforms aimed at improving the organization and overall efficiency of the Bourbon state. These changes differed substantially from those of the previous reign, which had been obsessed with central government, regional administration, and the organization of the armed services. Ensenada, whose coherent, comprehensive program for reform – the first since that of Olivares – was presented to Fernando shortly after his accession in 1746, set out initially to record the resources of the nation. To this end he decreed a *catastro* (or tax-census) in 1749. By charting the distribution of both numbers and wealth in the population, Ensenada hoped to introduce fiscal reforms based on personal income, not expenditure. This would free mortgaged capital at the top, encouraging productive labor at the bottom.

Though the census was duly carried out, the unitary tax structure it was supposed to bring into being was opposed by the vested interests of the nobility and the clergy, and consequently shelved. Nevertheless, crown revenues benefited from the expansion of the domestic economy, and there was considerable investment in the strategic industries – arms and uniform manufacture, naval dockyards and above all shipbuilding. Inevitably these activities tended to be based around the peninsula's periphery, particularly in the three official state arsenals of El Ferrol, Cádiz and Cartagena.

However, improvements in communications – roads, bridges and canals – brought some benefits to the central regions.

One historian has described Ensenada's reforms as "Spain's first modernization program". Undoubtedly its greatest success lay in producing a navy that was technologically abreast of its potential adversaries and not too deficient in size compared with them. Yet, despite important advances in the powers and organization of the treasury, Ensenada was unable to achieve a great deal in terms of fiscal improvement, and effective social reform was still hardly even on the horizon at his fall in 1754.

Ensenada's census had revealed substantial gains in population – largely as a result of peace – particularly in the economically buoyant regions of Catalonia and the Basque Country. By the end of Fernando's reign, the population finally exceeded its previous peak in the late 16th century. At the same time, the census had exposed the existence of a huge underclass (more than one in four of the population) of agricultural laborers living on the edge of subsistence. In the northwest, inheritance and tenure laws had resulted in an extreme subdivision of landholdings into tiny plots (*minifundia*) that could scarcely sustain the families who worked them. At the other extreme, the huge, inefficient estates (*latifundia*) of the south were owned by largely absentee landlords. Employing only a small permanent staff, the *latifundia* survived by exploiting huge armies of landless laborers, hired and fired on a daily basis during the busy periods of the year. During the slack seasons, whole rural communities lived in conditions of near-starvation. The large landowners took the best land, forcing peasant farmers onto marginal plots where they endured frequent crop failures and high rents.

Faction and power

Against the Bourbon reformers stood the deep-rooted and highly conservative influence of the old nobility. Though they had lost all hereditary claim to places in government, they continued to gain office, ostensibly by virtue of their education. This did not mean they had become an intellectual elite, and even less that royal administration was a career open to talent. Most members of the middle and higher levels of the civil service were graduates of the *Colegios Mayores* ("Greater Schools") the socially rather than academically prestigious universities of Salamanca and Alcalá de Henares. Originally, many had belonged to the minor nobility (*hidalguía*), but as the *hidalgos* moved higher in the social scale, they became almost indistinguishable from the grandee class above them, with revitalizing effects on the nobility. Moreover, the nobility – largely educated by the Society of Jesus and choosing Jesuits for their confessors – had from the late 17th century onward come to form a close-knit group firmly allied to the enormously powerful Jesuit interest in Spain.

Their political adversaries, the men of the *Nueva Planta*, were in one sense merely a fresh generation of *hidalgos*. Unlike earlier generations, however, the new men were often products of authentically bourgeois backgrounds, instinctively opposed to corporate and private privilege. They increasingly identified the church – and the Jesuits in particular – as the custodians of an obsolete order. Naturally, none of the new men refused the ennoblement and wealth that sprang from royal favor. Tensions between the two factions

Right In the great age of the Grand Tour, when the flower of the young nobility of northern maritime Europe flocked south to France and Italy, the Iberian peninsula was completely ignored. One reason for this was the parlous state of its roads and communications. Despite sporadic attempts to improve matters, tracks were frequently unpassable and roadside hospitality primitive. Furthermore, band's still infested the countryside – especially mountain regions such as the Basque country. In this painting by Leonardo Alenza, a miserable traveler is set upon by nocturnal footpads as he approaches the safety of a typical Basque *venta* (rural tavern) at the end of a day's exhausting journey.

crystallized during Fernando's reign in a power struggle between Ensenada – a commoner turned marquis – and José de Carvajal y Lancaster (1698–1754), a Castilian grandee who claimed descent from the English royal house of Lancaster. The protagonists symbolized what was steadily becoming a struggle for fundamental political attitudes and beliefs as well as mere factional interests. Fernando refused to endorse either group, but since his own confessor was a Jesuit of noted orthodoxy, the conservative sympathies of the king were obvious. Both ministers were removed from office in 1754 (Carvajal by his death, Ensenada for his anti-Jesuit sympathies), leaving the issue to be resolved in the reign of Carlos III (1759–88).

Suppression of the Jesuits

Carlos was a mature, vigorous and abstemious man who, as the reformist king of Naples and Sicily since 1734, was already an experienced ruler. At last the movement for political reform had secured leadership from the center. While on his way to Madrid in 1760, Carlos granted concessions to the citizens of Catalonia and Aragon that softened some of the most sharply resented aspects of earlier centralism. Once in the capital, he dismissed the favorite Farinelli from the court and released the veteran leader of reform, Melchor de

Macanaz, from prison. The focus of reform switched back to the political and legalistic aspects of Spanish life and away from the fuller vision projected by Ensenada. Moreover, for the opening period of the reign, reform was distorted by the intense struggle against the Jesuits.

Carlos himself was no liberal, but a paternalistic, strong-minded puritan who loathed the Jesuits for their alleged encouragement of lax moral standards amongst the aristocracy, and suspected them of undermining the prerogatives of absolutism. Yet he was politically adroit compared with most of his predecessors. This was perhaps most evident in the fact that he was prepared to place long-term confidence in two successive competent and hard-working chief ministers, the marquis Grimaldi (1720–86) from 1766 to 1777, and the count of Floridablanca (1728–1808) from 1777 to 1792.

The first crisis of Carlos' reign came in March 1766, when without warning, Madrid erupted in a sequence of riots that had all the superficial characteristics of a premature French Revolution. The simple probability is that the inflationary pressures of war and taxation, combined with a series of unusually severe harvests from 1760–63, had engendered discontent. It is notable that the outbreaks took place during the spring, the season when food prices reached their highest in the conditions of pre-industrial Europe. Yet the mob's resentment was focused almost exclusively upon the unfortunate figure of the marquis of Squillace (c. 1741–85). This hated foreigner, who had been Carlos' principal leader of reform in Naples, had foolishly attempted to regulate the dress and other customs of the citizens of Madrid. In particular, he banned the wide-brimmed sombrero and the long *capa* worn as a protection against the sun and wind that constantly besiege that city, believing that they were an aid to criminal behavior.

Perhaps this insult was used as a spark to light the tinder of grievance by some obscurely motivated group or groups – by the antireform nobility, by supporters of the fallen minister Ensenada, even (indirectly) by Jesuit intrigue. Whatever the case, only Squillace's house and the royal palaces were the targets of the mob, and when trouble spread to various provincial capitals, in only one of them (Zaragoza) did protest take on a violently antiproprietorial character. The almost unanimous cry was the immemorial one of "Long live the king but down with his evil ministers". The crisis was overcome by rapid measures to ameliorate the food shortage, followed by a powerful crackdown on further disorder (20,000 troops were brought into the capital). Squillace returned to Naples. The Madrid riots proved an isolated and even bizarre episode, but they provided Carlos' new chief minister Grimaldi and his main assistant, Pedro Rodríguez de Campomanes (1723–1803), with a motive for reform and a stick to beat its opponents. Publicly charged with having fomented the uprising, the Jesuits were expelled from all the dominions of Spain in 1767, and the pope was persuaded to suppress the order officially in 1773.

Campomanes was a genuinely enlightened minister who ensured that the expulsion of the Jesuits was accompanied by the diversion of the Society's resources to deserving social and educational causes, and by the academic reform of the universities. In the mid 1770s, Grimaldi and Campomanes were eclipsed by the rise of the talented José Moñino, count of Floridablanca, who effectively became Carlos III's chief minister for the rest of the reign. Under his direction reform became a continuous process of fine-tuning the pragmatic efficiency of absolutism rather than changing the political conditions or economic bases of Spanish society.

There was one traditional feature of government that Carlos did not seek to change – the pursuit of policy and glory through war. Within a few years of his accession he involved Spain in the Seven Years War (1756–63), a wide-ranging battle between France and Britain for colonial supremacy on the one hand, and between Austria and Prussia for German domination on the other. After the Treaty of Paris, which ended the war, Carlos spent much of his time plotting ways to revenge the humiliation inflicted on Spain by Britain. He and Floridablanca finally achieved their triumph in 1783 by regaining Minorca and Florida (the latter having been ceded to Britain by the Treaty of Paris) but at such a colossal cost to the treasury that it undermined much of the work of economic reform.

Below The great Venetian painter Giambattista Tiepolo (1696–1770) had already made a European reputation as the most imaginative decorative painter of his day when he was invited by Carlos III to Madrid in 1762 to join the team of international artists working on the king's building projects. Ceilings were Tiepolo's speciality. This detail is from *The Glory of Spain*, one of three ceilings he conceived for the new Royal Palace, then nearing completion, and which were carried out with the help of his sons Domenico and Lorenzo.

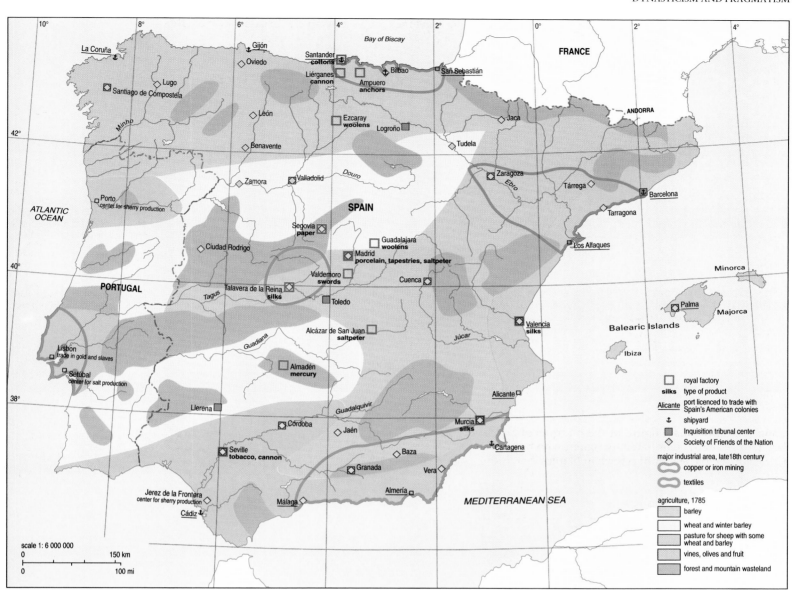

Key:
- ☐ royal factory
- **silks** type of product
- Alicante port licenced to trade with Spain's American colonies
- ⚓ shipyard
- ■ Inquisition tribunal center
- ◇ Society of Friends of the Nation

major industrial area, late 18th century
- copper or iron mining
- textiles

agriculture, 1785
- barley
- wheat and winter barley
- pasture for sheep with some wheat and barley
- vines, olives and fruit
- forest and mountain wasteland

scale 1: 6 000 000
0   150 km
0   100 mi

A flawed Enlightenment

Carlos' ministers clothed much of their reform in the fashionable rhetoric of the Enlightenment, the 18th-century movement in Europe that promoted rational, scientific, and humanitarian beliefs above superstition, privilege and religious intolerance. Though the reformers were bitterly attacked by conservative Catholics as heretics and traitors, the ideas of the Enlightenment barely touched Spanish society at large. The voluminous rationalist writings of the Galician monk Benito Feixó (1675–1764) had little contemporary influence. Though not fully abreast of avant-garde French ideas, Feixó had read the works of the French mathematician and philosopher René Descartes (1596–1650) and the British philosopher John Locke (1632–1704), and was one of the first orthodox Catholic thinkers to endorse the value of objective reasoning. In 1720, he published an encyclopedia that set out to combat the superstitious beliefs and prejudices of Spanish society. Feixó's acceptance that even the miraculous elements of Christian belief ought to be subject to scientific inquiry somehow escaped the attention of the Inquisition; he lived to old age in the confines of his cloister at Oviedo in remote Asturias. The Inquisition was, in any case, losing some of its hold, at least upon the ruling classes. A milestone in Spanish history had been reached in

1701 when Philip V refused to attend the *auto de fé* that was held, in accordance with the custom, to celebrate his accession to the throne. Nevertheless, as late as 1776, Pablo de Olavide (1725–1802), the anti-clerical *intendant* of Seville, was imprisoned by the Inquisition.

Though Carlos and his ministers had demonstrated the possibility of social and intellectual advance, the Spanish Enlightenment remained largely restricted to small groups of government officials who were always vulnerable to the forces of reaction. When Carlos died in 1788, Spain was poised delicately between two epochs: the old system of privilege and patronage and the new age of liberal democracy ushered in by the French Revolution (1789). Time was to show that the achievements of his reign, though real and with important consequences for the future, were incomplete and limited in their social penetration. For most Spaniards, especially those who lived in ultra-conservative Castile, radical change was still something dangerous, even frightening, to be associated with foreigners and heretics.

Pombal: the great dictator

Carlos III's reforms were influenced not only by his Italian experience and French ideas, but also by a striking example of reformism lying nearer home, in

Pombal and the Rebuilding of Lisbon

On 1 November 1755 – All Saint's Day – the great Gothic churches of Lisbon were crowded with worshipers. The city was then at the height of its 18th-century prosperity. But all this changed in just 10 minutes when, soon after 9.30 a.m., an earthquake of unparalleled severity struck, destroying most of the city's major buildings. The river Tagus burst its banks and inundated the ruins; flood was followed by fire. In a single day, two-thirds of the city was reduced to rubble and some 50,000 people perished. Disaster on such a massive scale was unprecedented in modern Europe, and the strength of its impact on 18th-century thought can be traced in writers as disparate as Voltaire, Goethe and Samuel Johnson.

The immediate situation was rapidly alleviated, however, by the actions of Sebastião de Carvalho (later the marquis of Pombal), the chief minister of José I. When asked by the despairing king what was to be done, Pombal is reported to have replied "Bury the dead and feed the living," and with typical flair and energy, that is what he did: aid was mobilized for the injured, shelter for the homeless, and food for the starving. Moreover, within a month of the disaster Pombal had prepared a plan for Lisbon's reconstruc-

tion. With the aid of five architects and an engineer, he remodeled the city center in what is now recognized as a classic example of enlightened town planning: the ruins of the royal palace on the Tagus made way for an arcaded square, leading to an elegant grid of narrow streets. All of Lisbon was rebuilt save one church, the Carmo, which was left in ruins as a memorial.

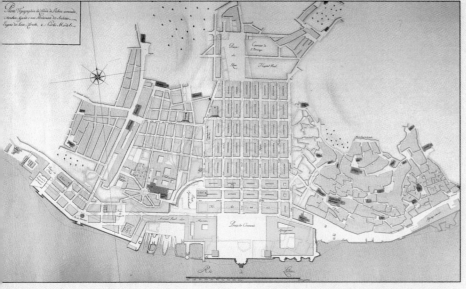

Portugal. During the last years of his reign, João V had become ill and apathetic, leaving much of the business of government to inept churchmen and secretaries of state. The country fell into neglect, with large areas of land lying uncultivated, roads rutted and impassable, and manufacturing industry and trade in serious decline. Though the flow of mineral wealth from America continued to sustain the crown, a crisis in the gold trade caused by the exhaustion of the most accessible of Brazil's gold mines and the high cost of new production, compounded the country's domestic economic problems. The new king, José I (1750–77), was aware of the need for strong action, though he himself had little inclination for government, preferring hunting, playing cards, music and the theater to the responsibilities of kingship. Fortunately for José, there was already someone close at hand who was only too ready to take over his duties: Sebastião de Carvalho, later marquis of Pombal (1699–1782), a largely self-made man of stunning charisma and self-confidence. The king delegated complete authority over his empire to Pombal, never wavering in his support despite Pombal's highly questionable methods and his frequent unpopularity. Throughout the whole of José's reign, Pombal was the brilliant, businesslike, and often brutal ruler of Portugal.

Pombal had been profoundly influenced by a period spent as Portuguese representative in London (1740–44). Throughout his career, he struggled to create in Portugal the conditions for trade and commercial prosperity he had observed in London: one of his earliest measures was to allow merchants to wear swords, thus putting them – in this respect at least – on the same social level as nobles. He tried to reform trade and industry, encouraging the manufacture of silk, woolens, ceramics and glass, mainly through the creation of chartered companies, both at home and in the colonies. These, however, frequently clashed with existing vested interests. Pombal's rise to power had offended the country's aristocracy – a small and highly exclusive group that guarded its privileges jealously. He was also implacably hostile to the Jesuits, whom he believed to be acting contrary to the crown's interests in South America. His economic reforms, coupled with his persecution of the Jesuits, soon brought active resistance.

As in Spain, the Society of Jesus had close links with the aristocracy, and when Pombal suppressed the Jesuit missions in South America, members of the order began to intrigue with certain nobles in Portugal. At the same time, they proclaimed from their pulpits that the Lisbon earthquake had been God's retribution on the people for supporting the atheistical usurper, Pombal. In 1758 members of two of Portugal's most distinguished noble families were implicated in a botched attempt on the king's life. The evidence against them was circumstantial, but in the course of the police investigations that followed – as unprecedented in their social daring as in their ruthlessness – confessions were extracted from the duke of Aveiro, the marquises of Távora and Alorna, and other noblemen under torture; they were then butchered to death in the tower of Belém. When a prominent Jesuit, the aged Father Malagrida (1689–1761), addressed a letter of appeal to the pope, Pombal seized the opportunity to outlaw the order. Most of its members were shipped to Rome, but Pombal invoked the Inquisition against Malagrida, who was garrotted and burned to death at an *auto-da-fé*.

Above left Lisbon's sufferings under the earthquake and its aftermath were extreme. "The fear, the sorrow and lamentations of the poor inhabitants are inexpressible," wrote an eye-witness of the disaster, "every one begging pardon and embracing each other, crying Forgive me, friend, brother, sister! Oh! what will become of us! Neither water nor land will protect us, and the third element, fire, seems now to threaten our total destruction! As in effect it happened." This contemporary engraving shows the horror of the earthquake, with people fleeing as burning buildings collapse around them.

Left The heart of the city remains today much as it was projected by Pombal and his architects after the earthquake, as can be seen by comparing this aerial view with Pombal's original plan (*above*). A new open space directly on the river, significantly named Praça de Commércio (Commerce Square) is linked to the Rossio (the main square) by a regular network of narrow streets. These were allocated, with Pombal's typical organizing style, to specific trades or professions: goldsmiths are still to be found in the Rua Aurea and silversmiths in the Rua da Prata.

Top Sebastião José de Carvalho e Mello, marquis of Pombal, was virtual dictator of Portugal throughout the reign of José I (1750–77), and for a high proportion of that time was the most hated man in the country. The brutal ruthlessness of his government, however, does not detract from the exceptional ability with which he handled the rebuilding of the ruined capital. Here he is portrayed at the height of his power, comfortably drawing attention to the plans and the reality of the new Lisbon, his greatest achievement.

Despite the brutality of his methods, Pombal was in many respects an enlightened despot. Having dislodged the Jesuits, he engineered a veritable revolution in education. New secondary schools were established in Lisbon and some provincial cities, with the best pupils receiving priority for entrance to the university of Coimbra. Here, he introduced a curriculum as advanced as any in Europe, with many new disciplines, especially in the sciences. As a result, Coimbra became a hothouse of liberalism in later generations. Though Pombal himself had no sympathy with liberal political ideas, many of his other reforms belonged to the liberal tradition. He reduced the Inquisition to a mere department of state, halted *autos-da-fé* (though not hesitating to employ them when it suited his own purposes, as against Malagrida), banned slavery in Portugal and removed the legal distinctions between Christians and converts. However, his attempt to restructure the flourishing slave trade between the Portuguese colonies of Angola and Brazil was prompted more by the desire to divert profits away from the Lisbon middlemen toward his own new companies than by humanitarian motives.

Toward the end of José's reign, Pombal summed up his own achievements for the king: greater literacy, expanded industry, flourishing artistic and literary activity, and prosperity (particularly evident in the rebuilding of Lisbon). These were not idle boasts. Pombal did much to remove privilege and modernize the institutions of the state. Perhaps his economic reforms were the least successful, for much of his effort was undermined by the continued decline of Brazilian gold production and the sudden contraction of the sugar trade, once a reliable source of colonial wealth. Nevertheless, they laid the foundations for the modest prosperity of the next reign.

With José's death in 1777, Pombal was swiftly removed from office; without the passive support of the king, he was powerless. José was succeeded by his daughter Maria I (1777–1816). She had married his brother, her uncle, who reigned with her as Pedro III (1777–86). Hundreds of Pombal's opponents were released from prison soon after she came to the throne, and the surviving members of the Távora family were retried at the queen's urgent insistence. All except one were acquitted. Pombal himself was accused of certain offenses. He defended himself vigorously, and was eventually allowed to live out his old age in obscurity in the village of Pombal. The queen, whose conscience had been much troubled by the Távora affair, became increasingly depressed after the death of her husband in 1786 and her eldest son two years later, and ceased to govern after 1792. Her second son, João, ruled in her name, becoming prince regent in 1799.

The end of the *ancien régime*
There is every reason to suppose that the Bourbon system of government would have survived the reign of Carlos IV (1788–1803), inadequate though he was, had it not coincided so fatally with the French Revolution. The whole of conservative Europe watched with mounting horror the events that unfolded in France after the fall of the Bastille in 1789. The Spanish Bourbons interceded to try to save the French king, and took steps to prevent revolutionary propaganda from infiltrating the peninsula. Perhaps one reason why the Spanish *ancien régime* seemed more secure – superficially at any rate – was that the opening of government to the bourgeoisie had gone several stages

Portuguese Tiles

Decorative tilework first found its way into the Iberian peninsula as one of the many contributions of Islamic culture: the Spanish and Portuguese word for tile – *azulejo* – is derived not, as might be imagined, from their predominantly blue color (*azul*), but from the Arabic *az-zulayj*, meaning "little stone". It was in Portugal that architectural and pictorial tilework attained its fullest glory. For nearly a century after the expulsion of the Muslims, tiles were imported, but by about 1550 *azulejo* workshops had been established in Lisbon, using Flemish artists. By the mid 17th century, the industry was self-sufficient, and the next 200 years marked the height of the *azulejo*'s popularity. Complex pictorial designs and lettering supplemented the traditional tile-patterns, and in the hands of skilled artists and craftsmen, the *azulejo* became a major artform, whose tradition continues to this day.

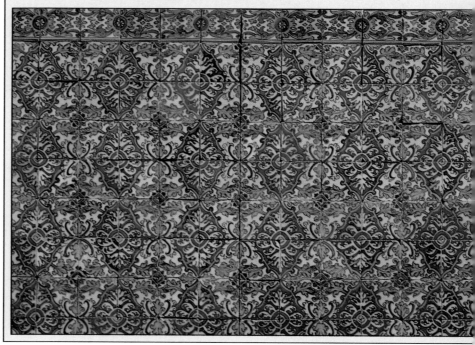

Right In the baroque period of the early to mid 18th century, the use of *azulejos* in the grand buildings of the aristocracy became a field for private ostentation – an ostentation that was made possible by the increased flow of gold to Portugal from Brazil. Tile-design grew increasingly theatrical in concept, with marvelous *trompe-l'oeil* effect and sumptuous classical landscapes. This splendidly armed gatekeeper stands on the grand staircase of the palace of Santo Antão de Tojal in Loures.

Left These tiles are from the Pombaline era (1760–80), when Lisbon was being rebuilt after the great earthquake of 1755. They show the grace and refinement of 18th-century *azulejo* patterns: the decoration is simple and flowing, with a notable reliance on plant motifs. It is in marked contrast to the panel *below left*, which dates from the first half of the 17th century. Its very richly and densely patterned design is based on imported oriental textiles. Panels like this were used to cover large wall areas in both secular and religious buildings.

Below Many 18th-century *azulejo* designs were in blue and white. This panel from the 1760s shows the crucified Christ within an elegant scalloped rococo frame; below are the figures of St Marcellinus, the saint who protects against fire, and St Antony of Lisbon, the patron saint of home and family. Originally from the facade of a private house, the whole panel can be seen as an invocation of heavenly protection against natural disasters - a very popular and understandable practice in Lisbon after the great earthquake.

Bottom The late 19th century saw a revival in the use of tilework to decorate the exteriors of public and private buildings. This design by José da Silva dates from the 1870s, and was originally the shop facade of a ceramics factory.

further in Spain than in France. This process reached its culmination with the rise to power of Manuel Godoy (1767–1851) in the early 1790s. But while Godoy was no grandee, he was hardly a representative of the middle classes, either: it might perhaps be argued that he was the last of the *validos*, or royal favorites. He came from Extremadura, the obscure region of harsh climate and small market towns that had produced most of the 16th-century *conquistadores*. His lowly origins – and some equally lowly aspects of character – might be compared to those of his infinitely more famous contemporary, Napoleon Bonaparte (1769–1821). Like him, Godoy had great ambitions, but he had none of Bonaparte's talents. He was merely the courageous lover of the Spanish queen, María Luisa (1751–1819). Acknowledged as such by Carlos, the favorite was gradually allowed to squeeze out of office the former ministers of Carlos III and assume control of government.

Spain declared war on France after the execution of the French king, Louis XVI, in 1793. The following year France invaded Spain, and seized the border towns of Bilbao, San Sebastián and Figueras. After initial resistance, Godoy surrendered, earning the euphemistic – even blasphemous – title "The Prince of Peace" from his royal patrons. Soon afterward, however, convinced that Britain was Spain's true enemy, Godoy entered an alliance with France. Once again, as during the era of Bourbon "family compacts", the Spanish and French fleets sailed together against England, to be crushingly defeated at the battle of St Vincent (1797). Moreover, it soon became apparent that with Bonaparte now in power in France, Spain stood to lose more than usual from this new Franco-Spanish

alliance. During the Italian campaign of 1796–97, Bonaparte's armies occupied a number of Spain's territories and within a short time Bonaparte was even directing policy in Madrid, reducing Spain to little more than a French satellite. Despite taking steps to establish his "revolutionary" credentials, Godoy was removed on Bonaparte's orders in 1798.

Peninsular war

Portugal was the key to the explosive events that now unfolded. Its destiny was controlled by Britain, which used Lisbon as a major naval base against the French. France was determined to break the Anglo-Portuguese alliance and subjected Portugal to extreme pressure. In 1801, Godoy was recalled to invade Portugal. The name of this campaign, "The War of the Oranges", has something of a comic-opera ring. When Godoy entered Portugal he picked some oranges, sending them to his royal lover with the message "I lack everything, but with nothing I will go to Lisbon." The war was quickly ended by negotiation, with almost no fighting. Portugal lost the town of Olivenza and had to pay an indemnity; more importantly, the Anglo-Portuguese alliance had been temporarily breached.

More and bloodier wars were on the horizon. French troops, ostensibly acting as reserves in the Spanish army in Portugal, now occupied parts of northern Spain, enforcing obedience to Napoleon's directives. Godoy, along with his royal patrons, survived for a few years by paying tribute to Napoleon (emperor of France since 1804) and sending a Spanish army to fight alongside the French in Germany. Godoy expected soon to be crowned in Lisbon, if not by the French, then by the British, with whom he was simul-

Left Goya's group portrait of *The Family of Carlos IV*, painted in 1800 on the eve of disaster, does not inspire confidence in the Spanish Bourbons' forthcoming match with the French. There is an evidently malicious delight, surely exceeding mere warts-and-all "realism", in the artist's treatment of the senior members of the doomed dynasty. The composition is untidy – perhaps deliberately so: a higgledy-piggledy assemblage of people who appear to have been hustled into the frame at the last moment. On the left, Goya has included himself standing at the easel – an obvious reference to Velázquez and *Las Meninas*.

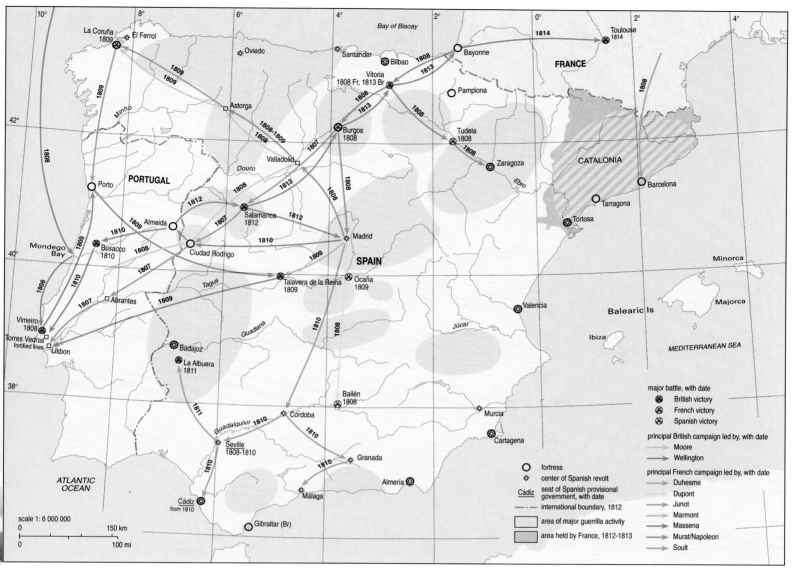

The map legend:

- La Coruña 1809
- El Ferrol
- Oviedo
- Santander
- Bilbao
- Bayonne
- FRANCE
- Toulouse 1814
- Pamplona
- Astorga
- Vitoria 1808 Fr, 1813 Br
- Burgos 1808
- Tudela 1808
- Zaragoza
- CATALONIA
- Barcelona
- Valladolid
- PORTUGAL
- Porto
- Douro
- Tarragona
- Tortosa
- Almeida
- Salamanca 1812
- Madrid
- Minorca
- Busacco 1810
- Mondego Bay
- Ciudad Rodrigo
- SPAIN
- Valencia
- Balearic Is
- Majorca
- Abrantes
- Tagus
- Talavera de la Reina 1809
- Ocaña 1809
- Ibiza
- MEDITERRANEAN SEA
- Vimeiro 1808
- Torres Vedras fortified lines
- Lisbon
- Badajoz
- La Albuera 1811
- Guadiana
- Murcia
- Bailén 1808
- Córdoba
- Cartagena
- Guadalquivir
- ATLANTIC OCEAN
- Seville 1808-1810
- Granada
- Almería
- Cádiz from 1810
- Málaga
- Gibraltar (Br)

Legend:

major battle, with date
- ⊕ British victory
- ⊗ French victory
- ✪ Spanish victory

principal British campaign led by, with date
- → Moore
- → Wellington

principal French campaign led by, with date
- → Duhesme
- → Dupont
- → Junot
- → Marmont
- → Massena
- → Murat/Napoleon
- → Soult

- ○ fortress
- ✿ center of Spanish revolt
- Cádiz — seat of Spanish provisional government, with date
- —·—·— international boundary, 1812
- ▢ area of major guerrilla activity
- ▨ area held by France, 1812-1813

scale 1:6 000 000
0 — 150 km
0 — 100 mi

The War of Independence 1808–14
The Madrid uprising of May 1808 against the occupying French troops sparked off resistance in towns throughout Spain. Despite its early success at Bailén and subsequent advance on Madrid, the ill-disciplined Spanish army was unable to match the superior forces of the French, who reoccupied Madrid in December. A provisional Spanish government (Central Junta) was established in Seville, and subsequently the Spanish war against the French took the form of terrorist action carried out by locally organized guerrilla groups. By 1813 they had come to dominate most of the land outside the cities; it has been calculated that they caused some 10 to 20 times more French casualties than did Wellington's armies. It was Napoleon's decision to withdraw troops from Spain to fight in Russia in 1812 that allowed Wellington to make his breakthrough from Portugal to Madrid and then to Toulouse.

taneously intriguing. His position could only be maintained as long as Napoleon was busy elsewhere.

By 1807, Napoleon was in control of most of mainland Europe. Only the British stood out against him. After the British naval victory at the battle of Trafalgar (1805), fought off the southwest coast of Spain, Napoleon set up the "continental system" of naval blockades, which was intended to cripple the British economy by closing all ports in allied or neutral European countries to British shipping. Since the War of the Oranges, Portugal had tried to remain neutral, but preserved a close association with Britain. Napoleon now seized the initiative. Without waiting for the formality of a treaty, he sent his forces marching straight across Spain to occupy Portugal. In November 1807, the royal court fled to Brazil in a fleet escorted by British vessels, and Andoche Junot (1771–1813), Napoleon's general in Portugal, declared the monarchy deposed: all symbols of royal and national sovereignty were removed. Britain responded by dispatching an army to Portugal under the command of Sir Arthur Wellesley, later the duke of Wellington (1769–1852). Reaching Portugal in August 1808, its early successes led to the withdrawal of Junot's forces.

Insurrection and independence
The great mass of ordinary Spaniards had come to despise Carlos IV for his capitulation to Napoleon.

The anticlerical excesses of French revolutionary politics, especially the massacre of priests in Paris and during the counter-revolutionary struggles in the Vendée (western France) coupled with the arrogant, irreligious behavior of the French army during their Spanish incursion, had sent panic signals throughout the country. Spanish patriotism was enflamed. Conservative opinion began to regroup under the leadership of the parish clergy and members of the traditional aristocracy. Suspicion of isolated groups of liberal intellectuals and local politicians hardened, and in time they became labelled with the contemptuous tag of *afrancesados* ("Frenchified ones").

With French troops now occupying much of Spain, Catholic and patriotic opinion became focused on the heir to the throne, Don Fernando (b.1784) – *el deseado*, or the "Desired One" – an unlikely figure who in the popular imagination became endowed with all the qualities of a heroic savior. In March 1808 the royal retinue had taken refuge at the summer palace of Aranjuez, southeast of Madrid. Here an angry mob forced Carlos IV to dismiss Godoy, whom they regarded as a liberal and quasi-atheist, the instigator of Spain's shame and a puppet of the French. Ejected from power, he was – like Napoleon – to die in exile, but in Paris and 30 years later.

Two days after these events, Carlos himself was forced to abdicate in favor of his son. The new king,

The Royal Palaces

Nearly all the royal palaces of Spain are in Madrid – the fixed capital city since the 17th century – or its immediate environs: the only exceptions are Charles V's unfinished Renaissance mansion in Granada and the little "palace" of La Magdalena in Santander, built in a much later epoch when the court took to spending its summers on the northern coast. Though the court had ceased to be peripatetic under Philip II, it still retained a fairly active calendar that dictated regular (if not continuous) movement. The palaces dotted in the landscape around Madrid were used to escape from the debilitating summer heat of the city and from the business of government that residence there always imposed upon the monarch. No doubt, too, the Bourbons wished to avoid the crowded and volatile capital for the same reason that Louis XIV, their model and patriarch, built Versailles at a safe distance from Paris. But the main objective was relaxation – above all to enjoy the pleasures of the chase.

The royal households grew inexorably in size and number, and enormously in cost, under the Bourbons, whose conspicuous consumption eclipsed even that of their predecessors. They extensively remodeled the buildings – and especially the gardens – of the Habsburg palaces in and around Madrid in the French style of the 18th century, even redecorating a wing of the Escorial, though they were not on the whole attracted to Philip II's austere palace. At La Granja, Philip V built a country retreat that was an imitation of Versailles. The court routinely existed within this "charmed circle" of luxurious watering-holes, and the kings themselves rarely left its comfortable orbit for long. It is little wonder that the increasingly resentful identification of the monarchy with Castile, and with Madrid, became a deeply rooted feature of Spanish politics.

Below This salon in the Royal Palace in Madrid (also known as the Palacio de Oriente) is still used by King Juan Carlos for formal occasions. The building occupies the site of a Moorish castle (or *alcázar*), destroyed by fire in 1734. Work on the new palace on the site began in 1738 under the direction of the Italian architect Juan Battista Sachetti (1690–1764) and was completed 30 years later for Carlos III. The heavy double-Palladian external staircase (*below left*), leading to the formal garden, gives an idea of the high baroque style of the exterior.

Below right The grounds of the Buen Retiro palace in Madrid are today a public park, criss-crossed by labyrinthine paths and adorned with cooling fountains. Little remains of the palace itself, built in the 1630s for Philip IV: Italian landscape gardeners, including Cosmo Lotti who had worked on the Boboli gardens in Florence, designed the original pleasure gardens.

Above Hunting on a huge scale was the purpose for which Aranjuez – about 30 kilometers south of Madrid on the road to Toledo – was first built. The original hunting lodge was extended by Philip IV and normally occupied by the royal household for a short period each spring. It was one of the few Habsburg palaces to meet with the approbation of their Bourbon successors, who remodeled the facade in rococo style.

Right La Granja, 11 kilometers southeast of Segovia, is rather less modest than its name ("The Farm") might suggest. It reflects the fashion for French taste that Philip V, the first of the Bourbon dynasty, introduced to Spain.

Fernando VII (1808–33), went to Madrid to ingratiate himself with Joachim Murat (1767–1815), Napoleon's military commander in Spain, but was given the cold shoulder. In April, the whole Bourbon family obeyed the French emperor's call to attend him at Bayonne in southwestern France, where he caused them to squabble publicly in front of his amused minions. The fortunes of the once-proud Spanish monarchy, defenders of the nation's honor, seemed to have reached rock bottom. Napoleon seized the opportunity to force Fernando to abdicate and hand the crown back to his father. Carlos then passed it to the emperor, who crowned his own brother Joseph Bonaparte (1768–1844) king of Spain.

Now the Madrid mob took control of events. On 2 May 1808 they rose against the French troops occupying the capital, attacking them in the Puerta del Sol, the commercial heart of the city. The event sparked off a chain reaction of popular resistance to the French. By 4 May, Asturias had joined the revolt, and within a week the whole of Spain was ablaze. If the French Revolution had been the catalyst, the Spanish nation in arms – and not Napoleon's Grand Army – was to decide Spain's destiny. Never before 1808 – and perhaps never since – did the nation exist more completely and intensely than in the early months of the War of Independence (1808–14). The greatest Spanish success came in July when a French army of 23,000 men operating in Andalusia capitulated at Bailén. The Spanish army then advanced on Madrid, forcing the French to withdraw.

The national uprising was conducted with almost equal fervor by Castilians, Basques, Aragonese, Valencians and Catalans. For the first time, the Spanish people acted as a coherent political force. Before 1808, many villagers had protested violently against being conscripted to fight for the French; now they flocked to join locally recruited guerrilla bands to fight against their well-organized and disciplined army of occupation (it was this war that added the term "guerrilla" – literally, "little war" – to the military vocabulary). Though all were united in the aim of driving out the French, the resistance movement was therefore localist in sentiment and organization. In a celebrated incident, the mayor and council of Móstoles, a small village just south of Madrid, unilaterally declared war against France under the rights of the village's ancient privileges. Everywhere, the people revived age-old, almost forgotten forms of self-government to organize bands of militia and exercise justice. Many tales of local resistance are recorded. At Zaragoza, the citizens rose up to protect the Virgin of Pilar from the French, and the cannonades that drove the invader back were organized by the washerwoman Agustina. Such myths were to provide glowing examples to the future apostles of the Spanish anarchist movement.

Despite their justified skepticism over Fernando, "the people's king", the sympathy of most liberals lay with the nation rather than the imperialist "liberator", Napoleon Bonaparte. Only a handful of the *afrancesados* threw in their lot with Joseph Bonaparte. Veteran liberals such as Floridablanca reappeared as leaders of the Central Junta, which had emerged to coordinate the politics of the independence movement. Of course, in such a prolonged, confused and frequently brutal conflict, there was bound to be local collaboration and many vicious reprisals. Some liberal mayors were murdered by fanatical Catholic mobs even before they had the chance to take sides.

Goya

Francisco de Goya y Lucientes was born in 1746 in Fuendetodos, a small village in Aragon. After intensive artistic training in Zaragoza, Madrid and Italy, he began his career in Madrid as a painter of religious subjects. His first major commission came in 1785: a series of cartoons (or preliminary paintings) for tapestries to be woven by the Royal Tapestry Factory of Santa Bárbara, depicting popular pastimes and scenes of country life. In 1786 he was appointed court painter, a post he was to retain under four successive kings. In this capacity, he painted many portraits of court and society figures, which are notable for their penetrating characterization. His output of paintings, drawings and engravings was enormous. A fierce social critic, he attacked the abuses of his day in a series of satirical etchings, *Los Caprichos* (1799), which were withdrawn from sale after only a few days. Following the Napoleonic invasion he remained in Madrid as court painter to Joseph Bonaparte, but left a compelling record of the horrors of the war: his monumental *The 2nd of May 1808* and *The 3rd of May 1808*, painted after the Restoration in 1814, commemorate the Madrid popular uprising. His later work shows increasing cynicism and despair: the enigmatic "black paintings" with which he decorated the walls of his country-house are sardonic portrayals of diabolism and violence. In 1824 he left Spain, deaf and embittered by the failure of liberalism, for exile in Bordeaux, France, where he continued to work until his death four years later at the age of 82. His influence on later 19th-century painting was profound.

Right Goya's social criticism was revealed in his 1799 collection of engravings, *Los Caprichos*. In perhaps his most famous engraving, Goya shows us the underside of the Enlightenment, with its belief in reason and the perfectibility of man: "The Sleep of Reason Engenders Monsters".

Below In the series of engravings entitled *The Disasters of War* Goya shows his horrified reaction to the brutalities of the Napoleonic invasion of 1808 and the subsequent guerrilla warfare. The caption to this one, in which civilian corpses sprawl in the ruins of a house after a French raid, reads "The Ravages of War".

Below left Goya was a supreme portraitist: the astonishing realism and pathos he could achieve can be seen in the *Self-Portrait with Dr Arrieta* (1820). In a composition reminiscent of Rembrandt, the artist is shown as a sick man being tended by Arrieta, his physician and friend. The inscription thanks the doctor "for the skill and devotion with which he preserved [my] life during a dangerous illness endured in [my] 73rd year".

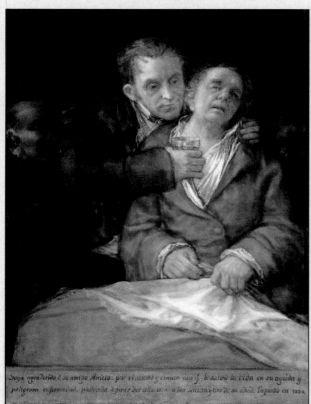

Right By the end of Goya's life disillusion and despair led him to the nightmare violence of the famous "black paintings" (1820–24). Perhaps the most powerful of the cycle is *Saturn Devouring his Son*, a subject taken from Greek mythology. The figure blindly tearing the flesh of his child has been interpreted as an allegory of Time, or possibly Reaction, but could also be seen as an example of Goya's morbid and sardonic humor: the picture was painted for his dining-room.

Below The last of Goya's cartoons for the Royal Tapestry Factory was *El Pelele* (*The Straw Mannikin*) painted in 1791-92, shortly before he was struck down by the serious illness that was to leave him totally deaf. Most of the tapestry cartoons are simple, unambiguous genre-paintings, but here for the first time we sense a darker undercurrent: a grotesque dummy flails its limbs against a lurid sky, as four girls smile knowingly upwards.

After the defeat at Bailén, Napoleon himself led a force of 300,000 men into Spain to retake Madrid. The defeat of a British army under Sir John Moore at La Coruña in January 1809 opened the way for the French to invade Portugal again, but later that year Wellington won a decisive victory against the French at Talavera in Spain before retreating to Portugal. Falling back to Lisbon, he constructed a defensive line centered on Torres Vedras just north of the capital. In 1810, yet another French army, under the command of Marshal Masséna, was despatched to Portugal, but was heavily defeated by Wellington at Bussaco near Coimbra. The French laid siege to Torres Vedras, but after four months their hungry and demoralized army was forced to retreat and finally withdrew from Portugal in 1811. A year later, the withdrawal of French troops to fight in Russia gave Wellington the opportunity to push forward into Spain once more. Madrid was liberated, and in June 1813, after the battle of Vitoria, Joseph Bonaparte fled Spain. Wellington went on to capture Toulouse, and in 1814 Fernando VII, released from house arrest in Valançay, France, returned to occupy his throne.

During the height of the fighting the Spanish Central Junta had ensconced itself first in Seville and then in Cádiz. In 1812, on the eve of Spanish independence, this semirepresentative assembly declared Spain's first liberal constitution and abolished the Inquisition. However, neither the king nor conservative Spain accepted the constitution of Cádiz. Wellington, himself a staunch conservative, discouraged radical change; most guerrilla leaders also wanted to purge Spanish soil of native liberals as well as the foreign invaders. Some also favored the restoration of the Inquisition or the revival of senorial jurisdiction, which had been swept away as one of the last acts of the old council of Castile. Spain, so briefly united in a common cause, had once more divided against itself.

Goya and the Disasters of War

All the events in Spain from Charles IV's accession to the atavistic chaos of guerrilla war were recorded by the greatest product of the Spanish enlightenment, the painter Francisco Goya y Lucientes (1746–1828). In his pictures of the Madrid uprising and the French reprisals of May 1808 (*The Disasters of War*), Goya helped to create the myth of Spanish nationalism. Yet his social inclinations lay with the French Revolution. Though he avoided any clear implication with the French, his attacks on the Inquisition, and on all forms of clericalism, were painted (as it were) in vitriol. The indiscriminate reaction of Fernando VII after 1813 forced him first into a species of internal exile, and then to Bordeaux, where he spent his last years painting a series of painfully accurate prophesies of Spain's future.

The turmoil of political events during the War of Independence and its aftermath also drove two talented musical figures, Fernando Sor (1778–1839), described by contemporaries as the "Mozart of the guitar", and Juan Crisostomo de Arriaga (1806–26) into exile in Paris, curtailing the early promise of their careers. As a result of Sor's sojourn in the French capital, Hector Berlioz (1803–69) was to be the only major musician of the 19th century whose instrument was the Spanish guitar. Arriaga, the author of some deeply moving and skillful instrumental works and of an opera, died in Paris tragically young, before his twentieth birthday.

CONSTITUTIONALISM AND CIVIL WAR 1812–1974

Restoration

With the end of the Napoleonic wars, monarchy, hierarchy and order were restored throughout Europe. Back in Spain, Fernando VII was greeted with adulation by some and with contempt by others. Those who were nostalgic for traditional order and hierarchy welcomed him; those eager for liberal progress hoped that the spirit of Cádiz would sweep away his despotic affectations. The latter were quickly disappointed: within two months, the restored monarch had revoked the 1812 Constitution, rounded up the liberal opposition and embarked on what was to be six years of government by royal decree.

From the standpoint of the liberals, the situation in Portugal seemed little more promising. In 1810, the country's few radical intellectuals had been deported to the Azores and to Britain, where some now met up with their Spanish coreligionists. War against the French had given the peninsula some of its most colorful liberal myths, but the long military action had left the Iberian states on the verge of bankruptcy. These once-great imperial powers were now seen as impoverished, marginal outposts. Since 1810, the Spanish colonies in America – cut off from Spain by the Napoleonic occupation – had been in revolt. Neither Spain nor Portugal could challenge for a place among the "Great Powers" who met at the Congress of Vienna (1815) to decide the future shape of Europe.

The legacy of empire
During the course of the 19th century, both Spain and Portugal were eclipsed as major colonial powers. Early in the century independence movements in Central and South America, inspired both by the rhetoric of the French Revolution of 1789 and by the remarkable career of Simón Bolívar (1783–1830), who led liberating armies from Venezuela to Bolivia, succeeded in shaking off the Iberian colonial yoke. Linguistic and cultural links, however, did not disappear with the loss of territory. As a result of the United States taking territory from Mexico in the aftermath of independence,

equatorial scale 1: 67 000 000

1974 — date of independence or cessation as colony
- - - - boundary at time of independance or cessation
— · — · — present day international boundary

former empire of
☐ Portugal
☐ Spain

▨ area subject to persistent Spanish colonial influence
▨ former colony with majority Roman Catholic presence

Spanish-speaking, Catholic areas in California and Texas were absorbed into the English-speaking, predominantly Protestant culture of North America. In the 20th century, migration from south to north has vastly increased the Hispanic profile in the United States. By the middle of the 21st century it is estimated that half the population of the US will speak Spanish. Spain had lost its few remaining possessions in the Pacific and the Caribbean by the end of the 19th century, but had acquired colonies in Africa in Equatorial Guinea, Morocco and Western Sahara. Portugal's reluctance to give up its African colonies led to increasingly bitter and costly fighting and, ultimately, to the downfall of the Salazar regime.

The War of Independence had left Portugal virtually a British protectorate. Portuguese representatives at Vienna, for instance, were largely ignored. João VI (1816–26) showed no desire for a speedy return from Brazil, leaving the governing of Portugal to a regency – whose power was little more than titular – and to William Carr Beresford (1768–1864), the commander-in-chief of the Portuguese armed forces. The illegitimate son of an Irish peer, Beresford was known for his administrative rather than his strategic talents. He completely overhauled the Portuguese army (which was never deployed as a united force, given its commander's shortcomings in the field), though his rigorous modernization of the country's dilapidated fighting forces made him many enemies. Disregarding family connections, Beresford had cashiered officers, shot deserters, introduced conscription and enforced discipline among troops supposedly terrified by his sightless left eye, which had been irreparably damaged in a shooting accident as a boy.

Beresford was, in part, resented because he was a foreigner. Yet the legend left by Fernando VII is far blacker than that of the British marshal. Liberal myth depicts Fernando as a vicious tyrant whose sadistic reign grossly impeded Spain's historical progress. However, the king was not without his supporters. Fernando entered Spain in 1814, secure in the knowledge that at least a faction of the army would uphold full monarchical rights. The conservative opposition from the Cortes of Cádiz, known as *serviles*, had called for the 1812 Constitution to be replaced by "traditional" government. Though the king was happy to comply with their rejection of the constitution, his desire was not to restore "tradition," but rather the ministerial government he remembered from before 1808. But he also remembered Godoy, and therefore displayed an obsessive need for private policy-making. The purchase of new Russian ships for the fleet, for instance, was kept secret even from the naval minister. Fernando always distrusted the governing classes. Fueled by memories of the rowdy welcome he had received from the Madrid mob in 1808, he believed his support came from the people and used his secret police to gauge the mood of the masses. Capricious in his exercise of power, he was determined to reinvent the old, imperial Spain, firmly

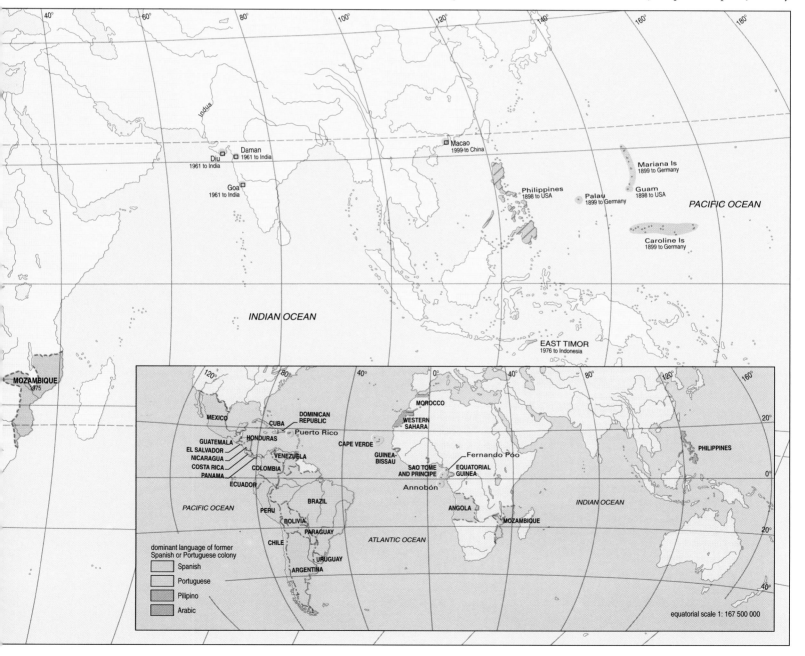

dominant language of former Spanish or Portuguese colony

- Spanish
- Portuguese
- Pilipino
- Arabic

equatorial scale 1: 167 500 000

believing the recapture of Spanish America lay within his grasp.

But South America could not be reconquered without an army, and the military was to be Fernando's undoing. Before the French invasion of the peninsula, local militias had largely conducted national defense; after the Napoleonic wars, the standing army was a fundamental fact of national life. In both Spain and Portugal, the wars had left armies swollen in numbers and short of cash, led by officer corps that were proving increasingly receptive to liberal ideas, particularly those associated with freemasonry.

The revolts of 1820

In January 1820, various batallions of the Spanish army rose in support of the Constitution of 1812. The rebellious troops were camped outside Cádiz, ready to depart for the American wars; their destination was unpopular, pay was short and some of the soldiers had been kicking their heels in Andalusia since 1818, waiting for the crown to raise sufficient funds to embark them. Liberal officers passed over for promotion and soldiers anxious to escape the trip across the Atlantic joined the civilian opposition and successfully rebelled against the crown. Fernando was forced to reinstate the 1812 Constitution and, as his liberal opponents returned from exile and incarceration, the "ministry of the jailbirds" initiated a new phase of government in Spain.

The Spanish Revolution of 1820 reverberated throughout Europe. The conservative system constructed at the Congress of Vienna had received its first real challenge; echoes of Spanish liberalism were heard among Russian Decembrist revolutionaries, Piedmontese army officers and Neapolitan constitutionalists. The loudest resonance, however, was felt in Portugal. Resentment against Beresford had risen since the summary trial and execution of a group of liberal plotters in 1817. British involvement in Brazilian affairs, particularly trade, was also helping the colony to become increasingly, and obviously, independent of the motherland. Dissent was hard to contain, even for a noted disciplinarian like Beresford and, in August 1820, the Porto garrison emulated its Spanish counterparts and staged a liberal coup d'état. João VI at last made the long journey back from Brazil, leaving his son Pedro to govern there. In 1822, the king accepted the newly promulgated liberal constitution, which was closely modeled on the Cádiz document of 1812.

The collapse of constitutionalism

The Portuguese constitution of 1822 had only a brief life. The following year, a reactionary revolt, known as the *vilafrancada*, led by João's second son, Miguel (1802–66), caused João to repudiate the constitution and reinstate absolute royal rule. Miguel was exiled. However, despite these draconian measures to protect his threatened throne, João was a relatively mild monarch, whose despotic period contrasted with the "ominous decade" Spain experienced between 1823 and 1833.

In April 1823, a month before the *vilafrancada*, a French army had entered Spain in order to restore Fernando VII's absolute authority. Its presence undoubtedly encouraged Miguel's rebellion, though British influence ensured that no foreign troops crossed the Portuguese border. Unlike the last French army to have trespassed on Iberian soil, the "hundred thou-

sand sons of St Louis" met no popular resistance when they crossed the Pyrenees. The 1820 revolution had been made by the army; now, with the liberals divided between moderates and the radical *exaltados*, the populace suffering from three years of drought, floods and yellow fever, and a foreign army occupying Spain, the generals lost no time in seeking to make peace with their king. The "three years of the constitution" were at an end.

In neither Spain nor Portugal could the parliamentary experiment of 1820–23 be counted a success. The pressures of government had driven the liberals of both lands into schism; with the exception of Cuba and Puerto Rico, the Central and South American colonies, including Brazil, had been lost for good; and constitutional government had been brought to an end by monarchical reaction. In Spain, Fernando's cruel repression, though short-lived, once again drove a generation of liberals into exile. Individual dossiers were drawn up on all serving army officers and Fernando's chosen ministers, while exercising despotic power, addressed him as *amo* (master), as if they were his household servants.

The real constraints on Fernando's power were financial. The treasury was empty, royalist opposition precluded reform of the archaic tax system and liberal

Above In 1831, General Torrijos led an ill-conceived invasion of his native land. The liberal general and his companions hoped to spark off a popular rising against the despotic King Fernando VII, but their action was an abject failure. The liberal invaders were captured and shot at Málaga, turning Torrijos into a martyr. In 1865, his execution was commemorated in a painting (a detail of which is shown here) by Antonio Gisbert (1835–1901), a major 19th-century Spanish artist who specialized in historical themes.

Regional revolt in the 19th century
During the mid 19th century, the Iberian peninsula was beset by revolt and rebellion. In many ways, two distinct cultures developed: the north remained conservative, Catholic and resentful of the incursions of central government while the south (particularly in Spain) became increasingly radical. Catalonia was home to both these traditions. The interior adhered to the conservative Carlist cause while, on the other side of the mountains that run parallel to the sea, the textile towns along the coast, including Barcelona, became strongholds of Republicanism. Both traditions fostered the cause of regional separatism. Similarly, in the Basque Country and Navarre, Carlism encapsulated local desires for autonomy. Miguelism, the Portuguese equivalent of Carlism, had no clear territorial identity, though the 1844 Maria da Fonte revolt in the Minho region - sparked off by new burial laws - showed the strength of rural resistance to central government interference with local customs. Support for the attempt by the Septembrists, the more radical of Portugal's two parties, to seize power in 1846–7 was quite widely spread throughout the country.

bankers blocked attempts to raise foreign loans. By 1825, there seemed to be some attempt at reconciliation as the king appointed more moderate ministers. Moderation, however, did not suit the ousted extreme royalists, or *apostólicos*. In 1827, former royalist army officers who had found no place in Fernando's "purified" forces and members of the lower clergy led a rebellion in the mountains of Catalonia. The "Revolt of the Aggrieved" was predominantly a local, peasant movement, based on the belief that the king's will was being thwarted by evil advisers. The rebels called for the restoration of traditional government, the return of the Inquisition and a purge of the army – demands that were to form the core of the Carlist program in the civil war of the 1830s. Though the king's brother, Don Carlos (1788–1855), had as yet refused to lead the rebels, the Revolt of the Aggrieved was, in fact, the first Carlist rebellion.

The Miguelist and Carlist wars
In both Spain and Portugal the conflict of liberalism and legitimism culminated in civil war. The supporters of these two contrasting creeds nailed their colors to the standards of competing dynasties as the succession to both thrones became unclear. Fernando VII's death in 1833 left the Spanish throne to his infant daughter, Isabel (1833–68). Her claim was inadmissable both to her uncle, Don Carlos, and to those traditionalists

who would not accept a female monarch. The opposition of the Carlists ensured liberal support for Isabel's cause. Though her mother, the regent María Cristina, had few, if any, liberal sympathies, the Royal Statute of 1834 granted a moderate degree of constitutional reform. A liberal monarchy, governing by consent, thus stood against an absolutist pretender, Don Carlos, whose claims to the throne rested upon divine right. Civil war, which was to rage for over six years, broke out almost as soon as Fernando had breathed his last.

Portugal too had a girl-queen. When João VI died in 1826, his eldest son, now emperor of Brazil, acceded to the throne as Pedro IV (March–May 1826). As he had little desire to return to Portugal, Pedro abdicated the European crown in favor of his seven-year-old daughter, Maria II (1826–53). She was formally betrothed to her uncle, Dom Miguel, on condition that he accepted a constitutional charter guaranteeing parliamentary government. Pedro did not return from Brazil – the hastily drafted and rather conservative charter was delivered to Lisbon by a British emissary – but constitutional monarchy gave new heart to the liberals. Joyful demonstrations in the streets of Lisbon and Porto, however, merely disguised the new government's weakness. Even before Dom Miguel had returned to his homeland, military action on his behalf had begun in the countryside. His Spanish mother,

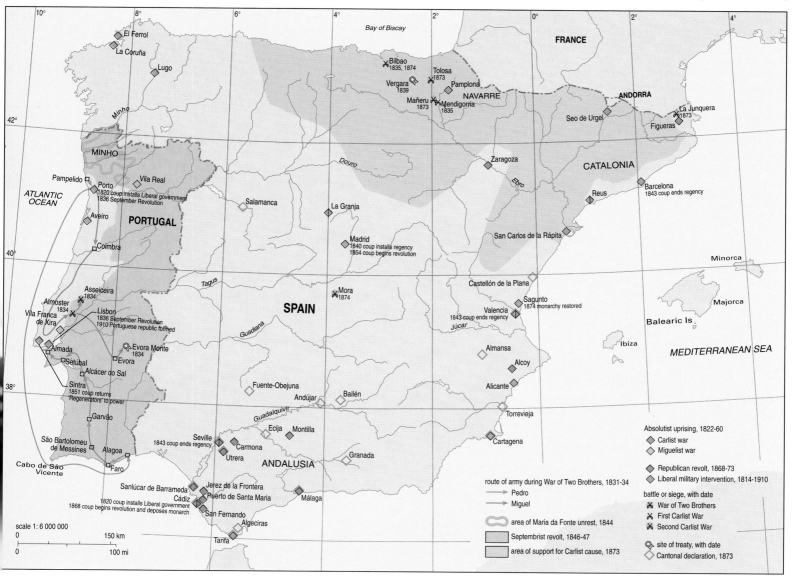

Carlota-Joaquina (1775–1830), won support from her brother, Fernando VII, whose troops began incursions into Portugal in 1826. In 1828 Miguel renounced the charter and usurped the throne, thereby starting the War of the Two Brothers (1828–34).

Popular support for both Miguelism and Carlism lay in the countryside, particularly in the north. Both were classic forms of counter-revolution; Miguelists and Carlists fought for what they regarded as the true king and the true religion. Legitimism and Catholicism proved potent rallying cries among the devout peasant farmers of the north, many of whom resented the prosperity of the towns. The movements attracted those whose traditional way of life seemed threatened: in Catalonia, for instance, where the market economy was most developed, bands of Carlists razed factories and pillaged commercial market-gardens. Carlism, like its Portuguese precursor, was essentially an inchoate protest movement, the direct heir to a long tradition of peasant risings against the encroachments of government – a particular cause for grievance among the Spanish Basques. Their demand for traditional regional liberties, the legendary *fueros*, became enshrined in the Carlist cry "God and the old laws". Even after defeat, the pretender's cause was preserved in the mountains of Navarre. It was only as a separatist tradition that Carlism was able to survive the government victories of the early 19th century. Miguelism, on the other hand, which had no such territorial heartland, could not long outlive defeat.

In contrast to these rural forms of reaction, liberalism was an urban phenomenon, and largely the preserve of the educated. Spain had a tradition of provincial radicalism, centered upon the cities of Andalusia and the Mediterranean coast, especially Barcelona. In Portugal, however, liberalism was mainly confined to Lisbon and Porto – the only cities of any size and the only seats of industry in the land. By 1828, after suppressing a military rising in Porto, Miguel controlled all of Portugal. Only the far-off Azores, a favorite destiny for liberal exiles, remained loyal to the young Maria.

If he was to depose Miguel, Pedro had no option but to invade Portugal. His inclination to do so rose after 1831, when a revolution in Brazil obliged him to abdicate in favor of his son. The ex-king left the Americas, landing in Terceira in the Azores in March 1832. Here, he assembled a motley fleet under the command of an English captain. As well as mercenaries and exiled Portuguese liberals, Pedro's 7,500 men included several hundred British and French volunteers, forced by their countries' neutrality – combined, it was said, with Lord Beresford's good offices for the usurper – to enroll by subterfuge. Pedro and the "settlers for Brazil" landed at Porto, where they were immediately besieged. After a year, and largely at the instigation of the idiosyncratic British admiral, Charles Napier (1786–1860), a force was sent to the Algarve, which promptly declared for Pedro. Napier's fleet defeated Miguel's ships off Cape St Vincent: as the admiral later recalled, "We had 176 guns against 372, and they were thrashed." Lisbon fell; the British and French governments recognized Pedro as king and, though Miguel could still command support in rural areas, the outcome of the war could not now be doubted. On 26 May 1834, at Evora-Monte, the usurper surrendered.

With Miguel's defeat, defense of the legitimist principle moved to Spain and the cause of Don Carlos. As

the upper echelons of army, bureaucracy and government had remained loyal to the queen regent, the pretender had to create an alternative administration as well as raise troops – unlike Miguel, who had controlled the entire state apparatus. Under the circumstances, Carlos enjoyed remarkable success. Much was due to his colorful Basque commander, Tomás de Zumalacárregui (1788–1835), who transformed the Carlist War from a series of local insurrections into a full-scale campaign that overran northern Spain. His strengths were those of the guerrilla commander, and it was in the mountains of the north, where irregular forces were helped by a sympathetic population, that Carlism was most successful. However, while the movement's rural *guerrillero* character made it difficult to defeat and impossible to eradicate, it also confined Carlism to an inaccessible heartland. The loyalties of the mountains did not translate to the plains, and certainly not to the cities, which remained liberal strongholds. Laying siege to Bilbao, for instance, as the Carlists did in the summer of 1835, simply wasted resources and led to Zumalacárregui's death in action.

Peace and parliamentary politics

Don Carlos' men reached the outskirts of Madrid in September 1837, but they could not defeat the Spanish state. The liberals were bolstered by the regular army, the machinery of government and, after the Quadruple Alliance of 1835, the support of Portugal, Britain and France. Though Carlism could not long withstand such superior strength, it left a long legacy. Under the strain of war, urban unrest was rife and liberalism became increasingly radical. Riot often coincided with the summer heat: in July 1834 an outbreak of cholera in Madrid led to rumors that the Jesuits had poisoned the wells and angry-mob attacks on monasteries. The contrast with pious Carlism could not have been more pointed. Indeed, clericalism and anticlericalism now became a counterpoint of politics on the Iberian peninsula – a struggle that would reach its

Above In 1833, the Spanish throne passed to a new-born infant, Isabel II. Her father, Fernando VII, said that his death would "let the cork out of the beer bottle" and so it proved. This contemporary French cartoon shows the child-queen, in leading strings, attempting to support the weight of a huge scepter. She is guided by her mother, the regent María Cristina. Against her is a conservative mob, the supporters of her uncle, Don Carlos, whose adhesion to the Salic Law, which excluded females from the line of succession to the throne, meant they refused to accept a queen as monarch. In the cartoon, the figures of Britain and France are shown tugging against the Carlists while a French arms dealer looks on in the hope of rich pickings from the civil war. This lasted from Fernando's death in 1833 to the liberal victory in 1840.

Above Portugal's "War of the Two Brothers" (1828–34) was ostensibly a conflict between reaction and liberalism. Supporters of the usurper, Miguel, refused to accept the girl-queen, Maria II. Eventually, the crown was reclaimed by her father, Dom Pedro, who defeated his brother Miguel with the help of a liberal army, foreign volunteers and the British admiral, Charles Napier. As this cartoon shows, Portugal was not a country in command of its own destiny. The warring brothers are depicted as childish puppets, their actions directed by foreign powers. Pedro is egged on by John Bull the Englishman while Miguel's actions are determined by absolutist Spain.

Right Much of the military success enjoyed by the Carlist rebels during the civil war of 1833–40 was attributable to their general, Tomás Zumalacárregui (1788–1835). He transformed a small, untrained fighting force into an extremely effective *guerrilla* army, which he deployed with great success in the Basque mountain country. Only when the Carlist forces abandoned *guerrilla* tactics for conventional warfare did their shortcomings become apparent. Besieging the fortified city of Bilbao in 1835 cost Zumalacárregui his life and severely weakened the rebel strength.

apocalyptic climax a century later in the Spanish Civil War of 1936–39.

The summer of 1835 saw a new wave of disturbances. Rioting broke out in Barcelona while a spate of minor radical revolts swept through the cities of the south. By 1836 there was full-scale revolution in Spain. Málaga rebelled in July; other provincial cities followed its lead and, on 13 August, a sergeants' mutiny forced the regent María Cristina to reinstate the 1812 Constitution. The Progressives – heirs to the former radical grouping, the *exaltados* – now held the upper hand.

In the same year, Portugal's September Revolution wrested power from the conservative constitutionalists, who had governed since the end of the civil war. The 1822 constitution was restored, though as in Spain, a new constitution soon followed. The victorious parties attempted to accommodate their radical programs to the realities of government, but neither the Spanish constitution of 1837 nor the Portuguese one of 1838 was to survive for long. The governing classes of both countries were now divided into two broad camps, both derived from liberalism's historic schism into radicals and moderates: in Portugal "Septembrists" opposed "Chartists", while Spanish "Progressives" stood against "Moderates".

In both countries, the less radical group was to become dominant. In Portugal, this process was gradual; Septembrist administrations fought off various Chartist challenges, but became increasingly authoritarian themselves. From 1839, power lay with the Secretary of Justice, António Bernardo de Costa Cabral (1803–89). He restored the Charter in 1842 and introduced a phase of constitutional despotism. Desire for order, strong government and a period of stability to make good the ravages of war was strong, particularly among the capitalist classes.

A similar solution had been reached in Spain. In 1841, General Baldomero Espartero (1793–1879) had been proclaimed regent in place of María Cristina. When a military revolt two years later brought about

his fall, government passed into the hands of the Moderates. Their hegemony, which lasted through the 1840s, ushered in a much-needed period of recuperation. A new age of parliamentary politics was beginning, but it was apparent to all that the army would be the ultimate arbiter.

The Romantic era

Among the soldiers who had marched into Porto with King Pedro the Liberator in 1832 had been the poet Almeida Garrett (1799–1854). Forced into exile in England when Miguel usurped the Portuguese throne, he had furthered his knowledge of English language and literature and – through the works of Sir Walter Scott (1771–1832) – absorbed the prevailing enthusiasm for all things medieval. Garrett's reforming Romanticism was predicated on the belief that "Nothing can be national if it is not popular." He rose to great prominence after the liberal restoration, becoming in turn a deputy, a minister for foreign affairs (1852) and, eventually, a peer.

Garrett did much to revive Portuguese literature, urging a reawakening of national spirit and native culture. He was joined in his task by the historian Alexandre Herculano (1810–77) – also a veteran of Dom Pedro's liberating army – whose great study of medieval Portugal caused fury in clerical circles. Unlike many of his contemporaries, Herculano was not looking for heroic myths of a glorious past. He discounted legends of divine intervention in the foundation of the nation and, in exploring the reasons for Portuguese backwardness, was not afraid to subject the Inquisition to scholarly scrutiny. He defended his work vigorously but eventually sought refuge in fiction. A poet in his youth, he ended his life as the peninsula's most distinguished writer of historical novels – a genre which, following the success of Sir Walter Scott, enjoyed a great vogue.

The Traveler in Spain

Until the end of the 18th century, the Iberian peninsula was scarcely known in northern Europe. Two things changed that. By following the campaigns of the Napoleonic wars in the newspapers, European readers were made familiar with the topography of the peninsula. At the same time, the rise of the Romantic movement glamorized the appeal of the picturesque and the remote. An early visitor to Portugal and Spain was Lord Byron (1788–1824), who journeyed across the peninsula in 1809; his epic poem *Don Juan* (1819–21) gave new expression to the story of the impious seducer that was first dramatized by the Spanish playwright Tirso de Molina (1571–1641) and was the subject of Mozart's opera *Don Giovanni* (1787). Another visitor was the American writer Washington Irving (1783–1849). Attached to the American legation in Seville from 1822, he was increasingly drawn to Andalusia's Moorish past and published a collection of legends and tales under the title *The Alhambra* (1832). Prosper Merimée published *Carmen*, the epitome of the Spanish Romantic novel, in 1845. However, it was the English writer Richard Ford (1796–1858) who brought the charms of the peninsula within the reach of the ordinary traveler. Ford's *Hand-book for Travellers in Spain*, published in 1845, was based on the copious notes and many sketches he made on horseback expeditions around the country when he and his wife were living at Seville and Granada in the 1830s. It provided the reader with a wealth of practical detail, and its pleasing style made it an instant bestseller. Many still regard it as the best guidebook to Spain ever written.

Left This portrait of Ford in the Andalusian costume that he wore during his riding tours was made in 1832 by the Sevillian artist Joaquín Bécquer, who became friendly with the Englishman during his stay in the city. Ford's great gift – which made his writings so vivid – was his curiosity, which led him to get to know the Spanish people at all levels of society.

Below left It was Washington Irving who suggested that the Ford should lodge in the Alhambra during their stay in Granada. Harriet Ford's sketch of the Mexuar, drawn in the summer of 1831, shows the window that opened on to her dressing room. The Alhambra in those days was run-down and neglected. In the *Hand-book* Ford describes the Mexuar as "a picture: it was made a sheep-pen . . . and since a poultry yard: one facade retains its original Moorish embroidery, and the beams of the roof are the finest specimens of the Alhambra."

Below Ford was a skillful watercolorist, and made many sketches during his travels. This view of *Seville from the Cartuja*, in gouache, shows the river Guadalquivir, the Giralda, the cathedral and the Torre del Oro.

The Romantic movement encompassed the entire peninsula, though in Spain there was no exponent to match the stature of Garrett or Herculano. Closest, perhaps, was the Byronic poet José de Espronceda (1808–42), author of some fine lyrics and a virtuoso verse treatment of the Don Juan legend. But the twin creeds of Romanticism and liberalism were espoused not only by intellectuals but also by the burghers and businessmen of the prosperous commercial cities of Porto and Barcelona, where the development of the textile industry – the production of Catalan cotton goods nearly tripled between 1830 and 1840 – had created the first industrial bourgeoisies. The cities of the peninsula were home to a rising generation of theater-goers and novel readers, eager for a taste of the fashionable Romantic.

Playwrights catered to their appetite. New theaters put on poetic dramas by Francisco Martínez de la Rosa (1787–1862), a veteran of the Cortes of Cádiz who had returned from exile in 1833 to become prime minister, the duque de Rivas (1791–1865) and José Zorrilla (1817–93). In contrast to the major plays of Almeida Garrett, however, the works of these Spanish Romantics are now seen as colorful period pieces. Garrett played an important role in the revival of Portuguese drama and was instrumental in the establishment of a National Theater in 1842. Camilo Castelo Branco (1825–90) used Portuguese themes and settings, particularly those of the Minho and his native Trás-os-Montes, to chronicle his novels of rural life. Indeed, Romanticism was so dominant in Portugal that it evolved into a sterile academism that held sway until the 1870s.

Spain itself was soon to become a character in the Romantic drama being played out in early 19th-century Europe. It was a favorite destination for northern travelers in search of the primitive and the picturesque. These Romantic pilgrims recorded or fictionalized their experiences. A journey to Spain by the French writer Prosper Merimée (1803–70) in 1830 provided the inspiration for his novel *Carmen* (1845). Thirty years later Georges Bizet (1838–75) based his successful opera on it, thereby perpetuating its popular clichés of Andalusian life.

The discovery of "the folk" was not confined to foreigners. Almeida Garrett made the first systematic collection of Portuguese ballads in the 1840s, the same decade in which an institute for the study of folklore was founded in Spain. Fernán Caballero (1796–1897) – the pseudonym adopted by the daughter of the Prussian consul in Cádiz – collected Andalusian folksongs and incorporated careful observation of southern life into her novels, a practice that was known as *costumbrismo*. In the field of painting, Goya's legacy was strong: some painters found new inspiration in landscape; others, like the Bécquer family of Seville – Joaquín (1805–41), his brother José and his son Valeriano (d.1870) – depicted Andalusian folklore and scenes of popular life.

Spanish Romanticism soon suffocated under the weight of so much national costume, though its legacy was longer lasting. Regional vocabulary and dialect were introduced into the literary language by the Romantics and accepted by writers such as the lyric poet Gustavo Adolfo Bécquer (1836–70) who, like all his family, was greatly influenced by his native Seville. Bécquer's contemporary, Rosalía de Castro (1837–85), wrote primarily in the language of her native Galicia (*galego*) and, within two decades, some of her verses were accepted locally as traditional songs. Spain's two greatest 19th-century poets were thus direct descendants of the Romantics. Castro's *galego* lyrics also contributed to a revival of Galician literature, just as the publication of a Romantic ode, "La Pàtria", in a Barcelona paper in 1833 began a profound renaissance in Catalan language and literature.

The consolidation of liberalism

The victory of constitutional government in both Portugal and Spain in the 1830s finally allowed the development of liberal society on the peninsula. The triumphant governments swept away the remaining legal anachronisms of the *ancien régime* in a series of fundamental reforms. Liberal legislators removed internal customs barriers, introduced the decimal system, reformed the post office, codified laws and standardized taxation. Much of this legislation imitated that of post-revolutionary France: the example of French centralization was particularly apparent in the revision of local administration. In 1833, Spain's historic regions were replaced by 50 uniformly sized provinces, each with a centrally appointed civil governor – the equivalent of the French prefect. The same model had been followed a decade earlier in Portugal when the country was divided into 17 districts (later to become 18). Though district administrators were appointed by the crown, centralization remained a contentious issue in 19th-century Portugal; attempts to introduce greater local autonomy in 1835 and 1878, though these came to nothing.

Reform, whether administrative or otherwise, did not come cheap. The civil wars had left the Iberian states in urgent need of funds; cash had to be raised, and economic prosperity increased, if the emergence of modern state structures was not to be severely hindered. As agriculture was the prime source of wealth – and land the most valuable commodity – the liberal governments of Spain and Portugal turned their attention to the agrarian sector in their efforts to raise revenue. According to every law of liberal economics, agriculture could not flourish while shackled by archaic laws of tithe and entail, which restricted the disposal of land. The constitutional regimes therefore set about creating a free market in land. In 1834, the Portuguese government abolished all convents and monasteries and put their lands up for sale, while all remaining ecclesiastical properties were made liable to tax. Two years later, similar action was taken in Spain when the government of Juan Alvarez Mendizábal (1790–1853) declared all monastic land to be state property. In the following decades, church, crown and, in Spain, common lands were sold by both governments on the open market. This generated considerable revenue for the national exchequers even if, in the haste to raise funds, much property was sold off below its market value.

Though in legal and political terms the land sales were revolutionary, their effect on the social structure of the peninsula was less far-reaching. Property could be bought only by those with capital; as land was the principal source of wealth, many disentailed plots went to existing landowners. Indeed, during the mid 19th century, the amount of land owned by noble families – who already controlled the vast *latifundia* estates in the south – actually increased. Nevertheless, the disentailments and land sales did enlarge the landowning class. Some of the largest ecclesiastical holdings were bought by financiers and politicians

Above The Fords visited Spain to try to restore Harriet's health. Her beauty was renowned. In this painting, after a print by J. F. Lewis, she is wearing the "splendid maja riding-habit . . . black with innumerable lacing and tagging, and a profusion of silver filigree buttons" described by Richard Ford in 1833.

from Madrid. Regional urban elites, such as the Catalan industrial bourgeoisie and the sherry families of Jerez, took the opportunity to buy local estates. On a smaller scale, wealthy peasant farmers, particularly in the north of Spain, made modest purchases in their own villages; in the Castilian province of Valladolid such people accounted for half of all buyers, but bought only 14 percent of the land offered for sale.

The effect of these massive transfers of land was twofold. On one level, they completed a legal revolution that, in its recognition of individual property rights and, hence, the equality of citizens before the law, set the parameters of the modern, liberal state. However, the disentailments also served to make landowners of the newly emergent urban and industrial elites. In effect, these dynamic social groups were co-opted by the old landowning classes: their interests were channeled into land; instead of challenging the power of the aristocracy, the new economic elites became concerned to preserve it. Disentailment, rather than modifying existing social and economic structures, reinforced and even exacerbated them.

Church and state

The appropriation of church lands was primarily a fiscal measure rather than an anticlerical one. Unsurprisingly, however, relations between church and state – already under strain in both countries – were badly damaged. The land sales were not unprecedented. Church property had first been expropriated under Carlos IV of Spain in 1798, but now liberalism and Catholicism seemed almost antithetical. Such an impression was, however, inaccurate. Though contemporary liberals often viewed the religious orders as bastions of reaction, constitutionalists were not, on the whole, anti-Catholic. Indeed, unlike their Republican successors, they often shared the faith and transcendental assumptions of their clerical opponents. But liberals were implacable opponents of superstition and privilege, and the wealthy monastic houses seemed to epitomize both.

The church was also discredited in liberal eyes by too close an association with absolutism. This was particularly true in Portugal, where Dom Miguel's regime had even been recognized by the pope. During the civil wars in Spain, the hierarchy had been more circumspect, though many of the lower clergy adhered to the Carlist cause, particularly in the north. Old allegiances were not easily put aside. In 1846, Carlist brigandage in Catalonia developed into a regional guerrilla war that lasted until 1849. The "War of the Early Risers" – so-called from the pious habit of attending early morning mass – showed that the concerns of the countryside were not always those of the government. The same point had been made during the Maria da Fonte unrest that erupted in much of northern Portugal in 1846. The men and women of the Minho – among them, supposedly, Maria da Fonte herself – rose in protest at a government prohibition on the traditional practice of burials inside churches. The measure had been decided on public health grounds, with no anticlerical intention, but the government had given scant thought to the effect its legislation would have on popular devotional practice. Enflamed by local clergy and nobility, many of whom were still loyal to Miguel, rural mobs marched on the Minho towns, burning official registers and other evidence of state interference in local life. Though the unrest subsided once the offending legislation had been repealed, the Maria da Fonte revolt gave early proof of the cleavage between the liberal towns and the Catholic countryside that would become a recurring theme in the modern history of the peninsula.

The church needed reform if it was to coexist with liberalism but, in the 19th century, there was no talk of disestablishment. In both Spain and Portugal, Catholicism was the religion of the state, the church hierarchy was represented in the senate, and the royal houses of Bourbon and Bragança retained the right of presenting their own bishops (though the severing of relations with Rome as a result of the sale of church land prevented episcopal appointments being confirmed). Once the land sales were accepted as a *fait accompli*, accommodation with the Vatican was soon reached: Portugal signed concordats with the Holy See in 1848 and 1857, while Spain did so in 1851.

Left Despite the legislative battles waged by church and state in 19th-century Spain, religion played an important role in civic life. This painting of 1862 by Manuel Cabral depicts Good Friday in Seville, when an elaborate and heavy float of the crucifixion was carried through the streets by hooded penitents. Fellow members of the confraternity, given anonymity by their raised hoods and robes, direct the procession as onlookers watch from pavements and balconies. The appearance of piety could, however, be deceptive. Despite its renowned Holy Week processions, Seville had one of the lowest rates of church attendance in Spain.

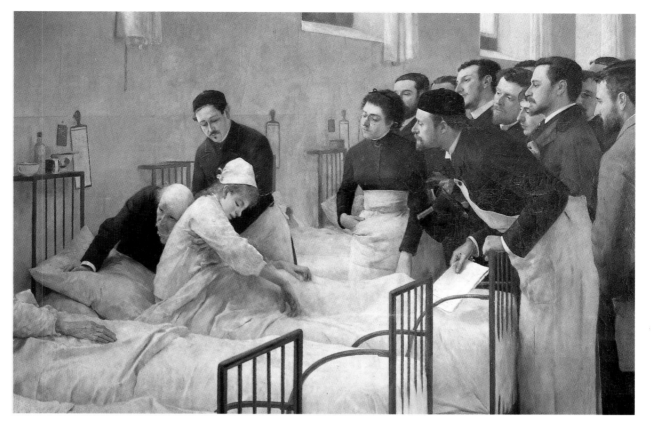

Right Though welfare provision remained rudimentary in 19th-century Spain, medicine developed along European lines. This realist painting by Luis Jiménez Aranda shows a doctor on his ward rounds. He listens to the chest of a tubercular patient; tuberculosis was a major cause of death until well into the 20th century and the focus of much medical attention. The doctor is observed by a group of medical students, one of whom is a woman. Spain's first woman doctor qualified in 1865.

The governing classes

In both countries, the institutions of the modern state coexisted with traditional social structures. Wealth remained largely tied to the land, and the landed classes were the governing classes. Though capitalist practices were introduced in certain agricultural areas – primarily by the fruit and vegetable growers of Spain's Mediterranean coast and the fortified wine producers of Porto, Jerez and Madeira – farming was generally backward. Spanish agricultural inefficiency was partly due to the hostile terrain and climate, but government protectionism in both countries safeguarded uncompetitive products, particularly wheat, with high tariffs.

The failure of agriculture to modernize in anything other than a sporadic fashion retarded industrial development on the peninsula. Constraints on food production – both Spain and Portugal were net importers of grain in the 19th century – acted as a brake on urban development. In 1850, for instance, Spain's urban population was proportionately no greater than in 1750. The lack of agricultural prosperity also reduced the size of the home market and thus severely restricted demand for industrial goods – a problem compounded by the difficulties of transportation in the interior of the peninsula. Only in Catalonia was there a thriving peasant market and, even here, demand was largely restricted to basic goods.

In these circumstances, industrial development remained confined to particular areas on the periphery of the peninsula and to certain sectors, notably textiles. In the mid 19th century – despite the prosperity of commercial centers such as Porto and Valencia – the only industrial city on the peninsula was Barcelona and the only true manufacturing region was Catalonia. The industrial bourgeoisie, such as it was, was composed of local manufacturing elites. These "good families" dominated municipal politics and policy-making, but at national level the wealthy, nontitled commercial classes remained both fragmented and small in number.

Elsewhere in Europe, the introduction of parliamentary government had been associated with the rise of the bourgeoisie. In Spain and Portugal the commercial and industrial classes were not sufficiently large or powerful to develop and staff liberal political institutions. Though limited suffrage was introduced and elections held, political institutions failed to evolve as they had done in Britain, France or the United States. The competing political factions – Progressives and Moderates in Spain, Regenerators and Historics in Portugal – actually represented different groups within the landed elite who, at a basic level, had more uniting than separating them. The franchise, for instance, was restricted by high property qualifications; the radical consititutions promulgated in Spain in 1812 and Portugal in 1822, which had given the vote to all literate males, had not lasted long.

The limits of the liberal state

Education was one area in which the modernizing state singularly failed to live up to expectations. Though liberal governments in both countries saw education as the responsibility of the state, shortage of funds meant that the provision of schooling remained woefully inadequate. Free, compulsory elementary education was introduced in Spain in 1857, but central government funding remained minimal – little more than one percent of the budget between 1850 and 1875. In Portugal in 1890, 76 percent of those over 7 years of age could not read or write. Though schools run by parishes and – where they were permitted – religious congregations made up some of the shortfall, educational provision in both countries was still vastly deficient.

The same pattern could be seen in the provision of orphanages, asylums, hospices and relief schemes, which was made on a haphazard and voluntary basis.

The Army in the Age of Pronunciamientos

The course of 19th-century Spanish history was punctuated by military rebellions when the army would rise in the name of the general will to take action against the perversions initiated by evil monarchical councillors or, later in the century, "anti-national" parliamentary politicians. Under Fernando VII military risings came to assume a set form: soundings were taken, the officers and sergeants won over, and all the conspirators bound to action. Finally, the leader issued a call to arms, addressed the assembled troops, and the revolt began. A successful officers' revolt would lead both to political change and to promotion for the triumphant rebels. The First Carlist War of 1833–40 enhanced the army's power. A new breed of soldier-politician emerged, ready to take over the reins of government itself. No longer content with occasionally determining policy through the *pronunciamiento*, politically ambitious generals used army rebellions to establish positions as permanent party leaders. Their persistent intervention in politics weakened the crown and made the evolution of a fully functioning parliamentary democracy all but impossible.

Below Isabel II, shown at an army review, was vacillating and unpopular. Her court was marked by scandal: she lived largely apart from her husband Francisco de Asís, who is riding beside her. Generals O'Donnell, Espartero and Narváez, grouped together in the background, were the real powers behind the throne. It was Narváez, leader of the Moderates, who deposed Espartero in 1843. O'Donnell headed the revolt that put Espartero back in power in 1854, and himself took control of government in 1856. He was Isabel's staunchest supporter. Unable to survive without military backing, she abdicated only months after his death in 1867.

Above General Baldomero Espartero was the first of Spain's soldier-statesmen. After defeating the Carlist rebels, he became sole regent for the child-queen Isabel II in 1841. Though ousted in 1843, he returned briefly to power at the head of the Progressives in 1854–56. Casado del Alisal's magnificent portrait reflects the esteem in which Espartero was held. After Isabel's abdication in 1868, he was even offered the vacant throne of Spain, but turned it down.

Right Barracks actions in which senior officers were not involved were swiftly suppressed. On 22 June 1866, the artillery sergeants of the San Gil barracks in Madrid mutinied against their elitist officer corps, which refused to allow promotion from the ranks. Professional grievances played a role in virtually all military rebellions, but only rarely did officers lose control of their men. After the San Gil mutiny, 60 sergeants were shot.

Despite the efforts of spirited reformers such as Concepción Arenal (1820–93) – who became Spain's first inspector of women's prisons in 1868, and later headed the national Red Cross – most charitable institutions on the peninsula owed their existence to individual philanthropy. Such provision, small as it was, that was made at national level, was in the area of medicine rather than welfare. The development of university medical faculties led to the establishment of public teaching hospitals in major cities. Doctors became increasingly highly trained, but there was no parallel development in related fields such as nursing. In Spain, the deficiency was made up by religious congregations, notably the Sisters of Charity of St Vincent de Paul. Their extensive charity work led to the congregation being exempted from Mendizábal's dissolution of religious orders in 1835–36. In Portugal, however, not even their record of welfare work could save the Sisters. They were first ordered to sever links with their superior in Paris, and then, in 1861, came the requirement to dissolve the Portuguese community. Without even the efforts of nuns, welfare provision in Portugal remained still more rudimentary than that in Spain.

In the social sphere, the discrepancy between liberal rhetoric and state action was acute; in politics the incongruity was less evident but just as real. While government was no longer an affair of autocrats and aristocrats, it was still the preserve of the elite: electoral results were brokered by the enfranchised minority rather than decided by a free vote at the polls. In Spain – and even more acutely in Portugal – the smallness of the political class, combined with the scarcity of national resources, culminated in factionalism and, particularly, personalism. Parties were little more than interest groups, existing for little reason other than to serve individual needs. Political allegiances shifted easily and regularly in the hope of employment, influence or position.

In such circumstances, parliamentary democracy was destined to have only a stunted existence, not least because it proved impossible to maintain stable party allegiances. Nor were the Spanish and Portuguese constitutions conducive to the development of representative government, not least because both left considerable influence with the "moderating power" of the crown. In the absence of a true two-party system, the monarch effectively "made" a government by inviting a minister to form a parliamentary majority. Like her mother, the regent María Cristina, Isabel II of Spain (1843–68) consistently favored the Moderates over their parliamentary opponents, repeatedly failing to invite the Progressives to form a government. However – perhaps in reaction to their meddlesome mother Maria II – both the mild Pedro V of Portugal (1853–61) and his brother Luis I (1861–89) proved, by Iberian standards, exemplary constitutional monarchs. This may have owed something to the influence of their father Ferdinand of Sachsen-Coburg-Gotha (1816–85), who was made consort, as Fernando II, in 1837 and ruled as regent to Pedro from 1853–55.

Given the fragmentation of the governing classes and the partiality of the crown, the army was by far the strongest power in the Iberian liberal state. Military intervention became embedded in the parliamentary system, in no small part because of the politicians' need for military backing. Soldiers – or, more accurately, generals – intervened to change governments or, as the century progressed, to lead them. Formalized coups d'état, whereby an army "pronouncement" (*pronunciamiento*) would usher in a change of government, replaced royal prerogative. Indeed, in Portugal the very word "revolution" (*revolução*) came to be applied to a military coup or barracks action that resulted in a change of civilian leadership; radical upheaval was described rather as a "political turnabout" (*reviralho*).

The armies of Spain and Portugal had made their first decisive intervention in civilian politics in 1820. A garrison revolt ensured the success of Portugal's September revolution in 1836, and another might have returned the Septembrists to power in 1846–47, but for the intervention of an Anglo-Spanish naval force at Queen Maria's request. Similarly, in Spain, military revolt ushered in the reign of the Moderates in the 1840s, while the army also orchestrated the revolution of 1854, finally ending it.

Such pseudo-parliamentarism could not continue indefinitely. With the army playing a pivotal role, it was inevitable that military commanders would begin to act as permanent party leaders. General Ramón María Narváez (1800–68), for example, became leader of the Spanish Moderates in the 1840s, and premier in May 1844. In Portugal the mantle of the soldier-statesman fell in the last years of Maria's reign on Pedro IV's elderly general, João Carlos Saldanha (1790–1876) who, after various brief incursions into politics, came to power in 1851. Saldanha introduced the concept of "regeneration" to peninsular politics: his administration aspired to a new beginning, bringing together the great and the good in a coalition government that held power from 1851 to 1856.

The first Spanish republic

The Spanish revolution of 1868 set a new precedent on the peninsula. It was started by the navy but, on this occasion, matters were not left in the hands of the officers: negotiations with civilian politicians had preceded the military action. Revolutionary *juntas* already existed in major cities, the Andalusian towns were ripe for revolt, and Barcelona was heavily republican. The combination of military coup and popular rebellion proved irresistible. Queen Isabel II – "that impossible woman", notorious for her extravagance, sexual immorality and favoritism – was driven into exile in France.

Though few mourned the queen's departure, only a small minority of the 1868 revolutionaries envisaged a republic. General Juan Prim (1814–70), head of the provisional government established after Isabel's flight, was determined to protect the nation from the extremes of radical democracy. Nevertheless, as local government was still largely in the hands of the revolutionary *juntas*, it was necessary to concede some democratic demands. In an attempt to forge a broadly acceptable revolutionary settlement, the provisional government introduced universal suffrage (that is, for men over 25), trial by jury, freedom of worship, of the press and of association. However, all republican demands were quashed. Instead, Prim sought to establish a constitutional monarchy that would embody traditional values of order and hierarchy while being governed by law.

The search for a suitable candidate led Prim round the royal houses of Europe, including that of Bragança. Luis I – who preferred literature to politics and translated Shakespeare into Portuguese – refused the throne with the words "I was born Portuguese and

Portuguese I want to die": a gesture that did much to earn him the soubriquet "the Popular". His father, Fernando II, kept alive the hopes of the peninsula's Pan-Iberianists, (who included the aged Marshal Saldanha). But his candidature did not survive Prim's lack of enthusiasm for a Portuguese king nor Britain's opposition to Iberian union. A plan to fill the vacant throne with a member of the German Hohenzollern dynasty failed as the affair became the catalyst for the Franco-Prussian War (1870–71). In these circumstances, with the peace of Europe threatened, the 26-year-old Amadeo of Savoy became king of Spain in 1871. As he set sail for his new kingdom, his mentor, General Prim, was assassinated in Madrid – the first, but by no means the last, modern Spanish leader to meet a violent death.

Amadeo I (1871–73) was an amiable, if unintelligent, man, with the best of constitutional intentions. But Prim's death had removed his main source of support and, as the revolutionary coalition disintegrated, no one else proved willing to guide the new king through the resulting chaos. Had the constitution been stronger, Amadeo might have proved an exemplary monarch. As it was, his ministers dismissed him as "a bearded child" or, more rudely, "an idiot". The press lampooned him as "Macarronini I", perhaps because he spoke a mixture of Italian and Spanish; opera audiences booed as he entered the royal box. The election of a republican-dominated parliament in 1872 was too much to bear; Amadeo used a military scandal as a pretext to escape what he termed the "lunatic asylum" of Spanish politics. The First Republic was proclaimed on the day he abdicated.

The Spanish revolution of September 1868 had also sparked off an insurrection in Cuba. This developed into a war of independence that lasted for 10 years. The exigencies of colonial war were already being felt by the Madrid government when the proclamation of a republic led to a resurgence of the Carlist cause. The supporters of the pretender (by now the third in the line) maintained their armed struggle until 1876, though the Second Carlist War, unlike the First, was largely confined to the pretender's Pyrenean heartland of Navarre. Though the piety of an army whose battalions were to be seen telling their rosary beads every sunset appealed to Catholics who were horrified by the actions of convent-burning radicals in the south, the Carlist cause remained fatally tinted by provincial obscurantism.

The combination of war in Cuba and revolt in Navarre proved fatal for the short-lived Spanish Republic. With the army stretched beyond its limits and the governing coalition in tatters, the revolution careered into radicalism, abandoning the unitary state for federalism. In its brief existence, the First Republic had no fewer than four presidents, the most influential of whom was the Catalan federalist Francesc Pi y Margall (1824–1901) who governed for a mere four months between April and July 1873. A veteran of the 1854 revolution, Pi was a freethinker and a convinced democrat who saw both church and monarchy as obstacles to progress. He was Spain's first theorist of regional aspirations, arguing for a consensual federalism, based on mutual association rather than the coercive power of the state.

Pi consequently rejected any imposed federalism just as he spurned centralizing government. He insisted on a legal solution to Spain's constitutional problems and resigned when he could not provide one.

Though his ideas were to be nurtured by Catalan nationalists, his time in power cannot be counted a success. His hopes for a national majority in favor of a federal republic were crushed between those who wanted a unitary state and provincial revolutionaries pressing for immediate devolution. The Republic disintegrated in his wake: army discipline collapsed and a flurry of independent cantons was hastily declared in the south. Power once again reverted to the generals. Conservatives throughout the land welcomed the final military intervention that restored morale among the troops, suppressed the cantons and, in 1875, restored a Bourbon king, Alfonso XII (1875–85), eldest surviving son of Isabel II.

Restoration and rotativism

The larger-than-life figure of Antonio Cánovas del Castillo (1828–97) presided over the Restoration monarchy. A superb orator, Cánovas aimed to create stable parliamentary government in Spain, encourage economic progress and free the country from the sterility of civil war. His ideal was the British two-party system – he had memorized the speeches of the British party leaders Gladstone and Disraeli and insisted that the king read the works of the English constitutionalist, Walter Bagehot. Cánovas's first aim was to create a monarchy that would refrain from meddling in parliamentary affairs. As the new king was a 16-year-old cadet fresh from the British military academy of Sandhurst, keeping the monarchy above politics proved a comparatively easy task. When Alfonso died ten years later of tuberculosis, the succession passed to the yet unborn Alfonso XIII (1902–31), whose mother María Cristina (1858–1929) was to prove a compliant regent.

No stable parliamentary government could hope to flourish with the continual threat of military intervention; keeping the army confined to barracks was perhaps Cánovas's most urgent task. He fostered a cult of loyalty to the soldier-king – the vestiges of which may still be seen today – while the extended war in Cuba (which erupted again in 1895) occupied the army overseas. After the experience of the First Republic, the army had become increasingly preoccupied with the problem of social order, though it was prepared to stay on the sidelines as long as civilians proved capable of maintaining order.

The British political system that Cánovas so admired was a representative one, with the composition of the lower house of parliament dependent on the will of an expanding electorate. Nevertheless, the Spanish statesman profoundly distrusted universal suffrage, which he described as "the dissolution of society". Until 1890, voting in Spanish elections was confined to property owners and tax payers, but Cánovas still feared electoral volatility. Though his desire for a parliamentary system that marginalized the electorate seemed paradoxical, such a system already existed in Portugal, which had long been trying to emulate British political stability.

Despite a continuing traditon of military interventionism, Portugal had suffered no large-scale civil conflict since the 1840s. The main political parties, the Regenerators and the Historics, had alternated in power more or less since the 1850s. After 1871, this system of power-sharing was formalized under António Maria Fontes de Pereira de Melo (1819–87). A third party, the Reformists, had arisen in the 1860s, but it joined forces with the Historics in 1876 to

Transportation

The difficulties of transportation on the Iberian peninsula consistently inhibited industrial and urban growth: none of the main rivers is fully navigable and all are liable to flooding and drought. The prospect of building canals first received serious consideration during the 18th century, but the difficulty and expense of carrying them long distance through mountainous terrain proved prohibitive. Overland journeys by road were long, dangerous and expensive: until late in the 19th century carters and muleteers had to be paid to conduct people and goods over poor tracks and to protect them from smugglers and bandits. Transportation was therefore mainly by sea, until the coming of the railroads. Though the Spanish government subsidized around 30 percent of the construction costs of the national railroad network, the companies were owned by foreign capitalists. Tracks radiated out from Madrid, which – though the national capital - was not a center of economic significance. Though some local industrial needs were served, the network failed to integrate the peninsular economies. However, urban centers developed rapidly from the late 19th century, as communications improved.

become the Progressive Party; henceforth they simply alternated in power with Fontes's Regenerators. Rotativism, as the Portuguese procedure was known, was replicated in Spain by Cánovas's Liberal Conservatives (later simply Conservatives) and the Liberal Party of Práxedes Sagasta (1825–1903). Both men were pragmatists; one would govern for as long as he could command a majority and then hand over to his rival. No other party was permitted representation.

This "peaceful turnaround" – the name adopted in Spain after 1876 – was at the heart of the rotativist system. Elections were held merely to obtain a governing majority while ensuring an adequate number of seats for the opposition. The actual outcome of elections was decided in advance, and at the center. Such a system, of course, depended upon clientelism – the traditional way of conducting business on the peninsula. Deputies were returned to office to obtain benefits for their constituents; if they failed to deliver the promised rewards, their clients would transfer their allegiance to someone who seemed more likely to do so. Politics was thus conducted through a series of face-to-face relationships; in effect, personalism assumed an advanced parliamentary façade.

Once an election was called, the desired result would be produced by local notables – known in Spain as *caciques* – drawn from the petty nobility and the landed bourgeoisie. As landowners, these men had

links with both local communities and the political party machine. At election time, favors were traded on a national scale with rewards handed out to those who voted in a particular way or eased the path of a certain candidate. Political office became simply a source of patronage. The parliamentary "pork barrel" was vast, not least because every new administration brought in its own bureaucracy. As government service was a principal source of middle-class employment, parallel bureaucracies developed. These rotated along with the politicians: those currently out of office – the *cesantes* – would while away their time in the cafés of Lisbon and Madrid, developing contacts and storing up favors for their next turn in power.

Rotativism ushered in a period of stable constitutional rule in the peninsula, free from regal caprice and military intervention. However, rotativism was essentially a means of keeping the old landed oligarchy in power. Spain's Conservative and Liberal Parties, for instance, broadly represented the wheat farmers of the north and the olive and vine growers of the south; there was no place for Catalan industrialists, nor for the increasingly important Basque ironmasters.

Rotativist stability brought economic progress but, as transport improved and industry developed, so new political forces emerged that could not be contained by the artifice of the "peaceful turnaround". Even when the system was working, the fixers and brokers could not "make" elections in big urban centers where the forces of mass politics were already playing their part. Here, clientelism was replaced by coercion and falsification. Thuggery was commonplace, glass ballot boxes were not unknown and, on numerous occasions, the inhabitants of the local cemetery turned out to be reliable voters. The interests of the electorate were sacrificed to the smooth running of a political machine. The increasingly corrupt and discredited system engendered apathy and alienation among the mass of the people, who turned instead to extra-parliamentary political movements such as separatism, socialism and anarchism. The articulation of working-class grievance and regional aspirations through these movements finally revealed the bankruptcy of the rotativist system.

Realism and urbanism

Though fervor for change during the "six revolutionary years" (1868–74) was not confined to the political sphere, artistic endeavor in the peninsula was sustained by years of peace and relative prosperity. During the late 19th century, prose – whether fictional, polemical or critical – prevailed. Contemporary poetry was largely unremarkable; the theater, though as popular as ever, was occupied with *zarzuelas*, an idiomatic form of operetta that, in the hands of composers such as Tomás Bretón (1850–1923) and Francisco Asenjo Barbieri (1823–94), made great play with folksong and regional dances.

From the 1850s, professional singers of traditional folk music, *fado* in Portugal and flamenco in Spain, began to appear in the cafés of Lisbon and Seville. However, the legacy of the Romantic movement was not confined to music. *Costumbrismo*, or the detailed observation of local life, gave rise to the regional novel in Spain. José María de Pereda (1833–1906), for instance, set much of his work in the mountain countryside of his native Santander, often examining the impact of new ideas on old ways, while Valencia gave Vicente Blasco Ibáñez (1867–1928) the setting for both his best novels and his later career as a federalist politician. Leopoldo Aras' *La regenta* (1884–85) dealt with adultery in a stifling provincial town – a classic theme of realist writing since the French novelist Gustave Flaubert (1821–80) created his masterpiece *Madame Bovary* (1857).

The most unusual of Spain's regional novelists was a Galician countess, Emilia Pardo Bazán (1851–1921). She wrote in Spanish rather than *galego* and was far from being merely a provincial figure. Though a devout Catholic, she was influenced by the naturalistic techniques of the French novelist Emile Zola (1840–1902), whose work – first translated into Spanish in 1877 – had been reviled by her coreligionists in France. Bazán was a noted feminist, who wrote literary criticism as well as fiction and, in 1916, became the first woman to be appointed to a professorship at Madrid university.

Novels of provincial life proved popular because so

Below The *zarzuela* – an idiomatic form of operetta with spoken dialog – was the characteristic musical entertainment of turn-of-the-century Spain. Madrid's *Teatro de la Zarzuela* was dedicated to the form – an indication of the popularity of musical theater. Like the contemporary Spanish classical music tradition, *zarzuelas* made extensive use of folksong and regional dance. Many had regional settings; this backdrop is from a 1912 production of Pablo Luna's operetta "Molinos de viento" ("Windmills").

Above In late 19th-century Spain, regional life proved as rich a source for painters as for novelists. Genre scenes proved popular with artists and purchasers alike. Joaquín Sorolla y Bastida (1863–1923) drew much of his inspiration from the fisherfolk of his native Valencia. This picture, *Valencian Fishwives* (1903) is typical of his work. His observation of nature on the Mediterranean coast led to a use of light – known as "luminism" – that anticipated the Spanish impressionists.

many of the Spanish reading public recognized the world they portrayed. Reading was essentially a middle-class occupation; in the constitutional security of the late 19th century, a recognizable bourgeoisie developed in Madrid and Lisbon, as well as Porto and Barcelona. However, the population of the capitals was still largely made up of immigrants: the greatest chronicler of 19th-century Madrid, Benito Pérez Galdós (1843–1920), was born in the Canary Islands. Similarly, José Maria Eça de Queiroz (1845–1900), whose diplomatic career took him from Lisbon to Cuba, Britain, and France, came originally from the northern Portuguese village of Póvoa de Varzim.

In Galdós and Eça, the Iberian peninsula produced two of Europe's greatest "realist" novelists. Both men's work had a moral purpose: several of Galdós' novels explore the conflict of progress and obscurantism, while Eça strove to make the Portuguese aware of their impoverished situation. They both saw national self-delusion as dangerous. They described the social reality of a fast-changing world and, though both set some novels in the provinces, their greatest works portray the bourgeoisie of the capitals. For Galdós in particular, the city was more than a mere backdrop. Like Dickens' London or Balzac's Paris, Galdós' Madrid is a human creation, the scene of momentous historical and social change. His pages reproduce the very language of the city, with its mixture of dialects and low-life colloquialisms.

Only in the last decades of the 19th century did modern urban society emerge on the peninsula. As migrants of all social classes flocked to the new urban centers, so medieval city walls were demolished and elegant suburbs constructed for the middle classes while crowded slums sprang up for the workers. The developing discipline of town planning was given new impetus by the cholera epidemics of 1855, 1865 and 1885. Coherent designs were accepted as blueprints for the extension of Madrid and Barcelona in 1860 and of Bilbao in 1876. Plans ranged from the functional to the fantastic. The Madrid architect Arturo Soria (d.1920), for instance, envisaged a linear "garden city" of one great street, with low-level housing linked by tram and trolley. The crowning achievement of urban planning and development on the peninsula is, without a doubt, Barcelona, whose turn-of-the-century architecture contains important buildings by Modernist architects such as Domenech i Montaner (1850–1924) and Antoni Gaudí (1852–1926).

The squares, cafés and shopping emporia of these new cities were not only captured in novels; townspeople had also caught the attention of painters. In part, this was a response to the market. The bourgeoisie bought paintings – or prints and other cheaper reproductions – just as they bought novels. The increasing demand for contemporary subjects led to many attractive, if unremarkable, genre paintings. Workshops, such as that in Lisbon run by the Bordalo

Barcelona's Modernist Architecture

Between 1857 and 1930, the population of Barcelona rose from 178,625 to over one million. Industrial wealth attracted migrants by the thousand and also financed the rebuilding and enlargement of the city after the medieval walls were demolished in 1854. The new Barcelona was to be a truly European capital, a fitting focus for the Catalan nation. Historic references to the Spanish past were discarded by Ildefons Cerdà (1815–76), a civil engineer who drew up plans for a city in which all citizens would have equal access to daylight, space and air. The *Eixample* – the only part of the city to resemble his original vision – nevertheless became a showcase for the luxurious villas of the new industrial bourgeoisie. By the end of the century, the expanding city had swallowed up the small town of Gracià, which gave its name to Barcelona's most elegant boulevard. Here was displayed work by the great Catalan architects Lluís Domènech i Montaner (1850–1923), Antoni Gaudí (1852–1926), and Josep Puig i Cadafalch (1867–1956).

Their work epitomizes the Catalan architectural and decorative movement known as *Modernisme* (1880–1910). Like Art Nouveau, its wider European counterpart, *Modernisme* made great play of asymmetry, curves and dynamic shapes. Ceramics, mosaics, metalwork and stained glass ornamented the private villas and public buildings whose sumptuously decorated facades bore witness to remarkable standards of craftsmanship. The naturalistic motifs and designs that decorated the buildings distanced them from the industry that had financed them, though the materials used placed the Modernist style firmly in the late 19th century. In its imaginative re-creation of civic space, Barcelona came to rival Paris or Vienna.

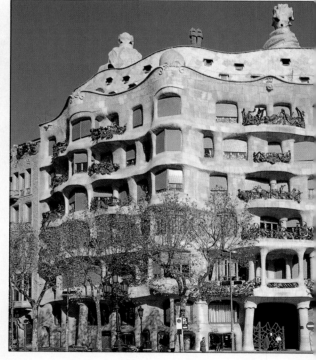

Above Gaudí's luxury apartment block the Casa Milá (1905–11) is one of Barcelona's best-known buildings. The remarkable undulating facade was made possible by the use of a steel-frame structure, which freed each floor from the restrictions of load-bearing walls. The asymmetric exterior uses a marine metaphor reflecting its "frozen wave" appearance. The forged-iron balconies resemble seaweed and coral while starfish and octopuses decorated the turquoise paving tiles outside on the Passeig de Gracià.

Left Across the way stands Puig i Cadafalch's Casa Amatller (1898–1900). Its Gothic style deliberately evokes Barcelona's medieval merchant palaces.

Top The decorative arts were fundamental to Catalan *Modernisme*. Perhaps the greatest synthesis of craftsmanship and architecture was achieved in Domènech i Montaner's Casa Lleó Morera (1905). The building itself was crassly remodelled in 1943 and much exterior ornamentation was lost. Many of the interiors, however, survived intact, displaying stone-carvings, ceramics, mosaics and stained glass. The rich colors and design of the 9-panelled curved window shown here reflect the stylized use of nature that was a recurrent theme of the Modernists, particularly in the work of Domènech, whose generous use of floral ornament was designed as a counterbalance to architectural rationality.

Right Gaudí's Casa Battló (1905–7) stands next to the Casa Amatller on the Passeig de Gracià; the top left-hand room was demolished so that the buildings would tie together. Gaudí's extraordinary, fluid skyline is in complete contrast to Puig i Cadafalch's Gothic crenellations. The facade of the existing building was enlivened with intricate mosaics of broken tiles and plates, which change in color from all-white on the bottom floor to blue, green and ocher above – a distinctive palette that Gaudí used only once. The house was to be a religious and patriotic symbol. The roof's humped ridges and glossy scales represent the dragon defeated by St George, Catalonia's patron saint, whose lance rises as a half-round tower set in the facade.

The Four Cats Café

Between 1897 and 1903, Els Quatre Gats, or Four Cats café, epitomized the bohemian life of turn-of-the-century Barcelona. Founded by the painters Santiago Rusinyol and Ramón Casas, who were both leading figures in the Modernist movement, it was housed in Josep Puig i Cadafalch's Casa Martí, where it served both as a meeting place and beer hall for the city's artistic and intellectual community. Its name derived from a Catalan slang term meaning "just a few people"; the "four cats", however, were commonly identified as Rusinyol, Casas, the folklorist and puppeteer Miquel Utrillo, and the café's idiosyncratic manager, Pere Romeu, who was also a painter, though not a very successful one.

The convivial intimacy of the café had long been a feature of urban life in Spain. Madrid had several famous literary cafés, such as the Café Gijón, where writers, politicians and intellectuals would meet in regular informal discussion groups (*tertulias*). Only The Four Cats was to achieve international renown as the Iberian equivalent of the bohemian cafés of the Left Bank in Paris – a reflection, in part, of the greater vibrancy of the Catalan capital.

Life at The Four Cats was one long *tertulia*. Regular customers included the artists Pablo Picasso and Isidre Nonell, along with the "four cats" themselves. Exhibitions and lectures were held there; musicians, including Enrique Granados and Isaac Albéniz, gave recitals, while the artists and writers associated with the café published their own illustrated review, *Pèl i ploma* (*Paper and Pen*). For these men, art was to provide a means of overcoming the materialism of modern, industrial Barcelona. Rusinyol believed in practicing "the religion of art and truth...dominating the based and profane world". To this end, he funded The Four Cats. However – though an artistic legend – it was not a commercial success. After a mere six years, the café closed.

Left The son of a textile manufacturer, Santiago Rusinyol used his considerable private means to fund artistic endeavors, including The Four Cats. Like his friend Ramón Casas – who left this sketch of him seated in one of the enormous ring chandeliers he had bought for the café – Rusinyol had lived in Paris where, with Casas and Utrillo, he established a Catalan artistic colony.

Above Pablo Picasso staged his first public exhibition at The Four Cats in 1900. He also designed this menu card for the café when he was 17. Picasso was only one of many young artists who benefited from the intellectual life of The Four Cats, which provided an escape from the stifling academicism of Spain's artistic establishment.

Above The architect Puig i Cadafalch designed the Gothic-style interior of The Four Cats (seen here in a photograph taken c. 1899) including much of the pseudo-medieval furniture; the wrought-ironwork reflected Rusinyol's interest in this traditional Catalan craft. The huge canvas by Casas that dominates the walls shows himself and Pere Romeu on a tandem. Bicycling was a favorite activity of Romeu's, but here his gangling figure surveys the café from the back seat while Casas does the work of two at the front.

Far left Among the most important legacies of The Four Cats are the portrait sketches of café regulars left by Casas and Picasso. This charcoal drawing of Picasso is one of hundreds of likenesses Casas made in the 1890s.

Left Casas also painted this poster for a Puchinel (Punch and Judy) puppet show. Both Romeu (shown here) and Utrillo had worked as puppeteers at the Chat Noir and gave avant-garde shadow puppet shows based on what they had learned there. But the hand puppet performances that drew on the local tradition of Punch and Judy attracted larger audiences. Given in Catalan, they reintroduced a forgotten popular art into the metropolitan culture of Barcelona.

Pinheiro family – Manoel-Maria (1815–80), his sister Maria Augusta and his son Columbano (1857–1929) – fed a growing market.

Inevitably, French Impressionism had a profound effect on peninsular art. Painters of landscapes and rural scenes depicted their subjects in a new way. The Spaniard Joaquín Sorolla (1863–1923) spoke of "luminism", and his shore scenes – usually set on the coast of his native Valencia – concentrate on light. Other artists, particularly in Catalonia, brought new techniques to urban scenes. Santiago Rusinyol (Rusiñol) (1861–1931) and, above all, Ramón Casas (1866–1932) left a record of bohemian and bourgeois life in Barcelona – which, for a time, rivaled Paris as an artistic center. Casas and Rusinyol painted each other, their friends, the cafés they frequented and the streetlife of the city, including the twilight world of whores and morphine addicts. Casas also earned money designing advertising hoardings and posters for Catalan-language publications; in the 1890s, he also courted notoriety with a series of highly critical political paintings. In cosmopolitan Barcelona, an artist was never short of a subject.

The crisis of rotativism

In his masterpiece, *The Maias* (1880), one of Eça de Queiroz's characters observes that there has been no news from Lisbon since the death of João VI in 1826. Though rather more had occurred in 19th-century Portugal than Eça cared to suggest, the middle years of the century had not been eventful. But oligarchic politics had at least brought constitutional stability to the country and, against all expectations, Portugal remained a colonial power. By the 1870s, under João de Andrade Corvo (1824–90: foreign minister 1871–77 and 1878–79), the Portuguese government was again dreaming of overseas expansion – a traditional recompense for the failure of domestic development. Seeing Africa carved up between the European powers, Portugal staked a claim for more colonies. In 1886, Portuguese expansionists drew up a "rose-colored map" showing a great swathe of Portuguese territory in southern Africa that would link the existing colonies of Angola and Mozambique. The proposal was not only unrealistic, but it also interfered with British plans for Rhodesia. In January 1890, the British prime minister, Lord Salisbury (1830–1903), demanded that Portuguese personnel be withdrawn from the disputed territory.

The Portuguese government had no choice but to comply with British demands, and thereby revealed its foreign policy as a sham. Colonial posturings could no longer disguise the lack of real power behind them just as, at home, impending governmental bankruptcy threatened to crack the representative façade of rotativism. From intellectuals of all kinds – including Eça and the future president of the Republic, Teófilo Braga (1843–1924) – came the demand that the nation "saw itself as it was" and accepted the need for modernization. Others advised a more active response. The Republican party, founded in 1878, was a growing force that, after the crisis of Lord Salisbury's ultimatum, also urged a new direction in national life. Under pressure, and faced with continuing financial constraints, the party of government began to disintegrate. Not even a spell of governing by degree, following the deferral of elections in 1894, could save the Regenerators from schism. The party split in 1901, and it was only an increased reliance on authoritarian tactics that allowed the remnants of rotativism to stagger on until 1910.

The national crisis of conscience that afflicted Portugal after 1890 was paralleled in Spain by the "disaster" of 1898. In this year, the long-standing Cuban troubles came to a head when the United States, anxious to establish American hegemony in the Caribbean, declared war on Spain. In the resulting military action, the Spanish fleet was wiped out. After a matter of weeks, the old imperial power was forced to cede its few surviving non-African possessions to the United States. The 1898 war destroyed all Spain's remaining pretensions to great-power status; public destruction of the imperial image turned defeat into abject national humiliation. As in Portugal, national pride had already been corroded by economic stricture and political dishonesty. Now, in the wake of moral disaster, the political system bore the blame for the defeat. As one, not untypical, Castilian polemic tellingly put it: "All is broken down in this wretched country: no government, no electors, no parties, no navy, no army. All is ruin, decadence."

The appeal for national renewal was taken up by intellectuals. The jurist and polemicist, Joaquín Costa (1846–1911), demanded "an iron surgeon" to cut out the gangrene of corruption. The call to open Spain to modern, European influences was echoed by the country's most prominent scientist, Santiago Ramón y Cajal (1852–1934), winner of the 1906 Nobel prize for medicine, and by a disparate group of young writers known as the "generation of 1898". Though never a coherent or organized group, the "generation of 1898" held up to scrutiny the malaise of their times. The name of the group was popularized by the writer Azorín (José Martínez Ruíz 1874–1967) who, like the poet Antonio Machado (1875–1939) and the novelist Pío Baroja (1872–1956), helped develop the prevailing intellectual themes of how to characterize both the national problem and the nature of the Spanish soul. In 1898, the common goal was regeneration, articulated by the philosopher Miguel de Unamuno (1869–1936) as the reconciliation of new ideas and eternal Spanish tradition. A rector of Salamanca university, Unamuno bridged the generational gap between the men of 1898 and younger scholars, such as José Ortega y Gasset (1883–1955), whose *Invertebrate Spain* (1921) again examined the gulf between the European and Spanish experiences.

The making of the working class

Before the 20th century, the peninsula's proletariat was largely composed of the rural laborers of Andalusia and southern Portugal. The retarded and patchy nature of industrial development ensured that the number of factory workers remained small: in 1917 the Portuguese industrial workforce numbered only 130,000 – 35 percent of whom were women and 15 percent minors – while the number of factories with over 500 employees was a mere 25. Though factory production was more widespread in Spain, the rural labor force in Andalusia was still equal in size to Spain's entire industrial proletariat at the turn of the 20th century.

In these circumstances, it is perhaps not surprising that anarchism – the political belief that all forms of governmental authority are unnecessary and which advocates a society based on voluntary cooperation and the free association of individuals – flourished on the peninsula. The first anarcho-collectivist federation, established in Spain in 1869, was dedicated to the destruction of state power through working-class revolution. Soon declared illegal, the federation went underground, only to reemerge under a different name – the beginning of a cycle of repression and toleration that was to persist into the 20th century.

The Spanish anarchists became enthusistic proponents of "propaganda by deed". Anarchist direct action encompassed traditional forms of rural social protest – riots, the destruction of property, and the mutilation of livestock – which, in southern regions, had long been the only protest available to malnourished landless laborers who were only too aware that work was short and workers plentiful. Anarchism first took hold in the south, and it has been argued that its utopian vision of a world to come had a particular appeal for these oppressed, illiterate and superstitious rural laborers.

Anarchist millenarianism was not confined to the *latifundia* areas of the south. Dramatic – and often highly symbolic – challenges to state power were undertaken in the belief that they would immediately usher in the revolution. Cánovas met his death at the hands of an anarchist assassin in 1897; two other prime ministers, José Canalejas (1854–1912) and Eduardo Dato (1856–1921) died the same way. A bomb was thrown at Alfonso XIII's wedding procession in 1906, just as, in 1896, anarchists had blown up the Barcelona Corpus Christi procession, simultaneously attacking not only the panoply of the state but also the sacramental presence of the Catholic God.

Though Barcelona was a prime focus for urban unrest, it was an unlikely anarchist stronghold. Nevertheless, Spain's most prosperous, modern industrial city became the center of the anarcho-syndicalist union, the Confederación Nacional de Trabajo (CNT: National Confederation of Labor) established in 1910. For anarcho-syndicalists the withdrawal of labor would, at some point, lead to revolution, the destruction of the state and the emergence of a new social order. With firm organizational backing, anarchism flourished in the "revolutionary triangle" between Barcelona, Valencia and Zaragoza. Night schools and other educational initiatives helped foster a discrete anarchist subculture with its own customs and folklore. Various minority forms developed; some anarcho-syndicalists were vegetarians, others teetotallers or nudists. More important was the feminist anarchism, that was to come to fruition in the 1930s.

The CNT was a broad church, but the extent of its appeal to industrial workers is hard to explain except in terms of the comparative failure of Spanish socialism. Though the Socialist Party had been established in 1879 and a corresponding trade union, the Unión General de Trabajadores (UGT: General Workers' Union), founded in 1888, the movement made little headway until 1914 when the UGT won converts among the foundry workers of the Basque Country and the miners of Asturias. Socialist organization was centrist, bureaucratic and firmly based in Madrid. Recruitment was confined to industrial workers in a land with little industry; the mass of workers were excluded because they labored on the land – only belatedly was the socialist landworkers' union established in 1931. The small size of the Spanish industrial workforce acted as a brake on all union activity. The UGT competed with the CNT for members and, even after the working class had begun to expand, socialists consistently refused to ally with anarchists.

Industrialization and urbanization
In both Spain and Portugal industrial development was patchy: the mining sector was very important, especially tungsten in Portugal, while Spain was rich in minerals including copper and, in the north, coal. However, only in the coastal regions of the north and northeast (where textiles were the leading sector), and in Portugal around Lisbon and Porto, was industrialization extensive. As late as the 1960s in Spain, and the 1980s in Portugal, most of the workforce was engaged in agriculture.

As a neutral power, Spain benefited economically during World War I. Sales of coal, iron and steel, textiles and even expensive Castilian wheat all boomed; the number of textile workers – virtually all of them in Catalonia – almost doubled. Economic success was, however, accompanied by rampant inflation and increased labor unrest. Separatist feeling in Catalonia reached boiling-point. The bourgeoisie wanted home rule and, not infrequently, a republic; the proletariat wanted anarcho-syndicalist revolution; neither wanted rule from Madrid.

From 1917, strikes, unrest and rebellion dominated all aspects of life in Spain. Faced with escalating crisis,

the government's only recourse was the use of force. The main police force, the Civil Guard, had been established in 1844 and became an integral part of the army in 1878. Civil Guards lived in barracks, separated from the local population, and never served in their native regions. In 1854, the force's deployment had been described as "a fully military occupation of the entire national territory" and, in the crisis of the Restoration monarchy (1917–23), they came to be perceived as a hostile army. The government became increasingly reliant on their repressive military presence. When, in 1917, troops machine-gunned strikers in the streets of Barcelona, it was clear that only the

147

crude use of armed force was preventing a revolutionary outburst in Spain.

The Portuguese Republic

An early Republican rebel in Portugal informed the judge hearing his trial that he "did not know what a republic was, but it could not help but be a holy thing". Such inchoate beliefs did much to bolster the initial popularity of the Portuguese Republic ushered in by the 1910 revolution. Visions of a better, even a utopian, future opened up before those who had not benefited under the monarchy, and they welcomed the new regime as a panacea for all ills.

The Portuguese Republic had come about, in part, because of the continuing tribulations of the house of Bragança. The assassination of King Carlos I (1889–1908) and his heir, Luis Felipe, in a Lisbon street on 1 February 1908 plunged the country into civil strife. Far from generating a wave of sympathy for the monarchy, the first regicide in Portuguese history led to a popular subscription being opened for the assassins' families. Carlos's successor Manuel II (1908–10) – known to history as "Manuel the Unfortunate" – ruled for under two years.

Manuel II abdicated when it became apparent that there was virtually no one left to defend his throne. In October 1910, a naval mutiny quickly sparked off a more general revolt. In the north, the peasantry – without whose acquiescence no revolution could hope to succeed in Portugal – marched on rural towns, though without any very clear idea of the "Republic" for which they were fighting. In the cities, urban workers were among the first to join the clamor for a republic. Though a Portuguese socialist party had been established in 1871, and anarchist-inspired labor unrest had become increasingly prevalent since the turn of the century, the industrial working class was so small as to be almost exiguous. In these circumstances, republicanism became a catch-all category, appealing to discontented workers, impoverished peasants and restless soldiers, as well as the petty bourgeoisie in the towns and cities. Excluded from the benefits of power by the governing oligarchy, these small merchants and professional men were the backbone of the republican movement and, therefore, the new political class.

The Portuguese Republic was to be an absolute break with the past. A new flag was introduced and the national anthem – which had previously hymned the virtues of the Constitutional Charter of 1826 – was replaced with a song full of yearning for lost maritime glories: "Oh sea heroes, oh noble people . . . raise again the splendor of Portugal . . . may Europe claim to all the world that Portugal is not dead."

Along with this dream of resurgence went a new political order that was intended to lay the foundations of modernity and strength. The old regime was to be swept aside and replaced with parliamentary democracy. To this end the Republicans separated church and state and introduced freedom of worship. Some bishops were deposed and others banished, religious instruction was removed from the school curriculum, public manifestations of cult, including the wearing of habits, were prohibited and all religious communities were dissolved. Catholic holidays were replaced by national ones, civil marriage and divorce were introduced and even the cemeteries were secularized. A new social order was legislated into existence while government-inspired propaganda preached scientism and warned of the dangers of

Left As an industrial working class formed in the city of Barcelona, and the anarchist movement grew in strength, so labor unrest became increasingly prevalent. Strikes and protests were invariably brutally repressed. Ramón Casas' picture *The Charge* shows the hated figure of a Civil Guard riding down a vulnerable worker who has fallen to the floor. Other Guardsmen, sabers drawn, charge the crowd of unarmed protesters who flee in panic. Casas painted this picture in 1899 but later he changed its date to 1903 and its title to *Barcelona, 1902* – a political statement that commemorated the general strike of that year.

"superstition". Secularism, agnosticism and even atheism were actively encouraged.

The government's actions met with bitter protests. Though the new constitutional arrangements would have had little practical impact on the great mass of Portuguese Catholics, the devout northern peasantry was grossly offended by state interference in traditional pious practice. Under the new laws, church bells were muffled, processions outlawed and new arrangements had to be made for burying the dead. The Republican government also proved unable to replace church personnel in education and social work; those previously reliant on Catholic schooling or religious charity often found nothing to replace them.

After the initial euphoria, the Republic fueled conflict and discord just as the monarchy had done. Hailed as a remedy for all woes, the Republic could only disappoint. Its revolutionary program was largely confined to abolishing the monarchy and extirpating Catholicism; the latter was far from being an unqualified success. The lack of any social program, combined with continuing economic problems, contributed to escalating social unrest. As the labor and syndical movements grew in strength, so the government found itself pitted against both urban and rural workers in north and south.

Most importantly, the Republic failed to establish democracy in Portugal. Women were never given the vote, supposedly because of their greater attachment to the church, and the suffrage remained restricted. Promises of devolving power to the provinces came to nothing as government was centralized and bureaucratized. Press censorship was common and, in the fluid politics that characterized the change of regime, personalism and factionalism flourished as never before. The Portuguese Republic had 45 governments in under 16 years. Prime ministers were changed not by the electorate but by the army, whose frequent insurrections were one of the few constants in political life after 1910.

In 1916, the Portuguese government, eager for a glimmer of international prestige and mindful of the ancient alliance with England, entered World War I on

Right By the time the Portuguese Republic was declared in 1910, the ruling house of Bragança had lost virtually all popular support. As this Republican lampoon shows, the royal dynasty was perceived – at least in some quarters – as a motley collection of cuckolds, gluttons, snobs and idiots. Portugal's last king, Manuel II (1903–10) abdicated when it became clear there was no one to defend him. He died in exile in Twickenham (London) in 1932, leaving no children.

open fighting broke out in the streets of Lisbon.

As social unrest combined with military conspiracy and endemic political crisis, some took refuge in dreams of a messianic savior. To such people, Sidónio Pais (1872–1918) seemed the heroic Sebastião of national legend. Sidónio's coup d'état of December 1917 created Europe's first modern Republican dictatorship. A highly charismatic figure, Sidónio's presidential style of politics had little sound administrative support. By the time of his assassination in December 1918, the New Republic was already in crisis. Yet, Sidónio left an important legacy, for his rule led conservatives to abandon monarchism. As the Catholic parties regrouped after 1917–18, they left the house of Bragança to its fate and concentrated instead on winning power for themselves.

Chaos and the avant garde

The Portuguese Republic, like Spain's Restoration monarchy, ended in turmoil. In both cases, years of constitutional sterility were ended by authoritarian intervention. In 1923, General Miguel Primo de Rivera (1870–1930) staged a military coup in Spain, with the acquiescence of Alfonso XIII. Ruling as a dictator, he put an end to six years of civil strife in which the most dynamic political force had been Catalan nationalism. Three years later, the Portuguese army overthrew democracy and instituted a provisional government under the leadership of General Oscar Carmona (1869–1951), who was elected president in 1928. In both Spain and Portugal, extreme political instability had been succeeded by the suppression of democracy and rule by the army. Despite these

the side of the Allies. The Republic was now less radical and some reconciliation was taking place, particularly in the area of church–state relations. However, entry into the war led to economic hardship, while the raising of troops to fight in France proved desperately unpopular. A new period of social turmoil ensued; a wave of strikes spread over the country in 1917 and

Right The democratic Portuguese Republic was to be a complete break with the corrupt monarchical past. The new regime quickly set about creating its own myths and symbols. This commemorative montage shows the allegorical figure of the Republic rising above the statesmen and politicians who formed the new government. The surrounding scenes emphasize the regime's popular origins and commemorate the naval mutiny that acted as a catalyst for a general revolt. The forces of reaction, epitomized by the clergy, are shown being led off by armed civilian defenders of the Republic.

Federico García Lorca

Federico García Lorca (1898–1936) is Spain's most famous 20th-century literary figure. He was born into an affluent and affectionate professional family in the southern city of Granada, but his talent and his homosexuality placed him outside conventional bourgeois society. Lorca, then a young graduate in Madrid, met the surrealist painter Salvador Dalí in 1923, and a passionate friendship developed. The relationship was a formative influence on Lorca's life, but he merely flirted with surrealism: his early successes – a play, *Mariana Pineda* (produced in Madrid in 1927) and a collection of poetry, *Gypsy Ballads* (1928) – which brought him sudden fame, drew on the stories, language and imagery of his native Andalusia rather than surrealism's shocking posturing. The banning of his next play, *Don Perlimpín*, by Primo de Rivera's dictatorship coincided with Dalí's departure to Paris, and

Lorca became acutely depressed. In 1929 he left Spain for New York. A direct result of his stay in the United States was his *Poet in New York* (1929–30), which represented a radical new departure in his poetry. But one observer commented that Lorca was now more Spanish, more Andalusian than ever. In 1930 he returned via Cuba to Spain and began to concentrate on writing for the theater. In the liberal climate of the Second Republic, his career flourished: he was a leading supporter of the new regime and produced his major plays while it was in power. His Republicanism led directly to his death. On the outbreak of civil war in July 1936, Granada fell to the rebel generals. On 18 August 1936, Lorca was executed by firing squad in Víznar, a village outside Granada. His body was never identified and, in the early years of the Franco regime, his works were banned.

Left Lorca's dark hair and coloring marked him out as a native Andalusian. As this portrait by Federico Toledo suggests, he experimented with image, though the impeccably dressed poet was never outrageous, unlike Salvador Dalí. A concern for convention perhaps explains Lorca's anxiety to keep his homosexuality hidden. It was a secret from his Catholic family, to whom he was close, and seems to have been a source of anxiety to Lorca, not least because of the extreme intolerance of contemporary Spanish society. Homosexuality remained unacknowledged even in liberal intellectual circles.

Above All Lorca's best-known works as a playwright were produced in the brief but exciting period between his return to Spain in 1930 and his death in 1936. The German artist Siegfried Bürmann – who had helped transform the art of scenery design in Spain – collaborated with Lorca on the sets for *The Shoemaker's Prodigious Wife*, staged in 1930.

Right The poster for the original production of *Yerma* (1934), one of three elegiac and powerful tragedies on Andalusian themes by Lorca – the others are *Blood Wedding* (1933) and *The House of Bernarda Alba* (1936). They are remarkable not just for their poetry but for the strength of their female roles.

Left In 1932, Lorca founded a traveling theater company, La Barraca, as part of an initiative to take culture and democracy to the people. The actors were all amateur students from Madrid University. Though the fame of Lorca's own plays was growing at this time, the company's repertoire was based on the Spanish classics. La Barraca's emblem of a mask within a wheel was designed by Lorca's friend Benjamín Palencia.

unpromising political circumstances, the first decades of the 20th century gave rise to some remarkable artistic achievements, particularly in Spain. Freed from the constraints of figurative representation by technological developments – most obviously photography – visual and plastic artists were exploring new ways of depicting the modern world. Art was again an elite intellectual activity with an international market. In this world, Paris was dominant and, after 1900, all the great modern Spanish artists lived and worked there, at least for a time.

Among those who moved to Paris permanently was Pablo Picasso (1881–1973). Born in Málaga, he later studied in Barcelona where he was associated with Ramón Casas and the young figurative artist, Isidre Nonell (1873–1911), whose striking paintings of gypsies and paupers influenced Picasso in his blue and rose periods (c.1901–05). After his move to Paris in 1900, Picasso became a prime force in the new Cubist movement. The Cubists, who included Picasso's compatriot Juan Gris (1887–1927) and the Frenchman, Georges Braque (1882–1963), together with more minor exponents such as Portugal's Amadeu de Sousa Cardoso (1887–1918), experimented with form and perspective, most notably by displaying several aspects of the same object simultaneously. The Spanish sculptors Pablo Gargallo (1881–1934) and Julio González (1876–1942) also worked with the Cubists in Paris. Both men worked with metal – a craft González had learned in his father's workshop – building on Spanish traditions in fine metal and wrought-iron work. Their Cubist representations not only combined the worlds of Parisian artists and Iberian artisans but also gave a new direction to Spanish sculpture.

Inevitably, the Cubist movement produced a backlash. The Catalan artist Joan Miró (1893–1983) said he had always wanted to "smash the Cubists' guitar", though he too had been influenced by Picasso's Cubist pieces. In 1924, Miró put his name to the manifesto issued by another self-consciously modern group of artists, the Surrealists. Strongly influenced by psychoanalysis, the Surrealists used incongruous images in an attempt to reflect the subconscious world. However, unlike his fellow-Catalan, the talented self-publicist Salvador Dalí (1904–89), or the Spaniard Oscar Domínguez (1906–58), Miró remained an individualist whose work shows a variety of styles and influences. Outside the galleries, Surrealism made its greatest impact on the cinema. Dalí collaborated with the Spanish film-maker Luis Buñuel (1900–83) on the Surrealist movies, *Un chien andalou* (1929) and *L'Age d'Or* (1931) and later worked with the English director Alfred Hitchcock (1899–1980) on the dream sequences in *Spellbound* (1945).

Dalí and Buñuel were also associated with the poet Federico García Lorca (1898–1936) whom they met while all three were students in Madrid in the early 1920s. Lorca belonged to the "generation of 27", a remarkable group of poets including Rafael Albertí (b. 1902), Vicente Aleixandre (1898–1984) and, in the 1930s, Miguel Hernández (1910–42) whose work was first recognized during Primo de Rivera's dictatorship. This remarkable flowering of Spanish poetry had no parallel in other branches of literature. Many of the "generation of 27" were Andalusian and shared a common sense of Spanish history, epitomized in their revival of the Golden Age poet Luis de Góngora (1561–1627). These same Andalusian roots, together with a sense of the past, were shared by the greatest of

(1888–1935). Though he was born in Lisbon, Pessoa was educated in Durban (South Africa) and his first poems were written in English. His contribution to Portuguese literature was extraordinary, not least because it was the product not of one man, but of four. As well as writing metaphysical poetry under his own name, Pessoa created three "heteronyms" – Alberto Caeiro, Alvaro de Campos and Ricardo Reis – all of whom wrote in different styles. Caeiro was a logical positivist for whom appearance was the only reality, Campos was a futurist writer of enthusiastic verse, while Reis was a classical humanist.

Pessoa strongly denied that his heteronyms were mere pseudonyms, arguing that they were rather manifestations of the multiple personalities found in all human beings. So real were they to him that each had his own biography, appearance and intellectual personality. Ricardo Reis, for instance, was supposedly born in Porto in 1887, educated by the Jesuits and became a general practitioner after taking a medical degree. A freethinker and fatalist, he wrote poetry in his spare time and, as a monarchist, went into exile rather than submit to a Republic. Though he found little recognition in his lifetime, since his death Pessoa has been hailed as the greatest Portuguese poet since Camões in the 16th century. His influence on younger generations of writers has been profound, while his extraordinary literary personality – or personalities – even became a character in a contemporary Portuguese novel, José Saramago's *The Year of the Death of Ricardo Reis* (1984).

Above Manuel de Falla (1876–1946) – depicted here in a sketch by the young Pablo Picasso – is the best-known of all 20th-century Spanish composers. With its haunting Andalusian themes, his music has come to define what is thought of as "Spanish" music.

Left The Catalan cellist Pau Casals (1876–1973) was one of the 20th century's greatest instrumentalists. After Franco's victory, Casals went into exile and between 1945–50 refused to give public performances in protest at the Allies' failure to intervene in Spain after World War II. This statue is by Josep Viladomat i Massanas (1899–1989).

the peninsula's 20th-century composers, Manuel de Falla (1876–1946).

A close friend of García Lorca, Falla was a pupil of the Catalan musicologist Felipe Pedrell (1841–1922). Founder of the modern school of Spanish music, Pedrell encouraged a knowledge and understanding of traditional music, believing that any truly national music must have indigenous roots. The first major exponents of the new music were, perhaps ironically, both Catalan. Isaac Albéniz (1860–1909) – also a pupil of Pedrell – and Enrique Granados (1867–1916) dominated music on the peninsula at the turn of the century. Both incorporated stylized folk-song and popular dance measures into their works and are now best remembered for their piano pieces, which make delicate use of local color.

The use of traditional music in modern composition was continued by, among others, Joaquín Turina (1882–1949) and, in a younger generation, Falla's pupils Ernesto and Rodolfo Halffter (1905–89 and 1900–87). None exceeded the achievements of Falla himself, who has won more renown outside Spain than any other modern Iberian composer. His most popular pieces are the Andalusian ballets *El sombrero de tres picos* ("The Three-Cornered Hat") and, in particular, *El amor brujo* ("Love the Magician") which makes dramatic use of flamenco – a popular art that Falla attempted to revive. A native of Granada, Falla combined a deep love of his native region with a profound and ascetic Catholicism. He spent the last years of his life composing an opera, *Atlántida*, but this remained unfinished at the time of his death in exile in Argentina.

Undoubtedly, the artistic achievements of the early 20th century in the peninsula were predominantly Spanish. However, perhaps the outstanding literary figure was the Portuguese poet Fernando Pessoa

The Second Spanish Republic

By 1929 virtually all traces of the initial enthusiasm for General Primo de Rivera's dictatorship had evaporated. Though the general could never have satisfied all the groups that supported him at the time of the coup, nevertheless, he ended by alienating all of them. Even the army – outraged at Primo's heavy-handed attempt to introduce some much needed reform – had withdrawn its support.

By the end of the decade, only Alfonso XIII seemed more unpopular than Primo. The monarch had acted illegally in appointing Primo as head of the government and was widely blamed for the consequences. Just as the country was beginning to feel the effects of the international depression of the 1930s, the historically fragmented Republican movement built up strength and moved toward unity, finally agreeing to cooperate with the Socialist Party in order to bring about a democratic republic in Spain. In April 1931, municipal elections were held as a precursor to constitutional government. The polls returned a resounding victory for the Republicans, who won 45 out of 52 provincial capitals. The monarchist right disintegrated and even the king admitted defeat. Though he never formally abdicated, Alfonso left Spain on 13 April 1931. The Second Republic came into existence without a shot being fired.

Like the Portuguese Republic, the new Spanish regime was swept into power on a tidal wave of optimism. It was the first republic to be voted into power in the peninsula and, like its Portuguese counterpart, represented a revolutionary break with the past. The outward symbols of the old regime were swept aside by the new government – which replaced the traditional red and gold Spanish flag with a red, gold and mauve *tricoleur* – and attacked by the mob. Less than a month after the inauguration of the Republic,

churches were being burnt in cities across the land.

The provisional government had good reason for emphasizing the symbols of Republican triumph, for the desire for a democratic regime was virtually the only political aim its supporters had in common. When parliamentary elections were held in July, the Republican–Socialist coalition swept the board. It was only when the coalition was installed in power, that it became apparent that there was little unanimity over the form that the new Republic should take.

Eventually, the 1931 constitution defined the new regime as "a republic of workers of all classes" – a phrase reflecting a compromise between the liberal Republican desire for a European parliamentary democracy, which would guarantee private property, and Socialist aspirations to a more radical framework, which would allow for collectivization. This same tension affected every clause of the constitution. Virtually all those on the left wanted a secular republic – a prospect that was anathema to their opponents on the right – but while many wanted to institute an anti-clerical regime, others simply wanted to divorce religion and the state. In the end, the measures introduced were similar to those instituted by the Portuguese Republic: the separation of church and state, the introduction of civil marriage and divorce, the exclusion of religious personnel from education and prohibitions on public manifestations of cult. As in Portugal, their effect was to alienate the devout while providing the right with a cause around which to rally. Henceforth, the fight against the Republic was deemed to be the cause of Christ – at least by those Catholic politicians

aiming to lead the right to electoral victory.

Though an assault on the Catholic church had already been witnessed in Portugal, in other ways the two regimes developed differently. Spain, for instance, had a powerful tradition of regional separatism that the new government had to address. Again, a compromise was reached that few found entirely satisfactory. The 1931 constitution defined the Republic as devolutionary but not separatist; the 1932 Statute of Catalonia gave the region a degree of autonomy, including its own parliament, but no sovereign powers. Increasingly, limited self-government failed to satisfy Catalan nationalists, while the army was horrified at any perceived attack on the territorial integrity of the Spanish state.

The land question

The fiercest battles were fought over property. The powerful presence of the Socialist Party in the government, together with the recognized strength of the non-parliamentary anarchist movement, ensured that the Republic would not simply confirm unqualified rights to private property. Indeed, the agrarian question was so acute, and the disparities in landed wealth so great, that there were few in government, even in the bourgeois liberal parties, who were prepared to leave the matter untouched.

Agrarian reform is the issue most often singled out by historians as the root cause of the extreme political polarization that led to the outbreak of civil war. Parliamentary debates on the land question were particularly bitter, not least because of the implacable opposition of the right which, by and large, refused to contemplate any reform of the land laws. Even when one of the right's own ministers introduced agrarian reform proposals in 1934–35, they were voted down by his own side. The issue was no easier for the Republicans. The Agrarian Law of September 1932 allowed for the expropriation of landed estates without compensation – a proposal that had already led to the resignation of various members of the drafting committee and was against the wishes of most liberal Republicans – but could not prevent a rising spiral of agrarian unrest and violence.

Rural agitation was, partly, the result of worsening economic conditions, in particular the international depression, over which the government had little control. However, some landowners had responded to the new law with lock-outs, and even left their land deliberately uncultivated. Nor did the Republic's agrarian reform satisfy the needs and expectations of all agricultural workers. The law did nothing for the Castilian smallholders, as it had been framed solely with regard to the landless laborers of the southern *latifundia* estates. Even in the south, agrarian reform failed to abate the revolutionary fervor of the countryside and still less to allay the hostility of conservative landowners. In the words of the UGT leader, Francisco Largo Caballero (1869–1946), the measures were "an aspirin to cure an appendicitis".

The descent into civil war

The Republican–Socialist government's failure to meet the enormous expectations engendered by the change of regime inevitably gave rise to a backlash. When the next set of parliamentary elections was held in November 1933, the number of Socialist deputies was halved; Republican representation almost disappeared. Power was given to a center-right coalition

Below Though he achieved little recognition in his lifetime, the Portuguese poet Fernando Pessoa (1888–1935) is now regarded as one of the outstanding literary figures of the 20th century. Much of his work was published after his death and his enigmatic character has attracted much attention. Between 1913–15, Pessoa created three "heteronyms" or *alter egos* who wrote poetry under their own names. This 1978 painting by Costa Pinheiro depicts the heteronyms as Pessoa's shadows. In fact, each had a different physical appearance as well as his own name, life history and prose style. Alberto Caeiro, for instance, the first heteronym to appear, was blond and clean-shaven with blue eyes. He had little education and wrote Portuguese badly.

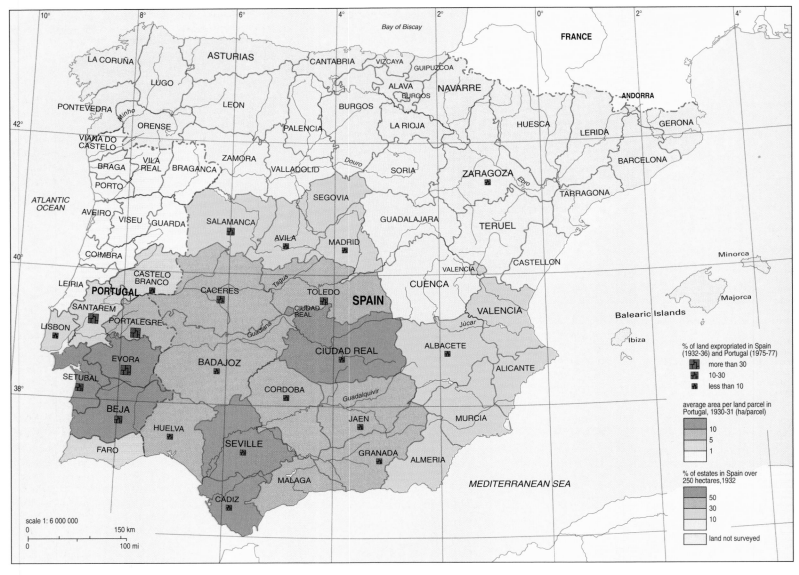

scale 1: 6 000 000
0 ————— 150 km
0 ————— 100 mi

% of land expropriated in Spain
(1932-36) and Portugal (1975-77)
- more than 30
- 10-30
- less than 10

average area per land parcel in
Portugal, 1930-31 (ha/parcel)
- 10
- 5
- 1

% of estates in Spain over
250 hectares, 1932
- 50
- 30
- 10
- land not surveyed

government determined to redress the injuries it felt had been inflicted by the 1931 constitution. Religious legislation was stalled, regional autonomy measures denied and labor legislation ignored as employers and landlords used the electoral victory as an opportunity to cut wages, evict tenants and raise rents.

The effect of such measures on workers and peasants already driven to violence by the perceived inadequacy of Republican reforms made conflict inevitable, especially as the left, now powerless within parliament, began to resort to revolutionary tactics. The Socialist leadership had more and more difficulty holding back its followers, particularly in the Youth Section, while "bolshevization" was encouraged by Largo Caballero, who had developed a weakness for revolutionary rhetoric.

During the course of 1934 it became clear that violence was no longer the preserve of recalcitrant libertarians. In that year a small Spanish fascist party, known as the Falange (or "Phalanx"), had been founded by José Antonio Primo de Rivera (1903–36), son of the late dictator; its members often brawled with left-wing youths. The Carlist movement – which had been given a new lease of life by the creation of a secularizing republic – was training militias in the mountains of Navarre in preparation for a future violent overthrow of the Republic. Even the largest parliamentary right-wing party, the Catholic Confed-

eración Española de Derechas Autónomas (CEDA: Spanish Confederation of Autonomous Right-Wing Groups), had a fascist-style youth movement whose members increasingly engaged in street battles with supporters of the left.

Matters finally came to a head in the fall of 1934 when the UGT called a general strike that turned into an abortive separatist rising in Catalonia and an armed insurrection in the northern mining province of Asturias. The miners' commune held out against the army for several days, using dynamite from the mines as their main weapon. Defeat was followed by bloody repression as Spanish troops occupied the region as if it were conquered territory. In the retribution that followed the Socialist leadership – Asturian or otherwise – was rounded up and gaoled, political prisoners were detained without trial, all Socialist Party premises were closed and the Statute of Catalonia was suspended.

These actions merely produced a greater feeling of solidarity among all sections of the Spanish left than had existed since early 1931. The future president of the Republic, Manuel Azaña (1880–1940), campaigned alongside the Socialist leader Indalecio Prieto (1883–1962) for a renewed Republican–Socialist coalition. This took shape in 1935–36 as the Spanish Popular Front. Though elsewhere in Europe the Popular Front was a communist-inspired initiative, the

Landholding and agriculture
Spain and Portugal entered the 20th century with unreformed and inequitable patterns of landholding. The south of the peninsula was dominated by vast *latifundia* estates of at least 250 hectares, usually owned by absentee landlords and run by estate managers. Laborers were employed on a casual basis and often received only starvation wages: for several months in the year, employment was virtually unobtainable. By contrast, in the north, smallholders strove to scratch a living from small parcels of land. When, in the 1930s, Spain's Republican government set about tackling the agrarian problem by expropriating large estates and redistributing the land, the poverty of the northern smallholders went largely unrecognized. The 1974 Portuguese Revolution brought a similar commitment to redistribute land in the south, though again the problems of the north were largely unresolved. In contrast, when democracy returned to Spain in 1975, the bitter agrarian divisions of the past failed to resurface. Spain was no longer primarily an agricultural economy, and many farming regions were now prosperous commercial centers with agri-business replacing the subsistence agriculture of the past.

minute size of the Spanish Communist Party meant that here it represented no more than a marginal force in the coalition.

When elections were called for February 1936, the Popular Front stood on a deliberately moderate platform, calling essentially for the reassertion of the Republican constitution. The right, however, portrayed the elections as a struggle between Christianity and communism, claiming that they would decide the confrontation between Spain and "anti-Spain". Partly as a result of depicting the poll in such apocalyptic terms, the right was utterly confident of victory. Yet the Popular Front won, albeit narrowly. For the parliamentary right, this result was catastrophic. They had failed to win control of the Republic by legal means and, in the wake of the Popular Front's victory, the CEDA disintegrated. Its party funds were made available to army conspirators while the youth movement went over *en masse* to the Falange. The Popular Front's triumph had made a violent rising against the Republic inevitable.

Spain divides

On 18 July 1936 a body of generals rose against the Republic. Virtually all of the army and the overwhelming majority of the Civil Guard responded to their call to arms. Areas such as Navarre and Old Castile also rose in revolt, but the rebellion failed in

Madrid, Catalonia and the Basque Country. Though the rebels controlled around a third of the national territory, they had not achieved the overwhelming success they had anticipated. Far from instigating a swift coup d'état, the Nationalist insurgents were forced to embark on a war of conquest.

Both the navy and the air force had stayed loyal to the Republic. Some of the insurgents' most important troops – the Army of Africa – were consequently stranded in Spanish Morocco under the command of General Francisco Franco (1892–1975). The problem was only overcome with foreign aid: following hasty approaches to Europe's fascist dictators, Adolf Hitler and Benito Mussolini, German and Italian planes ferried the Army of Africa across the Strait of Gibraltar, thereby turning a faltering coup into a prolonged and brutal civil war.

Once Franco's troops were on the mainland, they marched north, leaving the conquest of Andalusia to General Quiepo de Llano (1875–1951), who had taken Seville in the first hours of the rising. At the same time, the forces of General Mola (1887–1937) were marching south from Navarre. The two columns met in Mérida (Extremadura) on 10 August 1936 and their combined forces then took Badajoz. The savage repression that followed the city's fall was witnessed by an American journalist, Jay Allen, who reported the atrocity in the *Chicago Tribune*. Such adverse

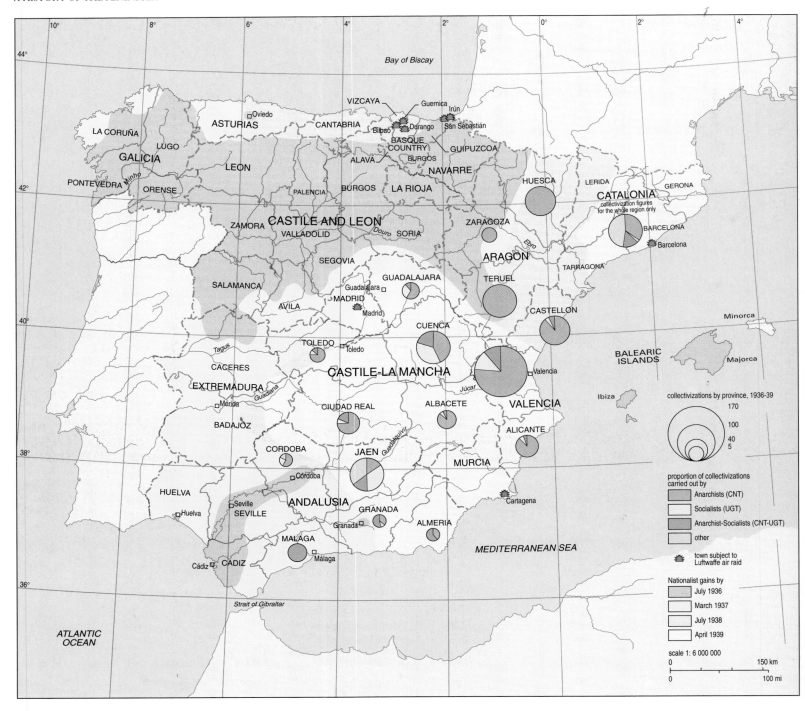

Map legend:

collectivizations by province, 1936–39

170
100
40
5

proportion of collectivizations carried out by

- Anarchists (CNT)
- Socialists (UGT)
- Anarchist-Socialists (CNT-UGT)
- other

town subject to Luftwaffe air raid

Nationalist gains by

- July 1936
- March 1937
- July 1938
- April 1939

scale 1: 6 000 000

0 — 150 km
0 — 100 mi

CATALONIA collectivization figures for the whole region only

publicity, however, could not stop the inexorable march of the rebel army toward Madrid, which was under siege by October.

Threatened by a disciplined regular army, the Republican militias defending the capital seemed to have little chance of success. The insurgents were bolstered by Italian supplies and German expertise – particularly in the air – while the Republic's attempts to rally international support were proving futile. The British government, in particular, was determined to avoid any escalation in the Spanish conflict that might result in a general European war. At British instigation, a policy of nonintervention was proposed by France's Popular Front government and formally adhered to by 27 countries. Nonintervention treated both sides as equally reprehensible, even though one was a legal government and the other a group of rebels who were acting outside the law. Despite the rhetoric of neutrality, both Germany and Italy – though signatories to the nonintervention agreement – were openly helping Franco. The legitimate Republican government had a right at international law to buy arms, but the refusal to supply it with them was effectively tantamount to providing aid for the rebels.

Faced with the imminent fall of Madrid, the left rallied to the Spanish cause. International volunteers made their way across the Pyrenees to defend the beleaguered Republic; the first contingents of the International Brigades reached Madrid on 8 November 1936, only three weeks after the first consignment of arms had arrived from the Soviet Union. Soviet aid, like Hitler's original help to the rebels, changed both the course and the nature of the Spanish Civil War. The supplies saved Madrid, but in return the Soviets demanded the right to intervene in internal Spanish affairs. Soviet assistance was systematically exploited to boost the Spanish Communist Party, which took an increasingly prominent role in the defense of Madrid.

The Spanish Civil War
The generals' rebellion of 18 July 1936 won the support of the mass of the army along with the populations of Navarre and Old Castile. Troops were airlifted by German and Italian planes across the Strait of Gibraltar to begin the war of conquest in the south. In the next three years, the Nationalist armies gradually gained territory from the Republicans; the war saw the first sustained use of aerial bombing against civilians. Within the Republican zones, the upsurge of revolutionary fervor sparked off by the Civil War led to the creation of agrarian collectives and in Catalonia to the collectivization of industry and services as well. From November 1936, the government became increasingly dependent on Soviet aid. Anarchists lost power to the communists, ending the revolution's early utopian ventures.

Above Capa's photograph of a woman refugee escaping Spain in 1936 is a stark portrayal of the personal suffering caused by war. Her horses have died where they have fallen in the road, and she must salvage what belongings she can from her cart before carrying on on foot.

The Spanish Revolution

The outbreak of civil war had sparked off widespread social revolution in many Republican areas, but especially in Catalonia. In Barcelona, the regional parliament was taken over by the anarcho-syndicalist union, the CNT. Wholesale collectivization took place – even the bootblacks were collectivized and their boxes painted in the anarchist colors of red and black. Tipping was outlawed, women no longer wore hats and the common form of address was "comrade". It was, in the words of the English writer George Orwell (1903–50) "a town where the working class was in the saddle". However, in other parts of the Republican zone, revolution was not such a priority. In Madrid, the atmosphere was somber and warlike, Valencia experienced no great social upheaval and, in Bilbao, life continued much as before. The devout Basques kept their churches open, in marked contrast to the Catalan capital where churches and convents were burnt and gutted.

Where it occurred, the Spanish revolution was violent. In the aftermath of the rebellion, law and order had broken down almost entirely, with courts being replaced by revolutionary tribunals. Though the government took steps to stop irregular executions, its measures had little impact in the first weeks of war. Suspected fascist sympathizers were summarily shot, hundreds of churches were burnt – often in a pecu-

liarly detached and unemotional way – and, in Barcelona, the bodies of nuns were disinterred and exposed to public curiosity. Anticlerical fury did not stop at the dead: in the early months of the war 12 bishops, 4,184 priests, 2,365 monks and 283 nuns lost their lives in the Republican zone.

If there is a difference in the atrocities committed in the two zones, it is that Republican killings were largely – though not entirely – the work of uncontrollable elements at a time of disorder, while those carried out in the Nationalist territory were ordered by the authorities. Nevertheless, at local level, much of the Spanish revolution was carried through by force. In Aragon, for example, the agrarian collectives, far from being the spontaneous creations of landworkers, were imposed by anarchist organizations. Even when collectives were in place, the revolutionaries had to contend with the constraints of war. It was the imperative need for unity on the Republican side that led three anarchists to take the step of entering the government in November 1936.

The creation of anarchist ministers – which divided their own movement – served as the catalyst for a major power struggle with the communists. Essentially, the conflict hinged on whether winning the war took precedence over completing the revolution or whether the creation of a new social order was, in fact, the only way to achieve victory. The anarchists, some

157

Socialists of the left and the dissident Partido Obrero de Unificación Marxista (POUM: Workers' Party for Marxist Unity), believed in furthering the revolution, pointing to the spontaneous enthusiasm which had strengthened the Republic's initial resistance to the coup. In contrast, the communists, backed by moderate socialists and Republicans, insisted on "discipline, hierarchy and organization". Their demand for a disciplined army to replace the people's militias was finally achieved after the militia- defended southern city of Málaga fell to the insurgents in a matter of hours on 3 February 1937. Indeed, there is little proof that revolutionary enthusiasm could have supplied victory over Franco who by now had emerged as the Nationalists' undisputed leader: the Republic lost more territory in the first 10 months of the war than in the remaining 33.

Controversy and bitterness still surround the methods the Communists used to carry out their aims. Acting on the orders of the Soviet dictator Joseph Stalin (1879–1953), the party attracted the support of small property owners alienated by the anarchist collectivizations and, with this essentially bourgeois membership, became a mass party for the first time in its history. In this sense, the Communists' victory over the anarchists reflected a more general recognition that the first priority must be to win the war. However, once they had achieved power, the Communists aimed to eliminate all opposition. The Barcelona "May Days" of 1937 – when POUM, anarchist and Communist gunmen fought each other on the streets – was a civil war within a civil war. Though the fighting ostensibly ended with a truce, the Communists proceeded to repress the revolution – often brutally – and destroy the POUM. Members of the party were purged as "Trotskyists" and their leader was tortured and executed by Soviet secret police. The Republic's new prime minister, Juan Negrín (1892–1956), was convinced that the only hope of victory lay with military discipline and Soviet arms. After May 1937, the communists conducted the war effort as they saw fit.

From then on, the Spanish conflict became a bloody war of attrition. Despite fierce resistance, Nationalist troops advanced slowly but inexorably, aided by plentiful supplies and total supremacy in the air. In April 1938, Franco's men reached the eastern coast, isolating Catalonia from the rest of the Republic's territory. Barcelona fell in January 1939 and the triumphant *generalísimo* marched into Madrid in April.

Franco and Salazar

During the Spanish Civil War, one of Franco's most consistent supporters was the Portuguese leader António de Oliveira Salazar (1889–1970). In 1928, this seminary-educated professor of economics had become finance minister of the New Republic under General Oscar Carmona. In his first year of office, the new minister achieved the hitherto apparently impossible task of balancing the budget. Insolvency had long been a national preoccupation and Salazar's success gave him immense prestige. From 1929, he was effectively in charge of the government of which Carmona remained the nominal head. Becoming prime minister in 1932, Salazar oversaw the legal foundations for the creation of the Portuguese "New State" a year later.

Salazar's New State was, in some ways, a clear precursor to Franco's. Defined as "a unitary and corporative republic", the Portuguese regime emphasized nationalism and strong government as a means of cre-

ating order out of the chaos of the past. Class conflict, and other dissolvent forces, had no place in the new state. Employers and employees were to work together in the new corporative structures that would facilitate cooperation in the national interest.

As in Nationalist Spain – where all these features were introduced after 1937 – strong government meant repressive government. Corporatism never amounted to more than a bureaucratic facade, while both regimes relied heavily on censorship. The police forces – particularly the secret police – became an essential tool of the state and unauthorized political activity was prohibited. The only political formation permitted in Franco's Spain was the regime's artificially created mass party, known as the "Movement", which had no Portuguese parallel. On Franco's order, the fascist Falange and the traditionalist Carlists had been forcibly merged into a single party in April 1937. Though the Falange's founder, José Antonio Primo de Rivera, who had been executed in a Republican jail, became the official martyr of the new regime, his party – like that of the Carlists – had been emasculated; the Movement had no ideological coherence and was allowed no autonomous role that might threaten Franco's preeminence. In effect, Franco's government – like Salazar's – was a personal rule.

Though fascist elements developed in the Portuguese New State under the impact of both the Spanish War and World War II, Salazar's dictatorship was never as brutal as Franco's. The Spanish regime's origins lay in a bitter civil war that had left over half a million dead and another half a million exiled. Thousands more had died in the hunger and repression of the 1940s as the victorious new regime purged erstwhile Republicans. However, Franco was no ideologue. He was, rather, a serving officer in the Spanish army who viewed political opposition as the civilian equivalent of mutiny. To the man who had been the

Above left When General Franco marched into Madrid at the head of his army, he ordered the construction of a triumphal arch to commemorate his conquest. It was here that the *caudillo* took the salute during the huge victory parade held on 19 May 1939.

Above Air raids carried out by the German Condor Legion left several Spanish cities with extensive bomb damage. This study by the Polish photographer David "Chim" Seymour (1911–66) shows water being collected from a pump in a Barcelona street that has been flattened by aerial bombardment. This picture was taken in 1938, as the war reached its close.

Right The post-war years in Spain were marked by hunger and privation. As this picture of harvest in the Alpujarras mountains of Andalusia shows, farming remained primitive. In 1941, police reported 357 sellers of grass in Córdoba market – a reflection both of the lack of food and the shortage of crops. Rationing remained in force until 1952 – the first year real per capita incomes regained their pre-war levels.

youngest general in the Spanish army, orders were to be obeyed without question. The good of the fatherland came before all else: the civil war had saved the true Spain from "anti-Spain", and sinister influences – commonly understood to be a conspiracy of communists, freemasons and Jews – were to be kept at bay.

The Spanish Civil War had saved Catholicism from communism – or so it was argued. Anti-communism became the watchword of both the Spanish and the Portuguese regimes. The moral norms of Catholicism held sway in both countries, with particular regard to public spectacles, film censorship and female fashions. Religious education was reinstated. In Portugal, however, no attempt was made to reunite church and state, and civil marriage and divorce remained on the statute books. In contrast, "national Catholicism" reigned in Spain: the church was reestablished, and the rhetoric of triumphalist Catholicism depicted Spain as the "spiritual reserve of the West". The Civil War was painted as nothing less than a latter-day crusade.

The ideology of both the Spanish and Portuguese dictatorships was deeply nostalgic. Rigidly opposed to modernism, the dictators created their highly conservative regimes against the preceding "disorder". The "true" nation would reemerge in the image of a mythical past. However, this did not mean that the regimes were unable to change. From 1943, for instance, when it became apparent that Nazi Germany would not avoid defeat, both governments distanced themselves from the Axis powers (Germany, Italy and Japan), abandoning the fascist trappings and rhetoric that had been increasingly apparent from 1939. By the end of the war, Portugal was aiding the Allies, though Spain's association with the Axis powers led to a period of ostracism by the international community immediately after the war.

The Soviet occupation of eastern Europe and the start of the Cold War ensured that the anticommunist bulwark of the Iberian peninsula would soon be viewed more favorably in the West. In the early 1950s, Franco's Spain – which now emphasized its Catholic nature – was rehabilitated by the United States. In 1953, the same year in which the Franco government signed a concordat with the Vatican, American air bases were located in Spain. In 1955, Spain was finally allowed to join the United Nations. Far from being a pariah, Franco was now a respected member of the international community.

This ability to change with the times undoubtedly contributed to the longevity of the Iberian dictatorships. Both Franco and Salazar lived to old age and died in their beds. Their regimes evolved internally to some extent; though both were ultimately dependent on repression, the brutality of Spain's "hungry 40s" did not survive the decade. There was also some experimentation with limited freedom of speech and, in Portugal, even some controlled opposition. Spain also experienced economic liberalization as the tourist boom of the 1960s finally led the country toward economic modernization – a policy that had been introduced and overseen by the Catholic laygroup, Opus Dei. In the short term, this new-found prosperity helped to create a large, depoliticized segment of society that was willing to accept better living standards instead of political liberties. However, there soon emerged an acute dysfunction between the reactionary regime and the ever-more dynamic society over which it presided. In the last years of the Franco regime, Spain was a land seething with discontent.

Posters of the Spanish Civil War

The Spanish Civil War was a full-scale propaganda war. For the first time, the radio was used as a weapon, while newspapers, both in Spain and abroad, were flooded with information and disinformation. The unending spiral of accusation and counter-denial reached fever pitch after the German Condor Legion's bombing of Guernica (1937), claimed by the Nationalists to have been carried out by a retreating "Red" army. Graphic artists contributed to this propaganda war by producing some of the most compelling visual images of any conflict.

Most Republican artists worked in Madrid and Barcelona. The Catalan capital had a tradition of graphic art: industrial prosperity had created a demand for advertizing. Under the Republic, posters had acquired political significance – electoral propaganda introduced the use of confrontational images, while the social struggle featured heavily in the posters produced by the parties of the left. The influence of the artists of the Russian Revolution was keenly felt.

The posters of the war bear eloquent testimony both to the spontaneous revolution that erupted in Barcelona and to the privation and heroism of the long defense of the Republic in Madrid, Bilbao and elsewhere. The Republic valued its intellectuals – culture was a way of fostering the war effort. Education was encouraged and immorality condemned. The poster art of the Civil War proved to be a vital means of communication as well as a striking artistic achievement.

Left "Spain, one, great and free." This Falangist poster incorporates Francoist Spain's most famous slogan. In comparison with Republican artwork, Nationalist posters were highly conventional. Here, the triumphant figure of the soldier stands above the broken and bestial body of anti-Spain. The imagery is religious: a latter-day crusader has defeated the devilish communist threat. Though the figures are clichés, the poster attracts the attention by its bold lines and colors. Subtlety has no role to play here; the poster depicts good and evil in absolute terms, contrasting the semi-abstract figure of the victorious soldier with the detailed and ugly drawing of the red monster it has vanquished.

Right "Worker! Peasant! Unity for victory!" Boldness and originality characterized the Civil War posters produced in Barcelona. The simple design of Jacint Bofarull's Catalan-language poster makes an arresting plea for unity. Overalled worker and shirt-sleeved peasant come together in a single figure. The muscularity of the male form shows that unity is strength. The sickle wielded by the peasant half of the body represents communism as well as agriculture, while the worker's fist is raised in a gesture reminiscent of the Marxist salute. Communism as depicted here was a broad camp; the poster was produced for the Anarchist CNT-FAI.

Far right "The commissar, sinew of our people's army." Produced in Valencia for the Communist Party, this poster by Josep Renau repeats the image of the clenched fist. The photomontage technique raises the arm amid a host of steel bayonets, representing the political commissar – a familiar figure in all Communist Party battalions – among fighting soldiers.

Per una potent Indústria de Guerra

Ier Congrés Metal·lúrgic de la U.G.T.

A CATALUNYA

2-3 i 4 SETEMBRE 1938

Grafos Collectivitzada - BARCELONA

El analfabetismo ciega el espíritu
SOLDADO INSTRUYETE

Above "Illiteracy blinds the spirit. Soldier teach yourself." The creation of an educated army was seen as a priority by the Republican government. Literacy campaigns were waged throughout the Republican zone, some directed specifically at soldiers, others at the general public. This poster was issued by the Ministry of Public Instruction in the name of the "cultural militias". It uses a particularly vivid visual image to convey its message to a population that was over 30 percent illiterate in 1930.

Left Victory on the battlefield depended upon continuing industrial output. Iron and steel production was particularly important for the continuing supply of armaments and artillery. This poster, which announces the first congress of metallurgical workers organized by the Socialist trade union (UGT), calls "For a powerful war industry". Written in Catalan, and directed at the workers of Barcelona, it lacks the originality of the earlier artwork produced in the city. Its representation is purely figurative and there is little inventiveness in the social realist design. By late 1938, when this poster was issued, the Anarchist revolution was long since over and the Republic was being pushed back on every front. Defeat was fast becoming the order of the day, and there was a growing sense that the entire war might be lost.

THE NEW DEMOCRACIES

The Portuguese revolution

On 25 April 1974, the Portuguese army once again entered politics. At twenty-five minutes past midnight, the Catholic radio station Rádio Renascença broadcast the agreed signal – a protest song, "Grândola, Vila Morena", later to become the anthem of the revolution. In response to the signal, army units throughout the land moved on key buildings, occupying government offices, military installations and the presidential palace. The New State collapsed without a shot being fired.

Military disaffection with the New State had been rumbling for some time. After 36 years as prime minister, Salazar suffered a stroke on 6 September 1968 and was relieved of office. He died two years later, on 27 July 1970, still believing himself to be head of government: in reality, however, the premiership had passed to Marcello Caetano (b. 1906), who governed until deposed by the revolutionary forces in April 1974. His accession to power had initially been welcomed by those disaffected from the Salazar regime. A personable, family man, Caetano's style contrasted sharply with Salazar's dour asceticism. He introduced a welcome element of informality into the Portuguese government; as well as staging televised "fireside chats", he relaxed the censorship laws and looked to broaden support for the regime. By 1971, however, the limits of Caetano's policy of "evolution within continuity" had been reached. The regime's anti-democratic institutions remained untouched by the reform process, perhaps because of the continuing strength of die-hard Salazarists in the government, but more probably because Caetano's own instincts were not those of a democrat. His policies vacillated, satisfying neither the establishment nor the increasingly clamorous opposition.

The key issue on which the regime foundered, however, was its determination to maintain Portugal's overseas colonies, against the trend of decolonization that had been taking place elsewhere in Africa since 1960. As a result, one of Europe's smallest and poorest powers became engaged in the longest colonial wars fought by a Western country since 1945. From 1961, the Portuguese army – which had not seen active service since World War I – was more or less continuously engaged in Angola, Mozambique and Guinea. Though Portugal had joined NATO as a founder member in 1949 – giving it access to sophisticated military hardware – the army's command structures remained resolutely pre-modern. By the 1960s, Portugal was the only European country to retain specialized staff officers who never saw active service but whose desk jobs were rewarded with higher pay and quicker promotion. Operational plans issued in Lisbon for the African theater of war were often inaccurate and were usually late: in 1973, the defense minister took the drastic step of issuing instructions to all staff officers to report for duties at 9 a.m. instead of their customary 2 p.m.

Promotion, for both staff and combat officers, depended on length of service rather than professional competence. Senior men in Lisbon often combined their military duties with lucrative directorships and business commitments; in contrast the junior ranks were among the worst-paid in Europe. The rising total of war dead did nothing to boost their morale. A decree-law of 13 July 1973, introduced to ease the shortage of soldiers, had a critical impact. By giving conscripted officers parity with career soldiers, it created an immediate sense of grievance amongst those who had spent years training and fighting before even reaching the rank of captain.

In September 1973, military discontent came out into the open when about 140 junior officers established the Movimento das Forças Armadas (MFA: Armed Forces Movement). Plans to overthrow the government, initiate peaceful decolonization and restore the honor of the army began in earnest. On 25 April 1974 a successful *coup* was staged, and General Antonío Ribeiro Spínola (b.1910) was installed as interim head of government; though he had agreed beforehand to support the plotters in principle, he had taken no part in the *coup*, which had been planned and carried out by those below the rank of colonel. When the MFA seized power, about 90 elderly brigadiers and generals were immediately relieved of their duties.

Spínola ruled with the help of the Junta de Salvação Nacional (JSN: Junta of National Salvation). It was, however, the MFA's program of democratic elections, an amnesty for political prisoners, freedom of association and a purge of high-level servants of the old regime that was implemented by the new government, a development that reflected the lack of ideological preparation for the *coup*. Tension soon developed between the two groups, the senior military men of the JSN favoring caution while the low-ranking officers of the MFA, looking to consolidate their gains, moved rapidly to the left.

Many later commentators have assumed that the MFA had a Marxist content and program, pointing to the radicalization of the Portuguese revolution and finding continuities between the actions of the MFA and those of the later Revolutionary Council. Individual officers may well have been influenced by the works of Marxist writers such as Che Guevara (1928–67), but in reality the MFA was the equivalent of an army trade union whose main concerns were professional. Its action on 25 April 1974 had served as a catalyst for revolution, throwing Portuguese politics into extreme confusion. In these circumstances, the Partido Comunista Português (PCP: Communist Party of Portugal) soon achieved a position of prominence, not least because it was the only organized political force in Portugal and had a clear sense of its own program and identity. Its leader, Alvaro Cunhal (b. 1913), had led the party from 1946 (when he retired in 1992 he was the longest-serving party leader in the Western world) and his opposition credentials, if not his democratic ones, were impeccable. The PCP was careful never to oppose the MFA, but its well-organized struc-

Above On 23 November 1975, the body of General Francisco Franco was interred at the Valley of the Fallen – the vast mausoleum in the mountains outside Madrid that had been built by Republican prisoners as Franco's monument to the Nationalist victory in the Civil War. The *caudillo* was buried amid much pomp and ceremony, yet the only foreign head of state to attend his funeral was General Pinochet of Chile. In contrast, presidential representatives and royal personages from all over the world attended the coronation of King Juan Carlos, held later in the same month.

ture enabled it to take over control of much of local government and the media, purging erstwhile supporters of the New State.

Radical pressure was also being exerted from below: the summer of 1974 saw waves of strikes sweep through the country, despite Communist Party opposition. Though law and order never broke down entirely, policemen virtually disappeared from the streets and the political situation became increasingly unmanageable. Spínola resigned the presidency on 30 September 1974, but on 11 March 1975 he attempted to seize power again; the *coup* was ill-prepared, and he fled. The timing of the *coup* attempt may have been influenced by *agents provocateurs*: the entire débâcle was televised by a Communist film crew.

The revolution now entered its most radical phase. Basic industries, including banks and insurance companies, were nationalized, and landless laborers occupied the *latifundia* estates on which they worked, turning them into vast collective farms. In response to this increasing evidence of expanding communist involvement, violence erupted in many parts of the north during the "hot July" of the same year. Smallholders and peasant proprietors attacked the homes of Party militants; in Braga, the PCP headquarters was burnt down. Unrest spread to the Azores and Madeira as the islanders issued a separatist challenge to what they saw as the communist-dominated mainland.

Rural revolt on this scale had never before been seen in Portugal. Only the far south remained relatively trouble-free. Those resisting the revolution had been encouraged by the elections, held on 25 April, which had seen the faction-ridden far left comprehensively defeated. Between them, the Partido Socialista (PS: Socialist Party) and the Partido Popular Democrata

(PPD: Popular Democrat Party) had taken more than two-thirds of the votes on a 90 percent turnout. As the intense period of anarchic disorder continued over the summer, the communists began to lose support and Mário Lopes Soares (b. 1924) emerged as the head of a wide-ranging pluralist coalition. However, unrest and uncertainty only came to an end in November 1975 when the MFA declared a state of emergency and disbanded all mutinous military units. The revolution had entered a new, more sober, phase.

The end of the Franco regime

Throughout the autumn of 1975, General Franco's protracted death agony drew the attention of the Spanish nation. His life was extended for days by modern science: his body was plugged into the most advanced medical technology available, while his hand clutched the incorrupt arm of St Teresa of Avila, a relic to which he had great devotion. Franco's deathbed served as a metaphor for the later history of his regime. The 1960s had seen Spain embark on an unprecedented period of economic modernization within the confines of an authoritarian political system. Greater affluence and material contentment was supposed to obviate the desire for political liberalization; at his death Franco's state remained ostensibly untouched by secularization and pluralism.

Between 1960 and 1974 the Spanish economy grew by an average of 6.6 percent per annum, a rate matched only by Japan. This new-found economic prosperity – which was fueled by tourism – may have enhanced satisfaction with the regime in the short term, but in the long term the gulf between Franco's oppressive, reactionary regime and the society over which it ruled became increasingly apparent. The ideo-

The Revolution of the Carnations

The army rebellion of 25 April 1974 marked the beginning of a truly revolutionary process in Portugal that lasted until November 1975. The first days, particularly in Lisbon, were euphoric. Not a shot was fired in defense of the dictatorial regime as soldiers took possession of the streets, greeted as heroes by the jubilant crowds. Observers commented on the numbers of happy faces in the streets; one even claimed to have discovered that the Portuguese had teeth "now that you can see us smile". The release of political prisoners was the occasion for wild rejoicing. Throughout the country, the prospect of democracy and an end to the unpopular colonial wars was broadly welcomed.

Within a mere two months, no fewer than 50 political parties had emerged in Portugal. The military remained in executive control but the future direction of the revolution was far from clear. A wave of strikes engulfed the country in the summer of 1974 and the increasing prominence of the Communist Party was viewed with unease. Support for the main political parties – the Communists, Socialists and the centrist Popular Democrats – expanded phenomenally in 1974–75, but by the summer of 1975, civil unrest had broken out in rural areas in reaction to the leftward swing of the revolution. Disorder took hold wherever wealthy peasants dominated the local economy; most disturbances occurred no farther than 120 kilometers from Lisbon within the farming area north of the city. Rural revolt changed the course of the revolution. In November 1975, moderate elements regained control of the military and the revolution was effectively over.

Above The army's re-entry into Portuguese politics in April 1974 is greeted with spontaneous enthusiasm in Lisbon. The carnival atmosphere of the early days of the revolution was broken only by a solitary gunman who fired into the crowd outside the secret police headquarters, killing four people. Elsewhere, the people of the capital indicated their delight with the turn of events by welcoming the rebel soldiers with food, drink and fresh flowers.

Below Mário Soares, leader of the Portuguese Socialist Party, campaigning in 1975. An exile since 1969, Soares returned to his native land to lead his party into all but one of the six provisional administrations that governed Portugal during the revolution. In the first democratic elections, held on 25 April 1975, the Socialists emerged as the clear winners – a personal triumph for Soares who served as prime minister in 1976–78 and again in 1983–85. In 1986 he was elected Portugal's first civilian president for 60 years.

Left "Down with the *latifundios*": peasants in the Beja district call for reform of the vast agricultural estates of southern Portugal. From March 1975, landless laborers invaded the *latifundios*, occupying and redistributing the land. The provisional government then conferred the transfer of title from the old absentee landowners to the new collective farms, many of which rejoiced in Soviet-style names such as "Red Star". Some farms struggled, but others succeeded, and the districts of the south were the only ones to escape the rural unrest of the "hot July" of 1975.

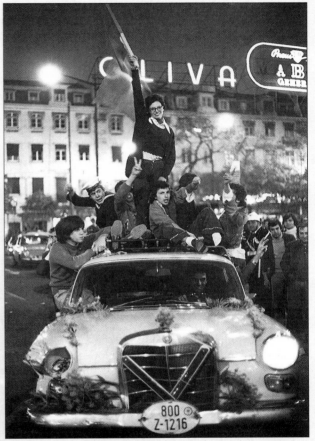

Top May Day, long recognized as international labor day, became the occasion for mass demonstrations of rejoicing rather than protest in 1974. New-found freedoms were celebrated in the streets of Lisbon as the revolutionary promise of liberation became a real experience. Cars, demonstrators and buildings were festooned with red carnations. At first, these seasonal flowers had been just one of the floral tributes offered to the insurgent soldiers but their ubiquity had rapidly led to them becoming the symbol of the April revolution.

Above Alvaro Cunhal, leader of the Portuguese Communist Party since 1946, presides over a rally. The PCP, banned between 1927 and 1974, proved virtually the only organized political force in the early months of the revolution. Its opposition credentials were impeccable: the 247 PCP candidates fielded in the 1975 elections were said to have served 440 years in prison between them. But the party of Marx and Lenin and the clenched-fist salute soon came to be seen as outmoded in the modernizing transition to democracy.

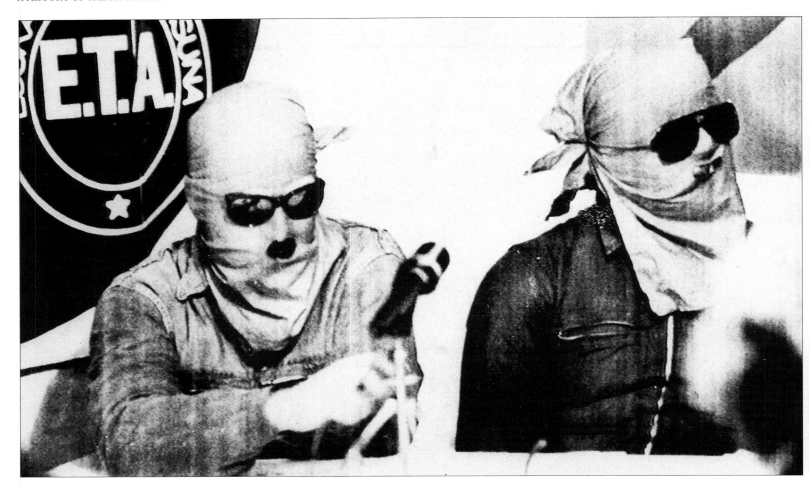

logical constructs of Francoism had idealized the countryside, emphasizing its stability, moral virtue and religious faith. Yet the rapid growth of the 1960s destroyed the agrarian basis of the Spanish economy, creating a service economy in its stead. As agricultural employment declined, so urban centers grew and the working class increased in both number and strength. Between 1964 and 1974 Spain experienced about 5,000 strikes; 1975, the last year of Franco's rule, saw a further 3,156 stoppages. Furthermore, 45 percent of strikes staged after 1967 were political in nature, as against a mere 4 percent of those called from 1963–67.

By the late 1960s, clandestine unions – notably the communist-organized Comisiones Obreras (CCOO: Workers' Commissions) – were experiencing considerable success among the burgeoning working classes. However, these were not the only groups calling for political concessions. Students played a major role in the anti-Franco opposition, often making common cause with the trade unions. The campus unrest of 1968 had a directly political character in Spain; by the end of the decade, police occupation of the universities was almost permanent. Students and workers came together in Catholic youth groups, which enjoyed a privileged status under the terms of the 1953 concordat with the Vatican; by the beginning of the 1970s, such groups had moved firmly into opposition.

Given the close identification of church and state that had characterized Spain in the 1940s and 1950s, the distancing of many Catholics from the regime in the 1960s and 1970s came as a surprise. The change was partly generational: on the eve of the Second Vatican Council (1960–65) most Spanish bishops were over 75 years old, but the clergy was among the youngest in the world. These young Catholics – who

had not fought in the Civil War but nonetheless lived in its shadow – were profoundly attracted to the universal church of Popes John XXIII (1958–63) and Paul VI (1963–78), with its language of human rights, democracy and ecumenism. Vatican II initiated an extraordinary period of *apertura* ("opening") in the Spanish church and, for once, its resonance could not be muffled by the state censors. Young Catholic militants, for instance, had always concerned themselves with social issues but now, as activists became increasingly vocal critics of human rights abuses, their involvement in wage disputes and strike action brought them into direct conflict with the state.

The language of human rights was also to be heard among those young Basques – many of them Catholics – who formed Euskadi Ta Askatasuna (ETA: Basque Homeland and Liberty) in 1959 as a revolutionary breakaway movement from the Partido Nacionalista Vasco (PNV: Basque Nationalist Party). This separatist terrorist group became the most spectacular and, arguably, the most effective of all the anti-Franco opposition groups. From its first assassination of a police torturer in August 1968, ETA gradually destroyed the myth of the regime's invulnerability. Widespread support for the organization in the Basque Country, coupled with the inaccessibility of much of the terrorists' native terrain, made ETA impossible to eradicate. Franco was forced to rely on "states of emergency". In the face of repression, ETA could command considerable public sympathy. Vivid proof of this came in 1970 in the Castilian city of Burgos when 16 ETA members were tried by a military court. The defendants – whose average age was 21 – gave vivid testimony of police torture; when six of them were sentenced to death the strength of protest,

Above Two masked ETA members address a news conference in March 1979 to announce the halting of their bombing campaign against tourist targets in Spain after their killing of six civilians had aroused widespread public condemnation. ETA – the terrorist group dedicated to winning an independent homeland for the Basque people – enjoyed overwhelming support in the Basque Country under Franco's repressive regime. Its campaign of violence continued during the transition to democracy after Franco's death, but the majority of Basques were satisfied with the granting of autonomous status for the region, and ETA gained less and less sympathy for its separatist goals. In recent years its violent attacks have been mostly aimed against police and military personnel.

Above In the months following Franco's death Spain found neither peace nor democracy. Though the delicate preparations for the transition to constitutional government began immediately in political circles, on the streets repression was as obvious as ever. Demonstrations were commonplace, the universities seethed with discontent and police brutality was rife. Here, a "special policeman" manhandles a demonstrator during a protest by assistant professors at Madrid university. He is being taken away for "interrogation" – at the time still often used as a euphemism for torture.

both at home and abroad, was so great that Franco commuted the punishments to life imprisonment.

ETA's most remarkable success came in December 1973 when it blew up the car in which Admiral Luis Carrero Blanco (1903–73) was traveling to mass. Recently appointed prime minister, he was regarded as Franco's probable successor; his assassination was to have profound repercussions for the history of Spain, for it created an immediate power-vacuum in the government. Cabinet circles were broadly divided between those who favored further liberalization in order to forestall a revolutionary deluge and those who – like Carrero Blanco – believed that modernization had already introduced an unwanted degree of license, requiring tougher police measures.

In a land seething with discontent, there were few political solutions on offer. The oil price rise of 1973 hit Spain hard, and, in the face of an energy crisis and economic recession, Carrero Blanco's successor, Carlos Arias Navarro (1908–89) announced the "opening" of the regime to democracy on 12 February 1974. The spiral of social unrest was, however, merely intensified by the worsening economic situation. The cleavages within Spanish society seemed to have become chasms. On the evening of 20 November 1975, when Arias Navarro wept on television as he announced Franco's death to the nation, the city of Barcelona was supposedly drunk dry of champagne.

Transition to democracy
In the autumn of 1975, both Spain and Portugal seemed to be on the brink of chaos. Yet, just over a decade later in January 1986, the Iberian states formally entered the European Community (EC) as functioning liberal democracies with stable parliamentary systems. The speed and success of the democratization process – particularly in Spain – came as a surprise to many and a relief to all. But, though Spain and Portugal both traveled a similar route in the late 1970s, their respective transitions to democracy were accomplished in rather different ways.

Portugal's transition was initiated by a military rebellion that served as a catalyst for social revolution. In contrast, Spain's armed forces were largely hostile to the prospect of democracy. Unlike many in the political elite, the military remained loyal to its Francoist inheritance. Though the army initially stayed moodily on the sidelines while erstwhile Francoists began to dismantle the regime from within, the threat of a military *coup* remained, and was a major constraint on policy-making. Spain's new head of state, King Juan Carlos (b. 1938), Alfonso XIII's grandson who had been named as his successor by General Franco in 1969, had a critical role in controlling the military. The virtues of hierarchy, discipline and loyalty to the monarch were emphasized not only by civilian governments but also by the king himself. On 23 February 1981 in a spectacular challenge to democracy, Civil Guards under the command of Lieutenant-Colonel Antonio Tejero held the Cortes hostage in Madrid while army tanks thundered through the streets of Valencia; the king immediately responded by appearing on television to remind soldiers of their oath of loyalty, roundly declaring that the crown would not tolerate the forcible interruption of the democratic process. With virtually the entire political class imprisoned in the Cortes, Juan Carlos' actions were decisive. The veteran general, Jaime Milans del Bosch (b. 1915), withdrew his troops from Valencia when the king made it clear that the rebels would only

Left On 23 February 1981, Lieutenant-Colonel Antonio Tejero of the Civil Guard stormed into Spain's parliament building with pistols blazing and took all those in the debating chamber hostage. He is shown here with the president of the Cortes and members of the government. Though he cut a faintly ridiculous figure, Tejero's attempted coup was Spanish democracy's most fragile moment. His actions were foiled, in large part by the brave conduct of the king.

silence him by force. The deputies were released from the Cortes at noon on 24 February and, the following weekend, three million people took part in pro-democracy demonstrations.

Though Juan Carlos's part in frustrating the 23-F (as Tejero's coup came to be known) was crucial, he did not institute democracy single-handed. Spain's transition to parliamentary government was the product of a series of pacts and negotiations, in which the king was one among several key protagonists. The initial process – whereby the dictator's chamber of deputies disbanded – was negotiated by a former Francoist *apparatchik*, Adolfo Suárez (b. 1932). By the time of Franco's death, the pillars of the regime were already crumbling. There was growing discontent among the economic and financial elites at the regime's immobilism, and many had come to regard liberal democracy as a more successful way both of governing an increasingly turbulent country and of conducting business. During 1976, Suárez, with the support of many elite groups, legislated Francoism out of existence and legalized political parties in preparation for the elections of 15 June 1977.

Those who framed and directed Spain's transition to democracy paid special attention to accommodating those who had benefited under Franco and were now left vulnerable. Particular care was taken to avoid infuriating the army; the legalization of the Communist Party, for instance – a highly sensitive issue – was accomplished just weeks before the 1977 elections. Even in Portugal – where there had been a radical social revolution – the old political class survived to implement the transition, even if individual landowners, financiers and industrialists suffered considerable loss. In both cases, after 1975, the extent of executive powers – wielded in Spain by the king and in Portugal by the president – provided some guarantee of stabil-

ity and limited radical excess. The right-of-center composition of Spain's transitional governments also proved reassuring while, in Portugal, the military remained committed to public order.

Unlike Portugal, Spain saw no purges of personnel associated with the dictatorship. Though, in terms of continuity, this was undoubtedly a strength, the uncertainty surrounding the loyalty of some of the new regime's servants posed its own problems. For example – the conciliatory tactics of Adolfo Suárez's Unión Centro Democrático (UCD: Union of the Democratic Center) – an *ad hoc* alliance of disparate interest groups that disintegrated during 1981–82 – proved remarkably successful in negotiating the transition, and were also able to circumvent the regional problem. However, they failed to reconcile or control the army. Nor was ETA pacified. Violence continued in the Basque Country even after Franco's death, the approval by referendum of a democratic constitution in 1978 and the introduction of regional autonomy for Catalonia and the Basque Country in 1980. The counterpoint between ETA and the Spanish military proved one of the main themes of the transition; though bitter enemies, the two groups represented separate but severe threats to the security of democracy in Spain. Indeed, ETA was deliberately seeking to provoke military intervention in the belief that a coup would spark off a revolutionary uprising. In fact, as regional autonomy measures began to take hold in the Basque Country, support for ETA began to fall, though the terrorists could always count on the loyalty of a small separatist minority.

Though the army in Portugal never permitted a return to the insurgent disorder of 1975, the country's fledgling democracy also experienced moments of extreme fragility. The 1976 constitution, which was agreed by all but one of the parties in the constituent

assembly, was not put to the people. It strengthened the executive and spoke of the "transition to socialism"; the collectivizations of 1975 were declared to be "irreversible". As in Spain, a method of proportional representation that normally gives an outright majority to a party winning over 42 percent of the vote was adopted in order to increase the likelihood of stable government. Even so, between July 1976 and July 1987, Portugal had eight separate governments; in 1978–79, the inability of any party to form a viable government forced the president, General António Ramalho Eanes (b.1935; president 1976–86) to appoint three successive non-party governments. Like Spain's 23-F, this potentially hazardous moment was successfully negotiated; the Portuguese elections of December 1979 were the first to result in a peaceful opposition takeover. This critical event was matched in Spain in October 1982 when, despite another abortive military coup, the Socialist Party took 48 percent of the vote and embarked on what was to be a decade of majority government.

Democratic consolidation

By the end of the 1980s, Iberian democracy seemed robust. The first party to win an outright electoral victory in Portugal was the Partido Social Demócrata (PSD: the Social Democratic Party, formerly the PPD) of Aníbal Cavaco Silva (b.1939), which took just over 50 percent of the vote in July 1987. However, the parliamentary system had already stabilized; from 1976–85, power had been shared between four main parties: the Socialists, the Social Democrats, the Communists and the Centro Democrático Social (CDS: Center Social Democrats). While the electoral support for each remained relatively constant, their shifting alliances led to considerable variation in government.

The presidential elections of February 1986 intro-

duced a new phase in Portuguese democracy. One of the most notable achievements of the 1980s in both Portugal and Spain was the military's return to barracks. In 1982, Portugal's revolutionary constitution was amended to enhance the power of the legislature. The Council of the Revolution – a constitutional body enshrining the military's role as guardian of the revolution – was abolished and the army relinquished its institutional presence without resistance. Four years later, the charismatic and experienced Mário Soares, who had headed Portugal's first socialist government in 1976, was elected Portugal's first civilian president since 1926, with overwhelming popular support.

The situation in Spain seemed more delicate. Following Tejero's attempted coup in February 1981, the UCD government had begun hasty negotiations with NATO, believing that membership would help professionalize and democratize the armed forces. Spain joined the alliance on 30 May 1982, in the face of considerable domestic opposition, not least from the Socialist Party. In October of the same year the Spanish Socialists – for the first time in their long history – formed a government. Faced with the apparently intractable problems of military subversion and ETA terrorism, the new premier, Felipe González (b. 1942), announced a reversal of government policy on NATO. When the question was belatedly put to a referendum in March 1986, the government – which had come under considerable pressure from both the United States and EC member states – campaigned vigorously for continued membership and won. Though it dismayed many Socialist supporters, this abrupt *volte face* did much to improve military–civilian relations. Levels of defense spending had increased: one of the reasons for the Socialists' reversal of policy on NATO was their desire to restructure Spanish industry with a high technology defense component. Furthermore, the ending of national isolationism through membership of NATO and the European Community (EC) (which Spain joined in 1986) had a profound affect on military attitudes. Unlike the UCD, the Socialist government dealt swiftly with mutinous officers; it also introduced a significant measure of military reform.

An important part of the army's Francoist inheritance was its unquestioning commitment to defend Spain's territorial integrity. The regional problem was thus inextricably linked to the military one; ultimately, a political solution had to be found. Though the Basque problem has never been fully resolved, the explosion of regionalist demands fostered by the repression of Franco's last years was largely defused in the 1980s by the Socialists' negotiations with the moderate Basque and Catalan parties. Tensions subsided, particularly after an extradition agreement with France led to a new offensive against ETA, but the regional problem did not go away.

Though the 1978 constitution emphasized the integrity of the Spanish state, under its terms Spain adopted a quasi-federal system that divided the national territory into 17 autonomous regions, each with devolved powers. Catalonia, Galicia and the Basque Country – the regions with clear historic and linguistic identities – moved fastest toward autonomous status; by 1983 this had been granted to all the regions. Autonomous status undoubtedly boosted nationalist feeling in the regions. Each now had its own flag, anthem and local institutions. Andalusia, which had no historic nationalist tradition, acquired a thriving regional party that won 10 seats in the regional parliament in June 1990. In Catalonia, where separatist demands are most prevalent, the break-up of the Soviet Union (1989–92), and in particular the recognition of the independent Baltic Republics in 1991, fueled popular demands for secession. Such demands, however, were not echoed by major political figures and the bloody conflicts that followed the break-up of Yugoslavia after 1990 dampened nationalist enthusiasm. Even in the Basque Country, where Herri Batasuna – ETA's political wing – retained a significant degree of popular support, only 17 percent of people in 1987 supported the party's demand for independence. Eight years earlier, 32 percent had favored a Basque nation state.

Portugal has no large-scale regional problem, though the question of local autonomy still features on the political agenda. The 1976 constitution declared Portugal to be a unitary state and regional parties were banned from standing at elections. However, the constitution did make provision for new regional government arrangements (due to be implemented in the early 1990s), while the island regions of Madeira and the Azores gained a considerable degree of autonomy, including some tax-raising powers. Under the terms of the constitution, each has an elected parliament, though members of the executive are appointed centrally. The Portuguese islands have historic aspirations to autonomy and, in the late 1970s, separatism seemed a powerful and increasing force, particularly on the Azores. In the immediate aftermath of the 1974 revolution the newly created Azorean Liberation Front received considerable backing from the United States. There was even some talk of the islands becoming the 51st state. However, when it was revealed that much of the separatists' American funding came from crime syndicates – who had great hopes of a mid-Atlantic gaming center – support plummeted.

Democratic deficit

Though Herri Batasuna was the only antisystem party in either Spain or Portugal to command a significant degree of popular support, in the later 1980s the Spanish electorate began to display some disenchantment with the national political system. The introduction of local autonomy engendered a new generation of regional parties, but the rise of such parties to electoral prominence reflected dissatisfaction with the ruling Socialist party, which – despite seeing its share of the vote cut significantly in the 1989 election – enjoyed almost undisputed power from 1982–93.

The electoral system in use throughout the Iberian peninsula creates large, multimember constituencies, whose representatives are chosen on a list system. In Portugal, there is virtually no link between deputies and those whom they represent: candidates are often unfamiliar with their districts and many show little inclination to visit them once elected. The list system also means that candidates are chosen by party bureaucrats and not by constituents. In effect, political careers depend more upon party officials – who determine which deputies will be reselected – than the voters. Conformism is the order of the day; independents are unknown and individualists are scarce.

The predominance of party elites is reinforced by the strength of the executives. Even under full democracy, they continue to enjoy considerably more authority than the legislatures. The long years of dictatorship have also left a legacy of state intervention, allowing the party in power to exert considerable influence over civil society. Many observers attributed part of the Socialists' success in the NATO referendum of March 1986 to the unsubtle manipulation of Spanish television, over which the government then had monopoly control. Three years later, in January 1989, the government-appointed head of the state broadcasting corporation (RTVE) was obliged to resign over accusations of political interference in programming. Though the situation eased somewhat after the tardy introduction of private television companies in 1990, the experience of government influence in broadcasting in the 1980s turned much of the printed media into virulent opponents of the Socialist Party. By 1990, some papers regularly referred to Felipe González as "Caesar".

In both countries, patronage plays an important

Above In October 1982 the Spanish Socialist Party won an outright electoral majority for the first time in its history. Felipe González became the new premier at the age of 42; the average age of his cabinet was only 40. For many Spaniards, the new government finally represented a complete break with the past. Under the Socialists, Spain formally entered the European Union and took its place as an up-and-coming world power. The lack of an effective opposition meant that González was still in power a decade later. By the 1990s, however, the euphoria of 1982 had evaporated.

The autonomous regions (*above right*)
Under the terms of the 1978 constitution, autonomous status was promised to the Spanish regions, with the possibility of their own elected assemblies. This was quickly granted to the Basque Country and Catalonia, which both had distinct cultural identities and a long history of regionalist demand. By 1983 17 autonomous regions had been created in Spain, including the Canary Islands. These have varying powers and responsibilities in relation to the central government: only the Basque Country and Navarre have independent tax-raising powers. A good indication of the strength of regional activities is the number of laws that were promulgated by each of the regional assemblies in the 10 years after 1982 – ranging from 232 passed by Catalonia to 43 by Extremadura. Portugal is a unitary state, though there is provision for the eventual introduction of some form of devolved government: the Azores and Madeira already have a degree of autonomy. The mainland is divided into 18 administrative districts, and regional parties are banned from standing in elections.

Right Under Franco, all public expressions of Catalan nationalism, even folk-dancing, were banned. Now Catalans have reclaimed their cultural heritage. Here, citizens of Barcelona perform the *sardana*, their traditional dance, in the cathedral square.

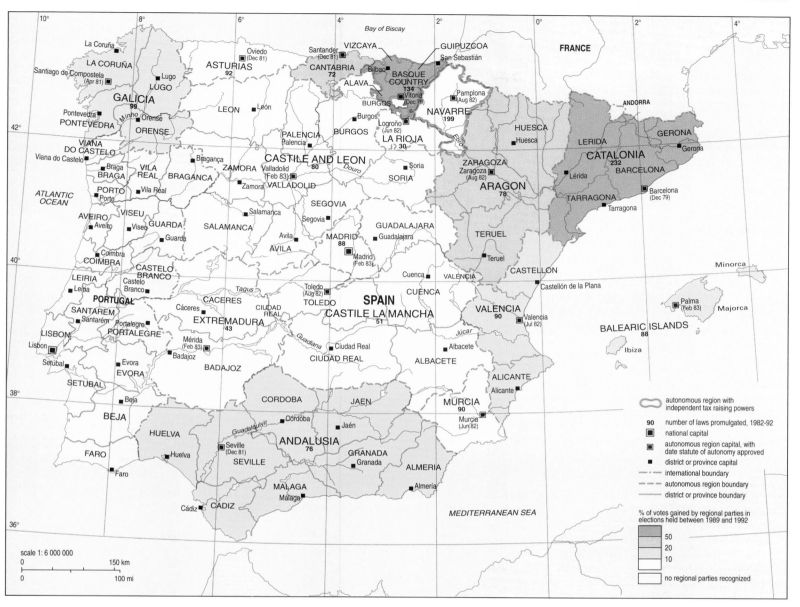

part in political life. The party in power seeks not only to take over state institutions but also to colonize other areas of public life, such as the bureaucracy, the media and even the universities. In Portugal, this process has been trammeled by the exigencies of power-sharing (particularly before 1987), but in Spain in the 1980s a rampant Socialist Party was able to appoint sympathizers to official positions in virtually every area of public life. This had the effect of expanding the party – whose actual membership was small – but the process also reflected the lack of any previous weeding-out of Francoist appointees and time-servers. In 1982, the new Socialist government had to make extensive political appointments, particularly in the civil service, to ensure that their policies were implemented. Similarly, in Portugal, the dramatic expansion of public sector employment during the late 1970s was related to the extensive nationalization program that was introduced in 1975, as well as to the desire to reward party loyalists.

Perhaps inevitably, the dominance of party elites brought wide-ranging accusations of corruption. In 1987 Spain's Socialist government, bowing to pressure, specified which bureaucratic posts might be political appointments and which were restricted to normal civil service promotions. In the same year,

Cavaco Silva won an absolute majority in the Portuguese election on a manifesto promising to curb the rise in patronage and scale down the public sector.

A decade of Socialist government in Spain, however, added a new dimension to the perennial problems of bureaucratic clientelism. In 1991, González's right-hand man, the deputy prime minister Alfonso Guerra (b. 1940), resigned after a long-running corruption scandal. Thereafter, an apparently endless series of revelations concerning irregular party funding, tax evasion and bribery eroded the Socialists' standing. In July 1993 Spain's party of the right, the Partido Popular (PP: Popular Party), achieved over 25 percent of the vote for the first time, depriving the Socialists of an absolute majority. The PP, which had been set up in September 1976 by a former Francoist minister, Manuel Fraga Iribarne (b. 1922), had taken some years to shake off its authoritarian image to become accepted as a catch-all party of the center right. In both Spain and Portugal the extremes at either end of the political spectrum won little electoral success in the 1980s, and self-styled center parties also became insignificant: in Portugal, the Center Social Democrats, which had disappeared into the wider Aliança Democrática (AD: Democratic Alliance) in 1979, was eclipsed by Cavaco Silva's PSD in 1987. Instead, those parties that most convincingly occupied the center ground, whatever their formal ideological designation, were rewarded at the polls.

Economic growth

Despite the scandals of the 1980s, the decade saw remarkable political, social and economic progress. The dramatic political upheavals of the mid 1970s had been compounded, in economic terms, by the energy crisis of 1973–74, when oil prices rose nearly 500 percent and the tourist-fueled Iberian economic miracle ground to a halt. It was all too clear that the expansion of the 1960s had been built on less than solid foundations. Both Spain and Portugal were highly dependent on imported energy, the financial sector was inefficient, outdated fiscal practices dominated the public sector and various restrictive mechanisms hampered the development of freely-working markets. In the 1970s, however, these economic issues had consistently been suppressed by the urgency of the political situation. It was democratization, not economic recovery, that set the governments' agenda. Structural weaknesses in the economy simply went unaddressed, with the result that by the early 1980s both Iberian economies faced urgent problems of recuperation and restructuring.

In Portugal, the position had been complicated, in the early days of the revolution, by talk of a command economy. This option, like that of a socialist state, was rejected after 1975. Portugal had to find a different solution to its acute economic problems. Though the tourist boom of the 1960s had introduced expansion, new levels of foreign investment had done little to reduce dependence on the colonies and nothing to regenerate agriculture, which remained highly traditional. After the 1974 revolution, the distribution of wealth shifted immediately to the workers, who had previously enjoyed neither collective bargaining rights nor the right to strike. Colonial markets contracted sharply – while the raw materials and agricultural products, previously imported at favorable rates from the overseas territories, were also lost. Decolonization also had a human effect. About 800,000 settlers from

the former colonies – known as *retornados* – returned to the motherland after 1974, many of them destitute. No longer a maritime, imperial power, Portugal's development came now to depend on integration with the European economy.

On 28 March 1977 both Portugal and Spain made formal application for membership of the EC. After lengthy and, at times, acrimonious negotiations, accession treaties were signed on 12 June 1985, leading six months later, on 1 January 1986, to entry into the Community. In the late 1970s, the principal reasons given for seeking admission were political. However the main effects of membership were to be economic. While the prospect of EC membership undoubtedly boosted Iberia's nascent democracies, by the time they joined the Community, both countries already had functioning parliamentary regimes.

In the early 1980s the Socialist government was committed to bringing Spain into the mainstream of European development. Modernization was to be achieved through a stringent package of austerity measures aimed at reducing inflation, encouraging foreign investment and restructuring declining heavy industry such as Basque steel. These far-reaching economic policies brought with them severe job-losses and cuts in public services. The economy had been

Above Seasonal agricultural work is still an important source of employment for Spain's gypsy community. Marginalized by much of society, gypsies find work where they can. Many women and children sell flowers, beg and tell fortunes. Though Spanish gypsies are not nomadic, they often live in camps or shanty towns on the outskirts of cities. This group of gypsies, together with their painfully thin dog, is returning to camp after harvest work on Majorca.

turned around by 1985, but the ties between the government and the union movement had declined markedly, largely because of legislation in 1984 to introduce greater flexibility in the labor market: by June 1991, over 32 percent of the wage-earning population were on fixed-term contracts.

Full membership of the EC opened the country to international trade, leading to a flood of foreign investment and providing the impetus for growth. Though some people expressed concern at the extent to which foreign, rather than Spanish, capital fueled the country's second "economic miracle" after 1986, Spain became a significant force in the EC. In 1992 the country hosted the Olympic Games in Barcelona and Expo92 in Seville. Massive expenditure on public works related to both the events reflected the government's commitment to modernization of the country's infrastructure. Nevertheless, though EC grants had done much to improve transportation and communications, as the Spanish economy entered recession in the early 1990s, it was apparent that still more was needed to bring about the country's full integration into Europe. Portugal, too, had experienced boom conditions after entering the EC in 1986, but in 1989 was still the poorest country in the Community, remaining heavily dependent on EC agricultural subsidies. Communications were still inadequate and few sectors of the economy had been fully modernized.

Education and social change

Education occupied a central place in the modernization programs of the Iberian democracies. Under both Franco and Salazar, its provision had been inadequate and its content obscurantist. Patriotism and religion dominated the curriculum, often to a suffocating degree. Both dictators were anxious to keep education free from demoralizing or corrupt influences (in the late 1950s, Salazar's concern to keep decadent forces out of Portugal had led him to ban Coca-Cola on both moral and aesthetic grounds). In such circumstances, convention was the order of the day. Students flocked to the law faculties – a traditional route to bureaucratic posts – despite a glut of graduates in this relatively uncontroversial discipline. Under Franco, religious instruction was made compulsory for all university students, yet theology faculties stagnated, isolated from new developments in philosophy and Biblical criticism. Modern history was left virtually unexplored as scholars sought the safer terrain of the medieval and imperial periods. Science was still more seriously affected. As Spain prospered in the 1960s, some attempt was made to remedy these deficiencies. Between 1962 and 1976 education's share of the budget more than doubled; in 1970 the General Education Law made schooling free and compulsory for all children aged between 6 and 14. These changes were, in part, the legacy of the Catholic lay group, Opus Dei, whose members had first been appointed to Franco's cabinet in 1957. Though theologically and politically conservative, Opus Dei was firmly committed to professionalism, education and technological development. Such an attitude contrasted sharply with that of the Portuguese elites, who remained largely uninterested in improving literacy levels.

Despite the expansion of the previous two decades, in the late 1980s an estimated 11 percent of Spaniards over the age of 14 were illiterate. The 1978 constitution had introduced the possibility of schooling in minority languages – a proposition adopted with gusto in Catalonia, the Basque Country and, to a lesser extent, Galicia – but education in the new Spain was still elitist. In 1984 the Socialist government made state funding for private schools conditional upon the adoption of standardized admission criteria, believing this would eventually lead to an egalitarian and secularized education system. The new law was bitterly opposed by sections of the church and many middle-class parents, and only came into effect after its opponents had appealed, unsuccessfully, to the constitutional tribunal. In 1990 the Socialists introduced a further education law that relegated religious instruction to an optional slot in the curriculum and introduced sex education – not least as a means of promoting greater equality between the sexes.

In Portugal the problems facing education seemed still more daunting. A survey in 1989 found 21 percent illiteracy among those over 15 – the highest level in the EC. The educational drop-out and failure rate stood at 33 percent, against an EC average of 10 percent. Not until after 1974 was schooling finally made available to all and the period of compulsory school attendance extended from four years to six. There was a considerable turnover in personnel after the revolution, with school heads being replaced by committees, but lack of funds and dilapidated buildings led to low morale among teaching staff. Though literacy rates rose dramatically among the young, it still proved difficult to enforce school attendance in those areas – particularly the poor industrial suburbs of Braga, Porto and Aveiro – where child labor remained an important part of the family economy.

Since the coming of democracy, particular attention has been paid to higher education. New universities were established to cope with burgeoning numbers of students. In 1970 Portugal had five universities, four public and one private; by 1990, there were 14 autonomous universities and colleges in the public sector and five in the private, together with a state-run open university. The rapid rise in university provision in both Portugal and Spain reflected the fast-changing nature of society on the peninsula. The greater prosperity of the 1960s had led to a mini "baby-boom" compared with the lean years of the 1940s and 1950s. This generation was ready to enter higher education in the 1980s, at a time when provision was greater than ever before, and government initiatives were encouraging young people to acquire qualifications, particularly in science and technical subjects. As women took their place in the workforce, so girls were taking up university places as never before. In 1940 only 13 percent of university students were women. Four years after Franco's death, the figure stood at 37 percent; by 1984, half of those studying for degrees were women.

The dramatic expansion of higher education notwithstanding, some issues have proved intractable. Students in both countries qualify for university entrance on successful completion of the secondary school certificate (*bachillerato*). Despite concern at the quality of some qualifications, attempts to introduce selectivity were met by bitter opposition: in Spain unrest among school and university students in 1987 led to the resignation of the education minister responsible for introducing the scheme. Though progress has been made in the development of science education, students still flock to the vocational subjects of law and medicine. The supply of trained lawyers on the peninsula perennially exceeds demand, while Spain has more doctors per head of population than any

Expo'92

In 1992 – as Spain's Socialist government celebrated ten years in office – Barcelona hosted the Olympic Games, Madrid acted as European Cultural Capital, and the Universal Exposition was held in Seville, capital of Andalusia. Since the first "Great Exhibition" was held in London in 1851, 26 world trade fairs have been staged in 17 countries. Yet, after Montreal, Canada, in 1967 and Osaka, Japan, in 1970, the popularity of such mammoth exhibitions had faded. The 1992 exposition was to have been a joint venture between Seville and Chicago but the American city pulled out in 1987, concerned at the expense.

Despite the misgivings, Expo'92 – as it was invariably known – provided a fitting climax to Spain's *annus mirabilis*. Held in part to commemorate the fifth centenary of Columbus' first journey across the Atlantic, the exposition provided an unrivalled showcase for the new Spain. It was staged on a 215-hectare site that occupied most of the island of La Cartuja in the Guadalquivir river. New bridges – several of them uncompromisingly modern in design – connected this previously abandoned site to the city of Seville. Pavilions were constructed on uncultivated agricultural land, while a deserted 15th-century monastery was renovated as an art gallery.

Modernity and internationalism were the watchwords of Expo'92. 110 countries participated in it; over 60 national pavilions were constructed. Though some countries chose to reproduce traditional architectural styles – the Hungarian pavilion was modeled on a wooden church – most looked to the future. The British pavilion, for instance, was built of steel and glass; its front facade was a wall of water, serviced by a pumping system powered by solar panels. Few of these innovative buildings were built to last, though it was planned to convert the Pavilion of Discovery, commemorating the Atlantic voyages, into a maritime museum. Expo'92 was open until 4 a.m. every day for six months from April to September 1992, and was seen by over 18 million visitors. Though the future use of the site remained uncertain, the benefits reaped by the city were considerable. The transport infrastructure of Seville, Spain's third largest city, which had previously possessed only a rudimentary communications network, was thoroughly modernized: in the run-up to Expo'92 the rail network was renovated, the city linked to Madrid by high-speed train (the AVE, modeled on the French TGV), the airport extended, and 75 kilometers of highway built.

Below The black-windowed pavilion of the Holy See and the spectacular peacock tail of the Indian pavilion form a dramatic backdrop for the cable cars and elevated monorail that ferried visitors around Expo'92. Pedestrians were shaded from the scorching Andalusian sun by creeper-covered walkways. In the background of this picture is the giant cooling sphere. This great globe was covered with micro-ionizers that exhaled clouds of moisture at regular intervals to lower the ambient temperature. The system, though extremely effective, consumed large amounts of water, leading to rationing among local farmers.

Above The magnificent Kuwaiti pavilion designed by the Spanish architect Santiago Calatrava was one of the architectural highlights of Expo'92. Above a spacious auditorium rose 19 movable "plumes": when closed these symbolized a pearl shell; half-open, they evoked a Bedouin tent; fully open, the sail of a ship.

Left One of the most impressive of the new bridges across the Guadalquivir was christened *La Barqueta* (the small ship), as its undulating lines rose and fell like the movement of a ship's prow.

Right Large expanses of the site were protected by canvas canopies strung between cooling towers that used water evaporation to alleviate the arid atmosphere. Traditional Moorish design, with its reliance on water, shade, plants and breezes, was harnessed to modern technology in the effort to keep visitors cool.

other country in the EC. This generous provision of medical practitioners disguises other failings in health care. Though the Spanish educational reforms of the 1980s helped improve medical training, related paramedical professions, such as physiotherapy, are still in their infancy. Even ward nurses have only a short professional history; hospitals have usually relied on patients' relatives to provide general nursing care.

Religion and cultural change

Under Franco and Salazar, religion defined national identity. Catholic morals and *mores* were enshrined by law, particularly in Spain, claimed by Franco as "the spiritual reserve of the west". Yet it was Portugal that produced the most spectacular display of divine interest in the peninsula. In 1917 – at a time when Portugal was governed by an anticlerical Republic – the Virgin Mary appeared to three cousins minding sheep outside the village of Fátima in Estremadura. Despite being imprisoned for two days by the local administrator, the children stuck to their story, and within weeks the site of the apparition was attracting pilgrims by the thousand.

The fame of Fátima, and the shrine's usefulness for the Catholic regimes of Salazar and Franco, did not depend solely on the original visions. The Virgin had apparently spoken of an anti-Christ: after the revolution in Russia the anti-Christ was widely identified with communism. The principal seer, Lucia, popularized this connection with accounts of further visions and revealed secrets, claiming in 1927 that, if Russia were not consecrated to the Immaculate Heart of Mary, "she will spread her errors throughout the entire world". During the Spanish Civil War, the Virgin Mary was proclaimed captain-general of the Francoist armies, guiding the soldiers who were extirpating the Red menace. After Franco's victory, the image of Our Lady of Fátima – already an invaluable source of propaganda for Salazar's New State – toured Spain, spreading its anti-communist message through tales of miracles, intercessions and severe punishment should the world not return to Catholicism.

In the harsh years following the Civil War, all Spanish citizens were expected to do just that. Huge public masses were celebrated in every city taken from the Republicans, Christian statues and religious place names hallowed the streets and squares, while swearing, blasphemy and immodest dress were proscribed by law. Though attendance at mass was not compulsory by law, many employers – including those in the public sector – made church-going a virtual condition of employment. Levels of Catholic practice were high, but they were never universal. The affluent were comfortable with Catholicism, the poor less so. As elsewhere in Europe, industrial workers were unlikely to attend church on a regular basis.

In the 1980s, over 40 percent of adults in northern Portugal attended mass, a figure that fell to around 10 percent in the south. More than 90 percent of the population, however, were baptized and the majority observed Catholic rites of first communion, marriage, burial and the commemoration of the dead. Similarly, in Spain a 1984 survey found that, though only 30 percent of the adult population attended Sunday mass, 47 percent identified themselves as practicing Catholics. The geographical distribution of regular church-goers was the same as in Portugal – mass attendance was usual in the north, unusual in the south. Rural areas were more religious then urban districts, at least in the

north; in Andalusia, the Alentejo and the Algarve, however, Catholic cities were marooned in an irreligious countryside. This pattern has been found in both countries for as long as records have been kept, and is also repeated in Italy. Possibly, the Moorish south was never truly "reconquered" for Christianity. Yet, in the 1980s, the numbers of Spaniards leaving the church were greatest in precisely those northern provinces that had historically been the most Catholic – Galicia, Asturias, the Basque Country and Navarre.

There can be no doubt that religious practice has declined since the days of Franco and Salazar. The number of practicing Catholics fell from 64.5 percent in 1975 – the year of Franco's death – to 40.9 percent in 1986. The proportion of non-believers remained small – 13 percent in 1990 as opposed to 9 percent in 1981 – but though 86 percent of Spaniards described themselves as "Catholic", there was some evidence to suggest that organized religion was still declining. An overwhelming majority (81 percent) believed in God, but fewer young people (68 percent) did so. The importance of festivals in family and community life has preserved Catholicism's ceremonial role and ensured that the church maintains a public presence unusual in secularized societies. Nonetheless, the fall in church attendance undoubtedly reflects a wide-

Above Since 1917, the site at Fátima where the Virgin Mary appeared to three children has become one of the Catholic world's most important place of pilgrimage. The devout come both to do penance – traveling the long path leading up to the basilica on one's knees is a common penitential devotion – and to give thanks. The shrine's most noted *devoté* is Pope John Paul II who believes his escape from an assassin's bullet to be due to the intervention of Our Lady of Fátima. He visited the shrine in thanksgiving, leaving the bullet in the crown that adorns the Virgin's statue.

spread adoption of secular cultural values. Despite the elaborate processions that take place in Holy Week and Corpus Christi, religion is now essentially a private affair; an individual's relationship with God, or the lack of it, a matter of personal conscience.

The relaxation of censorship

The rigorous imposition of a particularly puritanical style of Catholic morals had characterized both dictatorships. Toward the end of Salazar's long rule, newspapers were forbidden to print horoscopes, regarded as superstitious by the Catholic Church. In Spain, a censors' bureau established in wartime (1938) functioned for a further 30 years. The merest hint of eroticism had ecclesiastical censors reaching for their blue pencils. Painted vests discreetly covered bare torsos in photographs of boxing matches; dubbed soundtracks erased the dubious morals of Hollywood: mistresses were depicted as sisters, adding an uncomfortable hint of incest to films that began life as straightforward tales of adultery. Even in 1972, Spanish audiences for Steve McQueen's *The Getaway* were assured in an uplifting epilogue that the criminals they had just seen escape were apprehended off screen.

The old certainties were relaxed somewhat during the 1960s, not least due to the sudden influx of scantily-dressed northern European tourists, essential for economic recovery. In 1964 the censor allowed a bikini-clad woman on screen; a mere five years earlier, girls wearing such garments on Spanish beaches had risked arrest. In the months after Franco's death, more sensational elements of the press began to push back the frontiers of acceptability: nipples appeared on the pages of Spanish papers, then nudes. In 1978, the first sex shop appeared in Madrid and pornographic films were shown openly for the first time.

This heady freedom produced its own excesses. Yet, as the novelty of nudity and publicly proclaimed sexual freedom wore off, so pornography came to be no more and no less visible than in other Western countries. The church's role as arbiter of public morals had gone for good. In both countries today, religion is

Above As the legendary resting place of St James the Apostle, Santiago de Compostela has been a center of pilgrimage since the Middle Ages. The magnificent cathedral is the focal point of the celebrations for St James's Day and the square fills with people to watch the fireworks that commemorate Spain's patron saint. When St James's Day falls on a Sunday, it is declared a Holy Year and pilgrims traveling to the city gain the extra spiritual reward of a plenary indulgence and a year's absolution. In these years the *fiesta* is celebrated with extra vigor.

Right Spain's most noted film director, Luis Buñuel (1900–83), spent most of his life outside Spain, an opponent of both the politics and the aesthetics of the Franco regime. *Viridiana* (1961) was one of only three films shot in his native land. Though a worldwide critical success – and the first Spanish film to win the coveted Gold Palm at the Cannes film festival – *Viridiana* was condemned by the Vatican as blasphemous. Its anti-clericalism immediately attracted the attention of the Francoist censors and the film was not recognized as Spanish until 1983.

widely believed to have no role in politics. The separation of church and state is seen as desirable by a great majority even of practicing Catholics. The rigid confessional divisions of the past – when membership of a socialist party was unthinkable for Catholics – appear to have disappeared for ever.

Women and family life

The impact of secularization has perhaps been most profound in the realm of sexual behavior. The establishment of lay, democratic regimes in both Spain and Portugal has meant that moral offenses such as adultery are no longer crimes, elaborate state schemes encouraging large families (particularly favored by Franco) have been abandoned, and contraception is now freely available. Legal birth control, which is used by Catholic and non-Catholic alike, has led to a significant fall in the birth rate. In Portugal, 16.2 live births per 1,000 inhabitants were recorded in 1980, but in 1989 this figure had dropped to 11.5. In Spain, the birth rate halved between 1960 and 1990, falling from 21.6 per 1,000 to 10.2. The fall in the fertility rate was even more dramatic: in 1960 Spanish women bore an average of 2.86 children; in 1990, this figure had fallen to 1.36, the lowest level in the EC outside Italy. However, as there were more women of childbearing age in Spain than in many other European countries and – unlike Portugal – infant mortality was uncommon, the number of children being born was still considerable. In 1990, the Spanish and Portuguese populations were, along with Ireland, the youngest in Europe though, unlike Ireland, the fertility rate had dropped below generation replacement level.

Since 1984 in Portugal and 1985 in Spain women have been able to terminate their pregnancies legally, though only in the event of rape, incest, danger to the mother's life or fetal malformation. In the early 1990s, a majority of people in both countries opposed unrestricted legal abortion, even though backstreet terminations were still a problem, particularly among poorer women who could not afford to seek an abortion abroad. This has long been the case. In 1974, the year before Franco's death, official estimates put the annual number of illegal abortions in Spain at 300,000 while, in the early 1980s, nearly 10 percent of all terminations carried out in England and Wales were performed on Spanish women.

Divorce was legalized in Spain in 1981. In Portugal divorce was legal under Salazar, though only for those married by the courts rather than the church: the revolution made it available to all. Ecclesiastical opposition – fierce in Spain and rather more muted in Portugal – failed to convince the public that a comprehensive divorce law was undesirable. In Spain, divorce is available on the petition of either party two years after the break-up of a marriage. Most Spaniards support this, just as they do the availability of abortion in certain circumstances, young people being more likely to be in favor than their elders. However, though the number of couples seeking divorce rose by 140 percent in Spain between 1981 and 1989, the actual divorce rate was the lowest in Europe. As in Greece and Italy, the family has remained a central institution in Iberian society, regardless of the lessening importance of religious values. Young people usually remain in the family home until they marry. While this is often a reflection of practical need rather than personal choice, surveys conducted in 1990 showed that over 80 percent of young people between the ages

of 18 and 24 were satisfied with their life at home.

If the role of the family in Iberian society has not changed dramatically over the last decades of the 20th century, that of women undoubtedly has. At the height of his powers, Salazar maintained that "a wife who has in mind the care of her home cannot do good work outside" and declared that he would "always fight against the independence of married women" – a view shared by General Franco. The Portuguese constitution of 1933 established that all were equal before the law "except for women, the differences arising from their nature and for the good of the family". Yet, even under the dictators, many women had to go out to work in order to support their families. Though it was rare for middle-class women to work outside the home, except in cases of financial necessity, many working-class women – and some children – had to shoulder considerable economic responsibility. This was emphatically the case in those areas, Galicia and northern Portugal in particular, where the men

Above For decades after the Civil War, economic migration ensured that many men lived and worked away from home, often abroad. In the villages, their wives would tend the fields while the care of children was left to grandparents. Though this situation persists in parts of Portugal, Spain now receives migrants rather than creates them. While many working mothers still depend on relatives for childcare, others use nurseries.

migrated to northern Europe to find seasonal or un-skilled employment. Women worked in the fields and on the farmsteads, often entrusting the care of young children to elderly relatives; on marriage, it was common for the groom to move in with his bride's parents. Similarly, among fishing families on the Atlantic coast, when the men were at sea, the women ran the farms.

The identification of women and household meant that, historically, it was extremely difficult for a land-less woman to marry. In the first half of the 20th century 32 percent of Portuguese women over the age of 50 died as spinsters. In northern Portugal, despite the area's exceptionally high levels of Catholic practice, illegitimacy was common and pre-marital pregnancy was even more frequent. While pregnant women with dowries would expect their lovers to marry them, the landless were less fortunate, being left to raise their children alone, whether or not the relationship with the father continued. Illegitimacy rates began to fall from the 1950s and plummeted in the 1970s as the number of men seeking work in France and Germany rose enormously. The prospect of temporary employment abroad made these men and their families far less dependent on the land: men could now afford to marry regardless of how much – or how little – they or their prospective brides owned. However, a high proportion of households continued to be headed by women, at least while their husbands were abroad, though the numbers of families headed by unmarried mothers declined.

As Iberia prospered, so emigration rates began to decline. Female employment became more and more

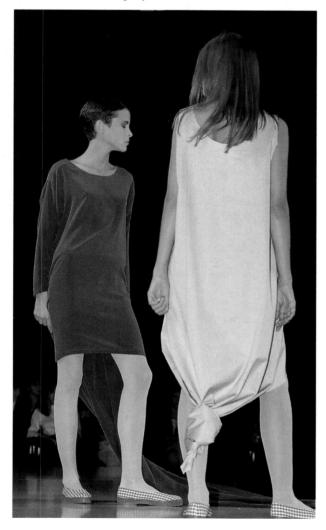

Right Fashion and design are important industries in democratic Spain. Now that women are no longer constricted by the rigid morals of the Francoist regime – which frowned on bare arms, short skirts and frivolity – they have acquired aesthetic freedom while fashion designers such as Agatha Ruíz de la Prada (whose clothes are pictured here) have won an international reputation.

common after the mid 1970s and families – far from having to rely on migrants' remittances – were increasingly supported by a double wage. By the 1990s the world of employment had become fully open to women, even though domestic service continued to account for a high proportion of their jobs.

During the transitions to democracy women's social and political expectations rose even faster than those of the population in general. One of the first blows for feminism had been struck in 1972 when the "Three Marias" – the poet Maria Teresa Horta, the novelist Maria Velho da Costa and Maria Isabel Barreno – published *New Portuguese Letters*. This attack on the suppression of women's rights in Portugal became a sensation, both abroad and at home, where it was banned as an outrage to public decency. The authors were arrested in 1973, held without trial and only acquitted after the 1974 revolution.

This completely changed the legal position of women in Portugal. After 1974, full civil and electoral rights were granted to women and men. A Commission on the Status of Women was established in 1977 to defend women's rights; the professions, bureaucracy and judiciary were opened to all, and women were appointed to top posts in government. In 1979, Maria de Lurdes Pintassilgo (b. 1929) – a chemical engineer by profession – became prime minister, the first Iberian woman to hold such office, albeit in a six-month caretaker post. In Spain, the position of women changed just as fast and in similar ways. The number of women in the work force rose rapidly from 27 percent in 1980 to 33.3 percent in 1990. Though this figure was still below the European average, over 50 percent of women aged under 40 worked outside the home. Since the coming of democracy women have played an increasingly prominent role in public life: they have been admitted to the police, the Civil Guard and the armed forces, and there have even been chair-women in leading football clubs.

Equal opportunities legislation has been enacted on various occasions since the establishment in 1983 of the *Instituto de la Mujer* (Institute for Women) designed to promote and protect women's welfare by the Socialist government. Individual women have always been prominent in literature and the arts, but are only now becoming major political figures. In 1992, there were two women ministers in the Social-ist government. In 1987, 3,652 women were returned as town councillors, and in 1989 13.4 percent of par-liamentary deputies and 6 percent of regional assemby deputies were women. These figures – particularly for the regional deputies – were not high compared with some other democratic countries, but the public posi-tion of women was clearly improving. The same was not necessarily true of their domestic position, how-ever: in 1990 a survey found that, even among liberal couples, 77 percent of women assumed sole responsi-bility for housework, while only 2 percent of men reg-ularly did the dishes.

The arts and leisure

Under Salazar, the cultural interests of the Portuguese were summed up as "football, *fado* and Fátima" – a reflection of the political conservatism of the regime rather than the artistic abilities of the people. Franco, too, fostered depoliticized pastimes. Regional diver-sity was reduced to folk-dancing, nationalist aspira-tions were played out on the soccer pitch rather than any greater political arena. Franco – who never missed

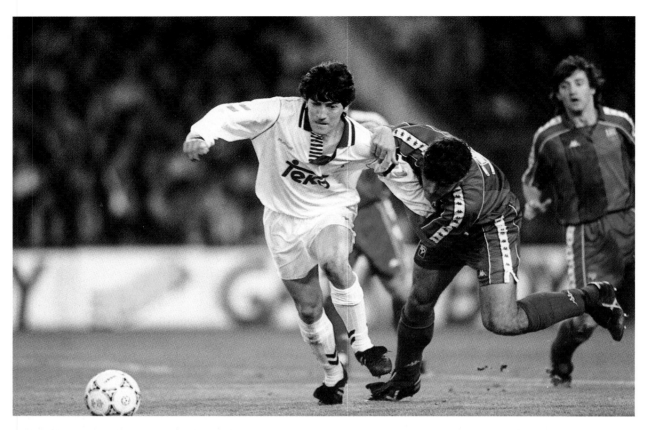

Left Soccer is a national obsession on the Iberian peninsula and has long since eclipsed bullfighting as the main spectator sport. Under Franco a great rivalry developed between Barcelona and Real Madrid. This sporting struggle owed much to the nationalistic conflict of Catalonia and Castile. Under the dictator, this fixture was virtually the only outlet for regionalist sentiment. Even today, the two teams attract fervent support and matches between them draw large and wildly partisan crowds.

televized soccer – unwittingly gave Catalan nationalism a new outlet with his encouragement of the game. The Spanish league came to be dominated by an intense rivalry between Barcelona F.C. (universally known as Barça) and Real Madrid.

Just as all Spaniards have a preference for either Barça or Real Madrid, even if their main support is given to another team entirely, every Portuguese supports one of the three big teams: F.C. Porto, Benfica or Sporting (both from Lisbon). Emigrants commonly follow the fortunes of home clubs: hundreds of Portuguese flags greet Benfica or Sporting when they play in Europe. For those at home, success on the soccer pitch is an occasion for patriotic rejoicing. Real Madrid's domination of continental soccer in the 1950s – when they won the European Cup five years running – was depicted by the Franco regime as a national achievement, despite the team's success being built around a Hungarian player, Ferenç Puskas. Later, in 1982, Spain's hosting of soccer's World Cup became a national *fiesta*, even though the Spanish team was eliminated by Northern Ireland in the second round of the competition.

The popularity of soccer reflects not only the legacy of Franco and Salazar, but also the historic poverty of the Iberian peninsula. Any child could play football on the street; far fewer could afford to take up tennis or golf, which required expensive equipment and club fees. These sports only became popular in Spain in the 1980s, not least because of the international success of golfers such as Severiano Ballesteros (b. 1957) and José María Olázabal and tennis players such as Arantxa Sánchez Vicario (b. 1971). In Portugal, however, the golf courses and tennis courts that were constructed in the 1970s and 1980s were largely for the benefit of affluent tourists.

By the 1960s soccer had replaced the bullfight (*corrida*) as the peninsula's most important spectator sport. Yet the traditional rituals of the bullring were not eclipsed, nor did they survive simply as a colorful tourist spectacle. The *corridas*, waged on horseback in Portugal and on foot in Spain, were encouraged by Franco and Salazar. However, Spanish audiences declined from the 1940s. The Civil War had greatly depleted the stock of fighting bulls; the reputation of the *toro bravo* (literally "brave bull") was damaged still further in the 1950s and 1960s when a small number of entrepreneurs acquired a virtual monopoly over Spanish bullfighting and demanded physically impressive but less dangerous bulls to send in against their often mediocre *toreros*. By the 1970s, some bulls had reached the point of physical collapse. Measures were taken to improve breeding standards and the development of new bullfighting schools led to a renaissance in the matador's art. A growing and increasingly vociferous minority of Spaniards regard bullfighting as neither sport nor art, but ritualized cruelty. Portuguese bullfighting also has its opponents but, as the bull is not killed in the ring, attracts less condemnation than its Spanish counterpart. In both countries, certain restaurants and butchers bid for the carcasses of bulls killed during *corridas* and the meat is sold to the public. Perhaps fittingly, in the European home of *machismo*, the beast's testicles can be expected to fetch a commanding price.

In the dictatorships' search for authentic native culture, they not only exalted the art of bullfighting but also corrupted and commercialized it. The same was true of *fado* and flamenco, both of which were relentlessly promoted as "typical" of their respective countries. Despite its obscure and possibly rural origins, Portuguese *fado* – the word literally means "fate" –had become the characteristic urban music of cafés, cabarets and night clubs. These songs of yearning, intimately associated with seafaring, were taken up by professional singers such as Amália Rodrigues (b. 1920). The *fado* houses of Lisbon and Coimbra became tourist attractions, yet they retained their distinct styles of singing. Certainly, commercialized *fado* lost much of its spontaneity, but it never became the source of cheap images for the tourist trade, in contrast to flamenco.

From the 1950s, Andalusia's gypsy flamenco dancers were promoted as representative of the whole of Spain. The form had enjoyed a great vogue in the late 19th century with the establishment of *cafés cantantes* in Andalusian cities and the appearance of the first professional performers. It later fell into decline and was only revived in 1956 when a competitive festival was reestablished in Córdoba. However – while state encouragement rescued the art from impoverished obscurity – the government's promotion of a bastardized version of flamenco first to a national and then to a tourist audience ran the risk of replacing one sort of decline with another. For a time flamenco seemed condemned to a half-life of lackluster performances in over-priced bars. But then performers such as the *cantaor* (literally, singer) Antonio Mairena (1909–83) revived a purer form by tirelessly promoting unadorned, undiluted flamenco. In 1977, the dancer and choreographer Antonio Gades (b. 1936), was appointed to lead Spain's first permanent dance company specializing in "ballet español", a fusion of flamenco and classical dance. The company achieved enormous critical and popular success in the 1980s, both in Spain and abroad, not least because of Gades' collaboration with the director Carlos Saura (b. 1932) in a trio of flamenco films, *Blood Wedding* (1981), *Carmen* (1983) and *Love the Magician* (1985).

It was only after Franco's death that artists and intellectuals were able to jettison bowdlerized versions of indigenous traditions and rediscover the folkloric roots of much of Spanish culture. The dressing-up of Spanish culture in flamenco flounces was lampooned in Luis García Berlanga's film, *Welcome, Mr Marshall* (1952), in which a small Castilian town disguises itself as Andalusian so as not to disappoint a visiting American official. In the same decade, a young generation of Spanish composers, all born around 1930, moved away from the national tradition of classical music and abandoned folksong. Roberto Gerhard (1896–1970), of Swiss ancestry, was the first Spanish composer who proved to be sympathetic to the atonal innovation of Arnold Schoenberg (1874–1951). His pupil, Joaquín Homs (b. 1906), introduced more cosmopolitan influences to Spain, though his own music remained in the national tradition. In the 1950s, Luis de Pablo (b. 1930) and Cristóbal Halffter (b. 1930) were at the forefront of a group of Spanish serialists, who looked more to the music of the German Karlheinz Stockhausen (b.1928) than to de Falla for inspiration. Innovative though these musicians were, by far the most successful post-war composer was Joaquín Rodrigo (b. 1902), whose evocative "Concierto de Aranjuez" (1939) – a classically "Spanish" piece of music – became popular throughout Europe.

While Rodrigo was happy to stay in Franco's Spain, others were not. A generation of writers, musicians and artists went into exile in 1939, among them Roberto Gerhard and the internationally renowned cellist Pau Casals (1876–1973), who died before Franco and so never returned to his native land.

Below Bullfighting continues to attract a considerable following in Spain, despite threats of legislation from the European Community and the actions of an increasingly vociferous – if still small – animal rights lobby within Spain. These posters are advertizing a *corrida* in Marbella. Bullfights are a major feature of civic *fiestas*; the most important date in the calendar is Madrid's San Isidro festival and the capital now houses Spain's most important bullfighting school.

Casals' fellow-Catalan Joan Miró, however, did come back: though never reconciled to Franco, Miró saw his regime as a scratch on the surface of Spanish – and particularly Catalan – culture, which he described as a carob tree, deep-rooted and evergreen. Though Franco's governments frowned upon modernism, painters and sculptors were not as circumscribed by the censors as were novelists, poets and journalists. Indeed, they were the first to make contact with the lost intellectual world of the 1930s. The early work of the sculptor Eduardo Chillida (b. 1924) continued the forged-iron tradition of Gargallo and González, though his increasingly metaphysical interpretation of the technique led him to more abstract installations. The first effective step toward modernism came in 1948 when a number of artists based in Barcelona established the journal *Dau al Set* to provide a focus for the emerging *avant-garde*. Originally surrealists,

Above Fado is now the characteristic cabaret music of Portuguese bars and restaurants. The word originally meant "fate" and the evocative music epitomized the *saudade* or yearning of a seafaring people. The songs are accompanied by the 12-string Portuguese guitar. While some of the most famous *fado* performers are women, they sing in the Lisbon style. The *fado* of the university city of Coimbra is exclusively masculine.

Left The art of flamenco, like that of classical ballet, is confined to professional performers, but the flamenco-style folk-dances known as *sevillanas* are enjoyed by all. Here, they are performed in traditional style by young girls during a *fiesta* in Seville, but they are also often seen in discos, bringing the night's dancing to an end.

most of the *Dau al Set* group later moved into expressive abstraction. Among them was Antoni Tàpies (b. 1923), perhaps the most influential of post-war Spanish painters, who later led the *arte povera* movement that used assemblage and collage techniques for the purposes of social criticism. Such was Tàpies' stature that, even under Franco, state galleries bought his work, recognizing it at least as a sound investment, if nothing else.

The visual arts have flourished in Spain since the 1960s and, with economic growth and an amenable democratic regime, state funding for the arts has reached record levels. The most important museum to open in Madrid in the 1990s, the Queen Sofía Center, was dedicated to contemporary art, while the works of Picasso and Miró were given pride of place in Barcelona. Picasso's searing condemnation of the Civil War, *Guernica* (1937), finally came to Spain after Franco's death and was housed in the Prado until 1993 when, amidst much controversy, it was moved to the Queen Sofía Center. In Portugal, limited state resources led to little being done to encourage the arts. The only systematic funding was provided by the Armenian petroleum millionaire and philanthropist, Calouste Gulbenkian (1869–1955), who came to live in Portugal after World War II and endowed his adopted country with a museum and art gallery, an orchestra, dance companies and choirs. Many of the Portuguese artists who exhibit today studied on Gulbenkian grants. The country's most influential contemporary artist, the abstract painter Maria Helena Vieira da Silva (b. 1908), has spent most of her life in France. In marked contrast to previous generations, women are now well represented among contemporary artists; Paula Rego (b. 1935) stands alongside the commanding figure of Vieira in the forefront of Portuguese painters.

While the lifting of political and moral censorship by the new democratic regimes had some impact on the visual arts in the peninsula, literature was transformed. In 1977, two years after Franco's death, the lyric poet Vicente Aleixandre – who was a member of

Far right Though best known as a painter, the Catalan artist Joan Miró (1893–1983), who studied in Barcelona, also worked as a sculptor, ceramicist and printmaker. In his mature work the picture plane is flattened, and use is made of schematized forms. Miró's particular concern was with the human emotional condition. He sought to represent "the things one cannot see" and, in his last years, used his art to search for "the sources of human feeling". This work, *Girl Escaping*, dates from 1968.

Right The music of the blind composer Joaquín Rodrigo (b. 1901) – pictured here with his wife at home in Madrid – has come to represent the traditional Spanish inheritance of classical music. Conservative in his technique, Rodrigo's best-known work is the haunting *Concierto de Aranjuez* (1939) – a concerto in three movements for orchestra and solo guitar. His numerous guitar compositions include *Fantasía para un gentilhombre*, written in 1954 for the renowned guitarist Andrés Segovia (1893–1987).

the "generation of 1927" and a contemporary of García Lorca – was awarded the Nobel Prize for Literature. Spanish culture, so long obscured by the shadows of the Franco regime, once again achieved international recognition. The artists and intellectuals who had opposed the dictatorships now returned to the peninsula. Though most were old and some came home simply to die, younger Communist Party activists such as Jorge Semprún (b.1923) and the Portuguese novelist José Saramago (b.1922) were also rehabilitated, becoming known as public figures rather than underground activists.

Those writers who had spent their creative lives under dictatorial regimes were finally given full and free expression. The Castilian novelist Miguel Delibes (b. 1920) had claimed that "by roundabout methods" he had always managed to say more or less what he wanted, but his naturalistic descriptions of rural Castile, which depicted hunger, backwardness and neglect, still attracted the censors' attention. The "social realist" work of novelists like Delibes had astonished post-war Spain. The greatest impact was made by Camilo José Cela's *The Family of Pascual Duarte* (1942), the brutal story of a peasant murderer from Extremadura set against the violence and poverty of fratricidal Spain. Cela (b. 1916) won the

Nobel Prize in 1989, like Aleixandre essentially for work done in his youth.

While social realists, working within an established tradition, might have been able to circumvent the censors' office, writers wanting to explore unconventional forms or explicitly sexual themes had little leeway. Juan Goytisolo (b. 1931) began his literary career in the 1950s as a social realist but moved on to explore language and text in novels concerned with the disintegration of human relationships. In a loose trilogy published between 1966 and 1975, Goytisolo launched an attack on the Spanish language as a means of destroying Spain's cultural past. The concluding passage of the work was written in Arabic. One of the first writers to deal openly with homosexuality, Goytisolo left Spain for Paris and then settled permanently in Morocco.

The transition to democracy finally allowed writers to address the questions of sexuality that had made late 20th-century writing so distinctive in other parts of the Western world. Between 1978 and 1980, the Catalan writer Esther Tusquets (b. 1936) published a trilogy that looked positively at the theme of female sexuality. Heterosexual, bisexual and lesbian relationships all featured in a lyrical depiction of affluent Catalan society in the 1960s and 1970s – a time when even oblique references to this kind of subject matter remained problematic.

Though, as everywhere, literary novels are a minority interest in Spain – and poetry even more so – publishing has expanded in the years since Franco's death. In 1976, less was read in Spain than anywhere else in western Europe, but the decline of illiteracy, the expansion of educational opportunity and the paperback boom of the late 1970s have helped to create a substantial novel-reading public. Some writers have tried to bridge the gap between literature and mass culture. The novelist and poet Manuel Vázquez Montalban (b. 1939) turned his hand to detective stories. The exploits of his cerebral, gastronomic investigator, Pepe Carvalho, have earned him millions of readers. In both Spain and Portugal, literature, whether highbrow, low-brow or middle-brow, is flourishing. The long years of censorship and repression have finally come to seem a mere parenthesis in the history of culture in the Iberian peninsula.

Above Eduardo Chillida (b. 1924) began his career as a sculptor by continuing the metalworking tradition of Gargallo (1881–1934) and González (1879–1942). His increasingly metaphysical approach led him toward environmental installations, of which *Wind Combs* (1975–77) is the most spectacular. These open metal structures interact with the elements on one of the wildest reaches of the Basque coast, literally combing the wind in Donostia Bay (San Sebastián).

PART THREE

THE GEOGRAPHICAL REGIONS

The Atlantic Coast
pp 212-219

The Ebro Valley
pp 206-211

The Center
pp 202-205

The Mediterranean
pp 194-201

The South
pp 186-193

STANDARD KEY TO REGIONAL MAPS

- ■ national capital
- ■ autonomous region capital
- ■ province or district capital
- ✈ international airport
- ⛴ ferry terminal
- ▬ ▬ ▬ international boundary
- ▬ ▬ ▬ autonomous region boundary
- ———— province or district boundary
- ———— expressway or major road
- ———— other main road
- ———— railroad
- └┴┴┴┘ canal
- ▲ mountain summit (height in meters)

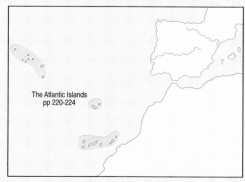

The Atlantic Islands
pp 220-224

place associated with

- 🧺 basketwork
- ⚱ ceramics or pottery
- 🧀 cheese
- ✚ embroidery or linen
- 🎸 guitars
- 💍 jewelry or filigree work
- lace
- 🧳 leather
- liqueur
- ⚒ metalwork
- rugs or carpets
- 🍇 wine

scale 1: 2 500 000

0   60 km
0   40 mi

Left Northern Spaniards often accuse Andalusians of never doing today what can be put off until *mañana* (tomorrow), just as foreigners see *mañana* as a national affliction. The customary *siesta* of the south is an effect of the summer heat rather than any regional proclivity for lethargy – in August, temperatures in Seville regularly pass 40°C. This man is taking his afternoon *siesta* under one of the ceramic historical scenes that decorate the city's Plaza de España.

Right Horse parades and events are held at the local *ferias* (fairs) of Andalusia, celebrated for its equestrian traditions. That of Jerez de la Frontera is one of the most famous, with riders demonstrating their prowess in racing, dressage and carriage competitions. Some customs have changed in recent years: the young women in the picture are wearing traditional male riding dress, albeit with ear-rings and hair ribbons. The pure-bred Carthusian horses that are on show at the fair can be seen at other times of the year in the town's School of Equestrian Arts.

resors
- ❄ ski
- ☂ summer
- ♨ spa

- 🏛 cathedral
- 🏰 church or monastery
- 🏯 castle
- 🏨 parador/pousada (hotel)
- 👑 royal palace
- ✝ Christian quarter
- ☰ Jewish quarter
- ☪ Moorish quarter
- ⚔ battlefield or memorial site
- 🏭 industrial center
- ⚓ major port

- built-up area
- arable
- citrus fruits
- olives
- other fruits
- vineyards
- grazing land
- forest
- nonagricultural land

Above The center of the sherry industry is at Jerez de la Frontera (from which the wine is named) though *bodegas* - sometimes called "sherry cathedrals" – are also found in Sanlucar de Barrameda and Puerto de Santa María. Here the wines are matured in barrels that are partly open to the air; the wine is protected by a natural layer of yeast or *flor*. As the wine ages, it is refreshed by the addition of younger wines. Tasting is a vital part of this process. The glass used is the traditional *copita*, which allows the wine to be "nosed" before passing the taster's lips.

(map labels) Guadalimar · Segura de la Sierra · Guadiana Menor · Cazorla · Velez Blanco · Guadix · Lacalahorra · ALMERIA · Albox · Vera · Garrucha · Cuevas del Almanzora · Mojácar · A NEVADA · Mulhacén 3482 · Tabernas · Sorbas · Solynieve · Alhama de Almería · Almería · Níjar · Carboneras · Berja · Roquetas de Mar · Almerimar · Cabo de Gata

THE SOUTH

Andalusia, southern Portugal and Extremadura

The most "typical" images of Spain and Portugal – though not necessarily the most representative – are almost invariably those of the south: the white-walled towns, sun-soaked beaches, flamenco, dramatic and somber Holy Week processions, Moorish mosques and castles. And if the south is commonly identified with Spain, then Andalusia is synonymous with the south. At 87,620 square kilometers – almost the same size as Portugal – Andalusia, which comprises eight provinces, is the largest of Spain's *autonomías* (autonomous communities); it is also its most populous, with 6.5 million inhabitants. Seville, the capital, is a thriving modern metropolis, a center of high-tech industries and the site of Expo92, for which many innovative buildings were designed.

Geographically, Andalusia is extremely varied. Extending from the Mediterranean to the Atlantic coast, it is bisected by the long east–west valley of the Guadalquivir, bordered on the north by the mountains of the Sierra Morena and on the south by the Sierra Nevada. In the arid east, the semidesert vegetation of Almería includes plants that are typical of North Africa, while in the west the Guadalquivir drains through marshes and wetlands, a haven for wildlife, into the Gulf of Cádiz.

Mineral wealth– silver, lead and tin – made the region an early center of metalworking: in the 1st millennium BC the indigenous Tartessian culture had its center in the Guadalquivir and Guadiana valleys. Subsequently, Phoenicians, Carthaginians and Romans settled in turn in the region. In 711, when the peninsula fell to the Arabs, they made Córdoba their intellectual and political center. From 1212 to 1492, Granada, in the mountains of the Sierra Nevada, was the sole surviving Muslim kingdom in Spain. Muslim civilization was urban-based, and to this day the people of Andalusia and the rest of the south live in comparatively large, far-flung settlements rather than the tiny hamlets and isolated farmsteads of the northern peninsula. Even the smallest village is regarded as a municipality and has its own mayor.

The legacy of the Islamic past is present not only in the splendid palaces and mosques of Córdoba, Granada and Seville but also in the whitewashed houses of many of its smaller medieval towns such as Ronda and Jerez de la Frontera, the center of the sherry industry. The Arab skill with water can be seen in colorful pleasure gardens like those of the Generalife, the summer palace close to the Alhambra in Granada – in common with all classical Islamic gardens, they are laid out according to the description of paradise in the Qu'ran, with running water and shady avenues. The tiled courtyards and fountains of many private houses are also an Arab legacy, as are the wrought-iron window grilles through which courting couples were expected to converse – a custom older people still remember. Arab sweetmeats of egg and almond are still common throughout the south. Gypsy culture has also been a major influence in southern Spain. The flamenco style of dance and singing –

regarded as typically Andalusian – is largely of gypsy origin (though there are also Caribbean and African influences), and traditional gypsy festivals such as the annual pilgrimage to the shrine of Our Lady of the Dew at El Rocio, near Huelva, are still observed.

In the past, Andalusia was known as "a rich land inhabited by poor men"; the naturally fertile soil was held in check by the dry climate and by the repressive *latifundia* landholding system of large estates with absentee landlords. However, improved irrigation and agricultural techniques, together with the development of silicon chip industries, is today giving it the name of "the California of Spain". In Almería, exotic crops such as kiwi fruit and bananas are extensively cultivated under plastic, though its arid soils are prone to wind erosion, which causes desertification. Increased irrigation, rapid urbanization and tourist development are placing growing pressure on scant water reserves, putting the region's wildlife at risk. The protected marshes of the Coto Doñana in the Guadalquivir delta are one of the most important wetland reserves in Europe and a haven for birds migrating between Europe and Africa. Around 80,000 greylag geese visit them every year, and they are home to several endangered species – among them the imperial eagle and the marbled teal – as well as to lynxes, deer and a rare European member of the mongoose family, the ichneumon. Yet Doñana's survival was threatened in the early 1990s by a proposed tourist development that would extract water from underground reserves.

Across the Guadiana river, the southernmost Portuguese district of Faro (the old province of Algarve) faces similar pressures from the tourist boom of the 1970s and 1980s, which caused unregulated development along the coast. Particularly threatened is the unique area of saltflats, marshes and lagoons around Faro, containing the Ría Formosa nature park, which is rich in birdlife. The lagoons are a valuable breeding ground for clams and oysters, producing 90 percent of Portugal's annual harvest. Like Andalusia, this part of Portugal retains many signs of its occupation by Romans and Arabs. It was these last who extended the system of irrigation canals – first introduced by the Romans – that transformed its landscape of gently rolling hills into the "garden of Portugal": the great Arab cistern at Silves is architecturally similar to the 13th-century water-tanks in the Middle East. Many varieties of fruit and vegetables are cultivated, including almonds, figs, carobs, melons, pomegranates, olives and tomatoes, many of which were introduced by the Arabs. Most are intended for domestic consumption, though citrus fruits are being increasingly grown for export. In the towns and villages, the flat-roofed, whitewashed houses, outlined with Tunisian blue, closely resemble those of North Africa.

Farther north are the plains of the Alentejo (the districts of Beja, Evora and Portalegre, with Setúbal in the west). The poet Fernando Pessoa summed up the Alentejo as "nothing with nothing around it and a few trees in between", a somewhat stark description of the *dehesa* landscape of scattered holm and cork oak trees that is characteristic of the Alentejo and of Spanish Extremadura, into which it merges imperceptibly. Alentejo produces over half the world's supply of cork – about 130,000 tonnes a year – followed by Extremadura. The cork is stripped from the trees by hand, as it has been centuries: this takes place every 9 years or so, and the trees can survive for up to 500

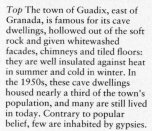

Top The town of Guadix, east of Granada, is famous for its cave dwellings, hollowed out of the soft rock and given whitewashed facades, chimneys and tiled floors: they are well insulated against heat in summer and cold in winter. In the 1950s, these cave dwellings housed nearly a third of the town's population, and many are still lived in today. Contrary to popular belief, few are inhabited by gypsies.

Above According to local legend, nothing is more cruel than to be blind in Granada. The city's exquisite Arab palaces and pleasure gardens are exemplified by the Generalife or "garden of the architect", which dates from the 14th century and once adorned the summer palace of the Nasrid rulers of this mountain kingdom.

Left Much 20th-century
architecture in Spain has sought to
recapture the past. The bridges,
canals and pavilions of Seville's
semicircular Plaza de España, built
for the 1929 Spanish-American
Exhibition, are reminiscent of
Spain's 18th-century Bourbon
palaces but have been decorated
with Moorish-style ceramic tiles in
an exuberant combination of
artistic traditions.

Below Other attempts to echo past
architectural styles have been less
happy. This opulent marina on the
Costa del Sol, for example, is a
cacophony of Moorish
architectural references while the
fluid lines of the roof turrets are
reminiscent of Gaudí's Barcelona.

Above The white hill towns
(*pueblos blancos*) of Andalusia,
with their flat roofs and dazzling
white walls, are reminiscent of
North Africa. Typical is Olvera,
near Ronda. Its narrow streets lead
up to the church, once the site of a
mosque, and to a fine Moorish
castle. Most of the white towns are
fortified and command majestic
views of the surrounding
countryside. Here, the land is given
over to wheat and olives, staple
crops of the southern uplands.

years. Portugal's traditional managed woodlands are threatened by plantations of quick-growing eucalyptus, which are a profitable source of pulp for papermaking. They are much disliked by ecologists since the trees take up heavy amounts of water through their roots and starve the soil of nutrients, thus reducing the opportunities for wildlife.

The capital of the Roman province of Lusitania was at Mérida (Augusta Emerita) in Extremadura. Today Extremadura remains the poorest region of Spain, as it has been for most of its history. About a third of the *conquistadores* came from here; most were the younger or illegitimate sons of noblemen, seeking to win their fortunes in the New World with their swords. Returning home, they built convents and palaces to celebrate their new-found wealth, but the region's brief moment of glory passed, and it faded once more into obscurity. As in the Alentejo, forestry is the region's economic mainstay, and fine cured hams and sausages are produced from pigs left to graze under the trees.

Extremadura means simply "beyond the Douro". The old province of Portugal that shares its name (Estremadura) has little else in common with it. This coastal area of productive farmland north of Lisbon (the districts of Lisboa and Leiria) has long grown food for the capital. When Portugal joined the EC in 1986, agricultural investment rose by 700 percent, most of it being directed toward the farms here and in neighboring Ribatejo (Santarém). There are many monuments connected with Portugal's past. Sintra, 24 kilometers northwest of Lisbon, was a favorite royal summer residence. Its ruined Moorish castle, palaces and monasteries make it one of Portugal's most visited sites. Tomar, the center of an olive, wine and fruit-growing area in the northeast corner of Santarém, contains the palace of Prince Henry the Navigator, rebuilt in Manueline style in the 16th century.

Lisbon itself, built on seven hills, developed around a superb natural harbor on the river Tagus. It owed its rise as one of the great Renaissance cities of Europe to the wealth that flooded into it into from Asia and the New World in the 16th and 17th centuries. A few churches and tall townhouses have survived from this period; the Baixa, on the waterfront, contains the grid of well-planned streets and the royal palace built by Pombal after earthquake had destroyed most of the city in 1755. Today the capital's rich cultural heritage is legally protected, and its buildings are being cleaned and renovated. New fire regulations have been introduced since fire swept disastrously through the historic Chiado quarter in the center of the old city in 1988, destroying its unique character.

Top right The white stork is one of the Iberian peninsula's most familiar summer sights. According to a Spanish proverb, the birds always return by St Blaise's day (3 February). After over-wintering in Africa, they come back to nest, always choosing high, conspicuous sites such as bell towers. The storks generally live close to human habitation. In recent years, as modern agriculture destroys old feeding grounds, they have taken to scavenging from municipal rubbish tips.

Right Many Portuguese fishing communities still preserve old customs. At Nazaré, north of Lisbon, sardines are being dried in the old way on racks on the beach. Traditional dress is becoming less common, but some women wear seven colored petticoats under a wide black skirt and, as in the picture, a black shawl over the head. Many men still choose tartan shirts but few now wear the old black stocking bonnets.

Above and right Holm and cork oaks flourish on the plains of Spanish Extremadura and the Portuguese Alentejo. In Extremadura, fighting bulls are pastured in their shade while in the Alentejo, the bark from cork oaks is harvested as it has been for centuries; it has to be stripped from the trees by hand as no machine can do so without damaging the tree.

Left Golf courses are a staple attraction of many tourist resorts. They do, however, have an environmental cost: this course, at Vale do Lobo on the Algarve, uses two million gallons of water a day to keep the greens green.

Overleaf The pilgrimage to the shrine at Moguer is popular with Andalusia's gypsies who use the occasion to demonstrate their horsemanship as well as religious devotion and community feeling. The women's flounced dresses are a reminder that flamenco's origins are largely rooted in gypsy culture.

THE MEDITERRANEAN

Catalonia, Valencia, Murcia and the Balearic Islands

Catalonia extends from the Pyrenees in the northeastern corner of the peninsula to nearly halfway along the eastern coast. It was once the heart of the powerful maritime trading empire formed by the 12th-century dynastic alliance between the count of Barcelona and the royal house of Aragon, and which looked outward to Italy, rather than inland to the rest of Spain. Both Valencia and the Balearic Islands came within its orbit of influence, and dialect forms of the distinct Catalan language are still spoken there. Catalans claim to have a European rather than a Spanish mentality, combining sound business acumen with a willingness to embrace progress: other Spaniards say that Catalans are hardworking but mean.

A strong nationalist movement was born in the 19th century, and in 1932 Catalonia was granted autonomy by the Second Republic. This, however, was rescinded by Franco, who banned the public use of the Catalan language, together with the Catalan flag and even the *sardana*, the traditional dance of the Catalans. With the Basque Country and Galicia, Catalonia was the first of the Spanish regions to be granted autonomous status in 1980. Catalan is now, with Castilian, the official language, and is understood by 97 percent of native Catalans.

Catalonia is the wealthiest region of the Iberian peninsula. Commerce and industry are centered on the historic port of Barcelona. A thriving medieval town, it declined in importance with the opening up of Atlantic trade in the 16th century, but boomed again in the 19th century with the development of the cotton industry. Immigrants came from all over Spain seeking work, the industrial sector rapidly expanded, and Barcelona became a leading center for the arts. It is now among the largest of the Mediterranean ports, and its industrial hinterland is a major area of chemicals and fertilizer production.

Outside the vicinity of Barcelona, irrigated agriculture is the principal industry, except for tourism. The coastal plains all along the Mediterranean seaboard provide some of the most fertile land on the peninsula. First irrigated by the Romans, the Valencian *huerta* (cultivated plain) is today one of the most developed agricultural areas in Europe, producing as many as four crops a year. The intensive cultivation of fruit and vegetables supplies a major export industry: until the

Above Since the 1960s, tourism has been the economic mainstay of the Mediterranean coast. Benidorm – once a small fishing village – is now synonymous with package holidays. Every year, visitors from sun-starved northern Europe flock to its highrise hotels and apartment blocks, passing the time in scores of English-style pubs and discotheques. The main attraction is the beach, which stretches for nearly 6 kilometers and has been refreshed with vast quantities of imported Moroccan sand.

Far right Not only tourists enjoy the pleasures of sea and sand. The municipal beach at Barceloneta is as much an amenity for the inhabitants of Barcelona as are the city's parks and gardens. Here, local people swim and sunbathe in the shadow of the industrial zone which, though ugly, has brought much prosperity to the city. Pollution is a constant worry, but does not deter most *barceloneses* from spending a day at the beach.

Left The Pyrenean villages of northern Catalonia preserve a unique cultural and linguistic inheritance. The area is Catalan-speaking on both sides of the Spanish/French border. Herding is the traditional way of life, though tourism, particularly in the skiing season, is increasingly important. Other visitors are attracted by the Romanesque churches that are preserved in many of these small Pyrenean settlements.

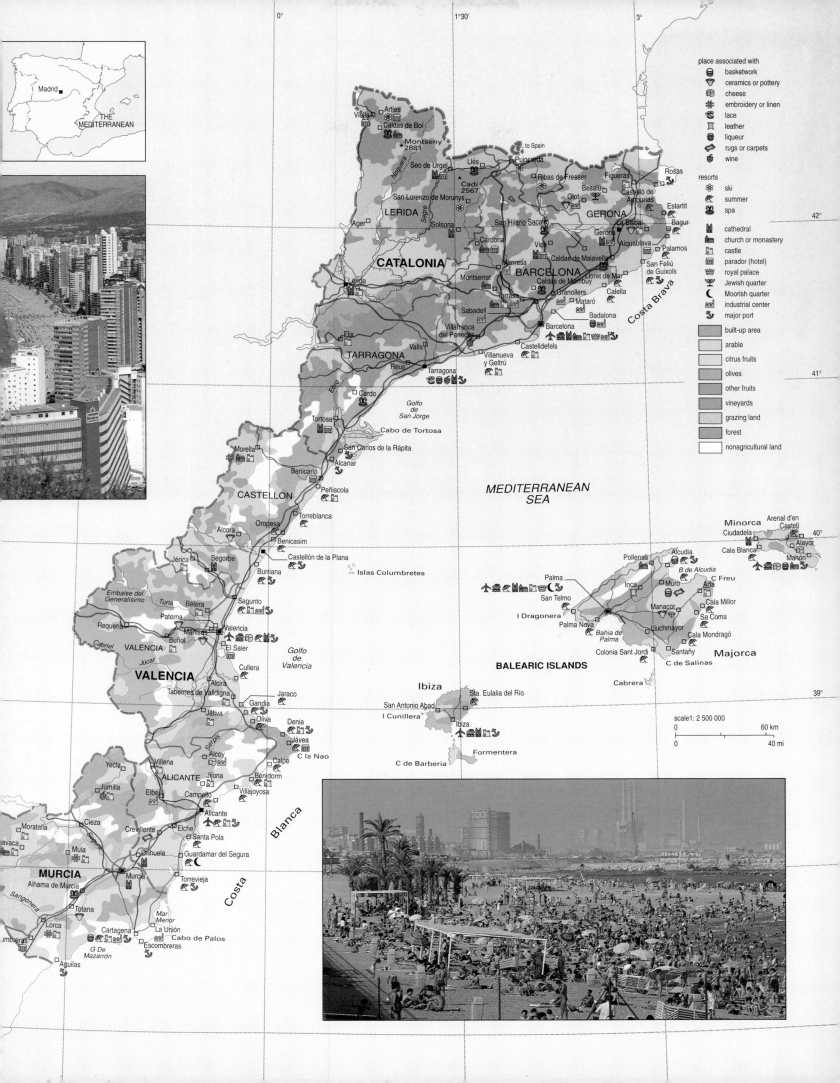

tourist boom of the 1960s, the orange – cultivated since Arab times – was Spain's main foreign currency earner. During times of unrest, armed guards were routinely posted in the citrus groves of Valencia to protect the valuable crop.

Mulberry trees serve as reminders of Valencia's once thriving silk industry, renowned throughout Europe in the 18th century. Cotton is also grown, though the raw material for the Catalan textile industry was imported from the Americas. Rice was introduced by the Arabs, who improved the Romans' ancient irrigation system, expanding and renovating its complex network of channels and conduits. The daily running of these waterways is still governed by the *Tribunal de las Aguas*, a committee of eight men – one for each of the original Roman canals – that meets outside Valencia cathedral every Thursday. It has been in continuous existence for 1,000 years; business is always conducted in Catalan.

Murcia to the south, hotter and drier, is also an area of irrigated *huerta*, with melons, tomatoes and peppers being widely grown for export, as well as lemons and limes and more exotic plants such as aloes and jojoba. The naval base at Cartagena and the surrounding mining district provide some industrial employment. Castilian is spoken in Murcia, and it forms a cultural bridge between the Mediterranean seaboard and Andalusia.

Coastal developments such as the sporting complex that has grown up around the Mar Menor are bringing more visitors to the area, but tourism is not as developed as it is in the Catalan-speaking regions to

Above Valencia is one of Spain's richest agricultural regions, and the center of the citrus industry. The sweet oranges grown here are still an important foreign currency earner, as are other citrus fruits such as tangerines and clementines. The large navel oranges seen here are, like the others, harvested in December. Most are then exported to meet the Christmas demand.

Left The great Benedictine abbey of Montserrat – founded in 976 – takes its name from the extraordinary serrated mountainscape that surrounds it. The Black Virgin venerated here was supposedly carved from life by St Luke and hidden in a cave by St Peter; the fame of her shrine made Montserrat the most important pilgrimage site in Spain after Santiago de Compostela. As a result, the abbey accumulated much wealth and enjoyed considerable autonomy. In 1811, however, it was sacked by Napoleon's troops. Under the Franco dictatorship it became a focus for Catalan nationalism.

Right While much of the scrubby vegetation in Murcia's Sierra de la Muela bears testimony to the thin soil and harsh climate, the olive trees that carpet the lowlands represent a considerable agricultural resource. The olive grows best in poor chalky soil. As it cannot survive winter frost, it is confined to the south of the peninsula. In Spain, olive groves cover over 1,000,000 hectares. Around 92 percent of the crop goes to make olive oil, with Andalusia alone producing some 20 percent of the world's olive oil.

Paella

Paella – by far the most famous of all Spanish dishes – is a regional rather than a national speciality. The original *paella* is supposed to have come from Lake Abufera, a freshwater lagoon outside Valencia, and to have been made with eels, snails and green beans. Today's classic *paella valenciana* is made with chicken or rabbit rather than seafood and always includes both green and butter (lima) beans. Like the original dish, it is a far cry from the medleys of chicken, seafood, sausage and lurid yellow rice all too often served to tourists.

Gastronomic purists claims that the Valencian version is the only true *paella*. The popular *paella marinera* is more accurately described as a seafood rice; its origins lie in the fishing communities of the Mediterranean coast, while those of *paella valenciana* are to be found among the market gardeners farther inland. Both are dry dishes, cooked uncovered in a large, flat, two-handled pan, known as a *paella* in the east and as a *paellera* elsewhere in Spain, that gives the dish its name. Short-grain rice grown in the paddy-fields of Valencia (first introduced there by the Arabs in the 8th century) is the essential ingredient for *paella*. Saffron from La Mancha adds both flavor and color to the classic Valencian dish. Other ingredients vary but they commonly include dried sweet peppers from

Murcia, olive oil from Andalusia, and fresh vegetables. Lemon juice from the local citrus groves is the traditional condiment.

Many other specialist dishes are made in the same way as *paella*. In Alicante, rice and seafood are served separately in a dish known as *arroz abanda* or "rice apart". *Arroz negro* ("black rice") takes both its name and its color from the ink sacs of the squid that are its principal ingredient. The southern province of Murcia specializes in vegetable *paellas*, while perhaps the most unusual of all is *fideuá* – a noodle dish cooked in exactly the same was as *paella*.

the north, especially in the densely urbanized corridors of Catalonia's Costa Brava and Valencia's Costa Blanca. Valencia in 1993 provided 78,415 hotel beds for holiday-makers, and Catalonia 198,264, but both were far outstripped by the 260,119 beds of the Balearic Islands – by far the largest figure for any of the autonomous regions. The beaches and dramatic mountain scenery of Majorca, the largest of the Balearics, make it one of Europe's most popular holiday destinations. Resorts such as crowded Magalluf on the south coast form a continuous strip of high-rise concrete hotels, discos and restaurants.

With its beaches in danger of being overwhelmed by mass development, Spain's tourist industry now promotes expensive holidays with a cultural or historical theme. Many visitors to Majorca come on architectural or artistic pilgrimages in the footsteps of writers and artists such as the composer Frederick Chopin, who visited the island in 1838 with his mistress, the French novelist George Sand: he wrote that life there was "delicious"; she hated it. In this century, the English poet Robert Graves (1895–1985) made his home on Majorca, heading a small artists' colony in Deiá. Today a similar community lives and works in the town of Pollença.

Minorca is the quietest of the Balearic Islands; the Georgian houses of its capital, Port Mahon, are a legacy of a period of occupation by the British in the 18th century. It boasts a unique wealth of prehistoric ruins that attract many archaeologists, both amateur and professional. Birdwatching on the Balearics is also extremely popular. By contrast, Ibiza is one of the liveliest youth resorts in Europe.

Unregulated tourist development has destroyed many areas of wildlife and natural beauty along the Mediterranean seaboard. But tourism does help to conserve some aspects of the region's traditional culture. Ceramics – particularly ornamental tiles, which substituted for tapestries as wall-coverings in the hot climate – have been been produced in Valencia since the 13th century. Unable to compete against cheaper imports, demand had fallen dangerously low, but now – thanks to the tourist market – it has risen again, and production has revived at the town of Manises, where some of the oldest potteries in Spain are found.

The elaborate festivals found all along the Mediterranean coast also attract visitors. Though less well-known than those of Andalusia, the Holy Week processions of Cartagena and Murcia are just as dramatic. People come from all over Spain for the extraordinary *fallas*, or fire festival, held on St Joseph's Day (19 March) in the town of Valencia. For much of the year rival teams prepare enormous papier-mâché figures that lampoon politicians and other personalities, local and national. For a week, the city is *en fiesta* and the figures are put on display amid much celebration. Then, on the final night, they are ceremonially put to the torch, creating such an extraordinary glow that Valencia itself seems to be alight.

Tales of the Reconquest are deeply rooted in local folklore: dances depicting the struggles of Moors and Christians are common, and there is even a regional dish that consists of a "Christian" ring of molded white rice filled with "Moorish" black beans. Various towns around Valencia and Alicante stage mock battles between "Moors and Christians". Those in Alcoy are held on St George's Day (23 April): after various processions and mock battles for possession of the castle, the saint himself intervenes to win the day for the Christians, just as he is said to have done in legend.

Above The island of Majorca is a favorite destination for the yachting fraternity. This marina development is at Port d'Andraitx, a small resort whose sheltered cove is fringed with hotel developments. The island's popularity has been enhanced by the Spanish royal family who visit it each summer. King Juan Carlos, Queen Sofia and the Prince of Asturias have all competed in Olympic yachting events.

Right The small town of Totana in Murcia is one of many Spanish communities to preserve a distinctive craft tradition. Totana pots, here being displayed for sale, have characteristic brown and cream coloring. Among the most unusual designs produced here are small covered jars with jagged edges; the cover and base fit together along these "teeth".

Previous page The castle at Peniscola, on the Castellón coast of Valencia, was originally built by the Knights Templar, but the promontory was made virtually impregnable by Pedro de la Luna (c.1328–1423), an Aragonese nobleman who in 1394 was elected pope in Avignon, in rivalry to the pope in Rome. Ruling as Benedict XIII, he rejected all attempts to reach an agreement to end the Great Schism dividing the church, and was eventually deposed by the Council of Constance in 1417. Two years earlier he had taken refuge in this beautiful citadel, declaring it to be the true Church and the ark of Noah. He died there, still defiant, at the age of 95 and is remembered in the town as "Papa Luna".

Left Much agricultural land in Spain and Portugal is characterized by steep gradients and mountain slopes, and must be terraced before it can be worked. The soil is plowed in narrow strips, behind low walls that prevent it being washed away down the hillsides after rain. These terraced slopes around Banyalbufar on the island of Majorca formerly grew the grapes used to make the island's famous sweet Malvoisie wine, until the vines were devastated by phylloxera in 1907.

Top Terracing is a highly traditional form of farming; where possible, Majorcan farmers make use of modern methods and equipment such as tractors and chemical fertilizers. However, many landholdings are characterized by their small size.

Above Though Ibiza is commonly thought of as a tourist paradise, much traditional vernacular architecture remains. The flat roofs, white-washed walls and wrought-iron balconies of the houses that line this narrow street are all characteristic of villages in the Balearic Islands. In rural communities – where the customary period of mourning for a husband may be as many as 10 years – older women often dress entirely in black; the habit of wearing strict mourning, however, is generally dying out.

THE CENTER
Castile and León, Castile La Mancha and Madrid

The vast tablelands of Castile, dotted with windmills and magnificent, decaying castles, form the heartland of the kingdom of Spain. As a local proverb puts it, "*ancha es Castilla*", "broad is Castile". Standing at an average height of over 600 meters, the great central plateau of the *meseta* spans the modern autonomous regions of Castile and León and Castile La Mancha, in the north and south respectively. Separating the two are a series of mountain ranges. In these harsh uplands, the sheep-herding traditions on which Castile's early prosperity was based are still maintained. Yet, all over Castile, rural communities are declining as people move to the cities. The ancient practice of transhumance – driving the flocks to summer pastures – once essential to the animals' survival in this stony mountain landscape, is today found only in a few isolated areas where it lingers as an archaic survival of a past way of life.

Castile derives its name from the Spanish word for castle, and most of Spain's 10,000 surviving castles are to be found here, for this was a much fought-over frontier region in the wars that marked the gradual southward expansion of the Christian kingdoms against the Arabs. Impressive fortifications – some of them renovated, others left to decay – tower over the flat landscape. The medieval walls of Avila are perhaps the most remarkable testimony of all to Castile's embattled past.

Northern Castile and the kingdom of León were re-Christianized early in the Reconquest, and the region today is one of tiny villages and small ecclesiastical cities. Burgos, with its magnificent twin-spired Gothic cathedral, is the burial place of El Cid, the legendary hero of the Reconquest. One of the world's finest surviving Roman aqueducts is to be found in the fortified town of Segovia. Farther west the magnificent Renaissance buildings of Salamanca's university and cathedral have won for the city the status of "national monument".

These beautiful cities stand marooned amid great swathes of agricultural land. Unbroken expanses of Castile and León are given over to the cultivation of wheat, using modern chemical fertilizers and mechanical harvesters. Waving cornfields beneath huge skies – one of the Iberian peninsula's most distinctive landscapes – have largely replaced the aromatic native scrubland of wild thyme and holm oaks. The losers are the rare birds and mammals of the *dehesa* and steppe grasslands – particularly the populations of black storks and bustards that are almost unique in Europe, and are now threatened by loss of habitat.

In the southern plains of La Mancha – immortalized in Cervantes' epic novel *Don Quixote* – settlements are larger and the land less fertile, though vineyards now cover an ever increasing area. La Mancha's most famous crop is saffron, gathered from the stamens of crocuses, fields of which carpet the landscape in fall. It was introduced by the Arabs to color and flavor the rice dishes for which Spain is now famous. Castile La Mancha preserves other signs of its centuries-long

Left Segovia's story-book Alcazar seems the perfect setting for tales of fairy princesses. The original citadel dated from the 14th century but was ravaged by fire in 1862. The restoration work faithfully reconstructed some Mudéjar features but contemporary taste dictated the addition of turrets and battlements. The result is a highly romanticized pastiche.

Right Cuenca's famous *casas colgadas* ("hanging houses") cling to the cliffs of the deep river gorges that cross the city. The cantilevered balconies hang in mid-air, offering views down to the river Huecar 180 meters below. One of these remarkable buildings houses Spain's Museum of Abstract Art and is as much part of the exhibit as the works it contains.

place associated with

- basketwork
- ceramics or pottery
- cheese
- jewelry or filigree work
- leather
- liqueur
- metalwork
- wine

resorts

- ski
- spa

- cathedral
- church or monastery
- castle
- parador (hotel)
- royal palace
- Christian quarter
- Jewish quarter
- Moorish quarter
- battlefield or memorial site
- industrial center

- built-up area
- arable
- olives
- vineyards
- grazing land
- forest
- nonagricultural land

scale 1: 2 500 000

0   60 km

0   40 mi

experience of Arab occupation. Metalworkers in the cathedral city of Toledo still practice the black-and-gold inlay work known as damascene – a name, derived from the Syrian city of Damascus, that is redolent of Arab culture.

At the heart of Castile, and of Spain itself, lies the national capital, Madrid. This has been the administrative center of Spain since Philip II settled his court there in 1560, the year before work began on his austere palace-monastery of the Escorial in the mountains a little way outside the city. It was the Bourbon kings who developed Madrid as a center for science and the arts in the 18th century, establishing a Royal Botanic Garden and a number of Royal Academies. The Italianate Royal Palace, which was completed in 1764, served as the primary royal residence until Alfonso XIII fled Spain in 1931.

The Bourbons' extravagant passion for building brought the Spanish crown to the verge of bankruptcy. Subsequently, the Napoleonic wars devastated the landscapes of Castile so that it became a backwater just at the time that Catalonia and the Basque Country were developing into prosperous industrial and commercial regions. Though Madrid's position as the national capital went unchallenged, its poor communication links with the rest of the country – it is the only European capital not situated on a major waterway – ensured that its economy did not begin to take

off until the middle years of the present century.

With a population of over 3.1 million in 1991, Madrid is now Spain's largest urban center. Commerce, retailing and finance have all expanded dramatically since the 1960s when multinational corporations flocked to Madrid, attracted by high growth rates and favorable conditions for foreign investment. This economic boom led to rapid urban growth and, for the first time, manufacturing industries were located within the city. Urban development continued apace. The extensive damage suffered during the Civil War was rebuilt, but the virtual absence of planning regulations meant that much was lost, particularly in the old city.

During the affluent 1980s, when the Spanish economy seemed to be the economic success story of Europe, property values in the capital rose astronomically: at one point, real estate in Madrid was the third most expensive in the world, only exceeded in value by property in Tokyo and Manhattan. Urban congestion is such that the affluent are now breaking the habit of generations and moving outside the city to form Spain's first commuter belt. Immigrants flock to the capital: most Madrid families have grandparents in other parts of Spain. Yet, as the population of Madrid grows, that of Castile continues to fall. The bustling prosperity of the capital stands in stark contrast to the empty plains that surround it.

Left The seemingly endless expanse of Castile La Mancha is broken by white windmills like those made famous by Cervantes' Don Quixote. Though Don Quixote is the most celebrated character in Spanish literature, and the windmills at which he tilted have passed into proverb, not many visitors come to these monotonous plains. The region is predominantly agricultural and there are few cities.

Top right Each June, the feast of Corpus Christi is celebrated with elaborate processions. The Toledo celebrations are one of Catholic Spain's most spectacular festivals. Children making their first communion lead the procession through narrow streets strewn with flowering thyme, known in Castile as "Corpus flowers".

Bottom right The sight of women sewing, embroidering or, as here, making lace outside their front doors is still common in rural villages such as Miranda del Castañar, in the mountains between Salamanca and Cáceres. However, the survival of these crafts is threatened as more and more people move to the cities and few younger women are left to continue the skills of centuries.

Below Madrid is a world-class cultural center. The Prado museum, in a neoclassical building commissioned by Carlos III, houses one of the world's finest art collections. Italian, Flemish and, above all, Spanish painting are particularly well represented and important conservation work is carried out in the laboratories and workrooms. Here, restorers are working on (to the left) a fine medieval *retablo*, or altarpiece, and (to the right) *The Dream of Jacob*, a work by Jusepe de Ribera, known as "Lo Spagnoletto" (1588–1656).

THE EBRO VALLEY
Madrid

43°
1°30'
3°
0°

Roncesvalles
Alsasua
Pamplona
NAVARRE
Estella
Javier
Canfranc
Sallent
Baños de Panticosa
Aneto Peak 3404
Monte Perdido 3353
Bielsa
Benasque
Jaca
Turbón 2492
Haro
Fuenmayor
Tafalla
Sangüesa
Sabiñánigo
Santo Domingo de la Calzada
Cenicero
Olite
Sos del Rey Católico
Loarre
HUESCA
Nájera
Logroño
Carcastillo
Aragón
LA RIOJA
Calahorra
Caparroso
Sádaba
Gállego
Arnedillo
Flumen
Huesca
Grávalos
Fitero
Tudela
Ejea de los Caballeros
Barbastro
Monzón
Tarazona
Cinca
Sariñena
ARAGON
Jalón
Zaragoza
Fraga
La Almunia de Doña Godina
ZARAGOZA
Mequinenza
Calatayud
Cariñena
Belchite
Ebro
Santa María de la Huerta
Caspe
Nuévalos
Alcañiz
Martín
Guadalope
Alcorisa
Jiloca
Montalbán
Monreal del Campo
Aliaga
Bronchales
Alfambra
Peñarroya 2019
Valdelinares
Albarracín
TERUEL
Teruel
Mijares
Mora de Rubielos

🍇 place associated with wine

resorts
❅ ski
♨ spa

🏛 cathedral
⛪ church or monastery
🏰 castle
🏨 parador (hotel)
👑 royal palace
🕎 Jewish quarter
☾ Moorish quarter
battlefield or memorial site
industrial center

arable
olives
vineyards
grazing land
forest
nonagricultural land

scale 1: 2 500 000
0   60 km
0   40 mi

THE EBRO VALLEY

Navarre, La Rioja and Aragon

Left Waterfalls are one of the most spectacular features of Aragon's mountain landscape. This particular cascade – known as *caprichosa* "capricious" – is in the Monasterio de Piedra natural park, south of Zaragoza.

Below left Despite divergent political traditions, the legacy of a common past with their Basque neighbors manifests itself in the language, culture and folklore of Navarre. Many Basque customs are preserved among its mountain communities. One of the most famous folk festivals is the *zampantzar*, a competitive Basque carnival held between the neighboring villages of Zubieta and Ituren.

Below Sos del Rey Católico is the most picturesque of the "Cinco Villas" ("five towns") of Aragon, found along the border with Navarre. All were given municipal status by Philip V for their loyalty during the War of the Succession (1701–13), though today none has more than 2,000 inhabitants. Sos del Rey Católico derives its name from the Catholic King, Ferdinand, who was born here in 1452. The town's past is reflected in the imposing mansions that grace its cobbled streets, overlooked by towering rock pinnacles.

Overleaf The climax of Pamplona's bullrunning *fiesta* is the *encierro* ("corraling") that takes place in the city's bullring. Young men and fighting bulls arrive together, having chased each other through the streets. These days the *fiesta* is a major tourist attraction, and nearly everyone, whether a local or not, wears the traditional red beret of Carlist Navarre.

The river Ebro – the second longest river on the peninsula, after the Tagus – rises in the Cantabrian mountains and flows southeast for 910 kilometers to its delta on the Mediterranean at Tortosa in Catalonia. Along its course, it forms the border between the *autonomías* of Navarre and La Rioja, and then flows through Aragon, once, with Catalonia, a powerful independent kingdom, and now Spain's least densely populated region.

The distinctive cultural and political traditions of Navarre have to some extent been shaped by its topography. The north is dominated by the mountains and valleys of the Pyrenees; here, herding communities were Basque-speaking until well into the 20th century, and they remain culturally Basque to this day. Farther south and east, smallholders along the fertile valleys of the Ebro and its tributaries traditionally had greater contact with the Castilian-speaking areas of Aragon and La Rioja.

Despite their close links with the neighboring Basques, the Navarrese have never shared their separatist ambitions, preferring their own version of local autonomy within the Spanish state. From 1512, when Ferdinand V acquired the kingdom of Navarre, until 1841, when it was reduced to provincial status, its towns and cities were guaranteed a degree of autonomy by the Spanish crown. In response to the centralization of government in the 19th century, however, Navarre became the heartland of Carlism – the movement formed in the 1830s in support of the Pretender Don Carlos' claim to the throne. This "Tradition", as it was known by its supporters, came to embody Navarrese aspirations to autonomy, together with a fervent Catholicism and a violent and anachronistic monarchism. Dressed in the red berets and sashes of the Navarrese peasantry, and with the Sacred Heart of Jesus emblazoned on their breasts, the Carlist militias, or *Requetés*, battled repeatedly against the forces of secular liberalism. During the Civil War of 1936–39 the *Requetés* provided Franco with some of his most zealous fighters. In return, he restored a number of the region's ancient privileges – a prerogative that was sternly denied to the Basques whose Republicanism was punished by the determined repression of their culture and language.

As Navarre forged its own local identity in the constitutional struggles of the 19th and 20th centuries, so its traditions and festivities came to seem distinctly Navarrese. For example, – though bullrunning festivals are found all over the northwest of the peninsula – they have become synonymous with the *fiesta* of San Fermín (St Ferminius), the patron saint of Pamplona, Navarre's capital. Every morning, from 6–14 July, fighting bulls are released into the medieval streets of the old city; hordes of agile young men, all wearing the red Carlist beret, run before them to the bullring in an ancient test of speed, courage and stamina. Ever since the American novelist Ernest Hemingway immortalized the bullrunning in his book *The Sun Also Rises* (1926), thousands of adventure-seeking tourists have

traveled to the *fiesta*, undeterred by the few fatal gorings that occur almost every year.

Pamplona today is a thriving industrial city, though many of its institutions remain conservative; the university of Navarre, for instance, is run by the Opus Dei, a Roman Catholic organization, founded in 1928, that emerged as a political force in Spain after the Civil War to provide leadership in lay society. Navarre has a prosperous modern economy: agriculture has been mechanized, and "agribusiness" is now more prevalent in the region than smallholding. Vegetables, wheat, maize and grapes are all widely grown in the Ebro valley.

La Rioja, south of the Ebro, was once part of Old Castile but now forms Spain's smallest autonomous region. Upper Rioja, west of the capital Logroño, is comparatively wet and mild, while Lower Rioja, to the east, has more in common with the barren plains of Aragon. Viticulture has long been the region's principal industry; the remains of a large Roman winery were found near Calahorra. The region's first wine laws were probably compiled by a 9th-century bishop named Abilio, and the monasteries that were founded along the Pilgrims' Way to Santiago de Compostela continued the tradition of wine-making. The first league of wine growers was established in 1520 but the practice of aging the wine in wooden barrels – which gives Rioja its characteristic "oaky" flavor – did not become widespread until after 1850.

The outbreak of phylloxera – the parasitic disease that ravaged the French vineyards in the late 19th century – provided the *bodegas* (cellars) of La Rioja with the opportunity to develop an export industry. Some 51,800 hectares were planted with vines: the greatest extent ever cultivated in the region. In the early 20th century, however, as the French vineyards recovered and colonial markets were lost, the industry went into decline, only to recover in the 1960s as new markets opened up in northern Europe. New *bodegas* were established and others modernized as up-to-date vinification methods were introduced. Though this boom also passed, it left in its wake a healthy, modern industry with thriving exports. Other agricultural industries, notably canning, have also been successfully

developed. The amount of land given over to vegetable crops, particularly asparagus, has doubled since the 1960s, often at the expense of vine-growing.

Aragon, by contrast, is much less fertile. Its hostile environment has contributed to the Aragonese reputation for stubbornness; locals are jokingly credited with an ability to drive nails into walls with their heads. The Pyrenees form Aragon's northern frontier, descending gradually to flatlands along the Ebro valley. South of the river are the bare, windswept uplands of Teruel. This whole area was heavily fought over during the Civil War; the ruins of the devastated town of Belchite have been left unrestored as a memorial to the dead. Apart from the fertile, irrigated areas around the regional capital, Zaragoza, the land is harsh and sparsely populated. New communications – in particular a trans-Pyrenean highway – are planned to revitalize the region, which remains largely ignored by tourists.

Aragon is home to some of Spain's most popular folk traditions, notably the *jota*. This lively dance-song is regarded as primarily Aragonese, though versions are also found in Navarre, Castile and Valencia. Best known as a dance, the Aragonese *jota* is also traditionally sung by agricultural workers and groups of seamstresses, but the lyrics are usually amatory and rarely refer to the task in hand. Despite its humble origins, the *jota* is a standard inclusion in the characteristically Spanish form of operetta known as *zarzuela* and was widely used by turn-of-the-century composers such as Enrique Granados.

Zaragoza – which derives its name from the Roman city, Caesar Augusta – has grown from a university and market town to a major trade and industrial center. Industry began to develop at the turn of the century, attracted by the city's position almost midway between Madrid and Barcelona, and by the relative ease of communication along the Ebro. The economic boom of the 1960s, fueled by hydroelectric power from dams in the Pyrenees, brought rapid expansion, while outlying areas of the region lost population at an unprecedented rate. By 1970, 42 percent of those living in Aragon were settled in Zaragoza. It is now Spain's fifth largest city.

Right This bridge across the river Ebro is at San Vicente de la Sonsierra in Upper Rioja. Though a wine-making area, the fertile alluvial plains on both sides of the river are used for market gardening and the bridge, one of a small number across the Ebro, has assumed new importance in facilitating the transportation of fruit and vegetables to the canning factories of La Rioja.

Left The grape harvest in La Rioja is carried out in the traditional way. Many pickers are gypsies, attracted by the seasonal work that according to custom begins on 10 October. Small sickles known as *corquetes* are used to cut the grapes, which are then placed in large wicker baskets. Black grapes make up 76 percent of the total harvest. Rioja is best-known for its oak-aged red wines – which must spend at least a year in wooden casks – but white wines are also produced. These are now generally fermented cold in stainless steel vats to produce a light table wine, though the classic "oaky" whites are still made by some *bodegas*.

THE ATLANTIC COAST

Madrid
Lisbon

Coordinates: 10°30' 9° 7°30' 6°
43° 42° 41° 40° 39° 38°

SPAIN

ASTURIAS

GALICIA

LA CORUÑA
LUGO
PONTEVEDRA
ORENSE

Cabo Ortegal Punta de la Estaca de Bares
Cervo Foz Cabo de Peñas
El Ferrol Mondoñedo Ribadeo Luarca Cudillero Aviles Gijón
Islas Sisargas La Coruña Villalba Navia Pravia Grado Oviedo Villaviciosa
Manzanares el Real Betanzos Guitiriz Valdediós Cangas de Onís
Cabo Touriñan Vimianzo Lugo Mieres Pola de Laviana
Santa Comba Tambre Mellid Peña Rubia 1930 Puerto de Pajares 2410 Peña Vieja 2615
Cabo Finisterre Santiago de Compostela Sarria
Muros Emb de Belesar Monforte de Lemos
Grove Cambados Sil
Sanxenxo Pontevedra Orense Puebla de Trives
Marin Mondariz Allariz
Vigo Minho Bande Verin
Bayona Tuy Melgaço Montalegre Bragança
Valença do Minho Monção Vidago Mirandela Miranda do Douro
La Guardia Vila Nova da Cerveira Canicada TRAS-OS-MONTES BRAGANÇA
VIANA DO CASTELO Viana do Castelo Cavado Braga Vila Real Sabor Douro
Barcelos Minho Guimarães PORTUGAL Vila Real Mateus Alijó
Esposende Caldas das Taipas Amarante Lamego Vila Nova de Fozcôa
Vila do Conde Leixões Tamega DOURO LITORAL
Vila Nova de Gaia Porto Douro
Espinho Lourosa Vila de Feira VISEU BEIRA ALTA GUARDA
Furadouro AVEIRO Vouga Carvalhal Pinhel
Myrtosa São Pedro do Sul Viseu Almeida
Aveiro Serém Caramulo Mondego Guarda
Costa Nova Curia Luso Gouveia Manteigas
Praia de Mira Bucaco Póvoa das Quartas Serra de Estrêla 1991
Cabo Mondego COIMBRA Zêzere
Figueira de Fóz Coimbra Lousã Barroca BEIRA BAIXA
São Pedro de Muel Montemor-o-Velho Penela Termas de Monfortinho
Marinha Grande BEIRA LITORAL LEIRIA CASTELO BRANCO Castelo Branco
Nazaré Batalha Leiria
Alcobaça Porto de Mós
I Berlenga Caldas da Rainha
C Carvoeiro Obidos
Roliça

ATLANTIC OCEAN

Legend:

place associated with
- basketwork
- ceramics or pottery
- cheese
- embroidery or linen
- lace
- leather
- metalwork
- rugs or carpets
- wine

resorts
- ski
- summer
- spa

- cathedral
- church or monastery
- castle
- parador/pousada (hotel)
- royal palace
- battlefield or memorial site
- industrial center
- major port

- arable
- citrus fruits
- olives
- vineyards
- grazing land
- forest
- nonagricultural land

scale 1: 2 500 000
0 60 km
0 40 mi

Right Iron and steel brought great prosperity to the city of Bilbao, the industrial heartland of the Basque Country, from the late 19th century. Today, as elsewhere in western Europe, heavy industry is in decline but, as these blast furnaces at the mouth of the river Nervión show, some still survives, despite an increasing dependence on the service sector and the growth of high-tech modern enterprises such as chemicals and computing.

THE ATLANTIC COAST

Basque Country, Cantabria, Asturias, Galicia and northern Portugal

The autonomous regions along Spain's rainswept Atlantic coast are strikingly different from the rest of the country. They are dominated by the massive Cantabrian mountains, which run from the Basque Country parallel to the north coast as far as Galicia before turning south toward the border with Portugal. Deep gorges are filled with the sound of rushing water and dense forests of oak and chestnut contain some of Europe's rarest – and most rarely seen – mammals such as brown bears and wolves. The wildness of the mountains, which in places are still virtually impenetrable, have long served as a barrier to communications with the rest of the country, fostering intensely local cultures with their own traditions, beliefs and social mores.

The Basques, ethnically distinct from the rest of the peninsula, are fiercely independent. Under Franco, political and cultural freedoms were severely constrained, fueling the growth of the separatist movement. Use of Euskera, the unique – and difficult – Basque language, had declined since the onset of industrialization, but the politicization of Basque culture boosted it enormously; it now has official status in the autonomous region and is taught in schools.

Basque cultural roots lie in its rural past. The Basques were pastoral farmers, rearing dairy cattle on the Pyrenean mountain pastures. Their traditional way of life centers on the large stone-built family farmsteads, or *caseríos*. Inheritance custom has helped preserve the large size of the farms, in contrast to other parts of northern Spain and Portugal; on the death of the parents, the farm passes intact to a single heir, who may or may not be the eldest child, whether male or female (though in practice inheritance favors sons). The Basque cuisine, based on the rich agricultural products of the region, is renowned as the best in Spain; all-male gastronomic clubs, whose members meet regularly to cook, eat and sing, are to be found in every Basque town.

Until recently, the northern coast was Spain's most

Above A stone and timber-built Basque farmstead, known in Spanish as a *caserío* and in Basque as a *baserri*, stands in the midst of closely worked fields: in front are the circular haystacks typical of the region. At the center of every *caserío* is the kitchen and adjoining stable. Generally three or four *caseríos* are built close to each other, forming a communal working unit whose members share certain tasks.

Right Amidst the dramatic scenery of the Picos de Europa in the Cantabrian Mountains is the shrine of Our Lady of Battles at Covadonga. It was here, according to Christian legend, that Pelayo of Asturias defeated some 400,000 Moors with a mere 30 men. Today the unique wildlife of these mountains is preserved in the Covadonga National Park.

Port

Port wine has its origins in the wine trade that developed between Portugal and Britain in the 17th century, when war with France prevented the wines of Bordeaux from reaching British dining tables. The Methuen commercial treaty of 1703 assured preferential entry for Portuguese wines into Britain; by the 1720s British wholesalers were shipping 25,000 pipes (large casks) of table wine a year from the northern city of Porto. The 18th-century vintners discovered that by adding brandy to the wine (a process known as fortification) they could slow down fermentation, thus preserving the wine's sweetness and flavor: this is still done in the same way today, by running partially fermented red wine, containing at least half its grape sugar, into barrels a quarter full of brandy. The port was then cellared in "lodges" built on the south bank of the Douro in Porto's wine suburb, Vila Nova de Gaia, to mature before being shipped to Britain. The marquis of Pombal, who created the first *zone d'appelation controlée*, or demarcated wine-making region, in 1756, attempted to regulate the trade, but Portuguese merchants were never able to accumulate the capital to break into it, and it remained largely in the hands of British port families such as Cockburn, Graham, Croft, Warre and Sandeman. Though these families were often substantial landowners in the surrounding countryside, they maintained an aloofness from the local population, and the great factory house in Porto remained a British enclave.

Most of the port made today is exported to France. In perhaps three years out of ten conditions are ideal for port-making. These harvests produce the great vintages, bottled after two years and best kept for twenty. Other port is blended and aged in wood; this process produces the fine pale wood ports known as tawny as well as ordinary ports such as ruby, usually drunk around five years old. White port, made from white grapes, is drunk as an aperitif.

Left The steep terraces of the port vineyards are linked by precipitous slate stairways. Mechanization is almost impossible and the harvest is still collected by hand. Workers carry the grapes on their shoulders in baskets weighing up to 50 kilograms. Traditionally the grapes for vintage port were trodden by a dozen men for a dozen hours, while the women danced.

Above Loading barrels on Porto's quayside. All port wine is matured "in the wood", though vintage port spends far longer in the bottle than in the barrel. The greatest ports are exported already bottled, but other wines, including tawny port, are exported in huge barrels, traditionally made either of Portuguese oak or chestnut or of Brazilian mahogany.

Left When the wine trade expanded in the 17th century the steep slate and granite slopes of the Upper Douro were laboriously terraced to make vineyards. Slate walls – often 4.5 meters high – were built by hand to contain the soil in which the vines are planted. Among the vineyards are the rambling white-walled farmhouses known as *quintas*. Here the grapes are trodden and the wines blended and brandied.

Below Wine kept up river develops a roasted flavor known as "the Douro burn"; traditionally, it was taken to Porto for cellaring on the flat-bottomed *barcos rabelos* that could be navigated through the treacherous Douro rapids. Today the boats are used for advertizing and the wine is transported by rail.

Bottom In the lodges of Vila Nova de Gaia, vintage port is aged in the bottle, usually for decades. A sediment or "crust" forms. This may break and mix with the wine if the bottle is moved carelessly.

heavily industrialized region but – as in the rest of the country – production is now in decline. The presence of iron ore in the Basque Country and Cantabria and coal in Asturias gave rise to iron and steel, shipbuilding and manufacturing industries in the 19th century, based around Bilbao in the Basque Country, Santander in Cantabria and Oviedo in Asturias. Bilbao is Spain's largest port. Paper manufacture, based on pulp timber supplies from the Pyrenees, and printing, are also important locally. The oil crisis of the 1970s hit all three regions very hard, and there is widespread unemployment.

Despite urban and industrial development – largely confined to the coast – and the introduction of tourism, life in the northwest is still largely centered around the village. Parish pump issues dominate political life, and business – political or otherwise – is conducted face to face. However, only in the most remote areas is Asturias' traditional language, *bable*, still spoken. Asturias was the only part of the peninsula never to be subjected to Arab rule; the beginning of the Reconquest is traditionally dated from the defeat inflicted on the Arabs by the Asturian king Pelayo at the battle of Covadonga in 718 or 719. A national shrine marks the site of this victory, high in the Asturian mountains, and Our Lady of Covadonga is venerated both as a guardian of Christian Spain and as patron saint of Asturias.

Galicia, farther still to the west, was once a kingdom in its own right but is now one of the poorest, if one of the most beautiful, of the Spanish *autonomías*. Culturally and linguistically, Galicia is Portuguese rather than Spanish: *galego*, the language that is spoken or understood by 86 percent of Galicia's native inhabitants, was the forerunner to modern Portuguese, though it is now recognized as a language in its own right. Like the Portuguese, Galicians are often depicted as a sentimental people, whose seafaring tradition has left a legacy of homesickness and melancholy – a feeling summed up in both languages as *saudade*. Yet Galicia was never part of Portugal. The great shrine of Santiago de Compostela, housing the relics of the apostle St James, made it a focus of unity for the medieval Christian kingdoms of northern Spain. Tradition maintained that "St James the Moor-slayer" would appear on the battlefield, mounted on horseback and brandishing a fearsome sword, to guide the Christian troops to victory.

In both Galicia and northern Portugal *minifundia* – minute parcels of land from which peasant households have to scratch a living – predominate. These have resulted from the custom of partible inheritance, whereby each child receives an equal share of property, and are a long-standing problem. In 1907 a government commission found that in Galicia a holding of as little as one hectare was considered a substantial property. One plot near La Coruña measured 32 meters square and had no fewer than three owners: one owned the land itself; another the chestnut tree growing on it; while the third was entitled to six eggs a year from the hens kept on the plot.

For centuries, the principal solution to this acute land shortage has been male emigration, either seasonal or permanent. Until the early 20th century Galician reapers would walk over the mountains each summer to bring in the harvest on the Castilian plains. From the mid 19th century, countless families sought a new life in Argentina and Brazil. It has been estimated that throughout the past 500 years one in three

Galician men has left his native region. The pattern of male emigration is equally strong in northern Portugal, where in some villages it is not uncommon for a third of the adult population to be away for some part of the year, sometimes finding work in the industrial suburbs of Porto or Bilbao but more often in the developed countries of western Europe.

The women are left to head the family, till the fields, and run the farms. Childcare is left to the grandparents. Women therefore assume an important role in local society, and some would argue that this reinforces the region's traditional conservatism and devout Catholicism. Nevertheless, when the men return to the village, their increased economic power strengthens rather than subverts their position as head of the household. Subsistence farming prevails – chestnut flour, maize and potatoes remain important parts of the daily diet. A staple dish in northern Portugal is *caldo verde* ("green broth"). This is made with kale so finely chopped that early travelers to the area believed

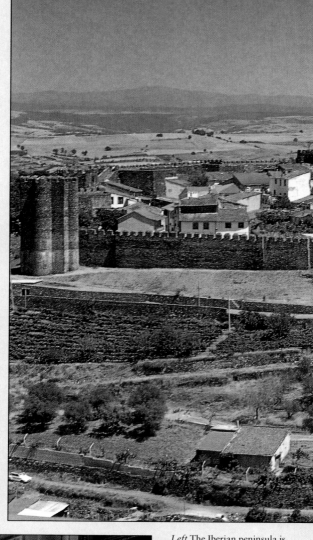

Below On a farm outside Santillana del Mar near the Cantabrian coast, a small boy pitchforks hay into a horse-drawn cart. This one is fitted with pneumatic tires, but wooden-wheeled ox-carts are still used on some peasant farms, particularly in northern Portugal. Livestock is housed in the lower storey of the farm building. The potted geraniums in the windows of the upper floor are typical of this rain-soaked region – the only part of the peninsula wet enough to support dairy cattle.

Left The Iberian peninsula is extraordinarily rich in folk song and dance. Street musicians are a common sight, their garb, instruments and style of song varying according to region. This small fife and drum band, pictured on the streets of Bilbao, is characteristically Basque. The black berets, or *boinas*, were once worn by all Basque men and are still common everyday wear, particularly among older generations.

Right Shellfish is a national obsession in Spain. The Atlantic coast of Galicia is reputed to produce the most succulent in Europe; locals claim its quality is rivaled only by that of Newfoundland. Razor clams (*navajas*) – much prized both as a *tapa* (snack) and as part of the seafood platters for which Galicia is famous – are gathered at low tide. Trucks travel through the night taking Galician seafood to landlocked Madrid before it has lost its freshness and quality.

Above The ducal city of Bragança –
home to Portugal's last royal
dynasty – is the ancient capital of
the often forgotten region of Trás-
os-Montes. The city walls, with
their 18 watch towers, are still
largely intact. The buildings within
are dominated by the fine 12th-
century castle, erected by Sancho I
(1154–1211), and a Renaissance
church, elevated to cathedral status
in 1770. Today, Bragança supports
a population of around 30,000. It is
the administrative capital of the
surrounding district and houses a
university college. Though
predominantly agricultural, there
are some potteries as well as a small
textile industry.

the locals supported themselves by eating grass.

Inevitably, the old ways of these mountain communities are declining in the face of modernization and economic development. Very few people around the remote border town of Miranda do Douro in the district of Bragança still speak *mirandês*, though other folk traditions – notably the bizarre male folkdancers known as *paulitieros*, who wear skirts and petticoats but wield large sticks – have survived. Some scholars believe that *mirandês* is descended from the language of the Sephardic Jews, and many Jews escaped expulsion in the 15th century by taking refuge in the mountains. The town of Belmonte in Castelo Branco nurtured a small community of "secret Jews" for centuries. Though nominally Catholic, they remained faithful to the Jewish tradition, observing the major festivals in private. Under Portugal's democratic regime, they were able to revert openly to Judaism and made plans to build a synagogue.

The historical heartland of the Portuguese kingdom lies in the mountains of the far north, in the old provinces of Minho, Trás-os-Montes and Douro. The first king of Portugal, Afonso Henriques, was born in the town of Guimarães, and the early state he forged developed around the archbishopric of Braga. It was at Porto – today the center of Portugal's largest industrial zone – that he persuaded a crusading army from northern Europe to join in the siege that freed Lisbon from the Arabs. Porto lies at the mouth of the river Douro, on whose steep, terraced banks the grapes are grown to make port wine.

The coastline south of the Douro is marked by lagoons: Aveiro is a town of canals and bridges, and paddyfields make a distinctive contribution to coastal cultivation. At the point where the mountains give way to the widening southern plains lies the city of Coimbra. This became the base for the reconquest of the south, and served as the national capital in the 12th and 13th centuries. A city of two cathedrals and many churches, it became in 1537 the permanent site of Portugal's only ancient university. In the east, the districts on either side of the Serra de Estrêla, Guarda and Castelo Branco (formerly Beira Alta and Beira Baixa), have the reputation of being the poorest areas of a poor country. Though predominantly agrarian, Castelo Branco is Portugal's only significant mining region; its tin fields, which contain Europe's largest wolfram deposits (a source of tungsten), dominate the local economy.

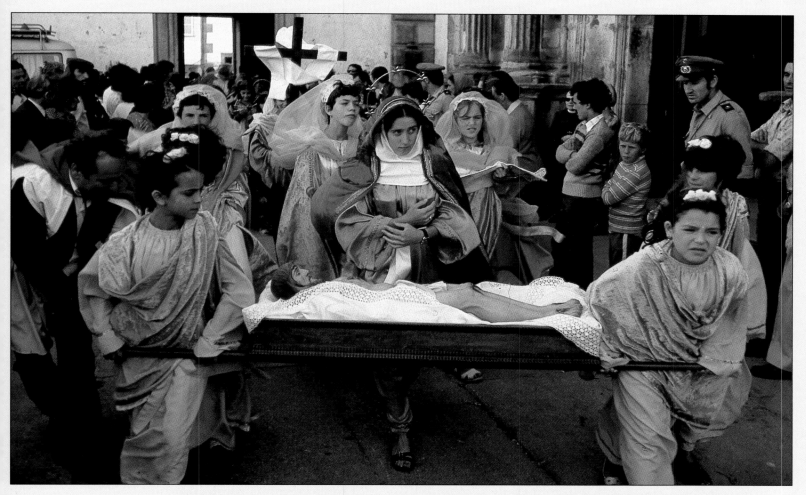

Above far left The highly stylized eyes typically painted on the prows of Portuguese fishing boats are reputed to be of Phoenician origin – they are certainly similar to those seen in the eastern Mediterranean, where they are said to represent the eye of the Egyptian goddess Isis. In Portugal they are called "eyes of God" and, as in the east, are supposed to ward off evil.

Above right Trás-os-Montes is the most devout area of Portugal. In Holy Week, the events of Christ's Passion are re-enacted in a *tableau vivant* by children. The Virgin Mary is played by a local girl, but Christ is represented by a statue.

Above left Blue and white *azulejos* (tiles) embellish buildings all over Portugal, giving a quite distinctive character to its city streets. This imposing mural adorns the church of São Ildefonso in Porto.

Right Dried salt cod, or *bacalhau*, has been a staple food in Portugal since the 16th century: the Portuguese claim to have a different salt cod dish for every day of the year. It is still sold in the small grocers' shops that, despite supermarket competition, are found on virtually every Portuguese street.

Left Coimbra is Portugal's only ancient university. Founded in 1290, it was settled on its present site in 1537 by João III (1521–57) whose statue overlooks the Patio das Escolas. The classical double-pillared doorway marks the entrance to the library.

THE ATLANTIC ISLANDS

Azores, Madeira, Canary Islands

Both Spain and Portugal possess island territories in the Atlantic – a lasting legacy of the voyages of exploration undertaken by Iberian navigators in the 15th century. The Azores, 1,200 kilometers due west of Lisbon, and Madeira, 1,000 kilometers southwest of the peninsula, belong to Portugal, while the Canary Islands – only 95 kilometers off the northwest coast of Africa – are one of Spain's 17 autonomous regions.

The volcanically active and often spectacularly beautiful archipelago of the Azores consists of nine major islands, forming three widely separated island groups. In the central group, mountainous Pico island rises to 2,351 meters, higher than any point on the Portuguese mainland. When the islands were discovered, reputedly in 1427, no traces of an indigenous population were found. The first settlers arrived a few years later, in about 1431, colonizing the island of Santa María. São Miguel, the largest island and the nearest to Portugal, was settled in 1444, and by the end of the 15th century all the islands were inhabited. During the 16th century, treasure fleets returning to Portugal from the Caribbean would stop off at the Azores to take on supplies and goods for trade with the mainland.

The islands lie on the major shipping routes of the Atlantic and are an important naval base. However, though both shipping and tourism are important, the economy of the islands is primarily agricultural; most of the islanders work on the land, growing tea, tobacco and a variety of tropical fruits. The gradient of the terraced volcanic slopes – here as in all the Atlantic islands – makes mechanization almost impossible. Over the centuries, generations of islanders have left the Azores in search of more prosperous work in the Americas; most of the numerous "Portuguese" communities of Canada and the United States are descendants of Azorean migrants – a link that helped to foster the separatist movements that emerged in the wake of the 1974 revolution in Portugal.

Colonization of the two main islands of the Madeira archipelago, Madeira and Porto Santo, discovered in 1420 (though it is likely that Genoese sailors had already sighted them in the early 14th century), was begun by João Gonçalves Zarco. He set fire to the dense forests from which the islands take their name – *madeira* simply means "wood" – to clear them for farming, but the flames raged hopelessly out of control and, according to contemporary chroniclers, were not extinguished for a biblical span of seven years. Prince Henry the Navigator took a direct interest in the islands' colonization, directing the import of sugar cane from Sicily and *malvoisie* grapes from Crete and Cyprus, along with wheat, barley and cattle. The soil, enriched by the ashes of the fires, was fertile, but the steep terrain was difficult to work. Slave labor was used in the sugar plantations, supplemented by convicts transported from Portugal. The *charamba* singing of Madeira and the Azores is considered by some authorities to be a slave lament of Arab origin, while the *cana-verde*, a circle dance associated with the sugar cane harvest, shows African influences.

Over centuries of cultivation, the mountain slopes of Madeira have been terraced and the problems of irrigation overcome by a remarkable system of *levadas* (aqueducts). The heavy rainfall on the northern slopes and high peaks replenishes the natural underground

Below "So much sea, so few fish" runs the old refrain. Tunny from around the Azores is in great demand on the Portuguese mainland. Including coastlines round the archipelagos of the Azores and Madeira, Portugal's offshore economic zone is some 20 times larger than its national land territory, but despite steps to modernize the fishing industry, many fishermen still rely on small, antiquated craft.

Below right Madeira's highest point, Pico Ruivo, rises to 1,862 meters. The precipitous slopes make terracing a necessity. In the south of the island every possible piece of land agricultural land is painstakingly walled. Pasture is so scarce that livestock is kept in sheds all year round.

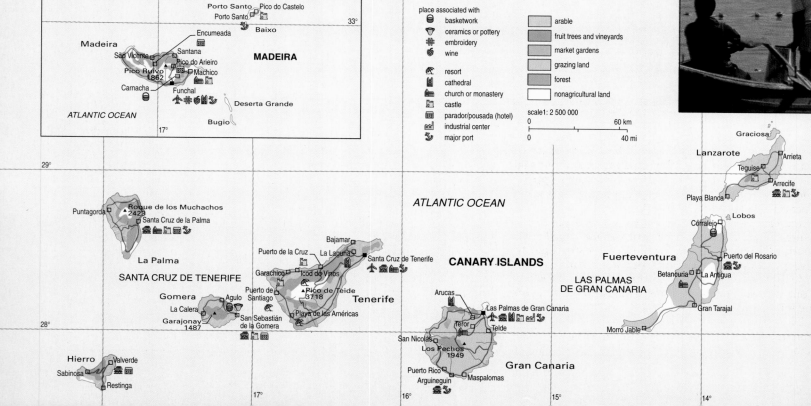

Corvo
Corvo

Flores
Santa Cruz-das Flores
ạã Grande

Graciosa — Santa Cruz-
da Graciosa

Terceira — Lajes
Praia da Vitória
Angra do Heroismo

São Jorge
Faial — Cedros
Velas
Horta
San Antonio
Pico ▲ 2351
Lajes do Pico   Pico
Topo

AZORES

São Miguel
Ribeira-Grande
Povoação
Ponta Delgada
Vila Franca-
do Campo

ATLANTIC OCEAN

place associated with cheese
cathedral
major port
arable
fruit trees and vineyards
grazing land
forest

scale1: 2 500 000
0   60 km
0   40 mi

Santa Maria
Santo Espírito
Vila do Porto

reservoirs – as much as 200 million cubic meters of water may be held beneath the surface. At about 500 meters above sea level, the water bubbles up in springs and is carried away in man-made channels and aqueducts to the lower-lying cultivated areas; here, sweet potatoes, avocados, custard apples and other exotic fruits and vegetables are grown for local use. Madeira's famous wine, fortified with cane sugar to give it its distinctive smoky flavor, is still a major industry, though sugar production is in decline. Tourism is increasingly important, visitors coming for the mild climate and spectacular scenery.

The seven major islands and numerous islets of the Canaries are topographically similar to those of the Azores and Madeira, consisting of rugged volcanic

221

peaks with fertile valleys and coasts, but unlike them they have an extremely long history of settlement, going back to prehistoric times. The indigenous people are commonly referred to as Guanches, though strictly speaking the term should be applied only to the aboriginal inhabitants of Gran Canaria. Archaeological evidence, including cave paintings and mummified remains, has linked these people to the Cro-Magnon culture of southwestern France. The Guanches are believed to have traveled to the Canaries from the North African coast about 2000 BC, though they subsequently lost the art of navigation, not even journeying between the islands.

The islands were known to the Romans, rediscovered by the Portuguese in 1341, and later came under Spanish control, confirmed by the Treaty of Alcaçovas in 1479. The Spanish *conquistadores* who took possession of the islands overran the native peoples, killing those who resisted them and capturing others for the slave trade; it took a five-year military campaign to take Gran Canaria. The present-day population of *canarios* is the result of intermarriage with the local women; the people of Gomera – which was less ravaged by war and slave raids than some of the other islands – are believed to have a higher proportion of Guanche blood. In contrast, many of the inhabitants of Fuerteventura are descended from the Arab and African slaves brought to work the plantations in the 16th century.

Tourism to the resorts and beaches of Tenerife, Gran Canaria and Lanzarote provides the islands with their main source of income, though agriculture is also important. Bananas, tobacco, potatoes and tomatoes are the main export crops, and have replaced wine and sugar. As on Madeira, aqueducts and storage tanks are used to collect water for irrigation; on Lanzarote a unique method of cultivation uses the moisture from the atmosphere that is trapped in the surface layers of volcanic ash by the natural humidity of the climate. The Canary Islands, like the Azores, are on major Atlantic shipping routes and its ports are duty free; Las Palmas de Gran Canaria is one of the largest ports in the western hemisphere.

The animal life of the Atlantic islands is particularly rich in birds: the Canary Islands have given their name to an endemic species of yellow finch (*Serinus canarius*), and the name of the Azores is derived from the Portuguese word for goshawk (*açor*). As well as birds, many unique species of reptiles and insects evolved in isolation on all the islands, free from natural predators. However, introduced mammals such as rats and cats, together with loss of natural habitats to farming and tourism, have caused havoc among these native species.

Even more spectacular and diverse is the plant life. Some 700 species of flowering plants are found on Madeira alone, together with 50 species of ferns and numerous types of trees. On the Canaries the variety of plant life is, if anything, still more extensive. The Canary pine (*Pinus canariensis*) and Canary palm (*Phoenix canariensis*) are among the islands' native trees, and types of juniper and laurel are also endemic, as they are on Madeira. The most distinctive indigenous plant, however, is the Dragon tree (*Dracaena draco*), also found on Madeira. Some individual specimens are believed to be over 2,000 years old. The unique native flora, the fertility of the soil, the variety of climates – which range from alpine to sub-tropical – make these archipelagos a horticultural paradise.

Right Columbus stopped at Las Palmas de Gran Canaria on his great voyage to America in 1492. This fine building – much of it restored in the 17th century – provided his lodgings on this and subsequent visits, and later became the official residence of the military governor. It now houses a museum that contains models of Columbus' ships, banners and firearms from the voyages, and a small statue of St Anne to whom Columbus prayed before setting out across the Atlantic.

Above left Triangular thatched houses are traditional to Madeira, though becoming increasingly scarce today. This well-preserved example is found in the village of Santana, where the typical pattern of a roadside church with scattered cottages can still be seen.

Above right Cruise ships once carried a select group of wealthy European visitors to the Canaries, but now cheap flights and year-round sunshine bring tourists flocking to the islands, particularly in winter when temperatures average between 17°C and 20°C. This beach at Puerto del Carmen is part of Lanzarote's main resort, stretching along 6 kilometers of coastline.

Far left Lanzarote's extraordinary volcanic landscape was largely formed when eruptions devastated the island in the 1730s. The luminous green lagoon at El Golfo on the south coast is the flooded crater of an extinct volcano, one wall of which has collapsed into the sea. A black sandbank of crushed lava separates it from the ocean.

Left Over half of Madeira's population live in the beautiful capital city of Funchal. Its coastal setting is sheltered by volcanic slopes and, in both the old and new towns, the architecture is small-scale. Balconied houses overlook the narrow, cobbled streets while white-walled villas with orange roofs are scattered on the steep hills above the town. Despite the absence of highrise development, Funchal is the center of tourism on the island though the Madeira wine trade and craft industries – notably wicker and needlework – are still important to the local economy.

RULING HOUSES OF SPAIN AND PORTUGAL
(All early medieval dates are approximate)

Visigothic kingdom
531–548	Theudis; assassinated
548–549	Theudigisel; assassinated
549–555	Agila I; assassinated
555–567	Athanagild
567–568	Liuva I
568–586	Leovigild
586–601	Reccared I
601–603	Liuva II; assassinated
603–610	Witteric
610–612	Gundemar
612–621	Sisebut
621	Reccared II
621–631	Swinthila; deposed
631–636	Sisenand
636–639	Khinthila
639–642	Tulga; deposed
642–653	Khindasuinth
653–672	Reccesuinth
672–680	Wamba; deposed
680–687	Erwig
687–702	Egica
702–710	Wittiza
710–711	Roderic

Caliphate of Córdoba (929–1031)
929–961	Abd al-Rahman III
961–976	Al-Hakam II
976–1009	Hisham II; deposed
1009	Muhammad II; deposed
1009–1010	Sulayman al-Mustain; deposed
1010	Muhammad II; restored
1010–1013	Hisham II; restored
1013–1016	Sulayman al-Mustain; restored
1016–1018	Ali b. Hammud al-Nasir
1018	Abd al-Rahman IV
1018–1021	Al-Qasim al-Mamun; deposed
1021–1023	Yahya al-Mutali; deposed
1023	Al-Qasim al-Mamun; restored; deposed
1023–1024	Abd al-Rahman V
1024–1025	Muhammad III
1025–1027	Yahya al-Mutali; restored; deposed
1027–1031	Hisham III; deposed

Kingdom of Asturias
718–737	Pelayo
737–739	Fáfila
739–757	Alfonso I, the Catholic (693?–757)
757–768	Fruela I (722–768); assassinated
768–774	Aurelio
774–783	Silo
783–788	Mauregato
788–791	Vermudo I; abdicated
791–842	Alfonso II
842–850	Ramiro I
850–866	Ordoño I
866–910	Alfonso III; deposed

Kingdom of (Asturias and) León
910–914	García
914–924	Ordoño II
924–925	Fruela II
926–931	Alfonso IV; abdicated
931–951	Ramiro II; abdicated
951–956	Ordoño III
956–958	Sancho I; deposed
958–959	Ordoño IV; deposed
959–966	Sancho I (restored); assassinated
966–985	Ramiro III
985–999	Vermudo II
999–1028	Alfonso V
1028–1037	Vermudo III
1037–1065	Fernando I, count of Castile
1065–1109	Alfonso VI
1109–1126	Urraca
1126–1157	Alfonso VII
1157–1188	Fernando II
1188–1230	Alfonso IX
1230–1252	Fernando III

Kingdom (County) of Castile
931–970	Fernán González
970–995	García I
995–1017	Sancho I

1017–1029	García II
1029–1065	Fernando I
1065–1072	Sancho II
1072–1109	Alfonso VI, king of León
1109–1126	Urraca
1126–1157	Alfonso VII
1157–1158	Sancho III
1158–1214	Alfonso VIII
1214–1217	Enrique I
1217	Berengaria
1217–1252	Fernando III

Kingdom of Castile and León
1252–1284	Alfonso X
1284–1295	Sancho IV
1295–1312	Fernando IV
1312–1350	Alfonso XI
1350–1369	Pedro the Cruel; assassinated
1369–1379	Enrique II
1379–1390	Juan I
1390–1406	Enrique III
1406–1454	Juan II
1454–1474	Enrique IV
1474–1504	Isabella I
1504–1506	Philip I
1504–1506	Juana; deposed
1506–1517	Fernando (Ferdinand) V, king of Aragon (regent)

Kingdom of Navarre (Pamplona)
905–925	Sancho I
925–931	Jimeno
931–970	García I
970–994	Sancho II
994–1004	García II
1004–1035	Sancho III
1035–1054	García III
1054–1076	Sancho IV; assassinated
1076–1094	Sancho V
1094–1104	Pedro I
1104–1134	Alfonso I
1134–1150	García IV
1150–1194	Sancho VI
1194–1234	Sancho VII
1234–1253	Thibaut I
1253–1270	Thibaut II
1270–1274	Enrique I
1274–1305	Juana I; married--
1284–1305	Philip I (IV of France)
1305–1316	Louis (X of France)
1316–1322	Philip II (V of France)
1322–1328	Carlos I
1328–1349	Juana II; married--
1328–1343	Philip III (Philippe d'Evreux)
1349–1387	Carlos II
1387–1425	Carlos III
1425–1441	Blanche; married--
1425–1479	Juan II, king of Aragon
1479	Eleanor; married--
1479–1483	Francis Phoebus, comte de Foix
1483–1517	Catalina (Catherine de Foix); married--
1484–1516	Juan III (Jean d'Albret)
[1515	Spanish Navarre formally annexed to Castile]

County of Barcelona
878–897	Wilfred I
897–911	Wilfred II (Borrell I)
911–947	Sunyer; abdicated
947–966	Miró
947–992	Borrell II
992–1017	Ramón Borrell III
1017–1035	Berenguer Ramón I
1035–1076	Ramón Berenguer I
1076–1082	Ramón Berenguer II
1082–1097	Berenguer Ramón II
1097–1131	Ramón Berenguer III
1131–1162	Ramón Berenguer IV
1162–1196	Alfonso (II of Aragon)

Kingdom of Aragon
1035–1069	Ramiro I
1069–1094	Sancho Ramírez (Sancho V of Navarre)
1094–1104	Pedro I, king of Navarre

1104–1134	Alfonso I, king of Navarre
1134–1137	Ramiro II; abdicated
1137–1164	Petronilla; abdicated
1164–1196	Alfonso II
1196–1213	Pedro II
1213–1276	Jaime I
1276–1285	Pedro III
1285–1291	Alfonso III
1291–1327	Jaime II
1327–1336	Alfonso IV
1336–1387	Pedro IV
1387–1396	Juan I
1396–1410	Martín
[1410–1412	Interregnum]
1412–1416	Fernando I
1416–1458	Alfonso V
1458–1479	Juan II
1479–1516	Fernando (Ferdinand) II

Kingdom of Spain
1516–1556	Charles I (Emperor Charles V); abdicated
1556–1598	Philip II
1598–1621	Philip III
1621–1665	Philip IV
1665–1700	Carlos II
1700–1724	Philip V; abdicated
1724	Luis I
1724–1746	Philip V; restored
1746–1759	Fernando VI
1759–1788	Carlos III
1788–1808	Carlos IV; abdicated
1808	Fernando VII; deposed
1808–1814	Joseph Bonaparte; deposed
1813–1833	Fernando VI (restored)
1833–1868	Isabel II; deposed
[1868–1870	provisional government]
1870–1873	Amedeo I; abdicated
[1873–1874	First Republic]
1874–1885	Alfonso XII
1886–1931	Alfonso XIII; deposed
[1931–1939	Second Republic]
[1939–1975	Francisco Franco, *Caudillo*]
1975–	Juan Carlos I

Kingdom of Portugal
1139–1185	Afonso I
1185–1211	Sancho I
1211–1223	Afonso II
1223–1248	Sancho II; deposed
1248–1279	Afonso III
1279–1325	Diniz
1325–1357	Afonso IV
1357–1367	Pedro I
1367–1383	Fernando I
[1383–1385	interregnum]
1385–1433	João I
1433–1438	Duarte
1438–1481	Afonso V
1481–1495	João II
1495–1521	Manuel I
1521–1557	João III
1557–1578	Sebastião
1578–1580	Henrique
1580–1598	Philip I (II of Spain)
1598–1621	Philip II (III of Spain)
1621–1640	Philip III (IV of Spain)
1640–1656	João IV, duke of Braganza
1656–1667	Afonso VI; deposed
1667–1706	Pedro II
1706–1750	João V
1750–1777	José I
1777–1786	Pedro III; married--
1777–1816	Maria I
1816–1826	João VI
1826	Pedro IV (I of Brazil); abdicated
1826–1828	Maria II; deposed
1828–1834	Miguel I; deposed
1834–1853	Maria II (restored)
1853–1861	Pedro V
1861–1889	Luis I
1889–1908	Carlos I; assassinated
1908–1910	Manuel II; deposed

GLOSSARY

al-Andalus
The Arabic name for the parts of the peninsula under Islamic domination. It is thought to be a corruption of *Vandalicia*, a name derived from the Vandal invaders.

alcázar
The Arabic word for castle: the protective fortress or palace of many town in Islamic Spain.

Almohads
A Muslim reforming sect originating in northwest Africa. They supplanted the ALMORAVIDS in Marrakesh in 1147 and gained control of virtually all of AL-ANDALUS in the next 50 years, but were defeated by the Christian monarchs at Las Navas de Tolosa (1212).

Almoravids
Originally a mystical religious movement among the BERBER tribesmen of North Africa. During the 11th century the Almoravids founded an empire in present-day Morocco and Algeria, and were invited into AL-ANDALUS to aid the Islamic cause in 1085. In less than twenty years they were in complete control of the region.

anarcho-syndicalism
A combination of the beliefs of anarchism (the replacement of the centralized state with self-sufficient local communities) and syndicalism (workers' control of the means of production and distribution). The docrine was influential under the 2nd Spanish Republic and in republican areas during the Civil War.

anticlericalism
Opposition to organized religion: a potent force in 20th-century Spain.

arbitrista
An advocate of economic reform in early 17th-century Spain.

Arian
Adherent of an anti-Trinitarian Christian heresy, emphasizing the distinction between the Son of God and the Father, regarded as a particularly heinous docrine by the Catholics of the early church.

audiencia
A court of justice or of appeal. In Spanish America *audiencias* were established as supreme judicial tribunals to assert the royal authority over that of the CONQUISTADORES and local chiefs.

auto de fe (in Portuguese, *auto-da-fé*)
The grand ceremonial (or "act of faith") of the Inquisition, at which reconciled heretics did public penance and received their sentences, while obdurate misbelievers were handed over to the secular authorities for execution (usually by fire).

autonomía
One of the self-governing regions of modern Spain, set up under the 1978 constitution.

bable
The dialect of Spanish spoken in Asturias.

baroque
An artistic style of the 17th and 18th centuries characterized by its richness and grandeur, together with an anti-classical fondness for emotional appeal. The style is particularly notable in Spanish church architecture and decoration.

Berbers
North African tribesmen who enthusiastically adopted the doctrines of Islam and supplied much of the manpower for the Muslim conquest of the Iberian peninsula. The warlike puritanism of the ALMORAVIDS and ALMOHADS has its origin among the Berber tribes.

bodega
A wine-shop or wine-store.

Bourbons
The French dynasty that became kings of France in 1549. In 1700 they also became kings of Spain under Philip V and reigned almost uninterruptedly until the abdication of Alfonso XIII in 1931; they were restored in 1975 with the accession of Juan Carlos. At one time the Bourbons also ruled Naples and several Italian duchies.

caballero
Originally meaning a mounted soldier or knight, the term came to be more or less equivalent to the English word "gentleman".

caliphate
The caliph of Damascus was the supreme ruler of the Islamic world. In establishing a caliphate of Córdoba, the ruling UMAYYAD dynasty was asserting its primacy over the Abbasid family that had supplanted it in Damascus.

Carlism
The docrine of the traditional, legitimist Catholic right in Spain, which refused to accept the liberal government of Isabel II and fought two wars (1833–40 and 1870–75) in support of the pretender Don Carlos. In the 20th century the party was subsumed into Franco's National Movement.

Carthaginians
The inhabitants of Carthage, a city on the north African coast close to the site of present-day Tunis, traditionally founded in 814 BC by PHOENICIAN traders. In the 3rd century BC it became the foremost city of the Mediterranean after Rome and extended its power into the Iberian peninsula, before being defeated in the Punic Wars. The city was totally destroyed by Rome in 146 BC.

Carolingians
The Frankish dynasty that supplanted the MEROVINGIANS as rulers of France in 751, and ruled until 987. During this period Charles Martel prevented the Arab advance across the Pyrenees and Charlemagne founded the HOLY ROMAN EMPIRE.

castro
A circular hilltop settlement occupied by the Celts, particularly found in the northwest of the peninsula.

Catholic Monarchs
The title awarded by Pope Alexander VI to Ferdinand II of Aragon and Isabella I of Castile as a reward for completing the reconquest of Islamic Spain and expelling the Jews.

caudillo
The title (meaning "chief") assumed by Francisco Franco during his 36 years as Spain's head of state.

Celtiberian
In parts of the pre-Christian peninsula the way of life of the Iberians and that of the Celtic tribes blended to form a distinct civilization, known as Celtiberian. This was particularly prevalent in northeastern and central Spain from the 3rd century BC.

Civil Guard
The quasi-military police force of Spain, established in 1844 by the central government to keep order in the countryside.

colonia
A Roman settlement of retired legionaries and landless freemen in the overseas provinces, which served as a center of Roman civilization.

Comuneros
The townsmen and minor gentry of Castile, involved in a revolt in 1520–21 against the absentee, foreign-dominated government of the young Charles V.

conquistador
Term applied to the explorers and soldiers who established Spain's empire in the Americas in the 16th century.

converso
A convert to Christianity from the Jewish faith.

convivencia
The generally harmonious coexistence of Islam, Christianity and Judaism in the Muslim parts of the peninsula.

cordillera
A chain or range of mountains.

corregidor
The chief magistrate or mayor of a Spanish town.

Cortes
The regional or national parliament.

costumbrismo
A literary and artistic genre of the 19th century concerned with the depiction of regional or local manners and customs.

Counter-Reformation
The attempted reestablishment of the Catholic Church in Protestant Europe in the 16th and 17th centuries. Though a political failure in much of Europe, the movement led to intensive missionary work in Asia and the Americas, and is associated in Spain with the MANNERIST and BAROQUE artistic styles.

Cubism
An influential style of 20th-century painting, practiced by Picasso, Braque, Juan Gris and others. A reaction against Impressionism, Cubism analyzes natural forms in geometrical terms and transforms them into semi-abstract arrangements of overlapping planes.

Enlightenment
The name given to the 18th-century development of a more questioning attitude toward revealed truth and a scientific approach to natural and social phenomena, which encouraged religious, administrative and economic reform.

Euskera
The Basque language.

fado
A plaintive Portuguese song and dance.

Falange
The authoritarian, centralist political movement founded in 1933 by José Antonio Primo de Rivera (son of the Spanish dictator). Falangism has been seen by some as a distinctively Spanish form of Fascism. Most of its ideas were adopted by Francisco Franco, and the Falange itself was eventually integrated into his National Movement.

flamenco
The vigorous rhythmic dance of Andalusia, accompanied by guitar-playing and the distinctive *cante hondo* ("deep voice") style of singing.

Franks
A Germanic tribe that settled west of the Rhine in the 3rd century AD in the area of the modern-day Low Countries and France, and after the collapse of the Roman empire became pre-eminent in northwestern continental Europe. Their kingdom reached its fullest extent under Charlemagne.

fueros
The local privileges and exemptions granted to specific regions of Spain during the period of the Reconquest. They became focuses of local pride and resistance to central government, but were progressively abolished during the 17th and 18th centuries.

galego
The language of Galicia in northwest Spain, in many ways more akin to Portuguese than to Spanish.

Germanías
Christian brotherhoods of Valencia and Majorca that rose in revolt in 1519 against the absentee government of Charles V. Partly fueled by social and racial tensions, the disturbances were savagely put down in 1521.

Habsburgs
The Habsburg dynasty began its rise to territorial supremacy in Europe in the 13th century by acquiring lands and titles in south Germany and Austria. In the following centuries the Habsburg domains were extended by marriage and diplomacy to include Burgundy and the Low Countries, and by the 15th century the family had gained possession of the title of Holy Roman Emperor. In 1520 Spain was added to their territories when Charles I of Spain succeeded as the Emperor Charles V. On his abdication in 1556 he divided his lands, creating a Spanish Habsburg line that ruled until 1700 and an Austrian Habsburg line that ruled until 1918.

hermandad
A Spanish militia, originally formed in the 12th century, that was revived by the CATHOLIC MONARCHS for the suppression of rural unrest and the maintenance of order.

hidalgo
A member of the minor nobility (*hidalguía*) in Spain. *Hidalgos*, generally untitled younger sons, played a leading part in the Spanish colonization of the New World.

Hispano-Roman
A Latin-speaking, Romanized inhabitant of Roman Hispania.

Holy Roman Empire
A conscious attempt to revive the glories of the Roman empire, the Holy Roman Empire was founded by Charlemagne in 800 AD. At its height it comprised much of western and central Europe, but by the 13th century had become a loose confederation of German territories under the suzerainty of the Emperor. Though an elected office, from the 15th century the Emperor was identified with the House of Habsburg. In theory he was the temporal ruler of Christendom, but this concept could not withstand the forces of nationalism and the REFORMATION.

huerta
An irrigated and cultivated plain, especially in Valencia and Murcia.

humanism
The RENAISSANCE concept, derived from classical antiquity, of man (rather than God) as the center of the universe. In theory (though hardly in practice) this idea led to a more humane social ethic of education, tolerance and peace.

infante
A prince or princess, the son or daughter of a Spanish monarch.

Inquisition
An ecclesiastical tribunal for the discovery and extirpation of heresy. Created by the Pope in 1233 as a weapon against the Albigensians, it was established under royal control in Spain in 1481 and in Portugal in 1536.

Jesuit
A member of the religious order founded by St Ignatius Loyola. In addition to the traditional vows of poverty, chastity and obedience, Jesuits were bound by an oath of personal loyalty to the Pope, and were thus seen as the storm-troopers of the COUNTER-REFORMATION.

jota
A popular dance of Aragon, Valencia and Navarre.

junta
A ruling council or governing body.

juros
Bonds issued by the HABSBURG kings of Spain, promising (*juro* = I swear) a fixed rate of interest. *Juros* were sold to raise money for the wars of Charles V and Philip II, and helped to cause Spain's financial collapse in the 17th century.

latifundia
Great landed estates, especially in Andalusia and southern Portugal.

letrado
A person of education, usually a university graduate in the legal profession.

Magdalenian
Belonging to the late Palaeolithic culture of about 15,000 BC represented by the remains found at La Madeleine in Périgord, France.

Maghreb
The region of northwest Africa including modern Morocco, Algeria and Tunisia.

Mannerism
An artistic movement associated with the Counter-Reformation, involving a reaction against the suave RENAISSANCE images of Raphael and his followers, and characterized by a contortion or elongation of natural forms as in the paintings of El Greco.

Manueline
The distinctive Portuguese style of architectural decoration, employing themes and motifs derived from the discoveries made during the reign of Manuel I.

mawla
The Arabic word for "client". Before about 750, all non-Arabs who wished to convert to Islam had to become clients, or lower-status members, of an Arab tribe.

Merovingians
The earliest ruling dynasty of the FRANKS. They extended the Frankish empire over much of France and Germany in the 5th and 6th centuries, but were displaced in 751 by the CAROLINGIANS.

meseta
The central plateau or tableland of the Iberian peninsula.

Mesta
The medieval Spanish sheep-farming and wool-producing guild, which enjoyed grazing rights over vast tracts of the country and was a prime cause of Spain's agricultural backwardness. The Mesta flourished until the end of the 18th century, and was not abolished until 1839.

Miguelism
The traditionalist, anti-Liberal movement in Portugal that supported Miguel I's claim to the throne over that of his niece Maria II. The "War of the Two Brothers" (between Miguel and his brother Pedro I of Brazil) lasted from 1828 to 1834.

minifundia
Modest farms and smallholdings (as opposed to LATIFUNDIA), particularly characteristic of northern Spain and Portugal.

Modernismo
A Spanish poetic movement flourishing between 1888 and 1914. Introduced into Spain by the poet Rubén Darío, *modernismo* reacted strongly against the materialism and naturalism of 19th-century literature and, in an attempt to create a poetry of timeless values, embraced an aestheticism and symbolism derived from French verse.

Moor
The word *moro*, literally meaning an inhabitant of Morocco, was applied indiscriminately in Christian Spain and Europe to all Muslims, whether from Spain, Africa or the Middle East.

morisco
In the 20 years following the fall of Granada (1492), all Spanish Muslims were offered the choice of exile or Christian baptism. Those who chose the latter alternative, though nominally Christian, were still seen as aliens and known as *moriscos*.

Mozarabs
The name given to the Christian inhabitants of Islamic Spain, living and practicing their religion under Muslim rulers (from *Mustaribun*, "Arabizers").

Mudéjars
The Islamic equivalent of the MOZARABS: Muslims permitted to live and practice their religion in Christian parts of Spain. This tolerance did not survive the end of the Reconquest: by 1526 all

Mudéjars had been forced to leave the country or become MORISCOS.

Neolithic
The New Stone Age: the last phase of the Stone Age culture, lasting in Europe from about 3000 to 1800 BC.

New State (*Estado Novo*)
The authoritarian and modernizing system introduced into Portugal under the 1933 constitution. The regime's founder and leading figure was António de Oliveira Salazar, finance minister from 1928 to 1940 and prime minister from 1932 until his retirement in 1968.

Opus Dei
A Catholic lay order that championed technical progress and the market economy in Franco's Spain.

Ostrogoths
In the late 4th century AD the Gothic nation divided into two parts: the VISIGOTHS ot the West and, in the East, the Ostrogoths, who settled in the Balkans. Under Theoderic (who ruled from 488 to 526) they invaded and conquered Italy.

Palaeolithic
The Old Stone Age, first and longest of the stages of human cultural development, extending from around 400,000 BC to 10,000 BC.

paria
The tribute paid by the Muslim TAIFAS to the Christian kingdoms of Spain from the 11th century onward.

Phoenicians
Descendants of a civilization originating in the Lebanese ports of Tyre and Sidon, who are chiefly remembered as skillful navigators and traders. In the 1st millennium BC their trading and and colonizing activities spread throughout the Mediterranean, and they founded Cádiz and other trading settlements in southern Spain. They were succeeded by the CARTHAGINIANS.

picaresque
The literary genre derived from the word *Pícaro* (= rogue) concerned with the travels and changing fortunes of a central character. The most famous Spanish examples are *Don Quixote* and *Lazarillo de Tormes*.

plateresque
A Spanish style of architectural decoration of the 16th century. Characterized by elaborate surface ornamentation, it took its name from the working and beating of precious metals (*platero* = silversmith).

plaza mayor
The main square of a Spanish town, frequently enclosed and arcaded (as in Madrid and Salamanca).

Popular Front
An alliance of left-wing parties formed to present a united opposition to Fascism in Europe between the wars. The Spanish Popular Front included socialists, communists, anarchists and trade unionists.

pronunciamiento (= pronouncement)
A distinctively Hispanic form of military *coup-d'état*, usually led by a group of senior officers.

Punic
From the Latin form of "Phoenician", the word is applied particularly to the Roman–Carthaginian wars of the 3rd and 2nd centuries BC.

Reformation
The 16th-century culmination of the movements for reform in the monolithic Catholic church. The growth of the doctrines of Luther and Calvin throughout Europe led to a split in Christendom between Catholicism and Protestantism, and eventually to the virtual disintegration of the HOLY ROMAN EMPIRE in the Thirty Years War (1618–1648).

Renaissance
The "rebirth" of classical culture in Western Europe at the end of the medieval period. In the arts this led to a revival of classical forms and ideas, while humanist ideals began to change the medieval concept of man in society.

repartimiento
The idea of dividing up conquered land (and its human resources) between those who conquered it seems to have originated in Valencia, and was extensively applied during the later stages of the Reconquest. The system was also employed, in a modified form, in the conquest of Spanish America.

ría
The estuary or delta of a major river.

rococo
An artistic and architectural style of extreme elaboration (French *rocaille* = shell-work), which developed from the BAROQUE in the early 18th century.

Romanesque
A style of architecture originating in 10th-century France, characterized by massive structure, simplicity of decoration and the round arch. In England the style is known as Norman.

sardana
The national dance of Catalonia, performed in a ring to the music of flutes and drums.

Sephardim
The Jews of Spain and Portugal (*Sepharad* is the Hebrew word for Spain). Sephardic Jews still live in parts of the Balkans and North Africa, having conserved their customs and their language from the 15th century, when they were expelled from the Iberian peninsula.

sierra
A range of mountains.

Suevi
A collective term applied to a number of tribes of northern Germany, some of whom accompanied the Vandals into Gaul and thence into northern Spain in 409 AD.

Surrealism
A literary and artistic movement originating in France in the 1920s. Surrealism is the art of the irrational, juxtaposing reality with contradictory and sometimes shocking images, frequently with Freudian overtones. Dalí is perhaps the most influential surrealist painter; Buñuel attempted to bring surrealism into the cinema.

taifa
A party or faction: the *reyes de taifa* ("party kings") were the local Muslim rulers who took power after the fall of the CALIPHATE of Córdoba.

Tartessian culture
The rich mining culture of prehistoric southwestern Spain, reportedly originating from a (lost) city named Tartessos, sometimes identified with the Biblical Tarshish. Little is known of the Tartessians beyond the fact that their tribes favored a strong kingship.

tercio
The standard regimental unit of Spanish infantry (consisting of pikemen, swordsmen and arquebusiers), which helped to make Spain's army the best in Europe during the reigns of Charles V and Philip II.

togado
A "gentleman of the robe", a member of the legal profession.

tramontana
The north wind, particularly as experienced in northern Spain.

Umayyad
The Muslim dynasty that controlled the CALIPHATE of Damascus from 661 to 750, when it was overthrown and virtually annihilated by the rival Abbasid family. Abd al-Rahman, a young Umayyad, escaped to AL-ANDALUS and founded the emirate of Córdoba; under his descendants it would become a rival caliphate.

valido
A royal favorite, or principal adviser, who came to assume many of the duties of a prime minister under the later HABSBURG kings.

Visigoth
In the late 4th century AD the Gothic nation divided into two parts: the OSTROGOTHS of the East and, in the West, the Visigoths, who withdrew from Italy (after sacking Rome) and founded an empire that stretched from Gibraltar to the Loire. Expelled from France in 507, they ruled Spain until the Arab invasion of 711.

Walloon
A French-speaking inhabitant of the southern Netherlands (modern Belgium).

zarzuela
A distinctively Spanish form of operetta that flourished in Madrid from the mid 19th century.

BIBLIOGRAPHY

General
David Birmingham, *A Concise History of Portugal*, Cambridge, 1993.
Gerald Brenan, *The Literature of the Spanish People*, Cambridge, 1951.
Americo Castro, *The Spaniards: An Introduction to Their History*, Berkeley & Los Angeles, 1971.
José Guidol, *The Arts of Spain*, New York, 1964.
Richard Herr, *An Historical Essay on Modern Spain*, Berkeley & Los Angeles, 1971.
Marion Kaplan, *The Portuguese: The Land and its People*, London, 1991.
J. Lassaigne, *Spanish Painting from the Catalan Frescoes to El Greco*, New York, 1952.
H.V. Livermore, *A New History of Portugal*, 2nd ed, Cambridge, 1976.
Rose Macaulay, *They Went to Portugal*, London, 1946.
A.H. de Oliveira Marques, *History of Portugal*, 2 vols, New York, 1972.
Stanley Payne, *A History of Spain and Portugal*, 2 vols, Wisconsin, 1973.
P.E. Russell (ed), *Spain: A Companion to Spanish Studies*, London, 1973.
Bradley Smith, *Spain: A History in Art*, New Jersey, 1979.
J.B. Trend, *The Civilization of Spain*, New Jersey, 1944.
Jaime Vicens Vives, *Approaches to the History of Spain*, Berkeley & Los Angeles, 1976.
Ruth Way, *A Geography of Spain and Portugal*, London, 1962.

The Peninsula to the Fall of the Visigoths
A. Arribas, *The Iberians*, London, 1963.
E. Bouchier, *Spain under the Roman Empire*, Oxford, 1914.
H. Galsterer, *Untersuchungen zum romischen Stadtwesen auf der iberischen Halbinsel*, Berlin, 1971.
J. Gonzalez, "*The Lex Irnitana*: a new Flavian Municipal Law", *Journal of Roman Studies* 76 (1986).
D. Harden, *The Phoenicians*, London, 1980.
R.J. Harrison, *Spain at the Dawn of History*, London, 1988.
Edward James (ed), *Visigothic Spain: New Approaches*, Oxford, 1981.
S. Keay, *Roman Spain*, London, 1988.
G. Nicolini, *The Ancient Spaniards*, Farnborough, 1974.
J. Richardson, *Hispaniae: Spain and the Development of Roman Imperialism 218–82 BC*, Cambridge, 1986.
H.M. Savoury, *Spain and Portugal*, London, 1968.
C.H. Sutherland, *The Romans in Spain*, London, 1939.
Edward A. Thompson, *The Goths in Spain*, Oxford, 1969.
A. Tovar, *Iberische Landeskunde*, Baden Baden, 1974/76.

Conquest and Reconquest
Eliyahu Ashtor, *The Jews of Moslem Spain*, Philadelphia, 1992.
Thomas Bisson, *The Medieval Crown of Aragon: A Short History*, Oxford, 1986.
Roger Collins, *Early Medieval Spain, Unity in Diversity, 400–1000*, London, 1983
Roger Collins, *The Arab Conquest of Spain, 710–797*, Oxford, 1989.
Richard Fletcher, *The Quest for El Cid*, London, 1989.
Richard Fletcher, *Moorish Spain*, London, 1992.
L.P. Harvey, *Islamic Spain, 1250 to 1500*, Chicago, 1990.
Jocelyn N. Hillgarth, *The Spanish Kingdoms, 1250–1516*, 2 vols, Oxford, 1976, 1978.
Edward James (ed) *Visigothic Spain: New Approaches*, Oxford, 1981.
Peggy K. Liss, *Isabel the Queen*, New York/Oxford, 1992.
Derek W. Lomax, *The Reconquest of Spain*, London, 1978.
Angus McKay, *Spain in the Middle Ages: from Frontier to Empire, 1000–1500*, London, 1977.
Evelyn S. Procter, *Curia and Cortes in León and Castile 1072–1295*, Cambridge, 1980.
Bernard F. Reilly, *The Contest of Christian and Muslim Spain*, Oxford, 1992.
Bernard F. Reilly, *The Medieval Spains*, Cambridge, 1993.
Edward A. Thompson, *The Goths in Spain*, Oxford, 1969.
Ludwig Vones, *Geschichte der iberischen Halbinsel im Mittelalter, 711–1480*, Sigmaringen, 1993.

The Catholic Empire
F. Braudel, *The Mediterranean World in the Age of Philip II*, London, 1972.

A. Dominguez Ortiz, *The Golden Age of Spain, 1516–1598*, London, 1971.
J.H. Elliott, *The Count-Duke of Olivares*, New Haven, 1986.
J.H. Elliott, "The Spanish Monarchy and the Kingdom of Portugal, 1580–1640" in M. Greengrass (ed) *Conquest and Coalescence: The Shaping of the State in Early Modern Europe*, London, 1991.
Felipe Fernandez-Armesto, *Ferdinand and Isabella*, London, 1975.
H. Kamen, *Golden Age Spain*, London, 1988.
H. Kamen, *Spain 1469-1714: A Society of Conflict*, London, 1983.
A.W. Lovett, *Early Habsburg Spain, 1516–1598*, Oxford, 1986.
J. Lynch, *The Hispanic World in Crisis and Change, 1598–1700*, Oxford, 1992.
J. Lynch, *Spain, 1516–1598: From Nation State to World Empire*, Oxford, 1991.
Garrett Mattingly, *The Defeat of the Spanish Armada*, London, 1959.
G. Parker, *The Dutch Revolt*, London, 1977.
G. Parker, *Philip II*, Boston, 1978.
Bradley Smith, *Spain: A History in Art*, New Jersey 1979.
R.A. Stradling, *Europe and the Decline of Spain, 1580–1720*, London, 1981.
R.A. Stradling, *Philip IV*, Cambridge 1988.
P. Vilar, *Spain: A Brief History*, Oxford, 1967.

Dynasticism and Pragmatism
W.J. Callaghan, *Honor, Commerce and Industry in Eighteenth-Century Spain*, Boston, 1972.
C. Esdaile, *The Spanish Army in the Peninsular War*, Manchester, 1988.
D. Gates, *The Spanish Ulcer: A History of the Peninsular War*, London, 1986.
C.A. Hanson, *Economy and Society in Baroque Portugal, 1668–1703*, London, 1981.
J.D. Harbron, *Trafalgar and the Spanish Navy*, London, 1988.
S. Harcourt-Smith, *Alberoni, or the Spanish Conspiracy*, London, 1943.
W.N. Hargreaves-Mawdesley, *Eighteenth-Century Spain, 1700–1788*, London, 1979.
R. Herr, *The Eighteenth-Century Revolution in Spain*, New Jersey, 1958.
A.H. Hull, *Charles III and the Revival of Spain*, Washington (DC), 1981.
H. Kamen, *Spain in the Later Seventeenth Century*, London, 1980.
H. Kamen, *The War of Succession in Spain, 1700–1715*, London, 1969.
J. Lynch, *Bourbon Spain, 1700-1808*, Oxford, 1989.
D. Ringrose, *Madrid and the Spanish Economy, 1560–1850*, Berkeley, 1983.
R.A. Stradling, *Europe and the Decline of Spain 1580–1720*, London, 1981.
G. Walker, *Spanish Politics and Imperial Trade, 1700–1789*, London, 1979.

Constitutionalism and Civil War
Franz Borkenau, *The Spanish Cockpit*, London, 1937.
George Borrow, *The Bible in Spain*, London, 1842.
Gerald Brenan, *The Spanish Labyrinth: An Account of the Social and Political Background of the Spanish Civil War*, Cambridge, 1943.
Raymond Carr, *Spain 1808–1975*, 2nd ed, Oxford, 1982.
António de Figueiredo, *Portugal: Fifty Years of Dictatorship*, New York & Harmondsworth, 1976.
Richard Ford, *Gatherings from Spain*, London, 1846.
Ronald Fraser, *Blood of Spain: The Experience of Civil War 1936–1939*, London, 1979.
Ian Gibson, *The Assassination of Federico García Lorca*, London, 1979.
Images of the Spanish Civil War (with an introduction by Raymond Carr), London, 1986.
Hugh Kay, *Salazar and Modern Portugal*, London, 1970.
Laurie Lee, *A Moment of War*, London, 1991.
George Orwell, *Homage to Catalonia*, London, 1938.
Stanley Payne, *The Franco Regime 1936–1975*, Wisconsin, 1987.
Paul Preston (ed), *Revolution and War in Spain*, London, 1984.
Paul Preston, *Franco*, London, 1993.
Richard Robinson, *Contemporary Portugal*, London, 1979.

Adrian Shubert, *A Social History of Modern Spain*, London, 1990.
Murray, A. Sperber (ed), *And I Remember Spain: A Spanish Civil War Anthology*, New York, 1974.
Hugh Thomas, *The Spanish Civil War*, revised ed, London, 1977.
Douglas Wheeler, *Republican Portugal*, Wisconsin, 1975.

The New Democracies
Carlos Alonso Zaldivar & Manuel Castells, *Spain Beyond Myths*, Madrid, 1992.
Peter Besas, *Behind the Spanish Lens: Spanish Cinema under Fascism and Democracy*, Denver, Colorado, 1985.
Raymond Carr & Juan Pablo Fusi, *Spain: Dictatorship to Democracy*, 2nd ed, London, 1981.
Robert P. Clark, *The Basque Insurgents: ETA, 1952–1980*, Wisconsin, 1984.
Tom Gallagher, *Portugal: A Twentieth-Century Interpretation*, Manchester, 1983.
Ian Gibson, *Fire in the Blood: The New Spain*, London, 1992.
Hugo Gil Ferreira & Michael W. Marshall, *Portugal's Revolution: Ten Years On*, Cambridge, 1986.
David Gilmour, *The Transformation of Spain*, London, 1985.
Lawrence S. Graham & Harry M. Maker (eds), *Contemporary Portugal*, Austin, Texas, 1979.
Lawrence S. Graham & Douglas L. Wheeler (eds), *In Search of Modern Portugal: The Revolution and its Consequences*, Wisconsin, 1983.
Robert Graham, *Spain: Change of a Nation*, London, 1984.
Richard Gunther, Giacomo Sani & Goldie Shabad, *Spain After Franco*, Berkeley & Los Angeles, 1986.
John Hooper, *The Spaniards: A Portrait of the New Spain*, London, 1987.
Diamantino P. Machado, *The Structure of Portuguese Society*, 1991.
José Maria Maravall, *The Transition to Democracy in Spain*, London & New York, 1982.
Victor Pérez-Díaz, *The Return of Civil Society*, Cambridge, Mass., 1993.
Paul Preston, *The Triumph of Democracy in Spain*, London, 1986.

The Geographical Regions
Gerald Brenan, *The Face of Spain*, London, 1950.
Gerald Brenan, *South from Granada*, London, 1957.
Penelope Casas, *The Foods and Wines of Spain*, USA, 1982.
Penelope Chetwode, *Two Middle-Aged Ladies in Andalusia*, London, 1963.
Roger Collins, *The Basques*, 2nd ed, London, 1992.
José Cutileiro, *A Portuguese Rural Society*, Oxford, 1971.
Hubrecht Duijker, *The Wine Atlas of Spain and Traveller's Guide to the Vineyards*, London, 1992.
Ronald Fraser, *The Pueblo: A Mountain Village on the Costa del Sol*, London, 1973.
Rodney Gallop, *A Book of the Basques*, London, 1946?; reprinted University of Nevada Press, Reno, Nevada.
Laurie Lee, *As I Walked Out One Midsummer Morning*, London, 1969.
Felipe Fernández-Armesto, *Barcelona: A Thousand Years of the City's Past*, London, 1991.
Robert Hughes, *Barcelona*, London, 1992.
Carmelo Lisón-Tolosana, *Belmonte de los Caballeros: Anthropology and History in an Aragonese Community*, Princeton, 1983.
James A. Michener, *Iberia*, New York, 1968.
John Payne, *Catalonia: Portrait of a Nation*, 1991.
Julian Pitt-Rivers, *The People of the Sierra*, 2nd ed, Chicago, 1971.
V.S. Pritchett, *The Spanish Temper*, London, 1954.
Jan Read, *The Catalans*, London, 1978.
Alicia Rios & Lourdes March, *The Heritage of Spanish Cooking*, London, 1992.
Francis Rogers, *Atlantic Islanders of the Azores and Madeira*, Massachusetts, 1979.
Edite Vieira, *The Taste of Portugal*, London, 1968.

LIST OF ILLUSTRATIONS

Abbreviations: t = top, tl = top left, tr = top right, c = center, b = bottom, etc.

AGE = AGE Fotostock, Barcelona; AIC = Arquivo Internacional de Cor, Portugal; AISA = Archivo Iconografico S.A., Spain; ALFA = Publicacoes ALFA s.a., Lisbon; AOL = Andromeda Oxford Limited, Abingdon; BAL = Bridgeman Library, London; CP = Camera Press Limited, London; M = Magnum Photos Limited, London; MAS = Arxiu MAS, Spain; MH = Michael Holford, Essex; RHPL = Robert Harding Picture Library, London; WFA = Werner Forman Archive, London; Z = Zefa Picture Library, London

GAZETTEER

INDEX

235

Evora-Monte 130
exaltados 131
Expo'92 173, 174, *174, 175*
Extremadura 12, 15, 17, 28, 32, 35, *71*, 120, *170, 188, 190, 191*

F

Facundus *46*
fado music 140, 179, 180–81, *182*
Falange 154, 155, 158, *160*
Falla, Manuel de 152, *152*
  El amor brujo 152
  Atlántida 152
  El sombrero de tres picos 152
family life 178–79
Farinelli, Carlo 112, 113
Faro 22, 188
fascism 154, 155, 157
fashion and design industries *179*
Fátima, Our Lady of 176, *176*, 179
Feixó, Benito 115
Ferdinand I, Holy Roman Emperor 79, 81
Ferdinand II, king of Aragon and Sicily, V of Castile and III of Naples 59, 66, 75, 77, 78–79, *207*
  see also Ferdinand and Isabella
Ferdinand and Isabella (Catholic Monarchs) 43, 47, 58, 66–72, *71*, 78
  legacy of joint kingship 72
  succession 72, 75, 77, 79
Ferdinand of Sachsen-Coburg-Gotha *see* Fernando II, king of Portugal
Fernando I, king of Aragon 59
Fernando III, king of Castile 43, 53, 57
Fernando I, king of León-Castile *43*, 46, 49, 50
Fernando II, king of León-Castile 50
Fernando II, king of Portugal 137, 138
Fernando VI, king of Spain 112–13
Fernando VII, king of Spain 121, 123, 125, 126, 127–29, 130, *130*, 136, *136*
Fernando, Don, brother of Philip IV *98*
Fernão, king of Portugal 61
Ferrante, king of Sicily *58*
fertility rate 178
feudalism 48, 58
Figueiredo, José de 62
Figueras 120
films 151, 181
  censorship under Franco and Salazar 177
fishing industry 15–16, *17*, *92*, *216*, *219, 220*
flamenco music 106, 140, 180–81, *182*, 187–88, *191*
Flaubert, Gustave 140
Florida 114
Floridablanca, José Moñino, count of 114, 123
Fluviá, river *57*
Foix, Germaine de 77
folklore, music and dance 133, 140, 144, 152, *170*, 199, 210, *216*, 218
Fontes de Pereira de Melo, António Maria 138–39
forestry 190

Four Cats Café 144, *144, 145*
Foz de Lumbier 38
Fraga Iribarne, Manuel 172
France
  Albigensian crusade 59
  and Catalan revolt 103
  French army 128
  French influence in Spain 52, 59
  French Revolution 115, 118, 120
  Napoleonic Wars 120–21
  Quadruple Alliance 130
  Seven Years War 114
  Thirty Years War 101
  Treaty of the Pyrenees 98, 103
  war with Spain 81, 85, 92
  War of the Spanish Succession 108
  wars of religion 85, *85*
Franche-Comté 108
franchise 135, 137, 148
Francis I, king of France 81
Franciscan Order 57–58, 71, *73*, 77
Franco, General Francisco 150, *152*, 155, 156, 158–59, *158*, *163, 163*, 166–67, 168, 207
  and Catholic church 176, *177*
  censorship under 177, 182
  Spanish culture under 180–02, *180*
  Spanish education system 173
  suppression of regional nationalism *170*, 194, 207, 213
  women and the family in Spanish society 178
Franco-Prussian War 138
Frankish March 46
Franks 37, 41, 42, 46, 48
French Revolution 115, 118, 120
frontiers 12, 48, 49
Fructuosus of Tarragona 38
Fuenterrabia, battle of 97
fueros 67, 69, 78, 91, 101, 109
Funchal *223*

G

Gades, Antonio 181
Gades (Cádiz) 34
Galba, Sulpicius 32, 35
Galdóz, Benito Pérez 141
galego 21, *21*, 133, 215
Galicia 17, 21, *21*, 170, 173, 178–79, 194, 213, 215–16
Gallaecia 37, 38, 39, *39*, 41
Gama, Vasco da 75, 86, *86*, 88
Gargallo, Pablo 151
Garrett, Almeida 131, 133
Gata 15
Gattinara, Mercurino 79
Gaudí, Antoni 141, 142
  Casa Battló *143*
  Casa Milá 142
Generalife 187, *188*
"generation of 27" 151, 183
"generation of 1898" 146
Gerhard, Roberto 181
Gerontius 38
Gibraltar 12, 42, 108, 110
Gibraltar, Strait of 12, 29, 42
Gisbert, Antonio 128
Goa 88
Godoy, Manuel 120, 121, 127
Goethe, Johann Wolfgang von 116
Golden Age 48, 78, 81, 83–84
Gomera 222
Gomes, Fernão *88*
Gonçalves, Nuño 62
  Altarpiece of St Vincent 62, *62*
Gonçalves Zarco, João 220

Góngora, Luis de 151
González, Felipe 169, 170, *170*, 172
González, Julio 151
Gothic architecture 52, 53, *54*, *55*
Goths 38
Goya y Lucientes, Francisco de 124, *125*, 133
  black paintings 124, *125*
  Los Caprichos 124, *124*
  The Disasters of War 124, *124*, 125
  The Family of Carlos IV 120
  El Pelele 125
  The 2nd of May 124
  Self-Portrait with Dr Arrieta 124
  tapestry cartoons 124, *125*
  The 3rd of May 124
Goytisolo, Juan 184
Gracchus, Tiberius 32
Gran Canaria 222, *222*
Granada *47*, 58, 60, 61, 66, 69–70, 78, 85, 187
  see also Alhambra
Granados, Enrique 144, 152, 210
Grand Alliance 108
grandees 105, 108, 111, 112–13
Graves, Robert 199
Greeks 29–30, *31*
Greenwich Cartoon *90*
Grimaldi, marquis 114
Gris, Juan 151
Guadalajara *115*
Guadalquivir, river 15, 17, 25, 29, 31, 35, 37, 42, 56, 57, *132*, 174, *175*, 187, 188
Guadarrama mountains 15, *47*, 80, 83
Guadiana, river 12, 15, 29, 35, 187, 188
Guadix *188*
Guanches 222
Guarda 218
Guerra, Alfonso 172
Guimarães 218
Guinea 162
guitar 106, *107*, 125, *183*
Gulbenkian, Calouste 183
Gumiel, Pedro de 69
Guzmán, Don Luis de *61*
gypsies 91, *172*, 181, 187–88, *188, 191*

H

ha-Levi, Samuel 61
Haarlem, massacre of 87
Habsburg dynasty 77, 79, *79*, 81, 83, 96, 104–06, *107*, 108
Hadrian *35*, 37
Halffter, Cristóbal 181
Halffter, Ernesto 152
Halffter, Rodolfo 152
Hannibal 30, 31
Hernández, Miguel 151
Hemingway, Ernest
  The Sun Also Rises 207
Henrique, Cardinal Archbishop of Evora, king of Portugal 88
Henry VIII, king of England 81
Henry II, king of France 81
Henry IV, king of France 81, 93
Henry the Navigator, Prince 61, *62*, 74, 75, 86, *86*, 190, 220
Herculano, Alexandre 131
hermandades 69, 94
Herodotus
  Histories 29
Herri Batasuna 170

hidalgos 69, 78, 79, 96, 112
Hisham II, caliph 46, *46*
Hispalis 34
Hispania Citerior 31, 32, *34*, 35
Hispania Ulterior 31, 32, *34*, 35
Hispaniola 106
Histories 135, 138
Hitchcock, Alfred
  Spellbound 151
Hitler, Adolf 155
Hohenstaufen dynasty *58*
Hohenzollern dynasty 138
Holanda, Francisco de 62
Holy League 85
Holy Roman Empire 48, 58, 79, *79*, 107, 108
Homem, Lopo 86
homosexuality 150, *150*
Homs, Joaquím 181
honoriaci 39
Horta, Maria Teresa 179
Hosius, Bishop of Córdoba 38
Howard, Admiral *90*
Huelva 28, 29–30, 35
huerta 194, 196
Huesca *13*, 32, 47
Huguet, Master 74
humanism 68, 77, 78, 82
Huns 38
hunting 92, *98, 122*
Hydatius 41

I

Ibáñez, Vicente Blasco 140
Iberian Mountains 15
Iberians 25, 29
  art 26, *26, 27*
  coinage 34
  interaction with Romans 32, 34
  weaponry 26, *27*, 34
Ibiza 199, *201*
ibn Rushd (Averroës) 56
Ilerda, battle of 32
Ilipa, battle of 31, *35*
illuminated manuscripts 46, 57, *61*
Imilce, wife of Hannibal 30
India 71, 73, 75, *75*, 86, *86*, 88
Indies road *73*
Indo, Iberian king 34
industrialization 135, 146, *147*, 215
Infantado, duke of 108
Inquisition 66–67, 69, 77, 85, 87, 88, 102, 109, 115, 117, 118, 125, 129
Instituto de la Mujer 179
intendants 109, 115
International Brigades *155*, 156
Irving, Washington *132*
  The Alhambra 132
Isabel II, queen of Spain 129, *130*, *136*, 139, 148
Isabel, daughter of Pedro II 107
Isabel, infanta, daughter of Philip II 93
Isabel, wife of Charles V 79
Isabella, daughter of Ferdinand and Isabella 75
Isabella, queen of Castile 59, 66, *68, 68*, 69, 72, 75
  see also Ferdinand and Isabella
Isabella Farnese of Parma 109, 110
Isidore, Bishop of Seville 41, *43*
Islam
  converts to 45
  convivencia 43, 45, 52–53, 54, 56, 58, 61, 62
  cultural contribution to west 53, 54

impact of 43–45
Ottoman war against Holy League 85
politics of 45–46
reforming sects 56
taifas 46, 49
  see also Arabs in Spain
Isma'il I, king of Granada 64, *65*
Italica 31, *35*, 37
Italy, Spanish intervention in 78, 81, 85, 97, 110
Ituren *207*
Iuvencus 38

J

Jaca 46, 52
Jaén 57, 58
Jamaica 103
James the Great, Saint 38
Japan 73, 86, *86*
Jaume I, king of Aragon 59, *59*
Jávea 27
Jerez de la Frontera 29, 49, *186*, *187, 187*
Jesuits (Society of Jesus) 73, 77–78, 82, *82*, 96, 101, 102, 104, 112–13, 130
  in Portugal 88, 117–18
  suppression 113–15, 117–18
jewelry
  Iberian 26, *27*
  Tartessian 29
  Visigothic *41*
Jews 54, 57, 60, 61, 218
  and Arab conquest 43
  Barcelona disputation 59
  conversos 61, 66, 70, 94, 97, 102–03, 118
  convivencia 43, 45, 52–53, 54, 56, 58, 61, 62, 75, 77
  expulsion from Portugal 60, 75, 218
  expulsion from Spain 60, 70, *70*
  Inquisition 69, 70
  settlement in Spain 43
  under Christian rule 43, 48, 54, 59, 60, 61
João I, king of Portugal 61, 74, *74*
João II, king of Portugal 62, *62*, 73, 74, 75, 86
João III, king of Portugal 74, 79, 87, 88, *219*
João IV, king of Portugal 103, 106
João V, king of Portugal 107, 111–12, *111*, 117
João VI, king of Portugal 118, 127, 128, 129
João, son of João III 88
John XXIII, Pope 166
John of the Cross, St 82, *82*, 83
John Paul II, Pope 176
Johnson, Samuel 116
José I, king of Portugal 116, 117–18
Joseph I, Holy Roman Emperor 108
jota 210
Juan II, king of Aragon *58*
Juan, son of Ferdinand and Isabella 72
Juan of Austria, Don 85
Juan Carlos, king of Spain *122*, *163*, 167–18, *168*, 169, *200*
Juan José, Don 104, 105, 106, 107
Juana, Queen (the Mad) 75–76, 79, *79*
Juana, daughter of Charles V 88
Julian, Count 43
Julius Caesar 32, 34–35
Junot, Andoche 121